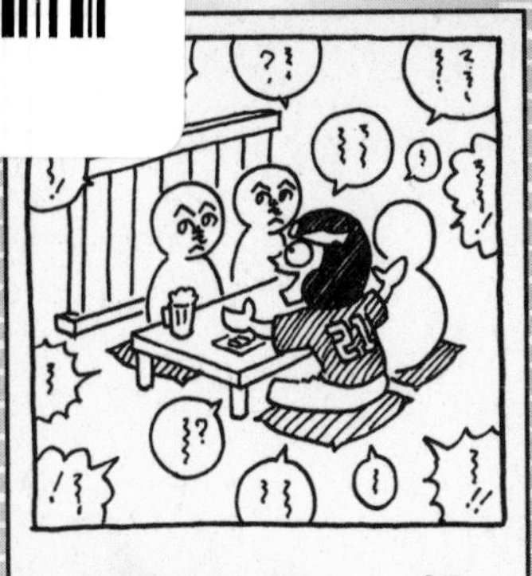

稲垣理一郎

Riichiro Inagaki

Recently, I've had several chances to talk with other manga artists and I've found them to be super easy to talk to. It's been a lot of fun. We're in the same line of work, so I guess it's to be expected.

My only worry is that people will avoid me because I'm such a chatterbox.

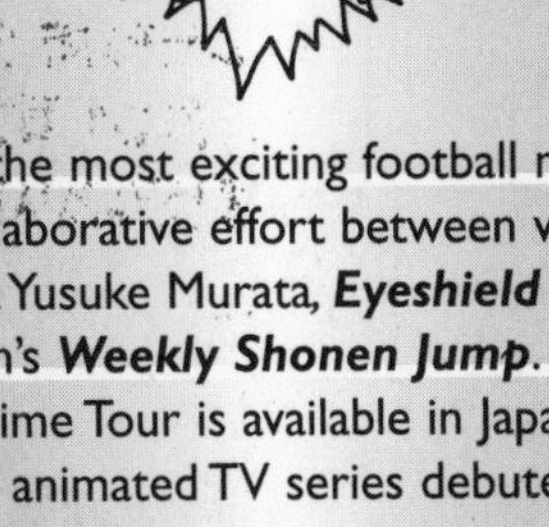

Eyeshield 21 is the most exciting football manga to hit the scene. A collaborative effort between writer Riichiro Inagaki and artist Yusuke Murata, ***Eyeshield 21*** was originally serialized in Japan's ***Weekly Shonen Jump***. An OAV created for Shueisha's Anime Tour is available in Japan, and the ***Eyeshield 21*** hit animated TV series debuted in spring 2005!

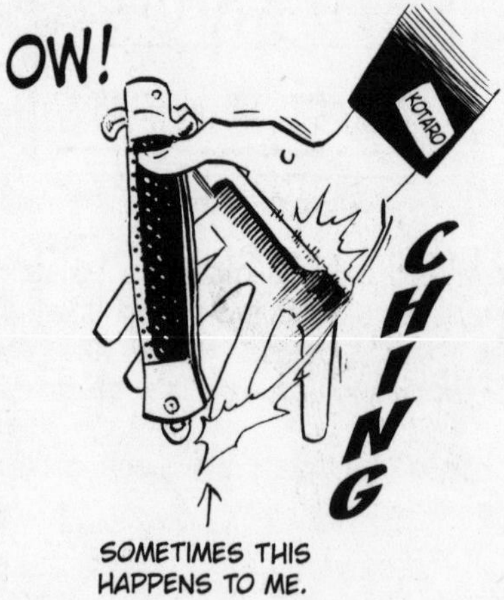
OW!
KOTARO
CHING
SOMETIMES THIS
HAPPENS TO ME.

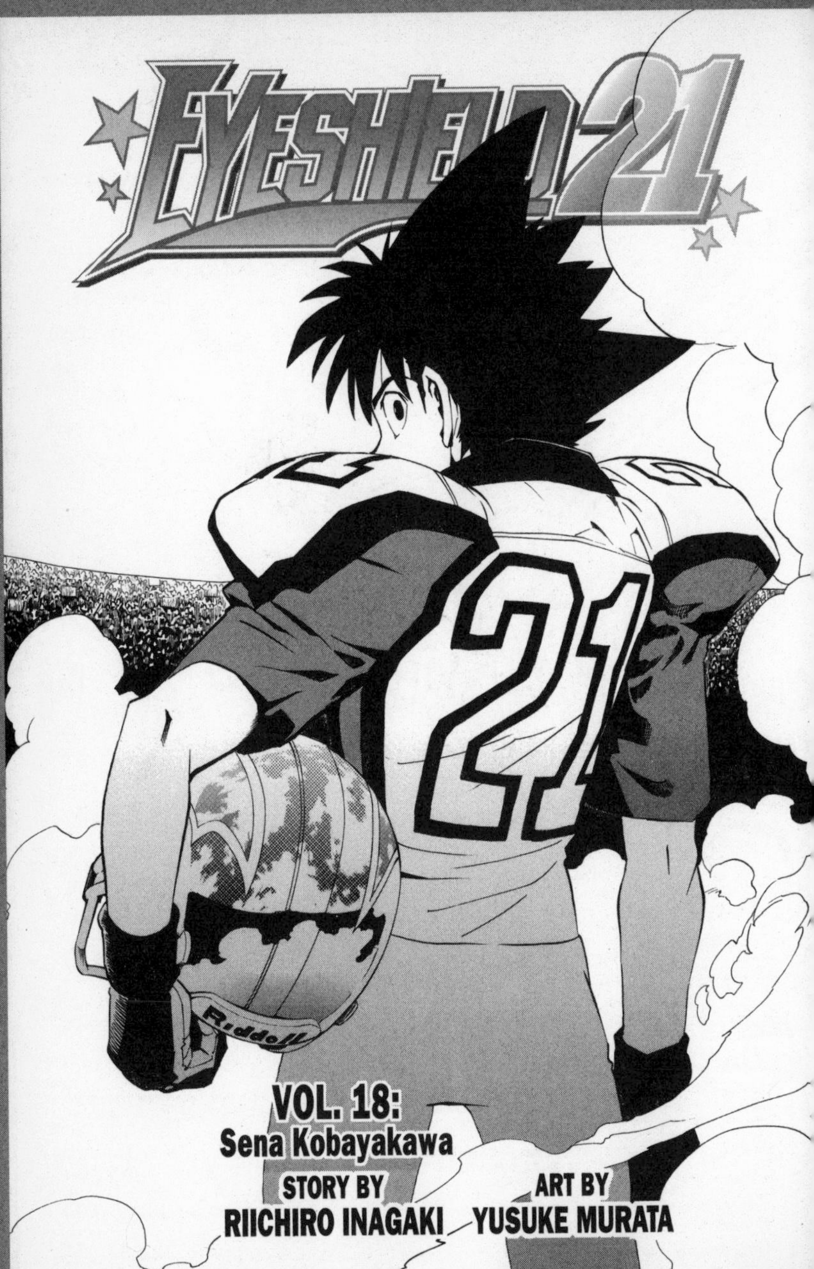

EYESHIELD 21

VOL. 18: Sena Kobayakawa

STORY BY
RIICHIRO INAGAKI

ART BY
YUSUKE MURATA

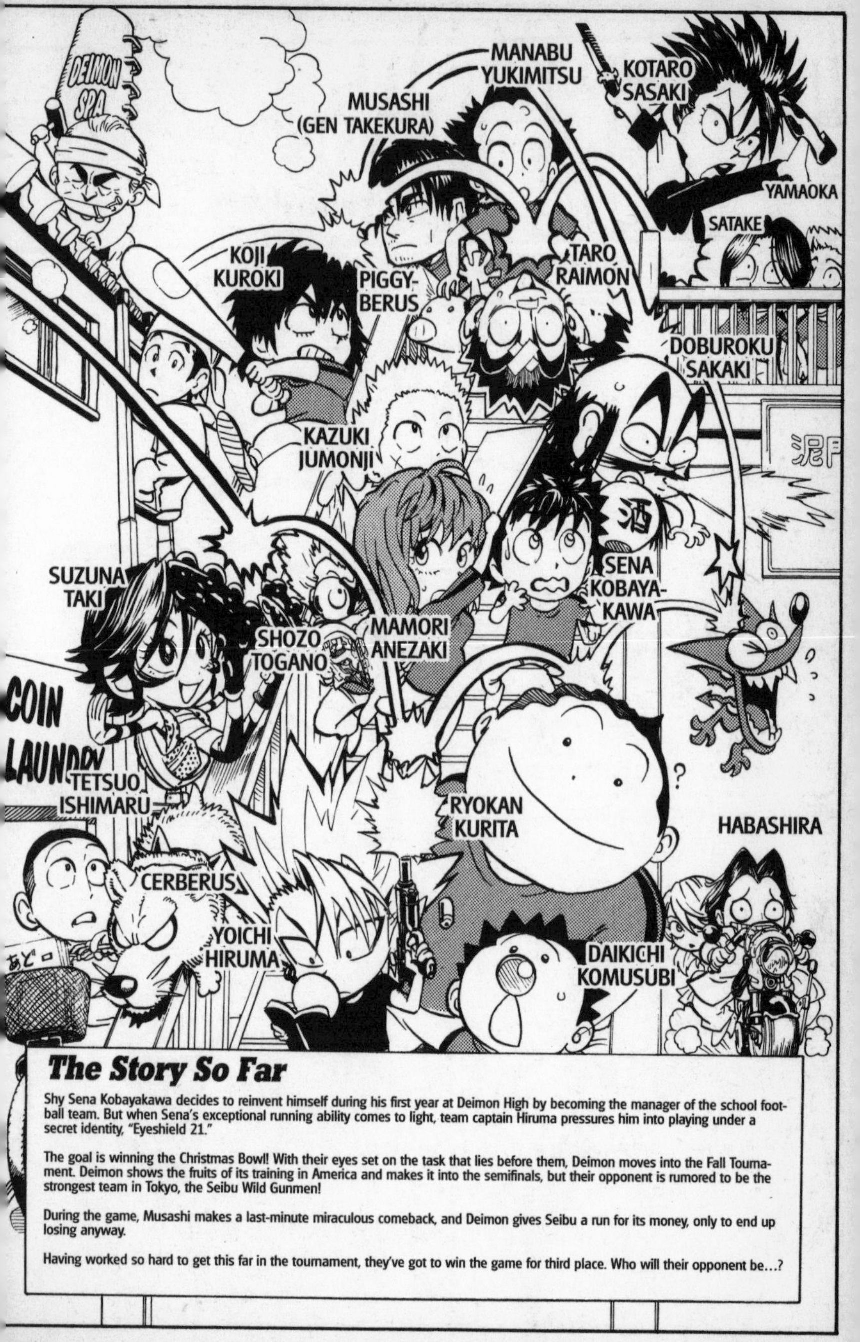
KOTARO SASAKI
MANABU YUKIMITSU
MUSASHI (GEN TAKEKURA)
DEIMON SPA
YAMAOKA
SATAKE
TARO RAIMON
PIGGY-BERUS
KOJI KUROKI
DOBUROKU SAKAKI
KAZUKI JUMONJI
酒
SENA KOBAYA-KAWA
SUZUNA TAKI
MAMORI ANEZAKI
SHOZO TOGANO
COIN
TETSUO ISHIMARU
HABASHIRA
RYOKAN KURITA
CERBERUS
YOICHI HIRUMA
DAIKICHI KOMUSUBI

The Story So Far

Shy Sena Kobayakawa decides to reinvent himself during his first year at Deimon High by becoming the manager of the school football team. But when Sena's exceptional running ability comes to light, team captain Hiruma pressures him into playing under a secret identity, "Eyeshield 21."

The goal is winning the Christmas Bowl! With their eyes set on the task that lies before them, Deimon moves into the Fall Tournament. Deimon shows the fruits of its training in America and makes it into the semifinals, but their opponent is rumored to be the strongest team in Tokyo, the Seibu Wild Gunmen!

During the game, Musashi makes a last-minute miraculous comeback, and Deimon gives Seibu a run for its money, only to end up losing anyway.

Having worked so hard to get this far in the tournament, they've got to win the game for third place. Who will their opponent be...?

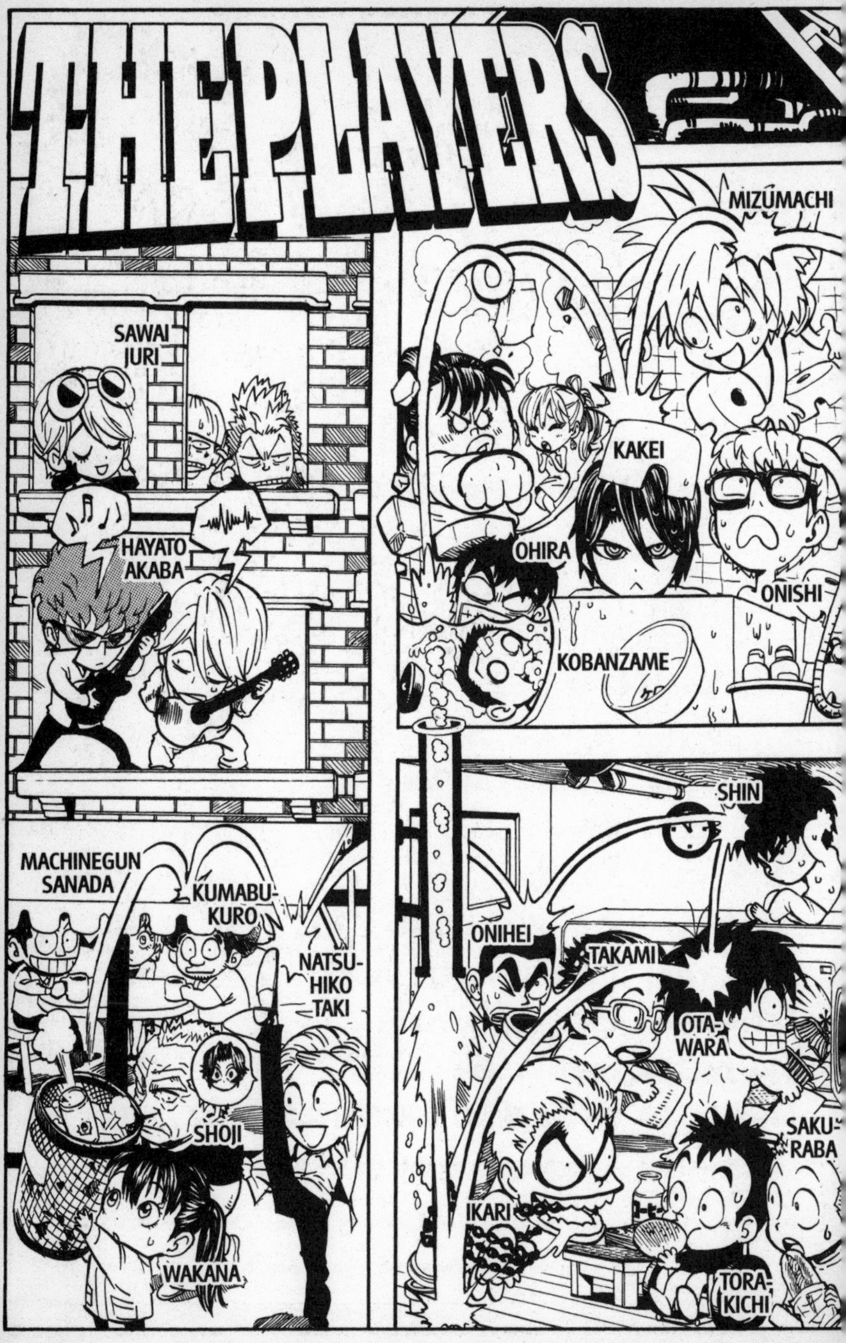
THE PLAYERS
MIZUMACHI
KAKEI
ONISHI
OHIRA
KOBANZAME
SAWAI JURI
HAYATO AKABA
SHIN
ONIHEI
TAKAMI
OTA-WARA
SAKU-RABA
IKARI
TORA-KICHI
MACHINEGUN SANADA
KUMABU-KURO
NATSU-HIKO TAKI
SHOJI
WAKANA

Vol. 18:
Sena Kobayakawa

CONTENTS

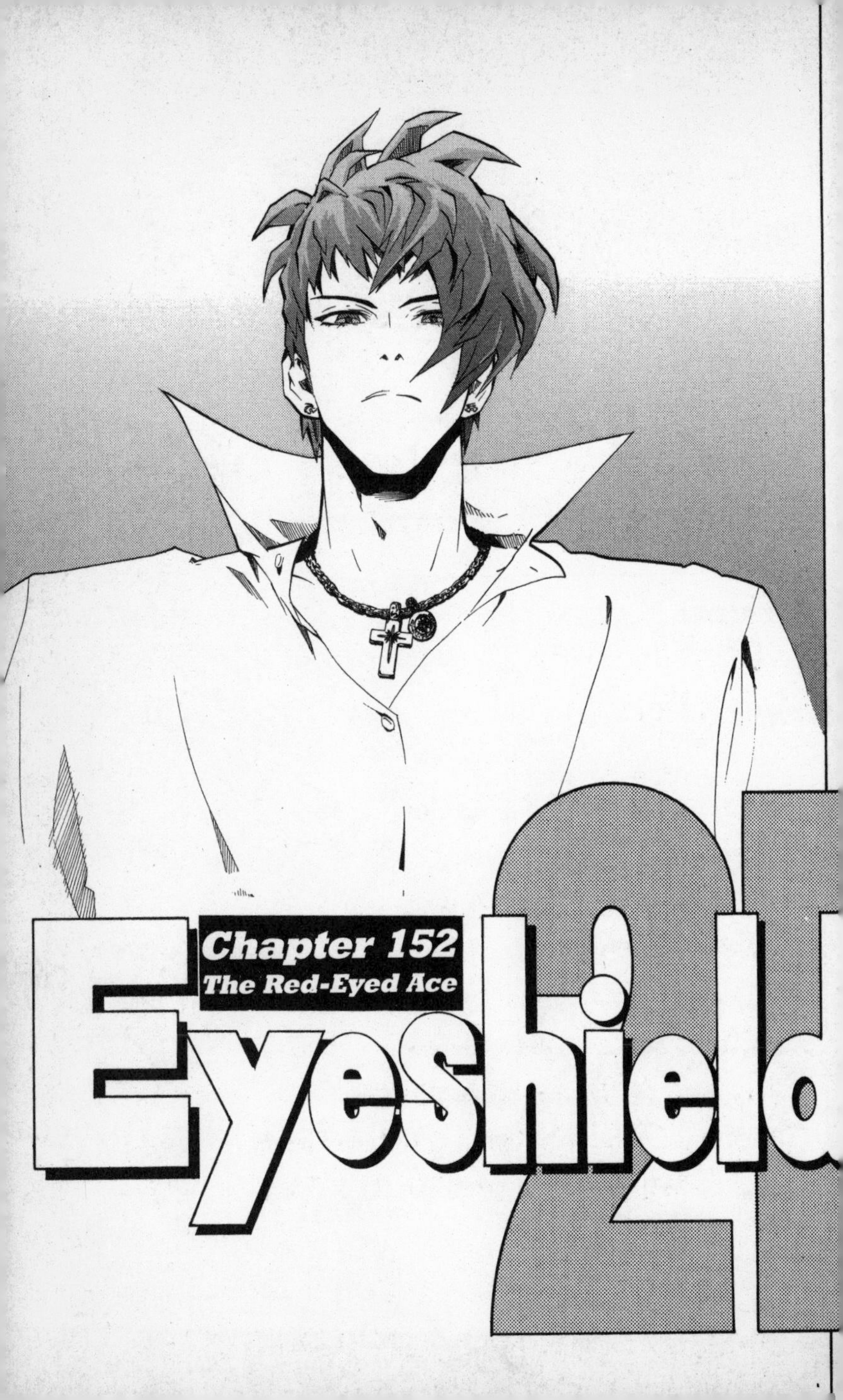
Chapter 152
The Red-Eyed Ace
Eyeshield 21

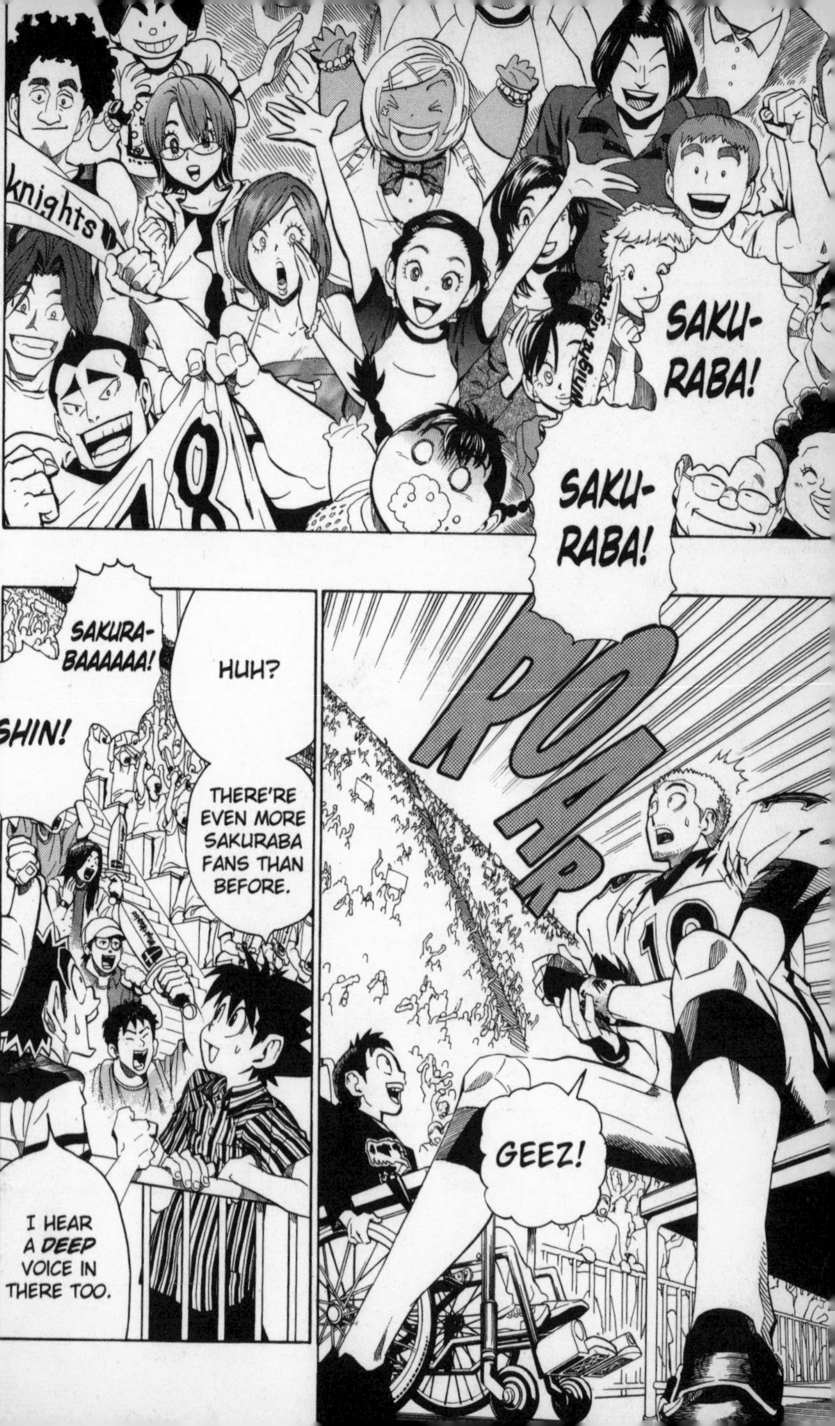
SAKU-RABA!
SAKU-RABA!
ROAR
GEEZ!
SAKURA-BAAAAAA!
SHIN!
HUH?
THERE'RE EVEN MORE SAKURABA FANS THAN BEFORE.
I HEAR A DEEP VOICE IN THERE TOO.

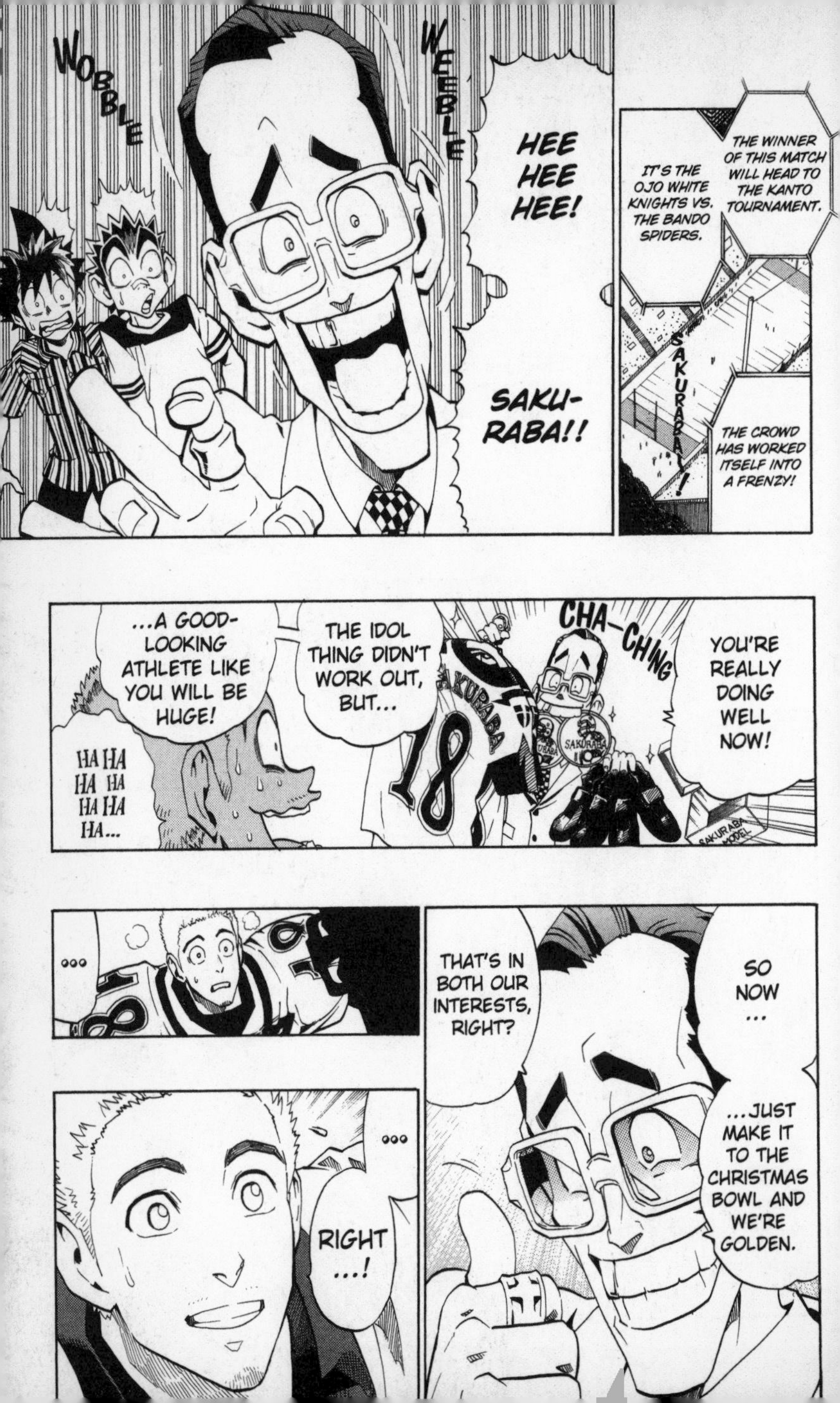
THE WINNER OF THIS MATCH WILL HEAD TO THE KANTO TOURNAMENT.
IT'S THE OJO WHITE KNIGHTS VS. THE BANDO SPIDERS.
SAKURABA!
THE CROWD HAS WORKED ITSELF INTO A FRENZY!
WEEBLE
HEE HEE HEE!
SAKU-RABA!!
WOBBLE
YOU'RE REALLY DOING WELL NOW!
CHA-CHING
SAKURABA
SAKURABA MODEL
THE IDOL THING DIDN'T WORK OUT, BUT...
...A GOOD-LOOKING ATHLETE LIKE YOU WILL BE HUGE!
HA HA HA HA HA HA HA...
SO NOW...
THAT'S IN BOTH OUR INTERESTS, RIGHT?
...
...JUST MAKE IT TO THE CHRISTMAS BOWL AND WE'RE GOLDEN.
...
RIGHT...!

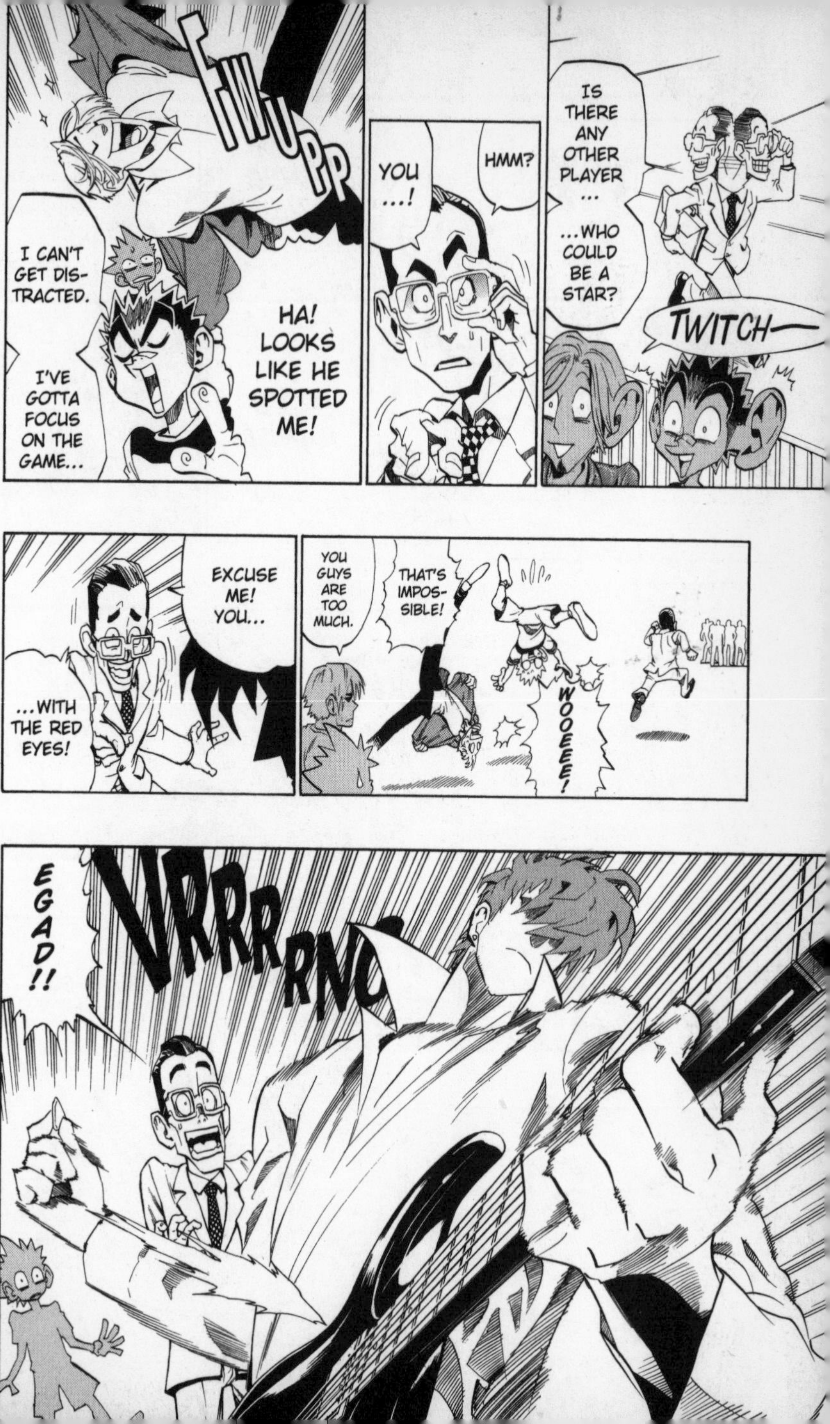
IS THERE ANY OTHER PLAYER...
...WHO COULD BE A STAR?
TWITCH—
HMM?
YOU ...!
FWUPP
HA! LOOKS LIKE HE SPOTTED ME!
I CAN'T GET DIS-TRACTED.
I'VE GOTTA FOCUS ON THE GAME...
THAT'S IMPOS-SIBLE!
YOU GUYS ARE TOO MUCH.
WOOEEE!
EXCUSE ME! YOU...
...WITH THE RED EYES!
VRRRRN
EGAD!!

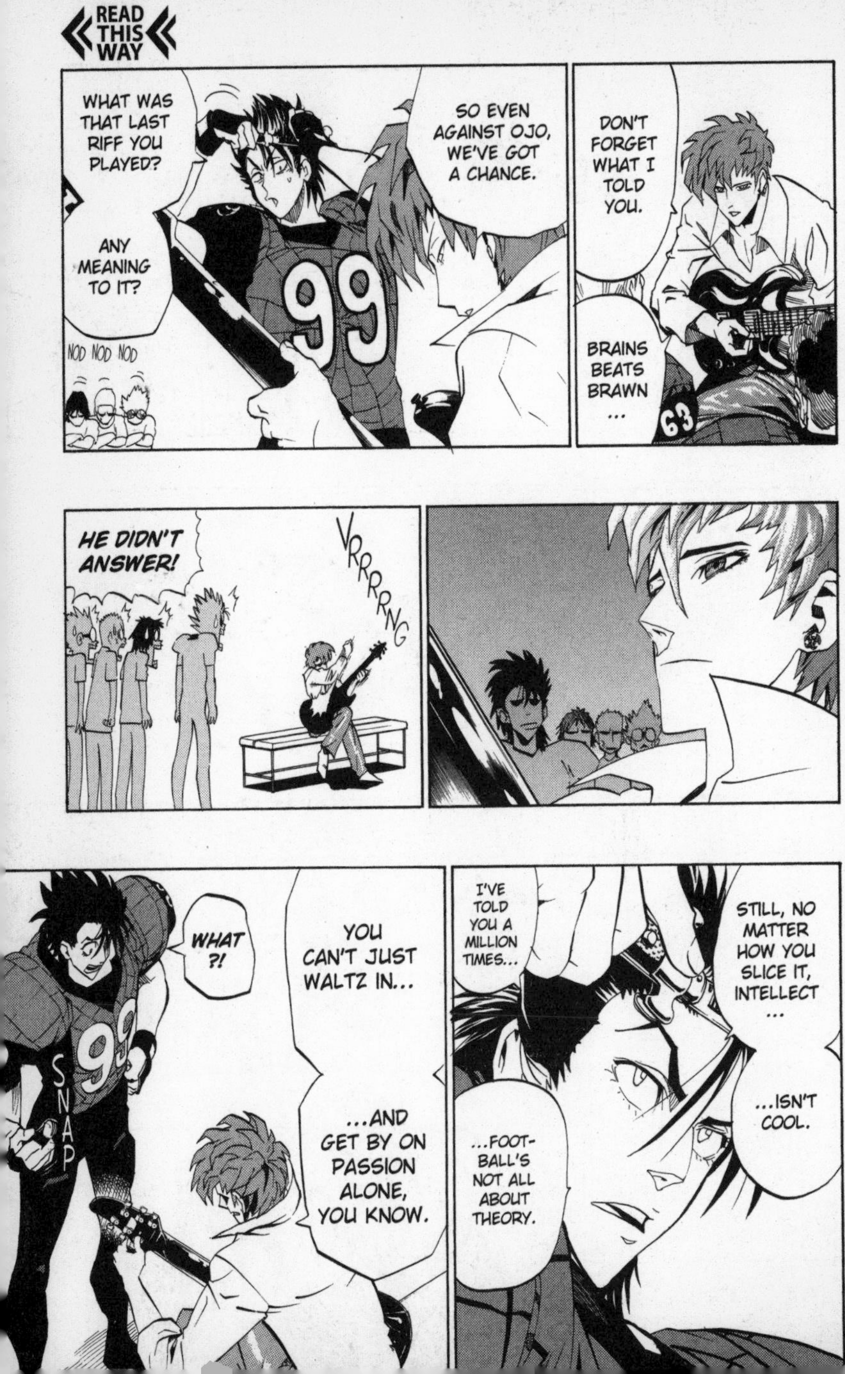
READ THIS WAY
DON'T FORGET WHAT I TOLD YOU.
BRAINS BEATS BRAWN ...
SO EVEN AGAINST OJO, WE'VE GOT A CHANCE.
WHAT WAS THAT LAST RIFF YOU PLAYED?
ANY MEANING TO IT?
NOD NOD NOD
VRRRRRNG
HE DIDN'T ANSWER!
STILL, NO MATTER HOW YOU SLICE IT, INTELLECT ...
I'VE TOLD YOU A MILLION TIMES...
...ISN'T COOL.
...FOOT-BALL'S NOT ALL ABOUT THEORY.
YOU CAN'T JUST WALTZ IN...
WHAT ?!
...AND GET BY ON PASSION ALONE, YOU KNOW.
SNAP

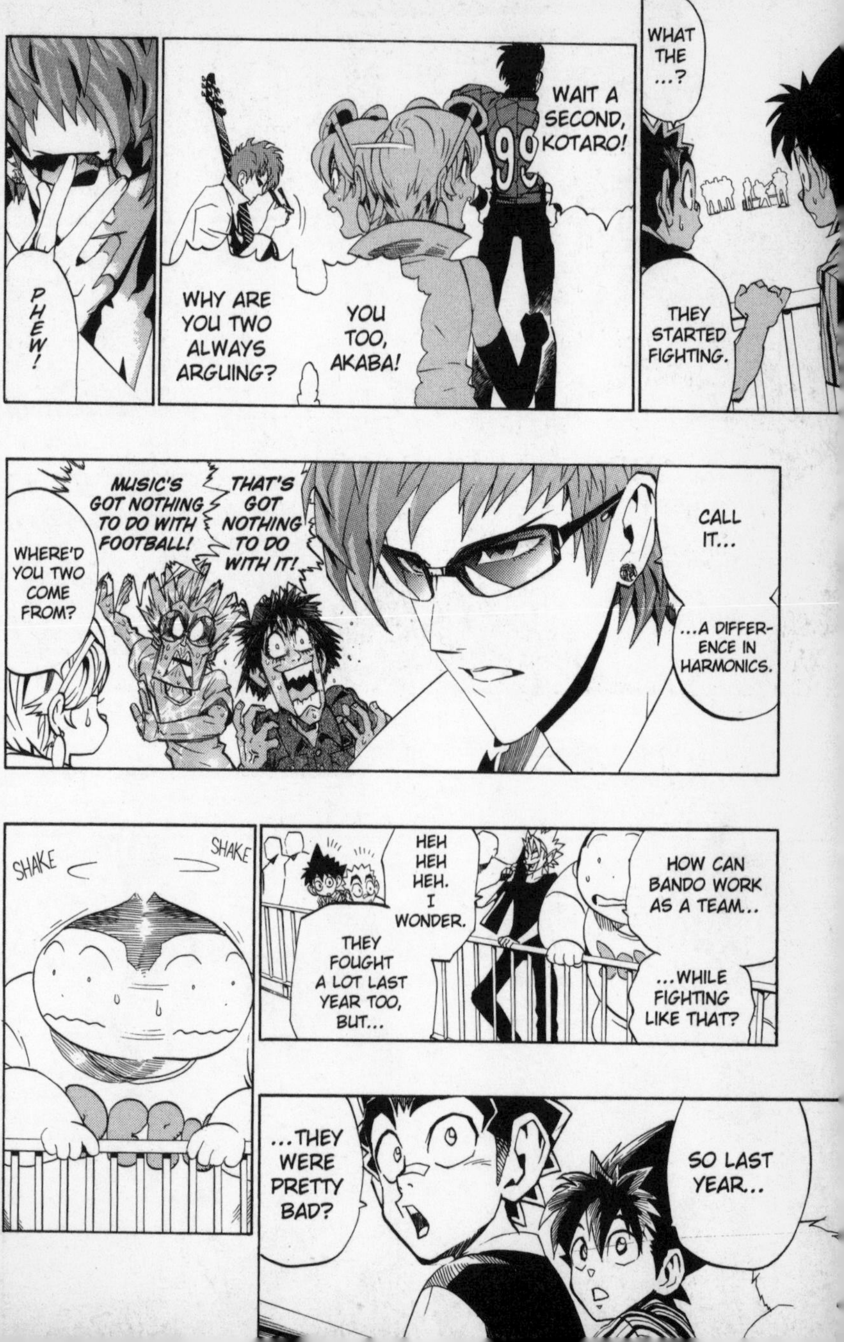
WHAT THE ...?
THEY STARTED FIGHTING.
WAIT A SECOND, KOTARO!
YOU TOO, AKABA!
WHY ARE YOU TWO ALWAYS ARGUING?
PHEW!
CALL IT...
...A DIFFERENCE IN HARMONICS.
THAT'S GOT NOTHING TO DO WITH IT!
MUSIC'S GOT NOTHING TO DO WITH FOOTBALL!
WHERE'D YOU TWO COME FROM?
HOW CAN BANDO WORK AS A TEAM...
...WHILE FIGHTING LIKE THAT?
HEH HEH HEH. I WONDER.
THEY FOUGHT A LOT LAST YEAR TOO, BUT...
SO LAST YEAR...
...THEY WERE PRETTY BAD?
SHAKE
SHAKE

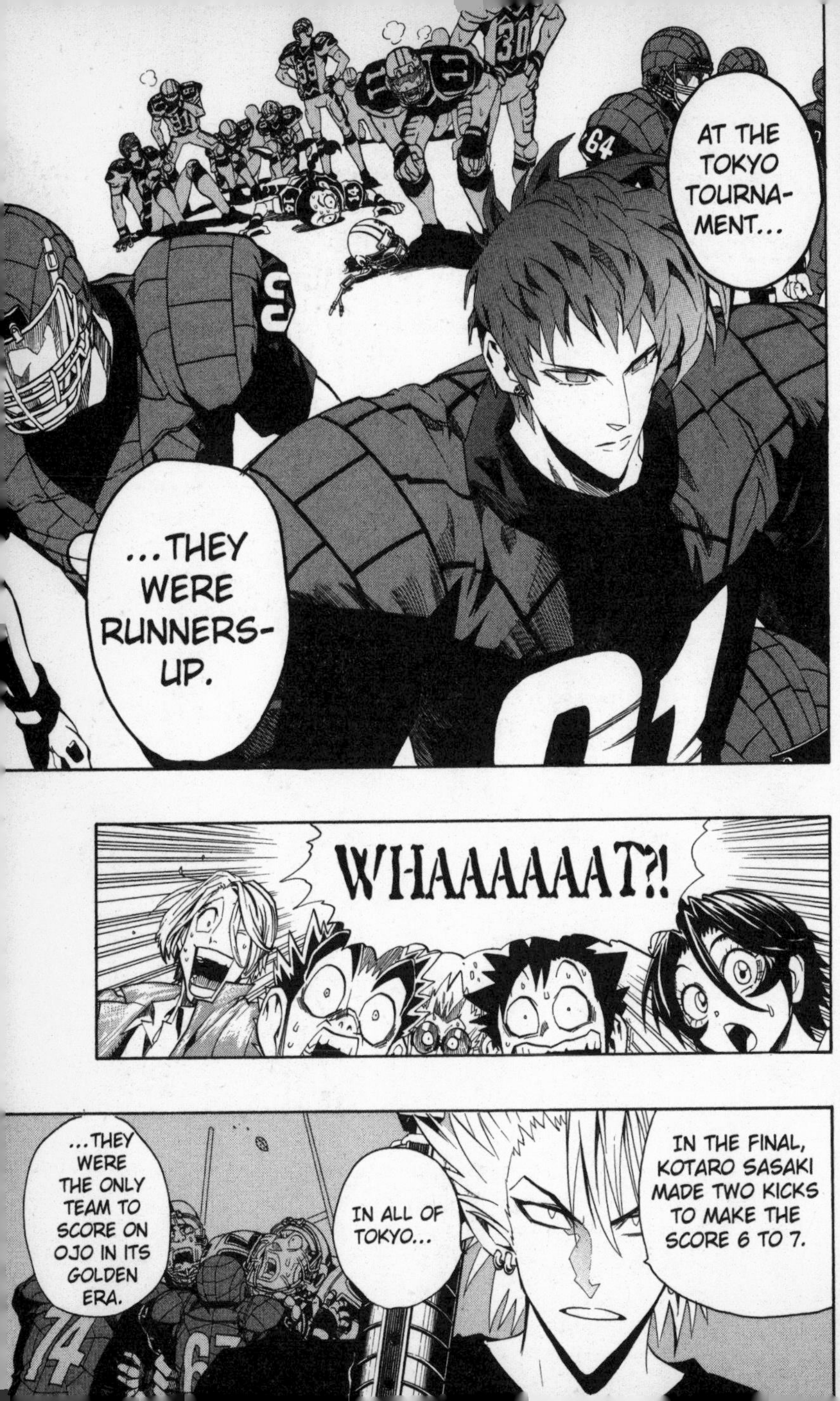
AT THE TOKYO TOURNAMENT...
...THEY WERE RUNNERS-UP.
WHAAAAAAT?!
IN THE FINAL, KOTARO SASAKI MADE TWO KICKS TO MAKE THE SCORE 6 TO 7.
IN ALL OF TOKYO...
...THEY WERE THE ONLY TEAM TO SCORE ON OJO IN ITS GOLDEN ERA.

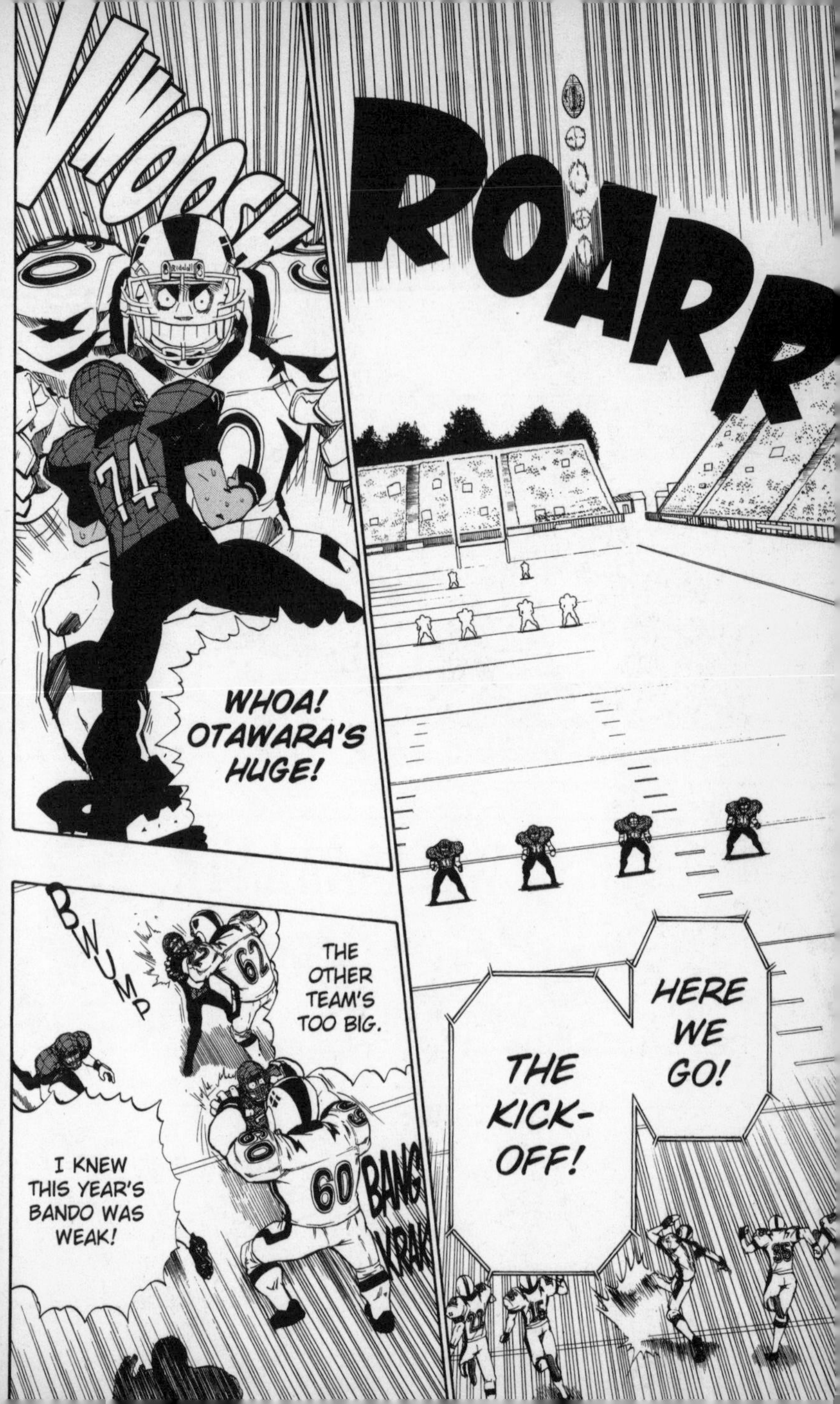
ROARR
HERE WE GO!
THE KICK-OFF!
WHOOSH
WHOA! OTAWARA'S HUGE!
BWUMP
THE OTHER TEAM'S TOO BIG.
BANG
KRAK
I KNEW THIS YEAR'S BANDO WAS WEAK!

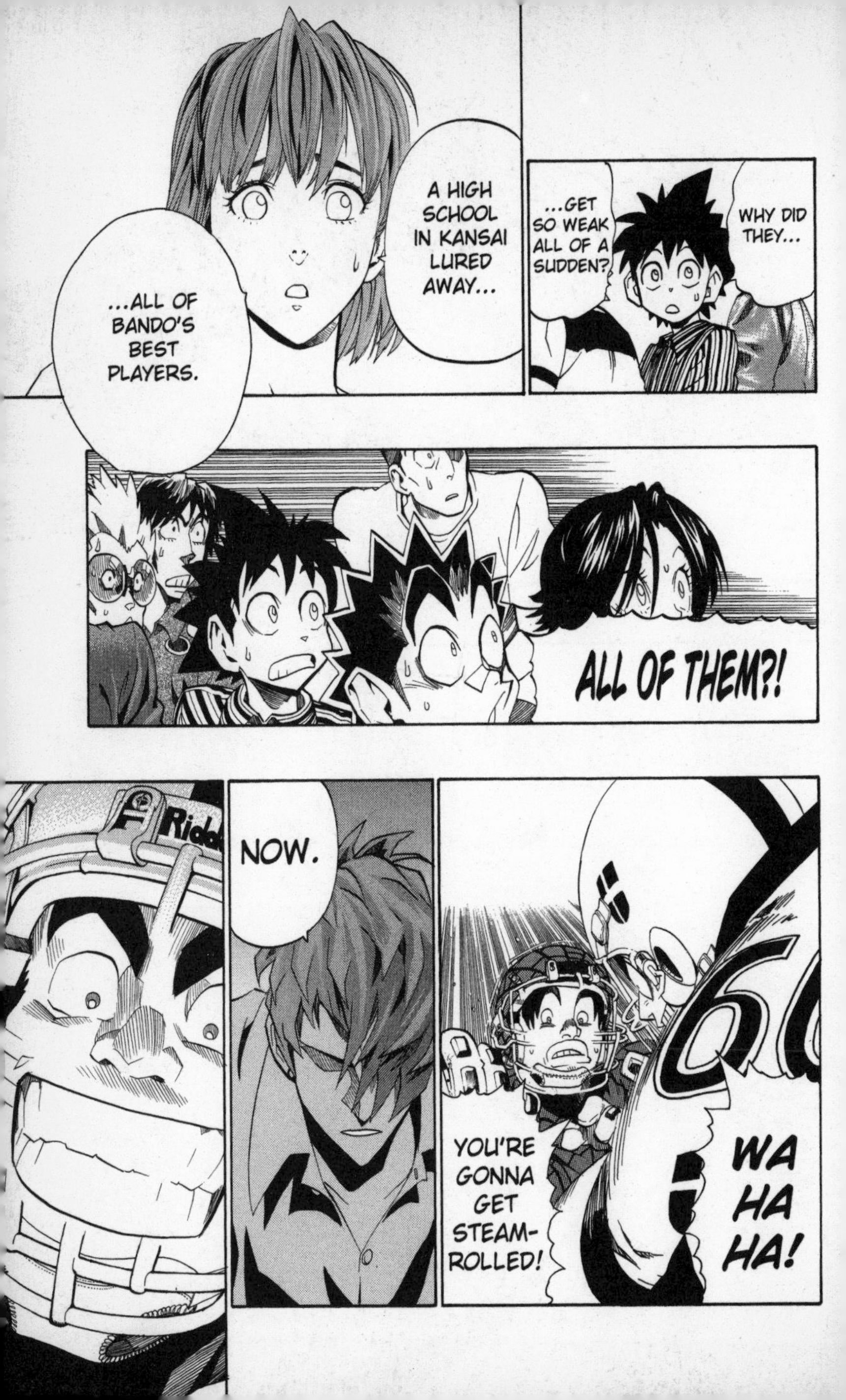
WHY DID THEY...
...GET SO WEAK ALL OF A SUDDEN?
A HIGH SCHOOL IN KANSAI LURED AWAY...
...ALL OF BANDO'S BEST PLAYERS.
ALL OF THEM?!
WA HA HA!
YOU'RE GONNA GET STEAM-ROLLED!
NOW.

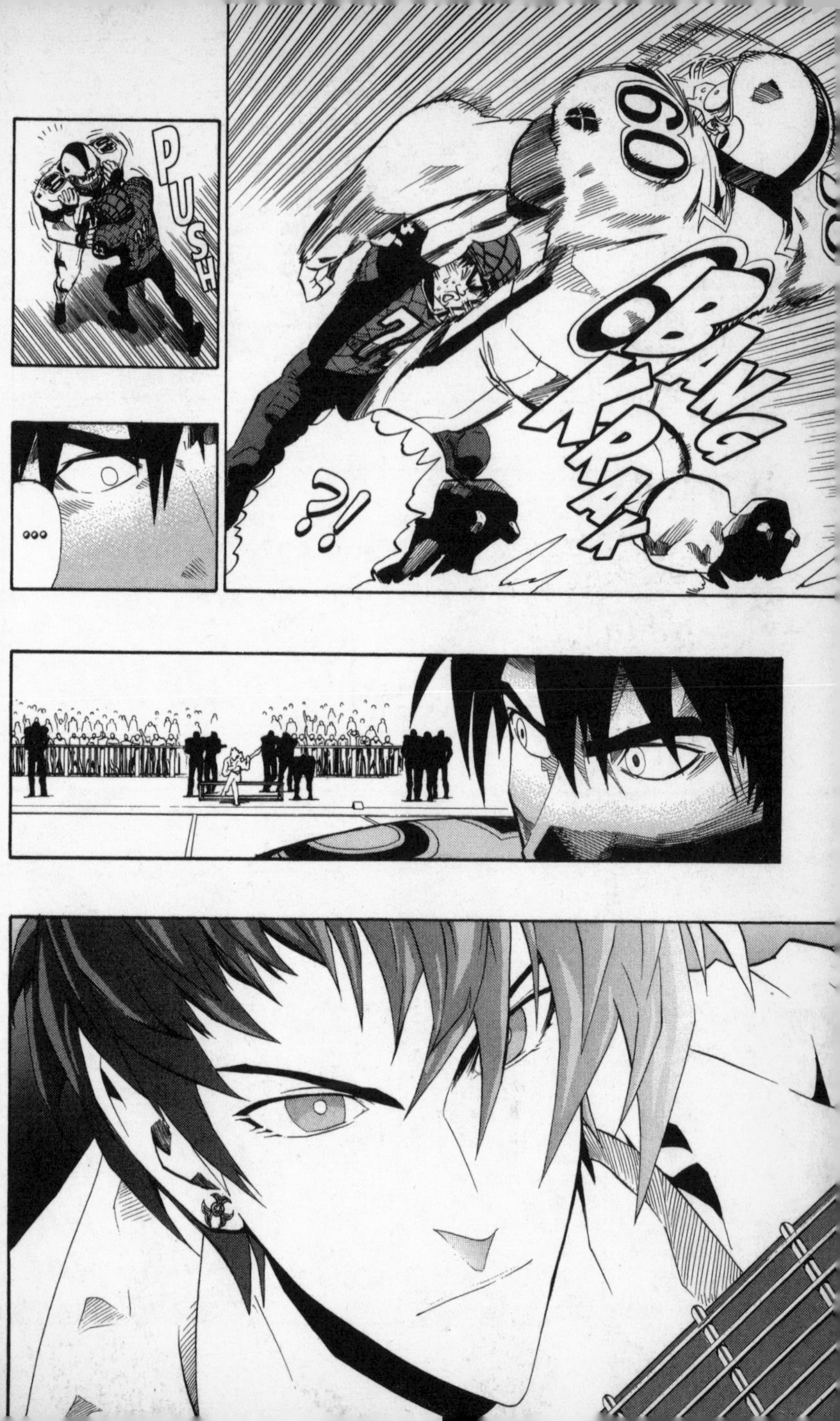
BANG
KRAK
?!
PUSH
...

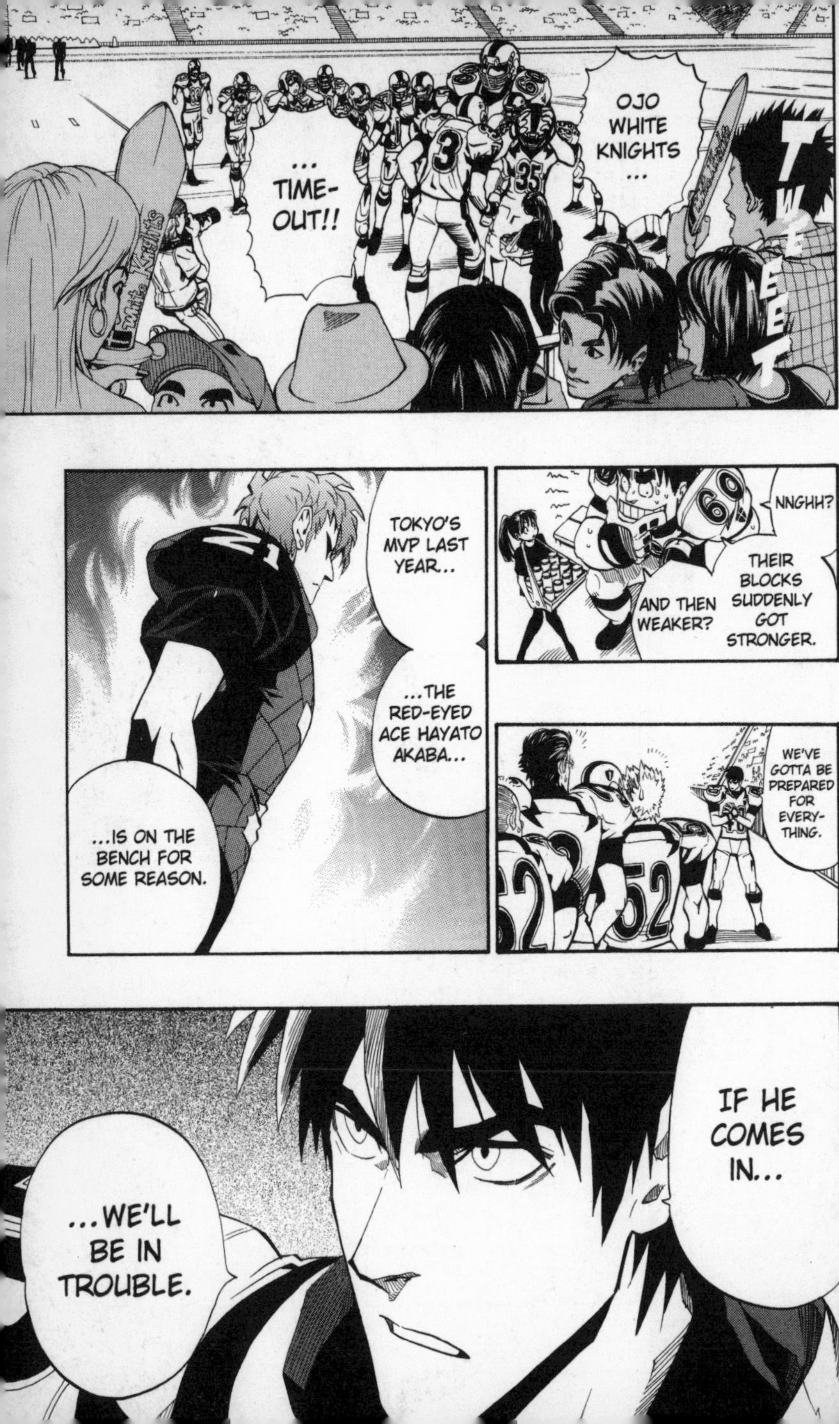
OJO WHITE KNIGHTS...
TWEET
...TIME-OUT!!
White Knights
NNGHH?
THEIR BLOCKS SUDDENLY GOT STRONGER.
AND THEN WEAKER?
WE'VE GOTTA BE PREPARED FOR EVERYTHING.
TOKYO'S MVP LAST YEAR...
...THE RED-EYED ACE HAYATO AKABA...
...IS ON THE BENCH FOR SOME REASON.
IF HE COMES IN...
...WE'LL BE IN TROUBLE.

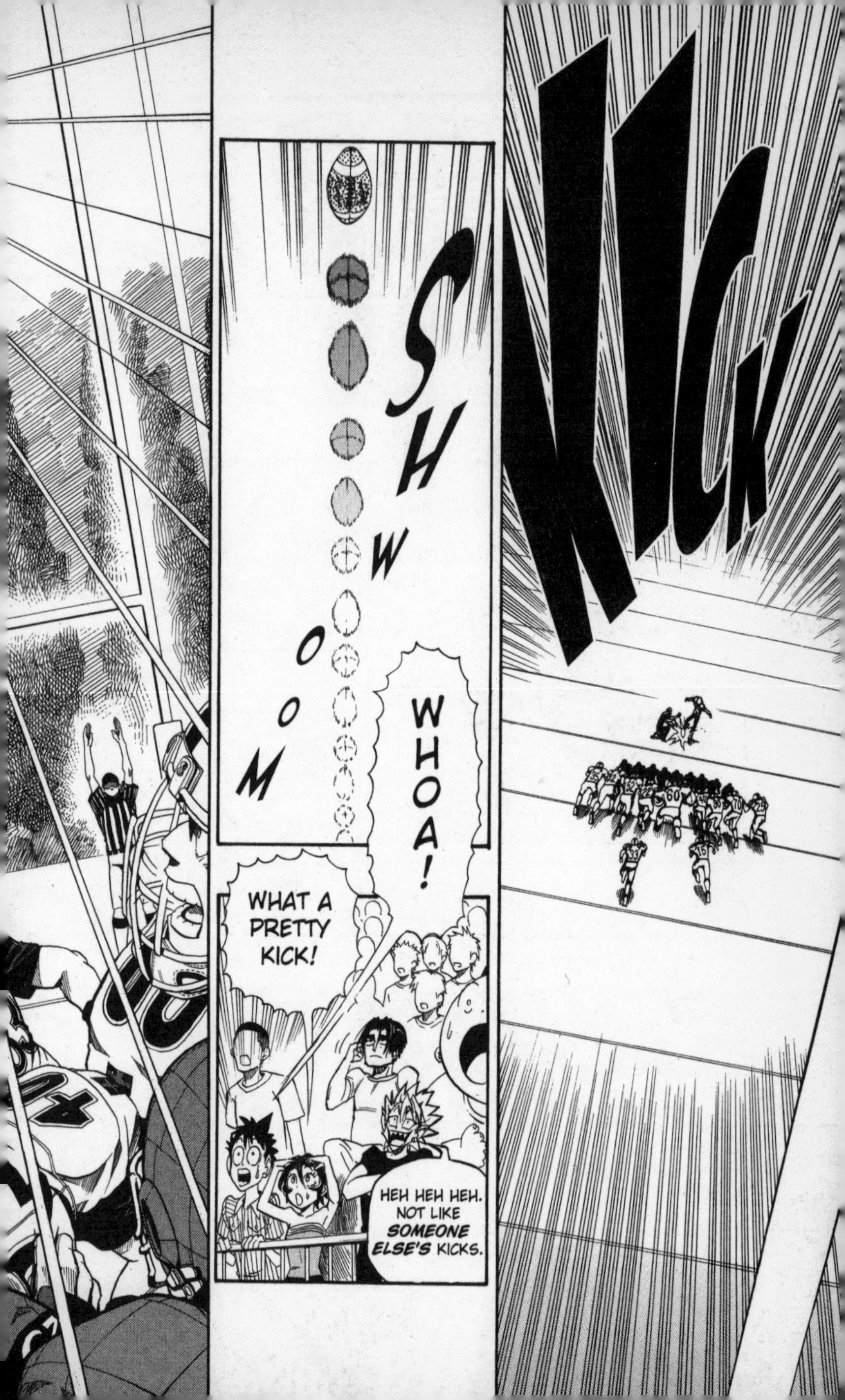
SHWOOM
WHOA!
WHAT A PRETTY KICK!
HEH HEH HEH. NOT LIKE SOMEONE ELSE'S KICKS.

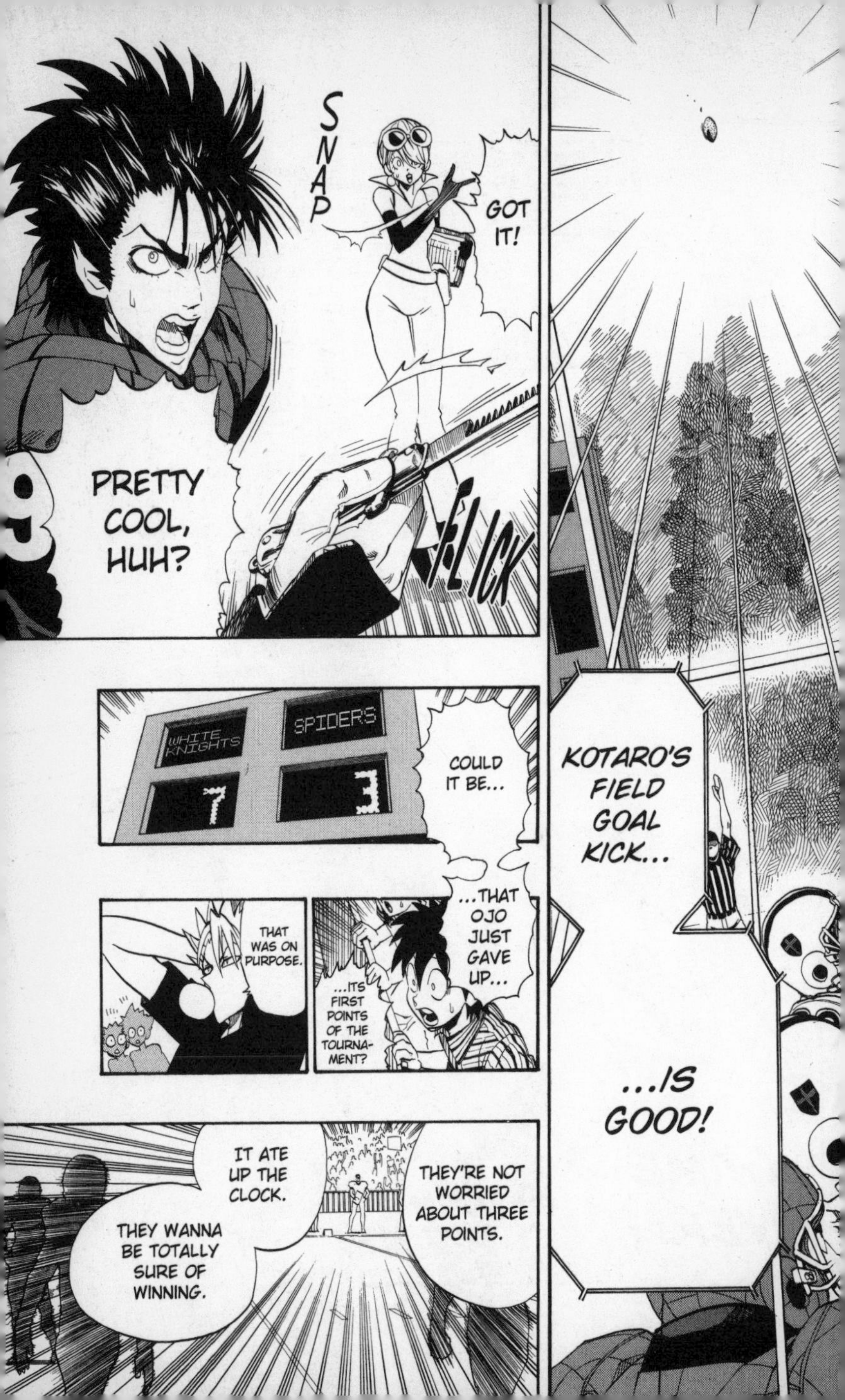
KOTARO'S FIELD GOAL KICK...
...IS GOOD!
SNAP
GOT IT!
F-LICK
PRETTY COOL, HUH?
WHITE KNIGHTS
SPIDERS
7
3
COULD IT BE...
...THAT OJO JUST GAVE UP...
...ITS FIRST POINTS OF THE TOURNAMENT?
THAT WAS ON PURPOSE.
THEY'RE NOT WORRIED ABOUT THREE POINTS.
IT ATE UP THE CLOCK.
THEY WANNA BE TOTALLY SURE OF WINNING.

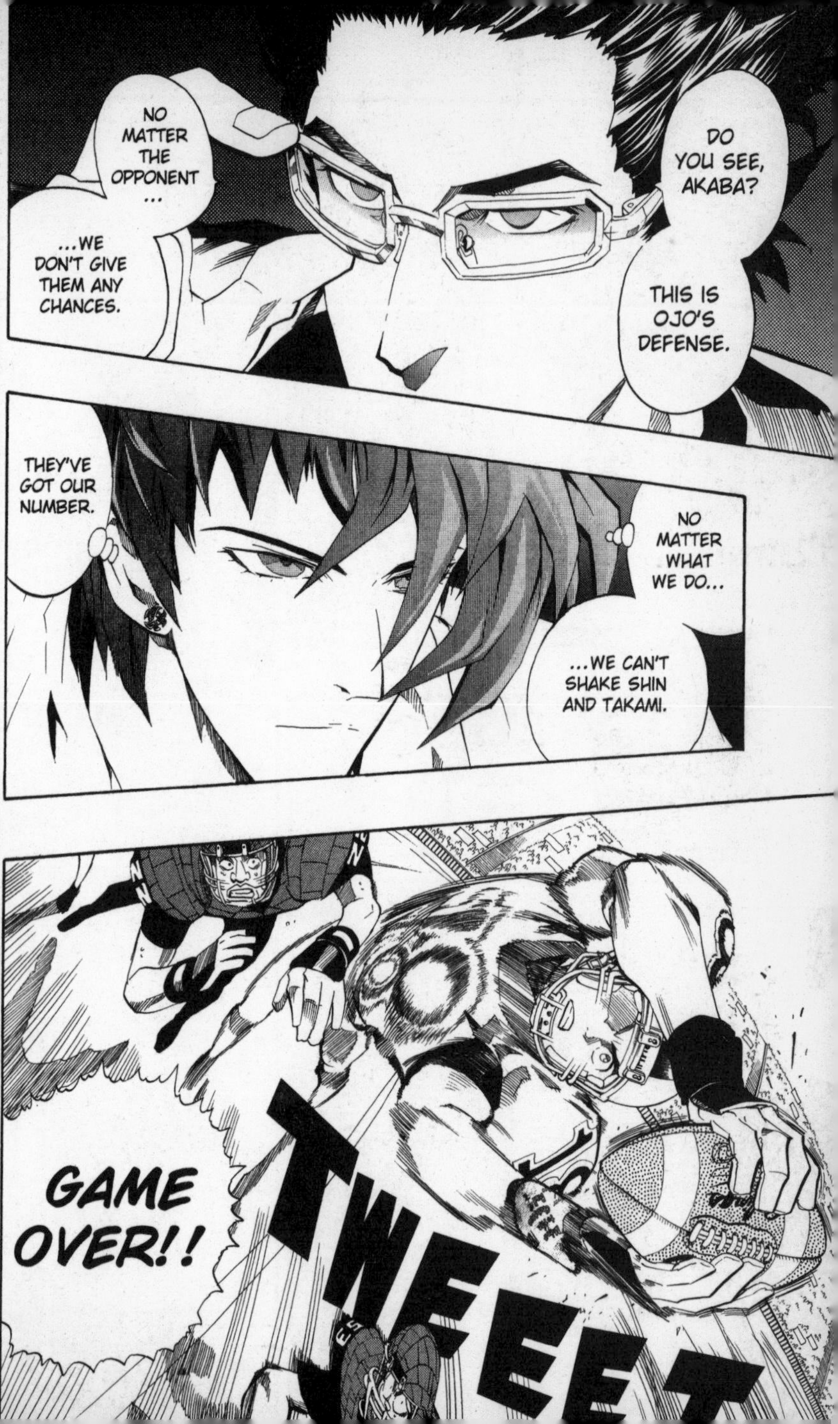

DO YOU SEE, AKABA?
THIS IS OJO'S DEFENSE.
NO MATTER THE OPPONENT...
...WE DON'T GIVE THEM ANY CHANCES.
NO MATTER WHAT WE DO...
...WE CAN'T SHAKE SHIN AND TAKAMI.
THEY'VE GOT OUR NUMBER.
TWEEET
GAME OVER!!

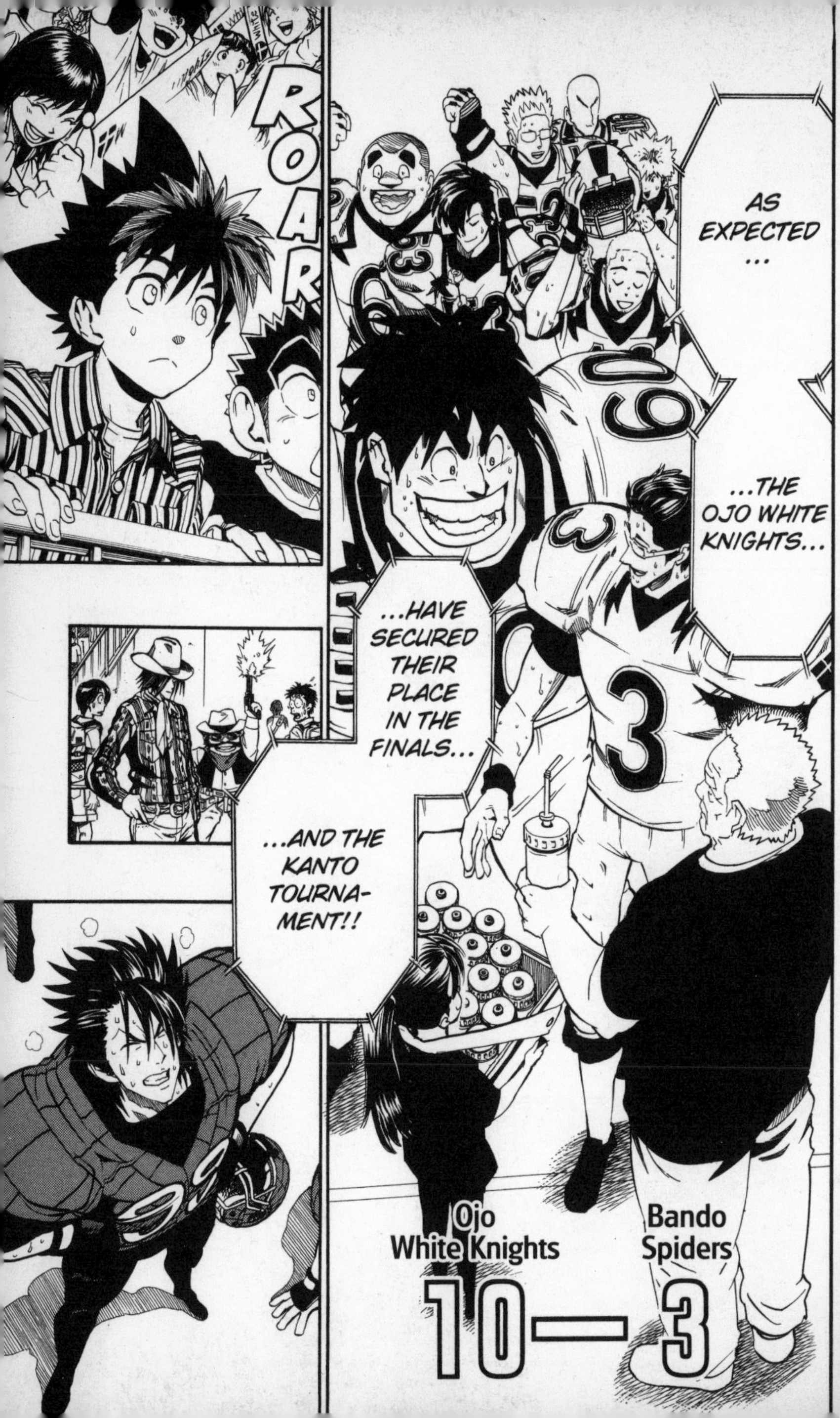
AS EXPECTED...
...THE OJO WHITE KNIGHTS...
...HAVE SECURED THEIR PLACE IN THE FINALS...
...AND THE KANTO TOURNAMENT!!
Ojo White Knights
Bando Spiders
10—3
ROAR

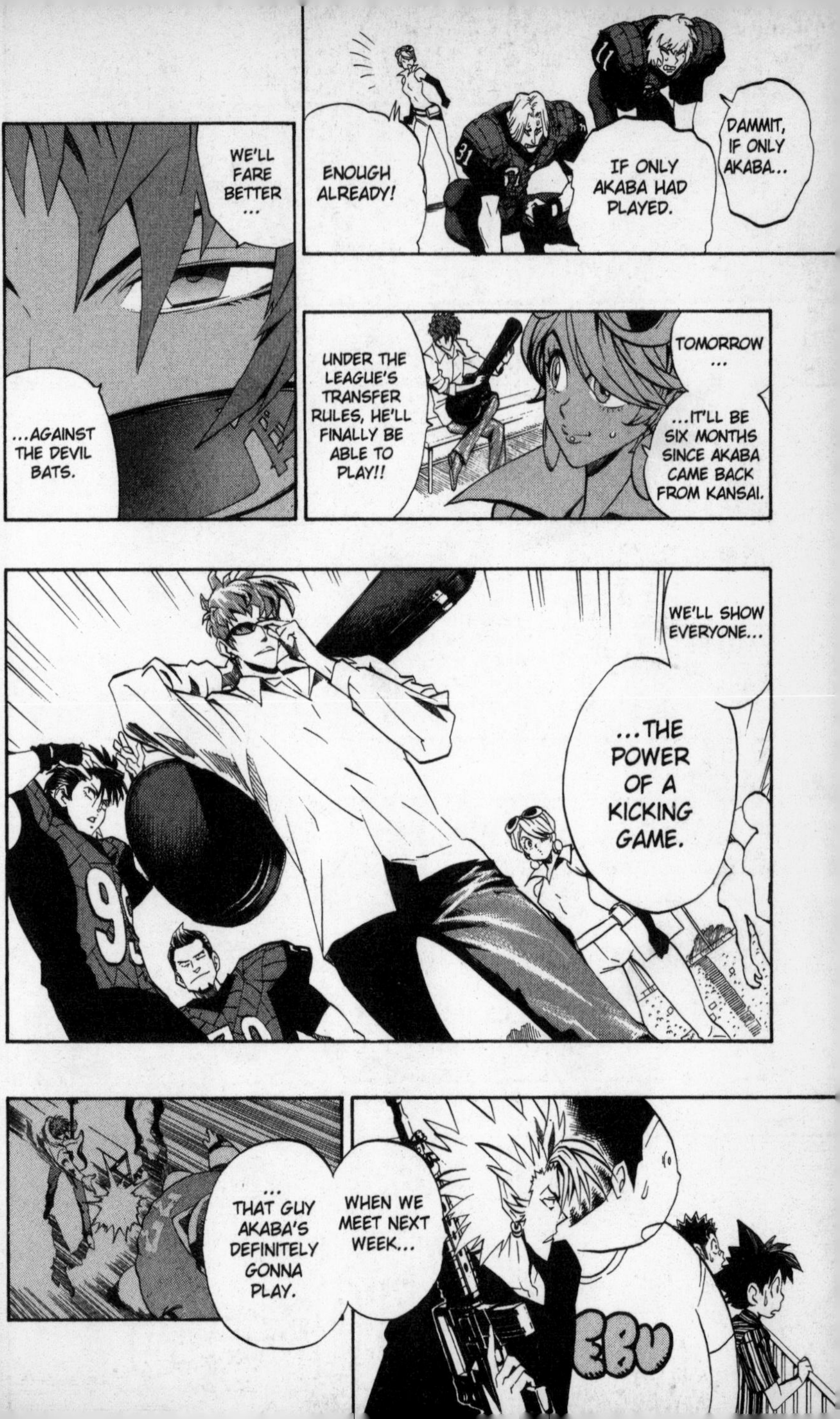
DAMMIT, IF ONLY AKABA...
IF ONLY AKABA HAD PLAYED.
ENOUGH ALREADY!
TOMORROW...
...IT'LL BE SIX MONTHS SINCE AKABA CAME BACK FROM KANSAI.
UNDER THE LEAGUE'S TRANSFER RULES, HE'LL FINALLY BE ABLE TO PLAY!!
WE'LL FARE BETTER...
...AGAINST THE DEVIL BATS.
WE'LL SHOW EVERYONE...
...THE POWER OF A KICKING GAME.
WHEN WE MEET NEXT WEEK...
...THAT GUY AKABA'S DEFINITELY GONNA PLAY.

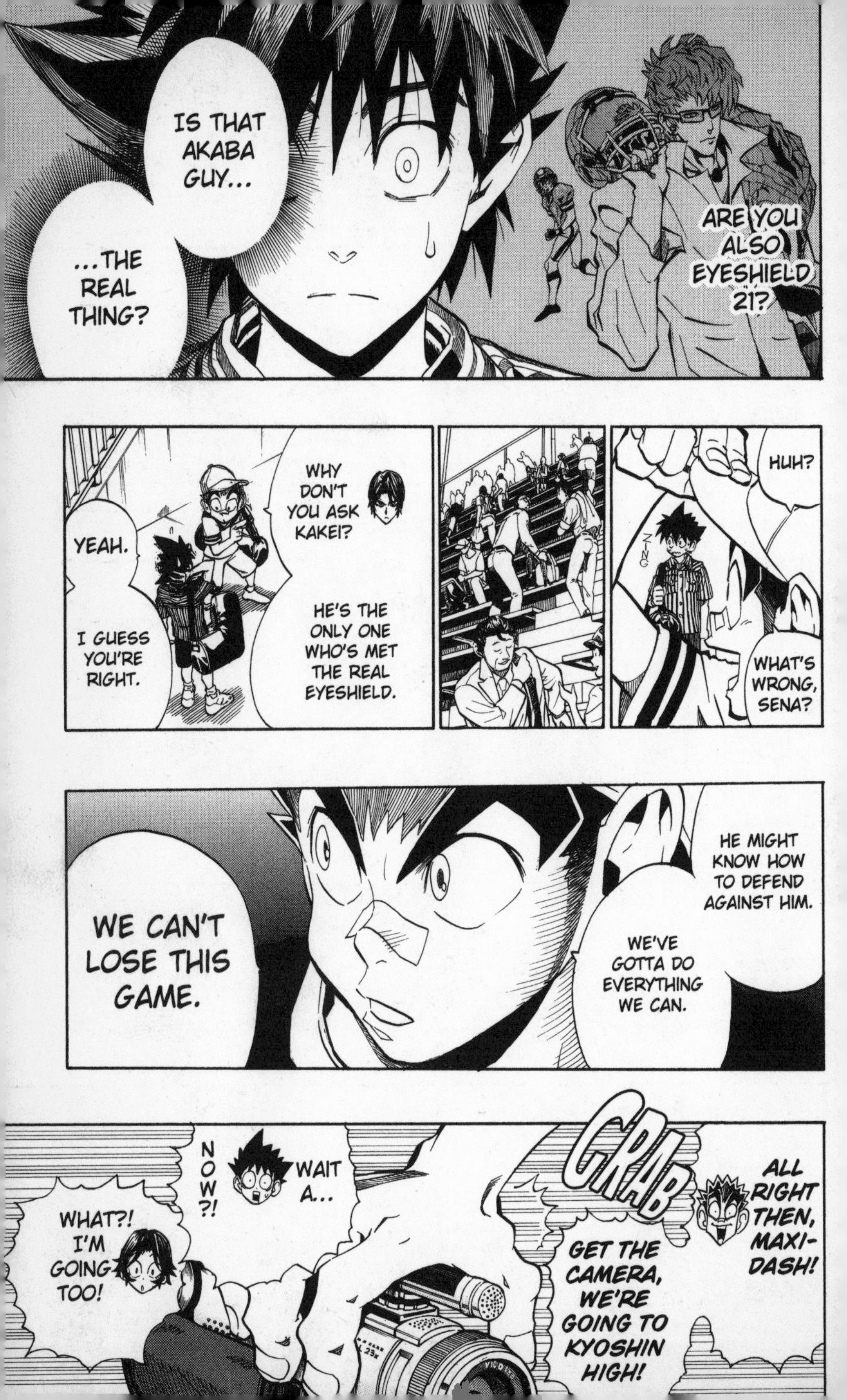
ARE YOU ALSO EYESHIELD 21?
IS THAT AKABA GUY...
...THE REAL THING?
HUH?
ZING
WHAT'S WRONG, SENA?
WHY DON'T YOU ASK KAKEI?
HE'S THE ONLY ONE WHO'S MET THE REAL EYESHIELD.
YEAH.
I GUESS YOU'RE RIGHT.
HE MIGHT KNOW HOW TO DEFEND AGAINST HIM.
WE'VE GOTTA DO EVERYTHING WE CAN.
WE CAN'T LOSE THIS GAME.
ALL RIGHT THEN, MAXI-DASH!
GRAB
GET THE CAMERA, WE'RE GOING TO KYOSHIN HIGH!
WAIT A...
NOW?!
WHAT?! I'M GOING TOO!

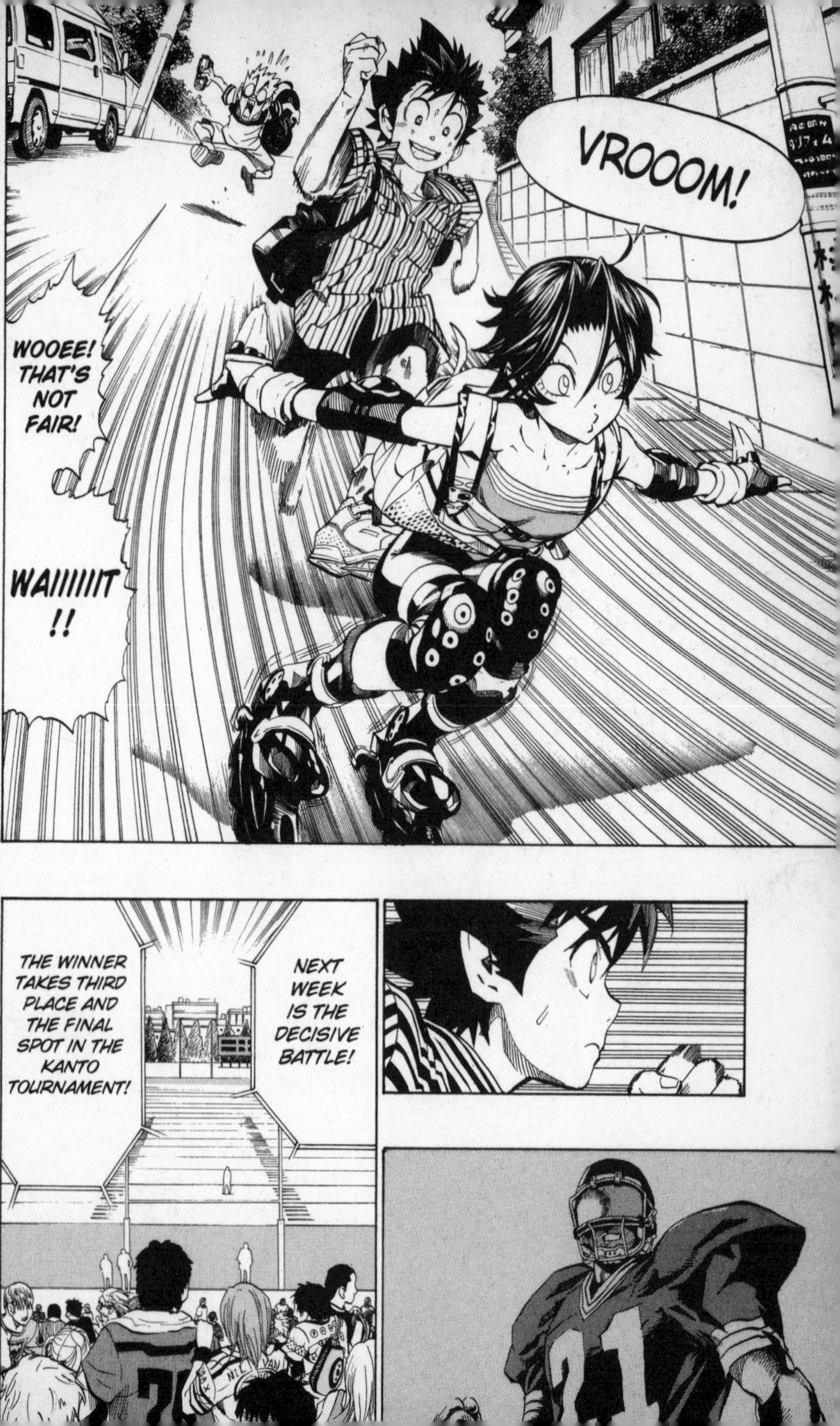
VROOOM!
WOOEE! THAT'S NOT FAIR!
WAIIIIIIT !!
NEXT WEEK IS THE DECISIVE BATTLE!
THE WINNER TAKES THIRD PLACE AND THE FINAL SPOT IN THE KANTO TOURNAMENT!

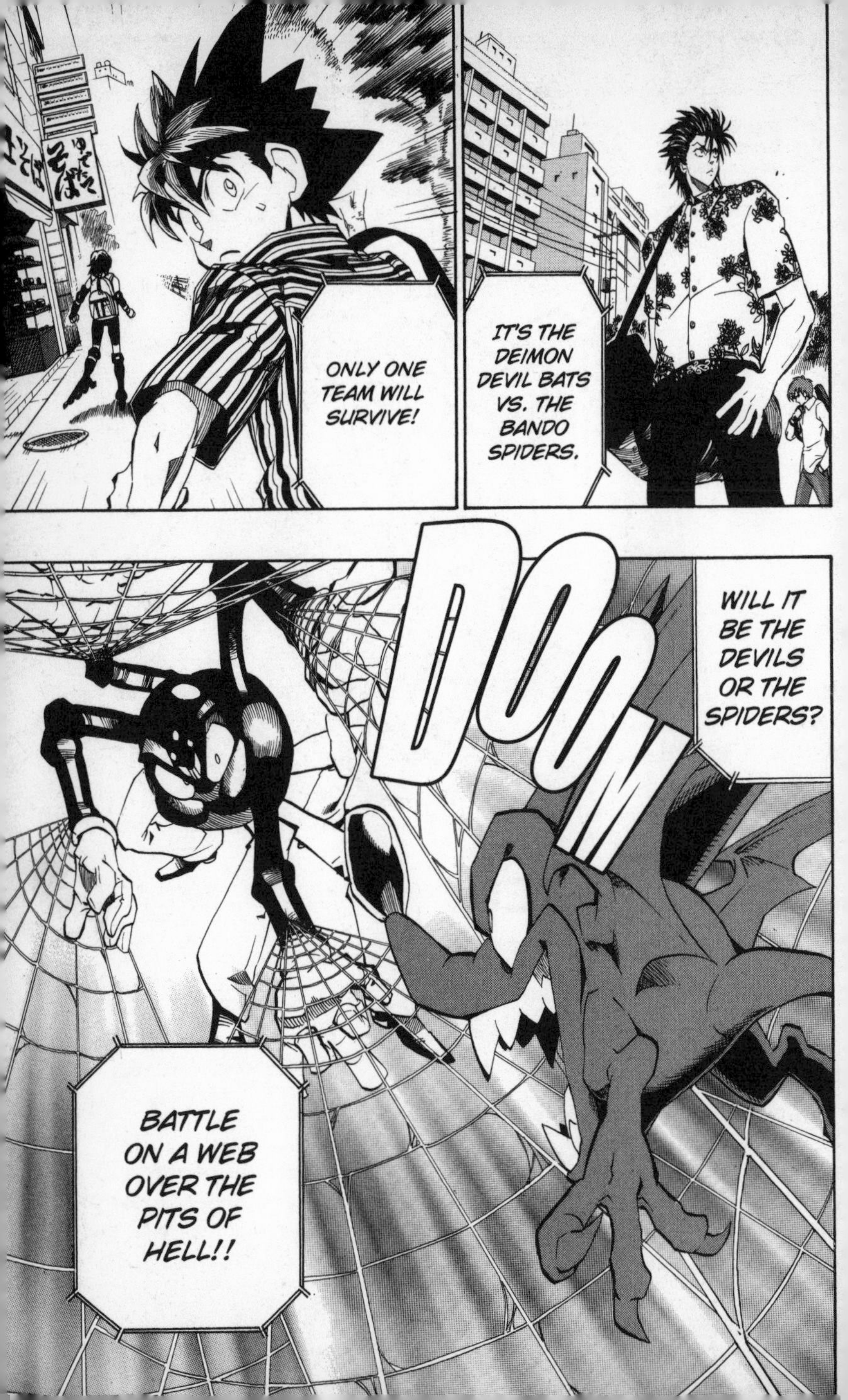
IT'S THE DEIMON DEVIL BATS VS. THE BANDO SPIDERS.
ゆでたて
そば
ONLY ONE TEAM WILL SURVIVE!
WILL IT BE THE DEVILS OR THE SPIDERS?
DOOM
BATTLE ON A WEB OVER THE PITS OF HELL!!

※This guide was put together by the principal of Bando High School for his students. Some students have been vocal about trying to get it abolished, but the principal expels anyone who refuses to accept it.

Hayato Akaba

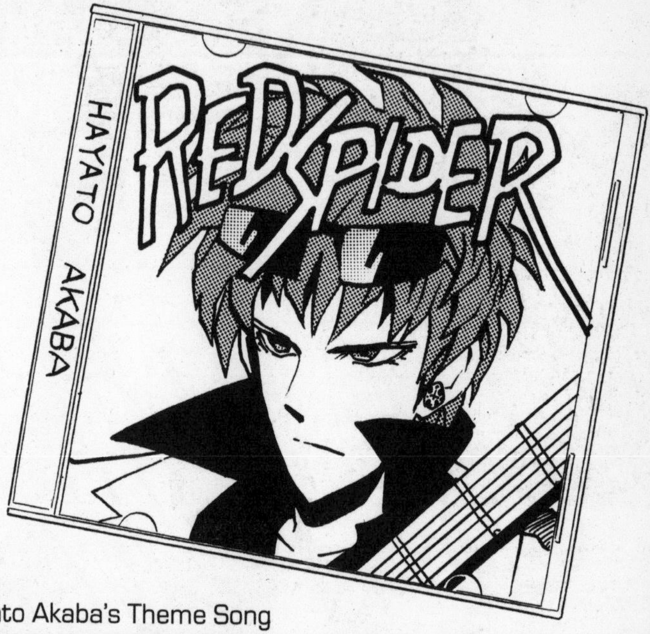
RED SPIDER
HAYATO AKABA

1. Hayato Akaba's Theme Song

"RED SPIDER"

Lyrics / Composition / Vocals: The Principal

Those red eyes that smolder
They're just colored contacts

With a light sigh
Coolly freezing everything

RED SPIDER–eight arms and unlimited power
RED SPIDER–a screeching guitar and a mystery

PRIVATE DATA

Family Members: Mother, father, younger sister

Favorite Food: Salad

Favorite Color: Red

Favorite Animal: Monkeys (because they're smart)

Personal Hero: Alfred Nobel

Most Important Thing in Life: Coolness

Most Important Thing in Football: The Kicking Team

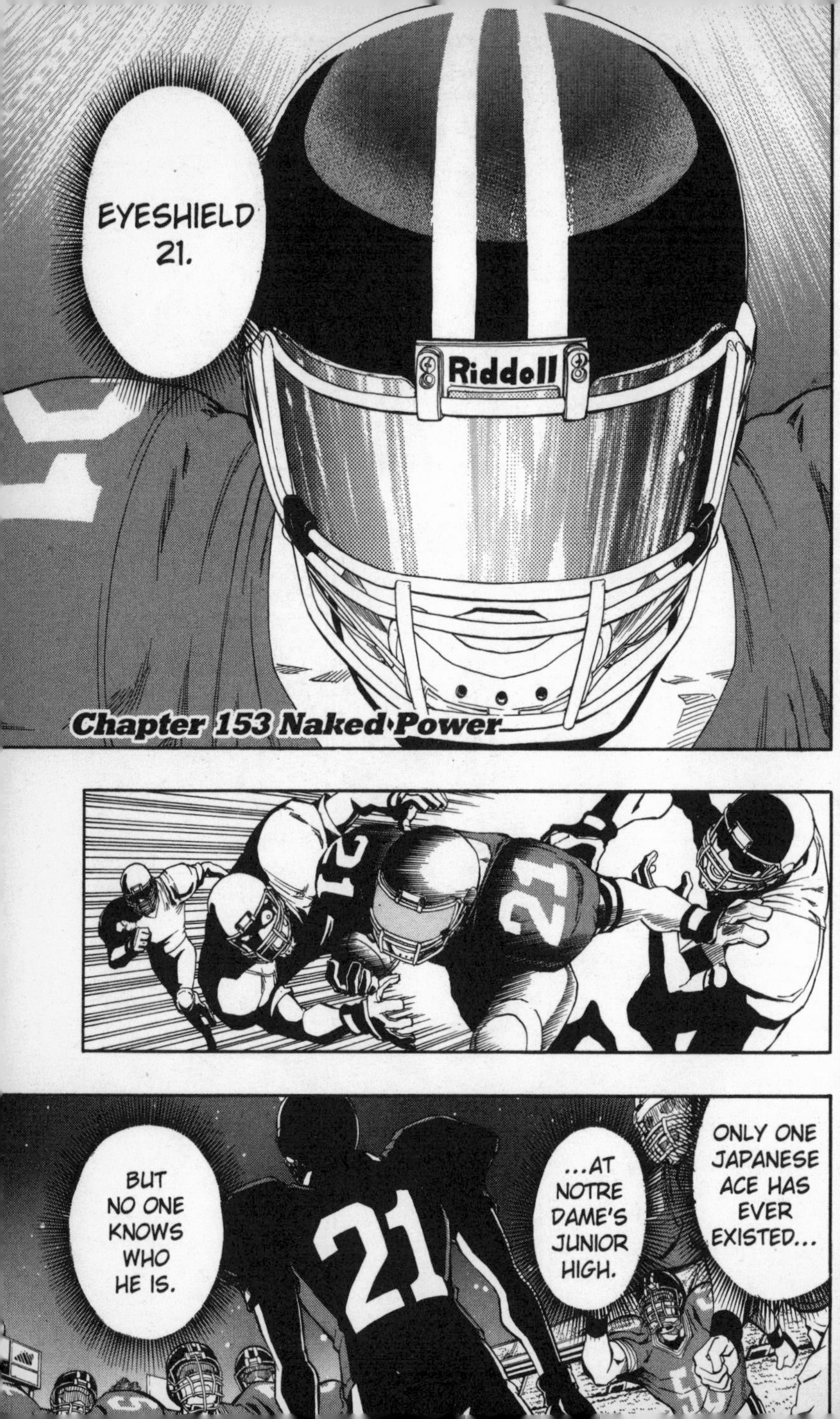
EYESHIELD 21.
Riddoll
Chapter 153 Naked Power
ONLY ONE JAPANESE ACE HAS EVER EXISTED...
...AT NOTRE DAME'S JUNIOR HIGH.
BUT NO ONE KNOWS WHO HE IS.

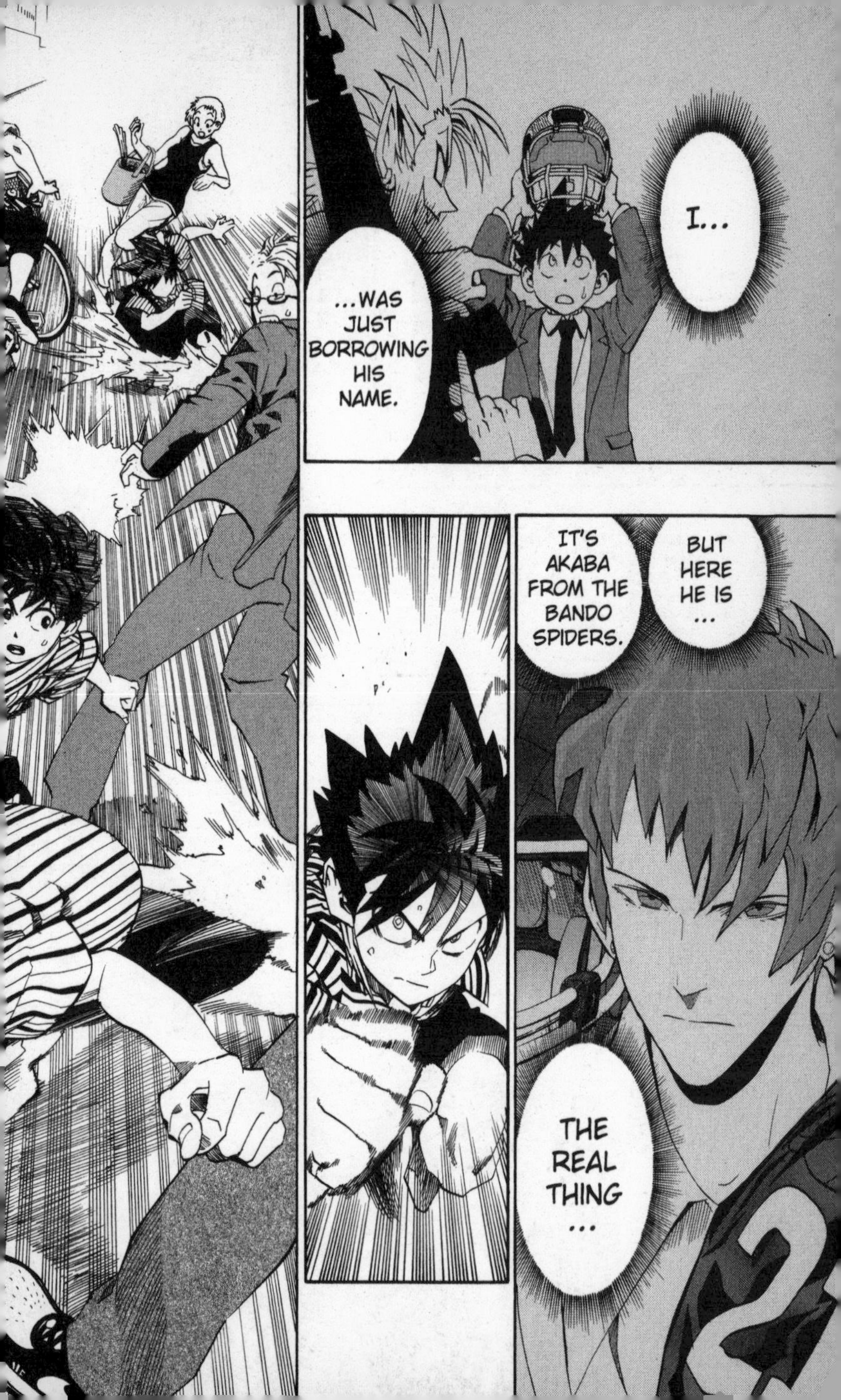
I...
...WAS JUST BORROWING HIS NAME.
BUT HERE HE IS ...
IT'S AKABA FROM THE BANDO SPIDERS.
THE REAL THING ...

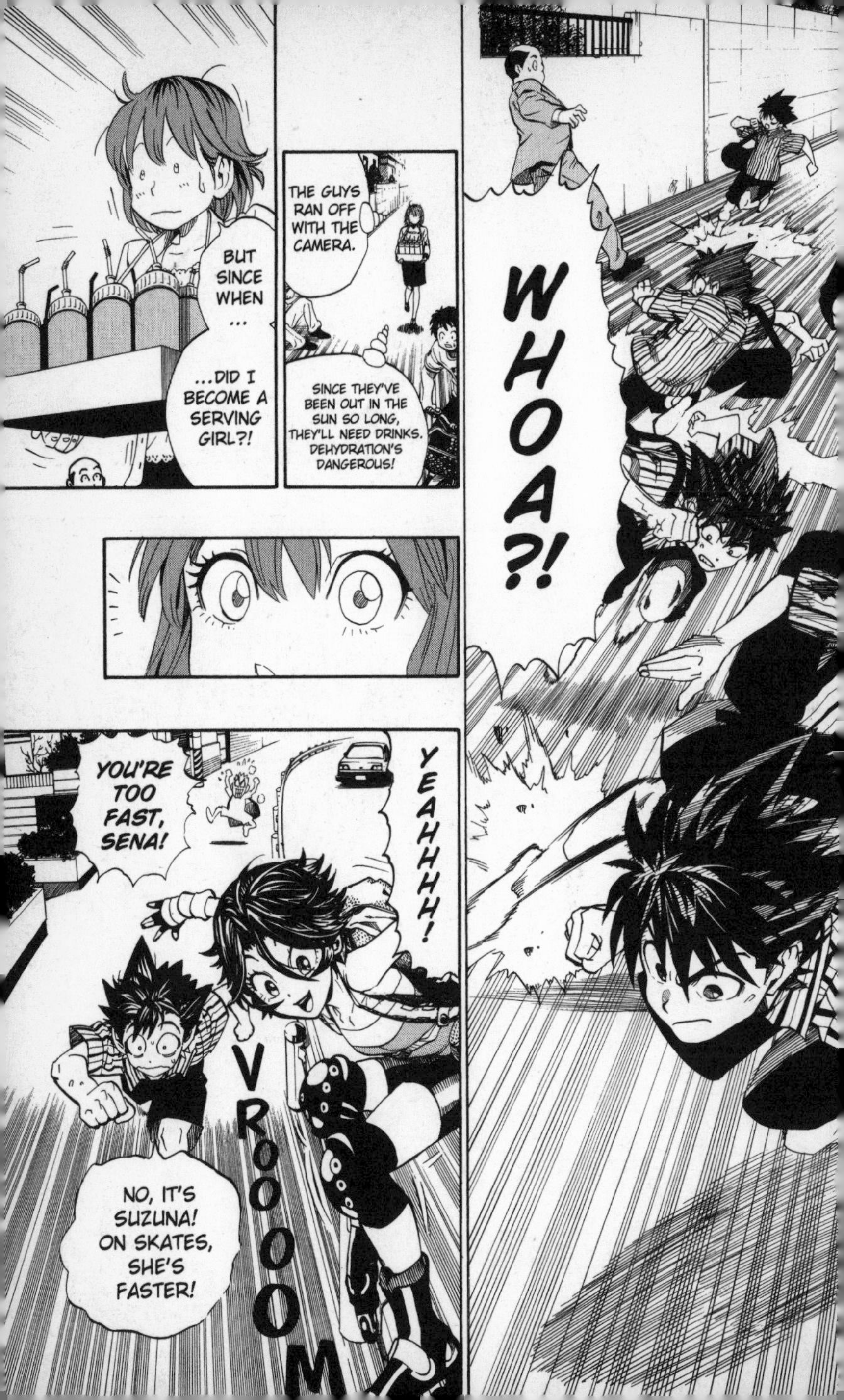
WHOA?!
THE GUYS RAN OFF WITH THE CAMERA.
SINCE THEY'VE BEEN OUT IN THE SUN SO LONG, THEY'LL NEED DRINKS. DEHYDRATION'S DANGEROUS!
BUT SINCE WHEN ...
...DID I BECOME A SERVING GIRL?!
YEAHHHHH!
YOU'RE TOO FAST, SENA!
VROOOOOM
NO, IT'S SUZUNA! ON SKATES, SHE'S FASTER!

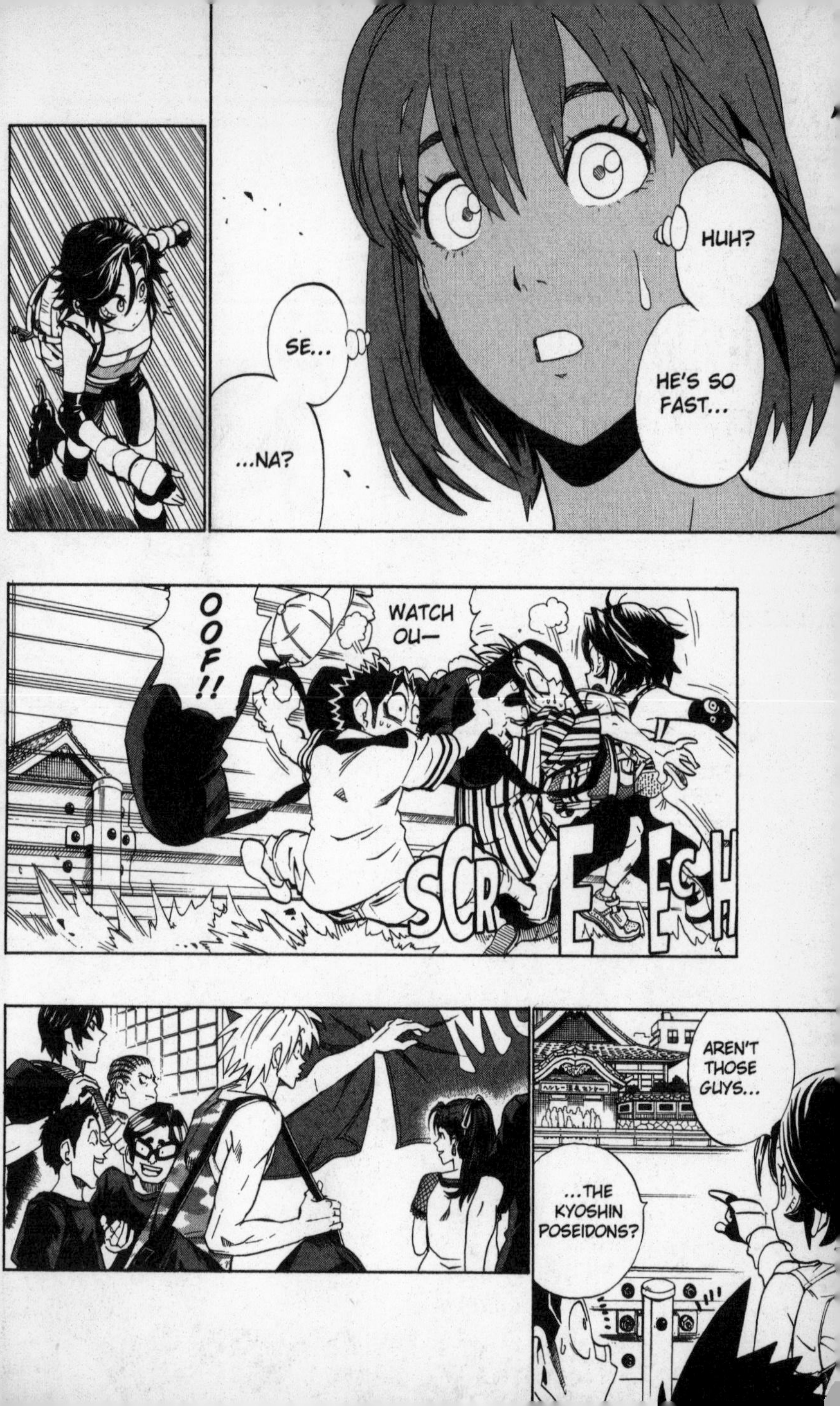
HUH?
HE'S SO FAST...
SE...
...NA?
WATCH OU—
OOF!!
SCREECH
AREN'T THOSE GUYS...
...THE KYOSHIN POSEIDONS?

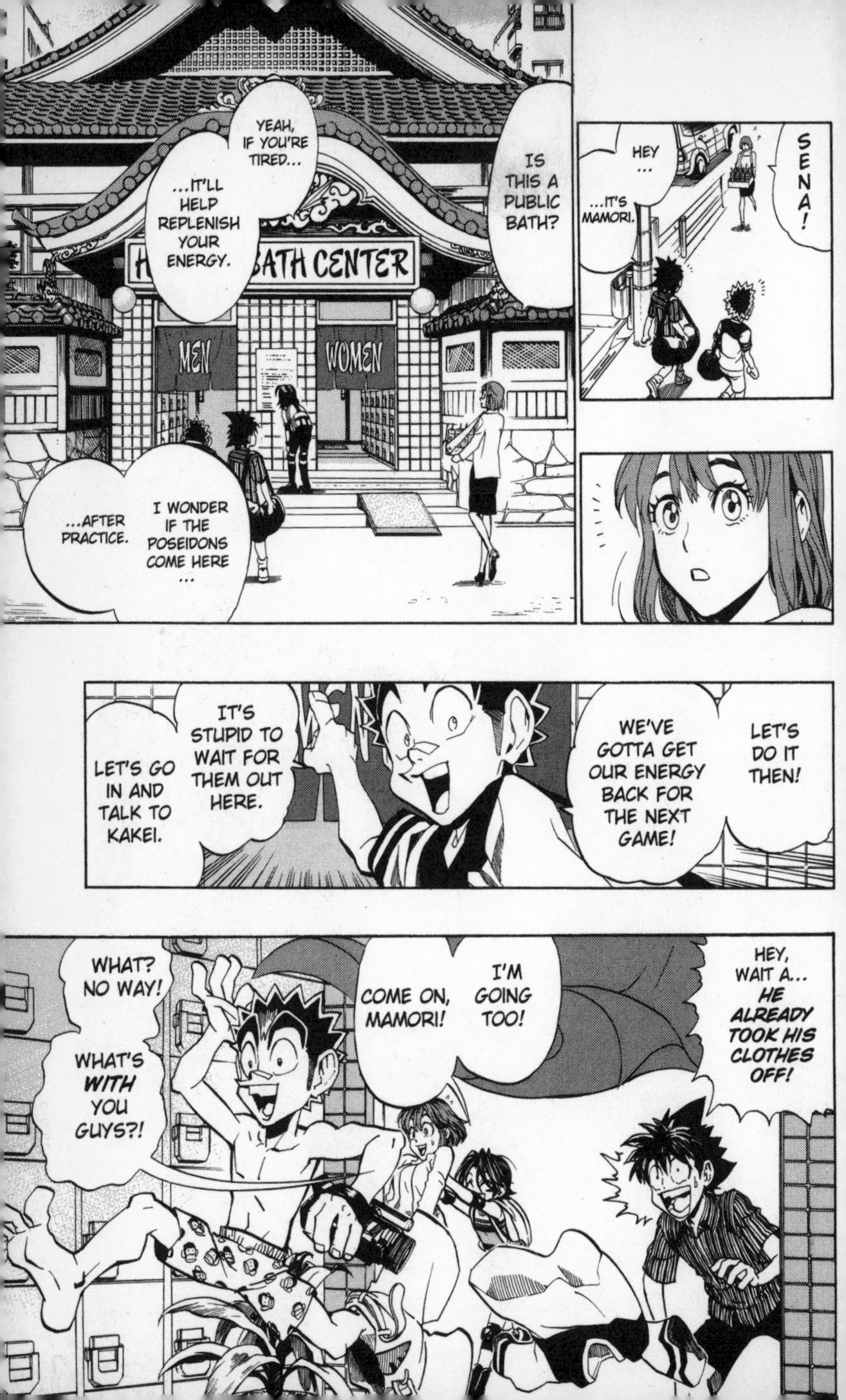
SENA!
HEY ...
...IT'S MAMORI.
IS THIS A PUBLIC BATH?
YEAH, IF YOU'RE TIRED...
...IT'LL HELP REPLENISH YOUR ENERGY.
BATH CENTER
MEN
WOMEN
I WONDER IF THE POSEIDONS COME HERE ...
...AFTER PRACTICE.
LET'S DO IT THEN!
WE'VE GOTTA GET OUR ENERGY BACK FOR THE NEXT GAME!
IT'S STUPID TO WAIT FOR THEM OUT HERE.
LET'S GO IN AND TALK TO KAKEI.
HEY, WAIT A... HE ALREADY TOOK HIS CLOTHES OFF!
I'M GOING TOO!
COME ON, MAMORI!
WHAT? NO WAY!
WHAT'S WITH YOU GUYS?!

Chapter 153 Naked Power

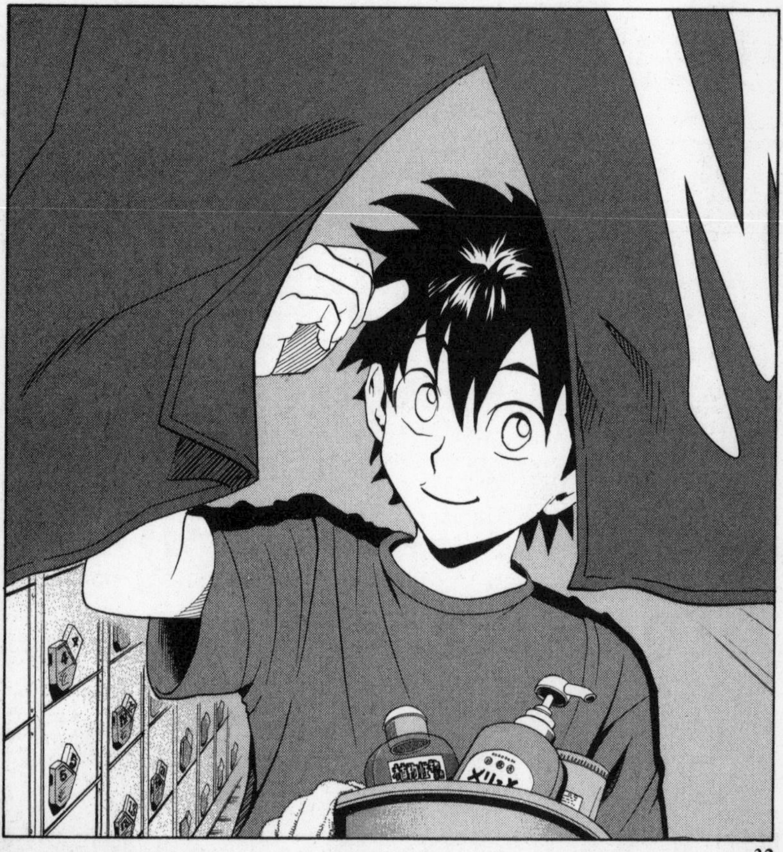

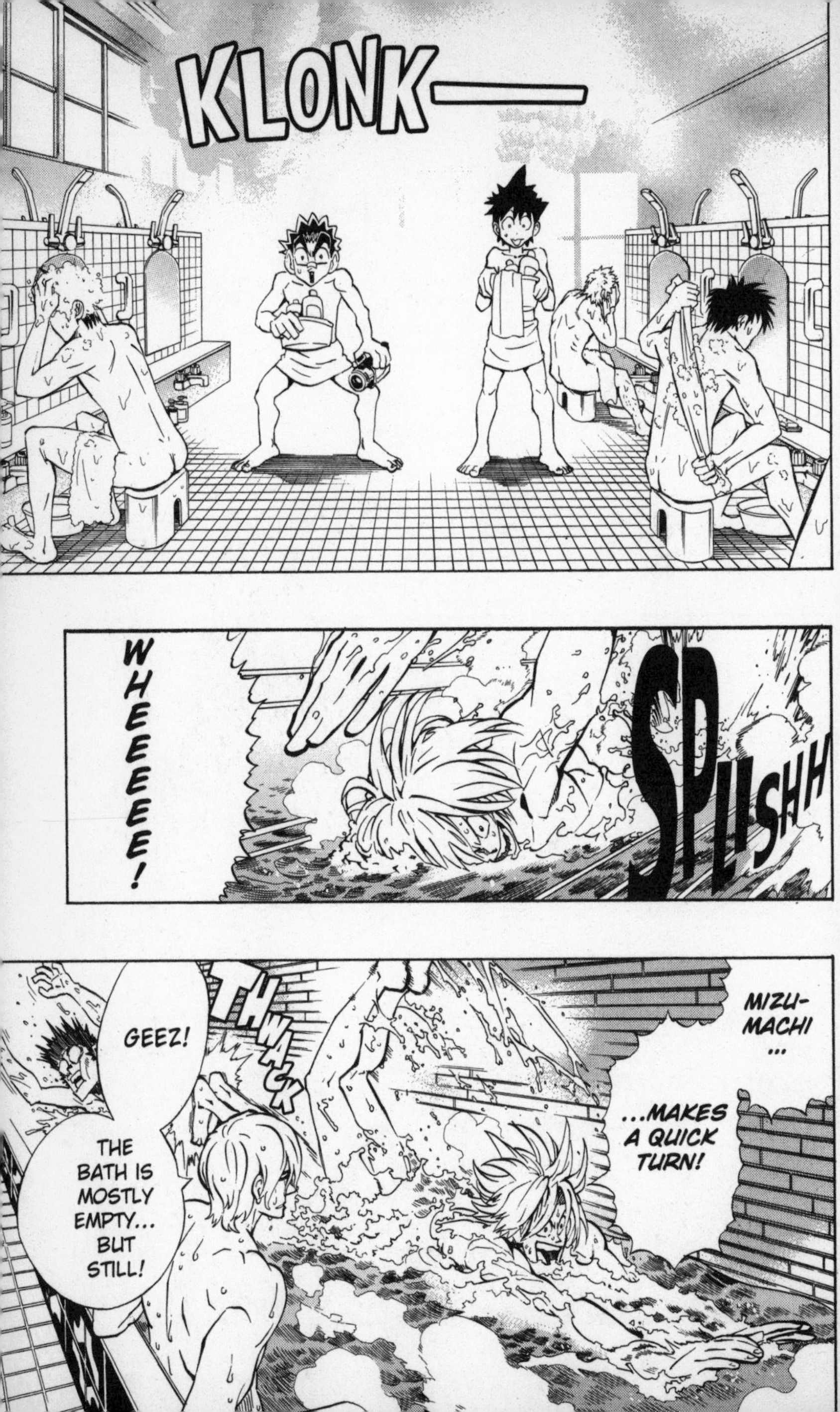
KLONK—
WHEEEEEE!
SPLISHH
MIZU-MACHI...
...MAKES A QUICK TURN!
THWACK
GEEZ!
THE BATH IS MOSTLY EMPTY... BUT STILL!

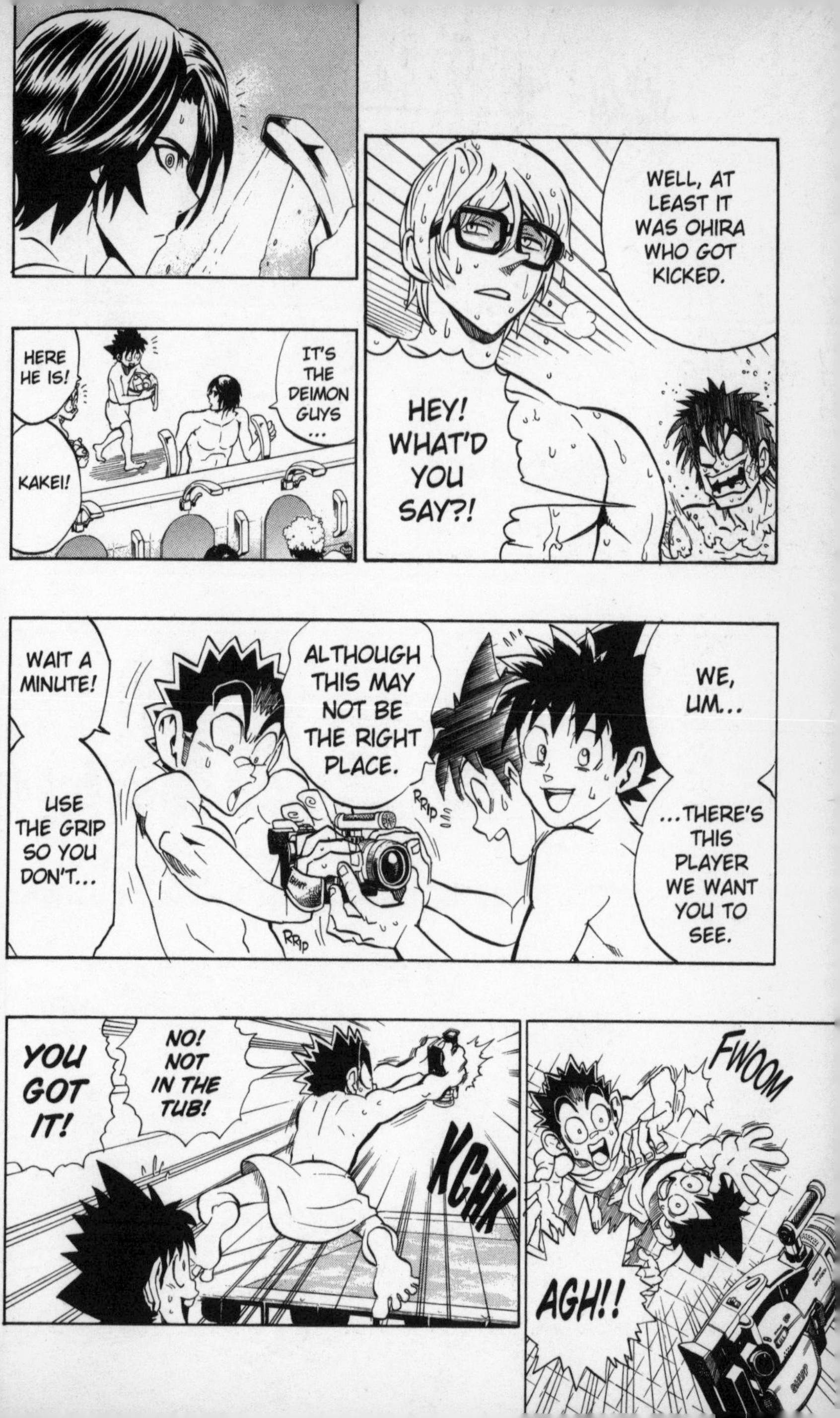
WELL, AT LEAST IT WAS OHIRA WHO GOT KICKED.
HEY! WHAT'D YOU SAY?!
IT'S THE DEIMON GUYS...
HERE HE IS!
KAKEI!
WE, UM...
...THERE'S THIS PLAYER WE WANT YOU TO SEE.
RRIP
ALTHOUGH THIS MAY NOT BE THE RIGHT PLACE.
RRIP
WAIT A MINUTE!
USE THE GRIP SO YOU DON'T...
FWOOM
AGH!!
KCHK
NO! NOT IN THE TUB!
YOU GOT IT!

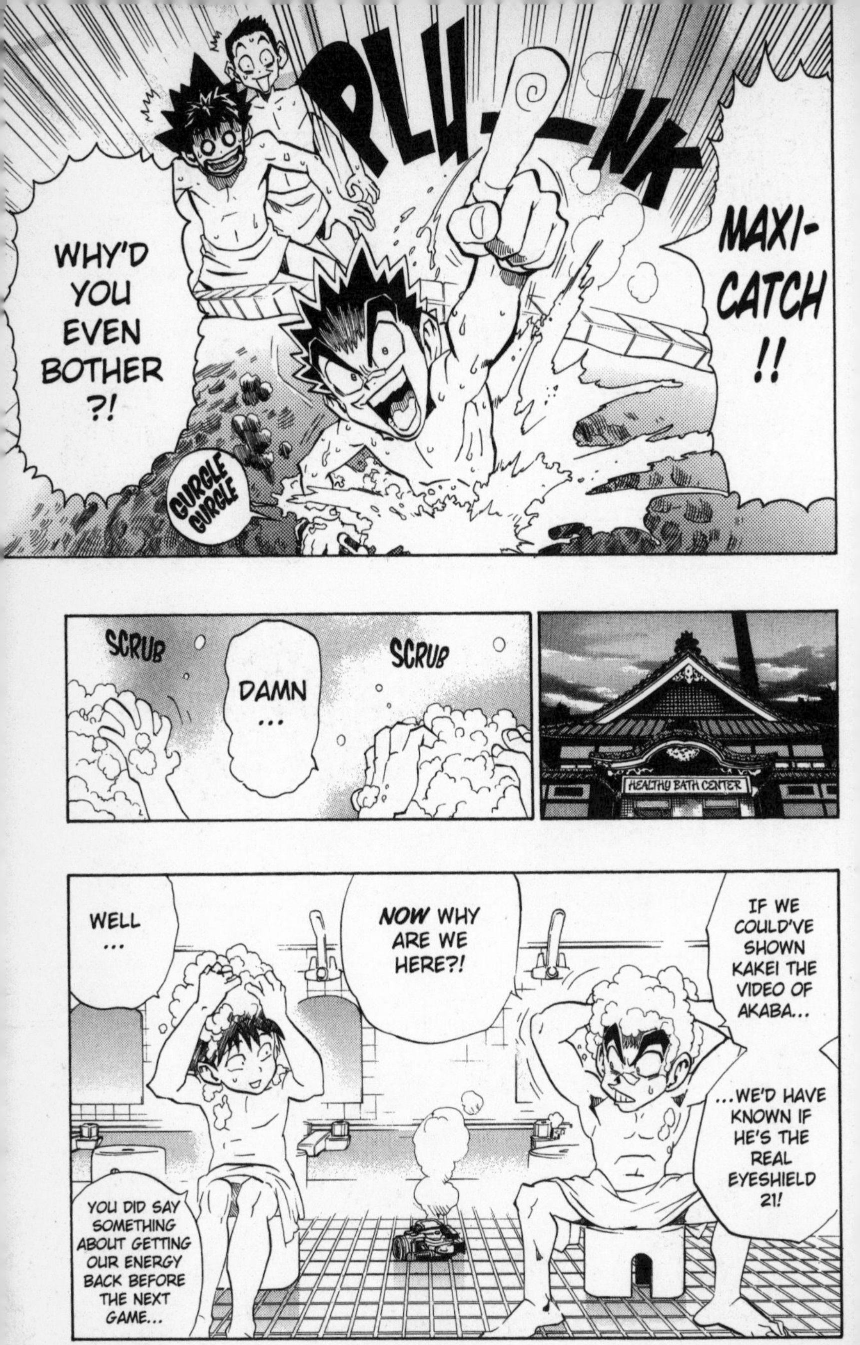
MAXI-CATCH!!
PLU---NK
WHY'D YOU EVEN BOTHER?!
GURGLE GURGLE
HEALTHY BATH CENTER
SCRUB
DAMN...
SCRUB
IF WE COULD'VE SHOWN KAKEI THE VIDEO OF AKABA...
...WE'D HAVE KNOWN IF HE'S THE REAL EYESHIELD 21!
NOW WHY ARE WE HERE?!
WELL...
YOU DID SAY SOMETHING ABOUT GETTING OUR ENERGY BACK BEFORE THE NEXT GAME...

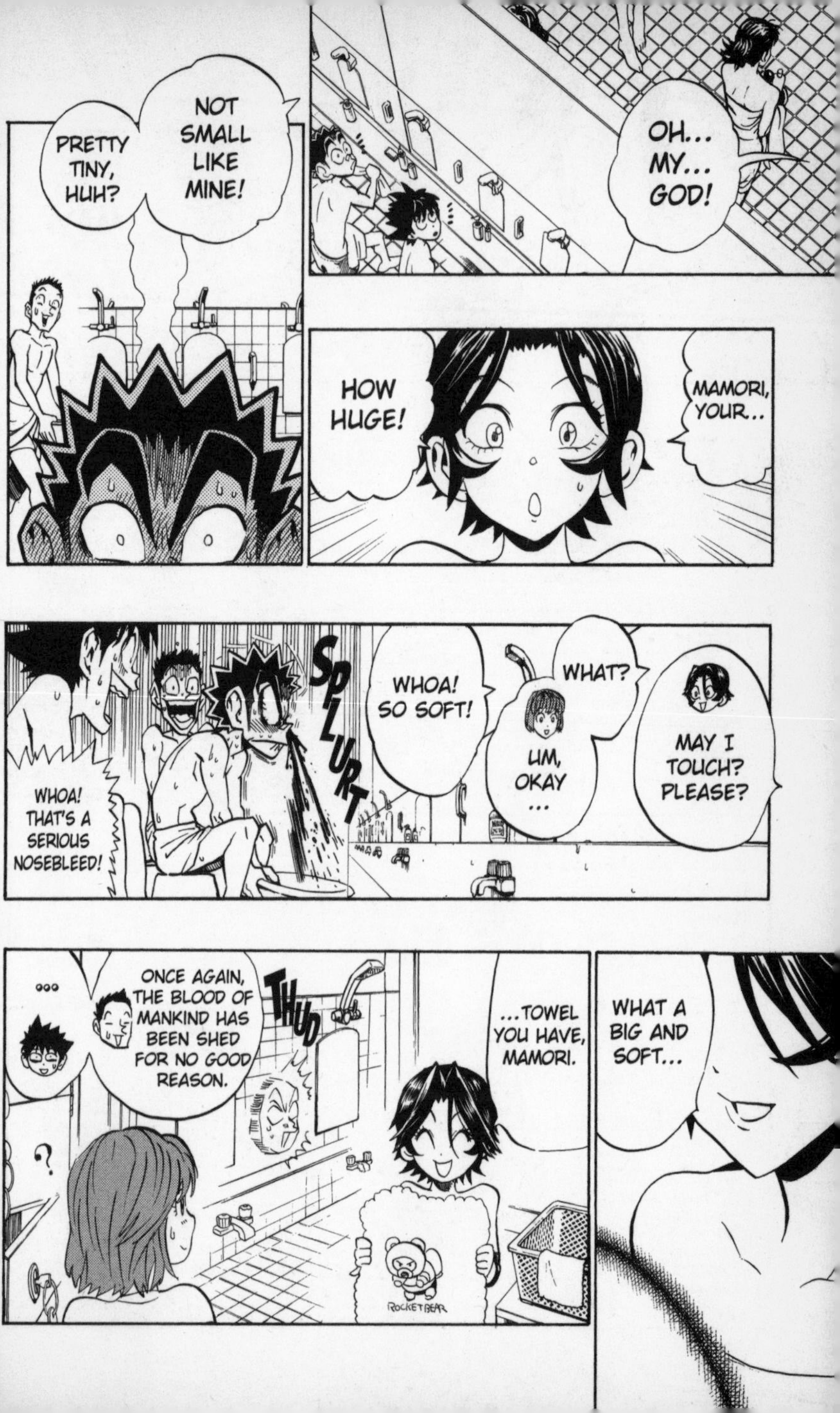
OH... MY... GOD!
MAMORI, YOUR...
HOW HUGE!
NOT SMALL LIKE MINE!
PRETTY TINY, HUH?
MAY I TOUCH? PLEASE?
WHAT?
UM, OKAY ...
WHOA! SO SOFT!
SPLURT
WHOA! THAT'S A SERIOUS NOSEBLEED!
WHAT A BIG AND SOFT...
...TOWEL YOU HAVE, MAMORI.
ROCKET BEAR
THUD
ONCE AGAIN, THE BLOOD OF MANKIND HAS BEEN SHED FOR NO GOOD REASON.
...
?

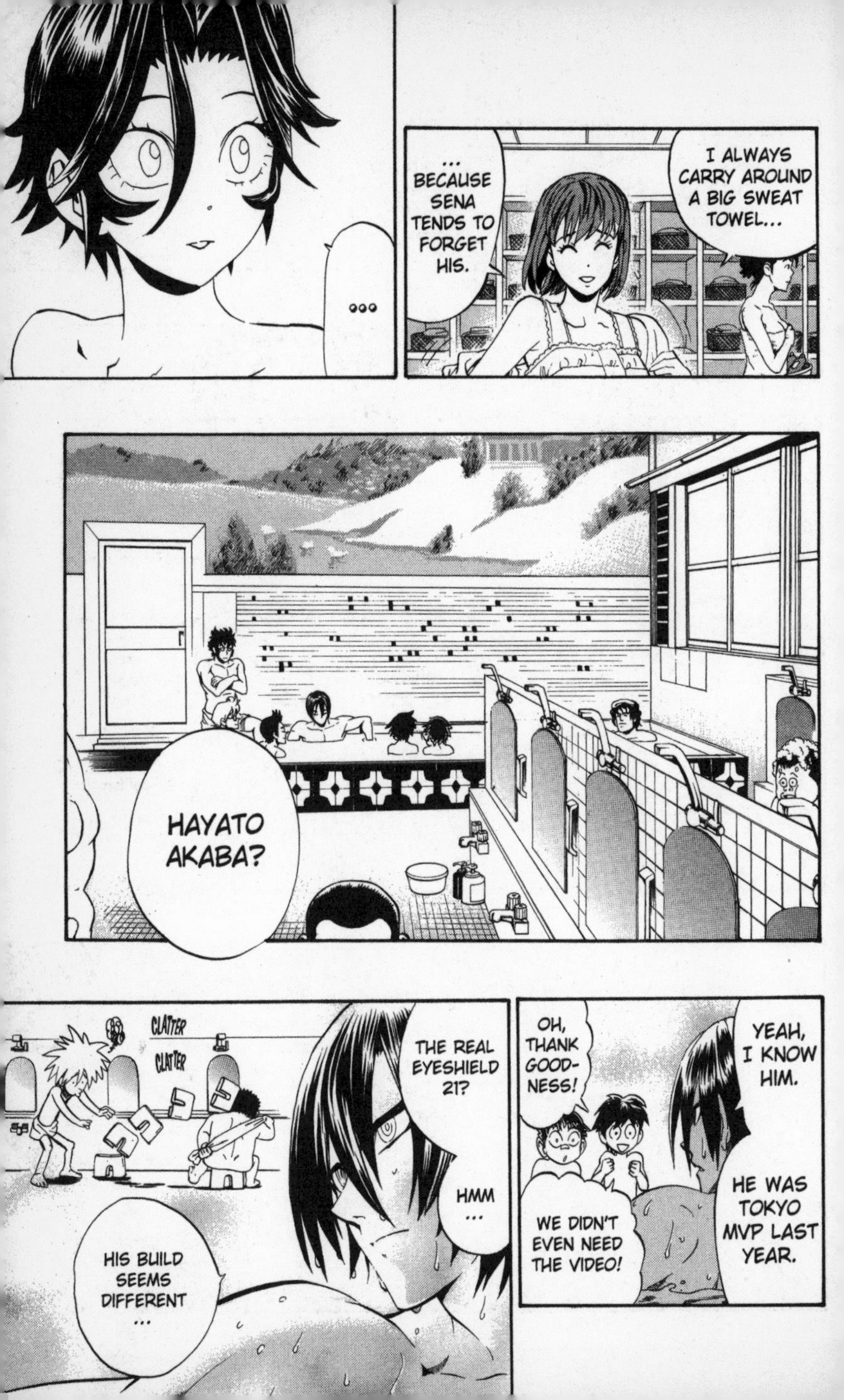
I ALWAYS CARRY AROUND A BIG SWEAT TOWEL...
...BECAUSE SENA TENDS TO FORGET HIS.
...
HAYATO AKABA?
YEAH, I KNOW HIM.
OH, THANK GOODNESS!
HE WAS TOKYO MVP LAST YEAR.
WE DIDN'T EVEN NEED THE VIDEO!
THE REAL EYESHIELD 21?
HMM...
CLATTER
CLATTER
HIS BUILD SEEMS DIFFERENT...

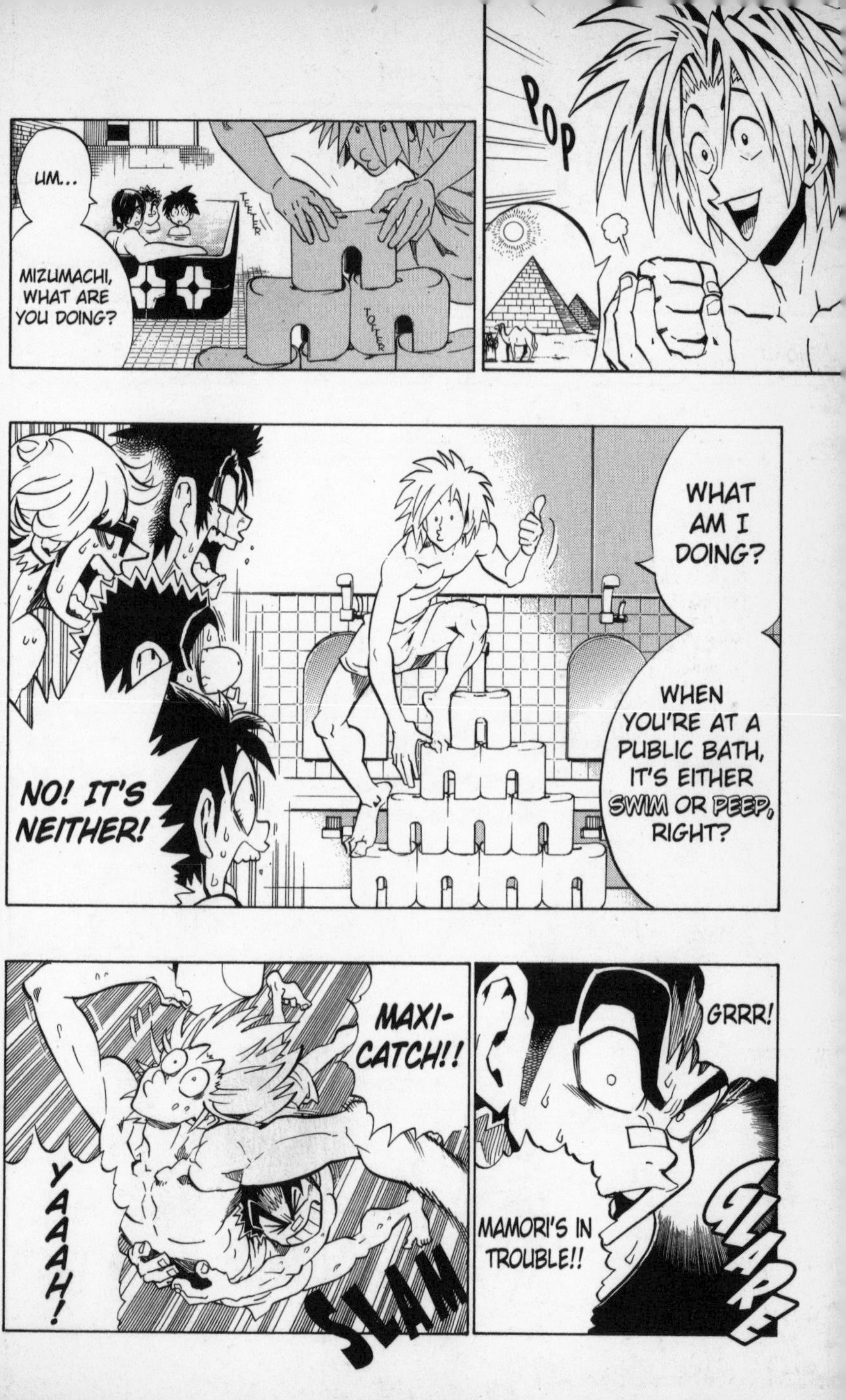
POP
UM...
MIZUMACHI, WHAT ARE YOU DOING?
TEETER
TOTTER
WHAT AM I DOING?
WHEN YOU'RE AT A PUBLIC BATH, IT'S EITHER SWIM OR PEEP, RIGHT?
NO! IT'S NEITHER!
GRRR!
GLARE
MAMORI'S IN TROUBLE!!
MAXI-CATCH!!
YAAAH!
SLAM

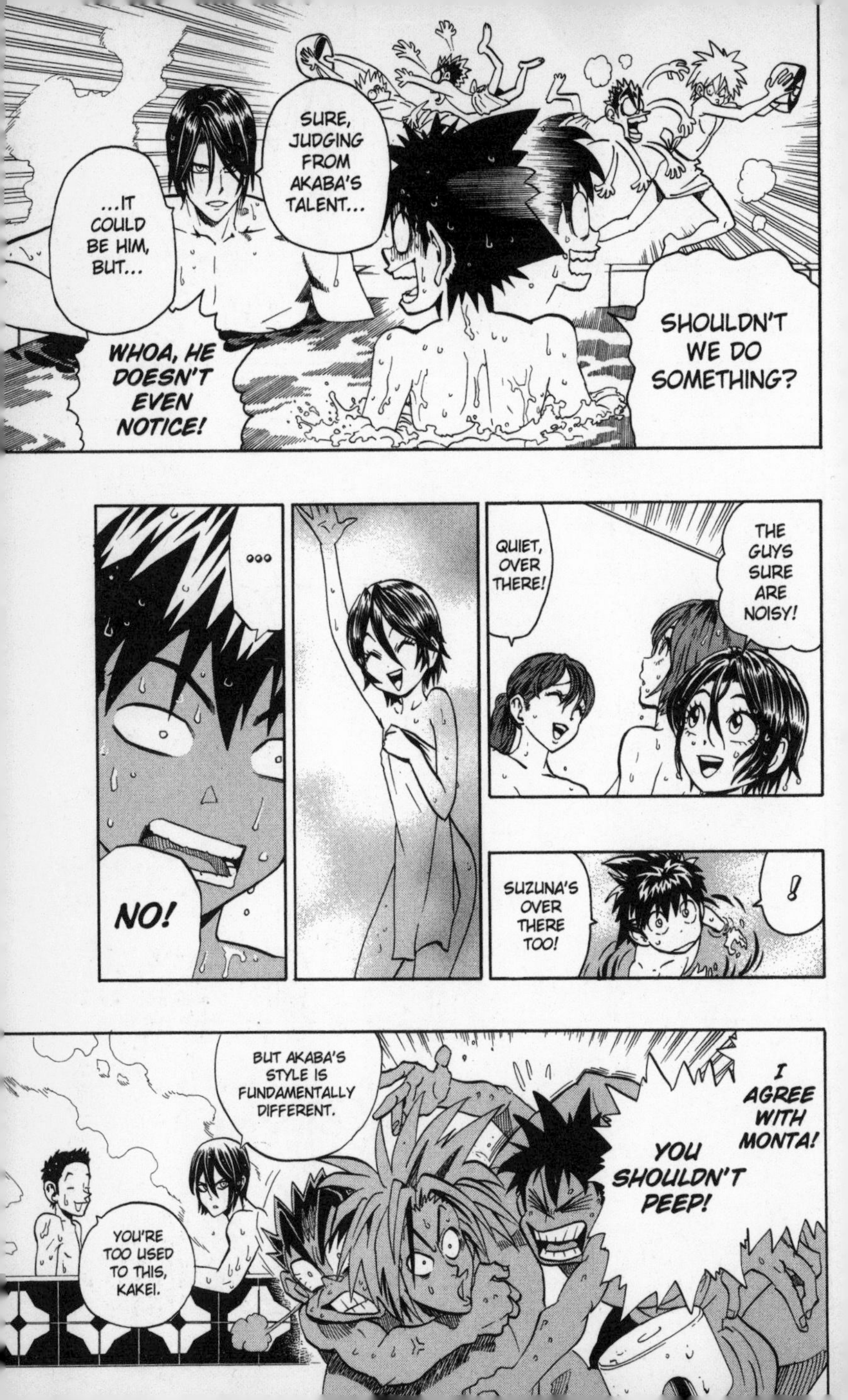

SHOULDN'T WE DO SOMETHING?
SURE, JUDGING FROM AKABA'S TALENT...
...IT COULD BE HIM, BUT...
WHOA, HE DOESN'T EVEN NOTICE!
THE GUYS SURE ARE NOISY!
QUIET, OVER THERE!
!
SUZUNA'S OVER THERE TOO!
...
NO!
I AGREE WITH MONTA!
YOU SHOULDN'T PEEP!
BUT AKABA'S STYLE IS FUNDAMENTALLY DIFFERENT.
YOU'RE TOO USED TO THIS, KAKEI.

...

YOU KNOW ...

I WONDER IF SENA'S OKAY.

IT SOUNDS PRETTY WILD OVER THERE...

BUT HE...

...SENA'S NOT AS VULNERABLE...

...AS YOU THINK.

SPLOOSH

I WANT TO TELL HER MYSELF.

WHEN I'M GOOD ENOUGH OF A PLAYER THAT SHE DOESN'T HAVE TO WORRY.

...?

WHEN A GUY'S SET ON SOMETHING...

...IT'S BEST NOT TO INTERFERE.

SORRY, MAMORI.

I...

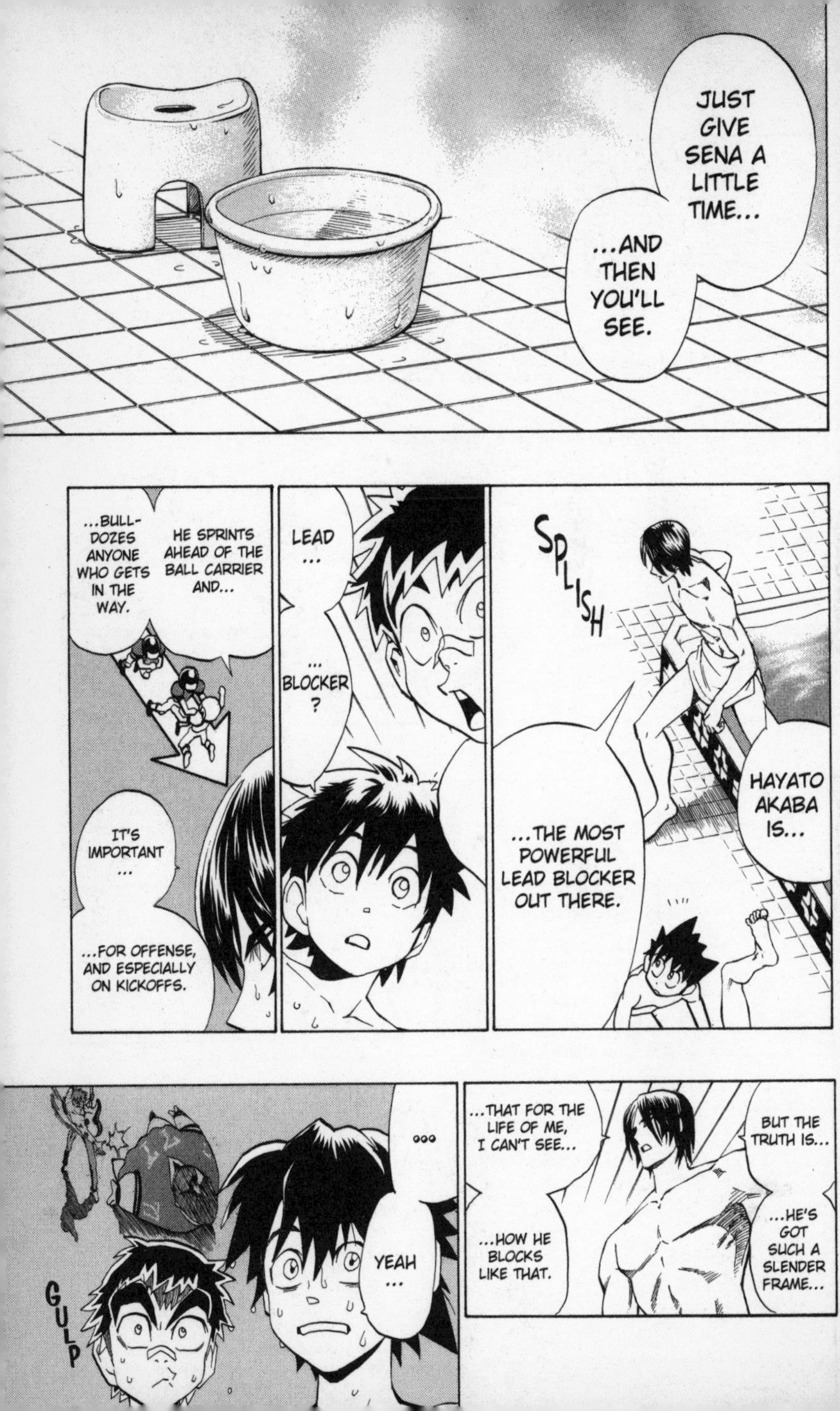

JUST GIVE SENA A LITTLE TIME...
...AND THEN YOU'LL SEE.
SPLISH
HAYATO AKABA IS...
...THE MOST POWERFUL LEAD BLOCKER OUT THERE.
LEAD...
...BLOCKER?
HE SPRINTS AHEAD OF THE BALL CARRIER AND...
...BULLDOZES ANYONE WHO GETS IN THE WAY.
IT'S IMPORTANT...
...FOR OFFENSE, AND ESPECIALLY ON KICKOFFS.
BUT THE TRUTH IS...
...HE'S GOT SUCH A SLENDER FRAME...
...THAT FOR THE LIFE OF ME, I CAN'T SEE...
...HOW HE BLOCKS LIKE THAT.
...
YEAH...
GULP

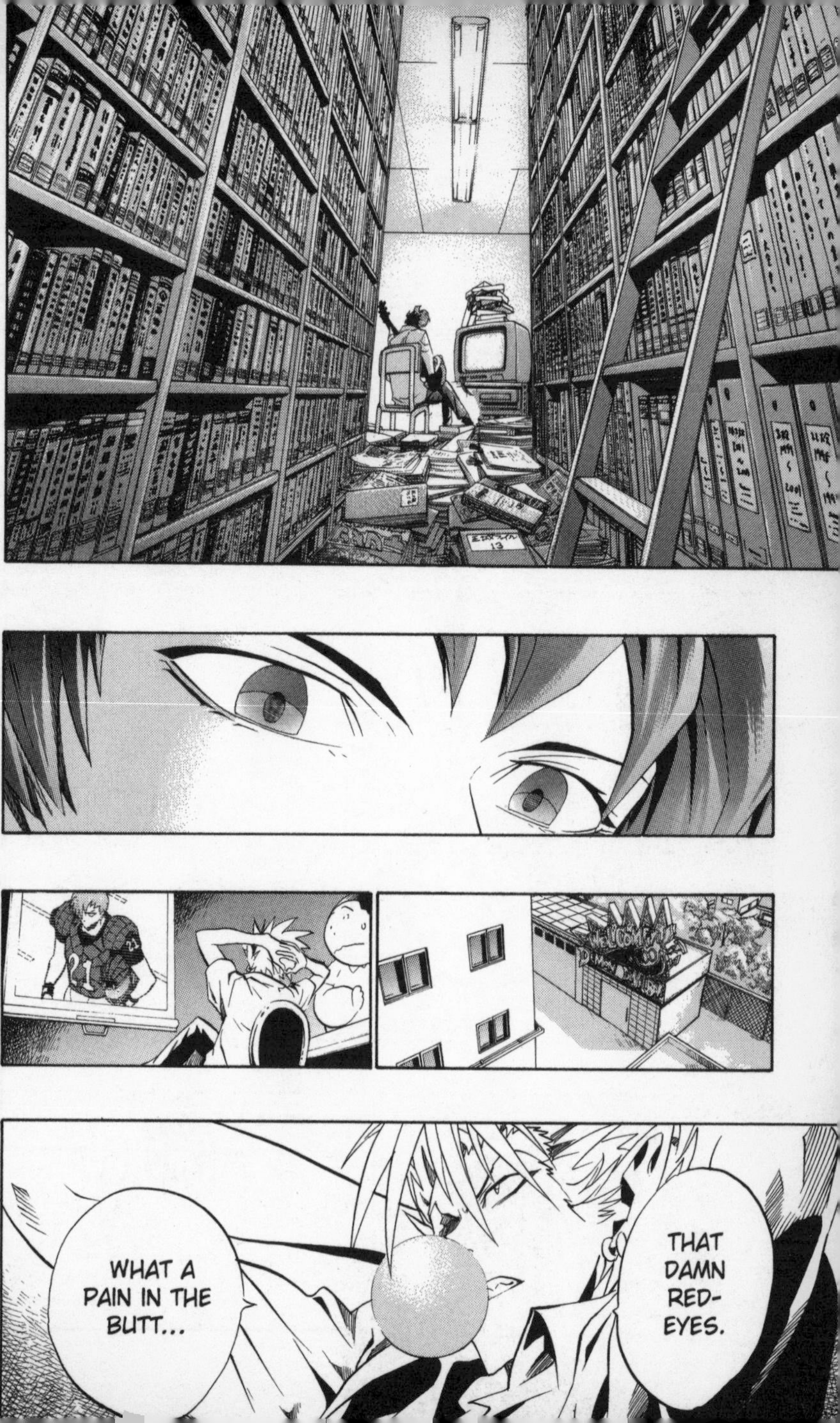
THAT DAMN RED-EYES.
WHAT A PAIN IN THE BUTT...

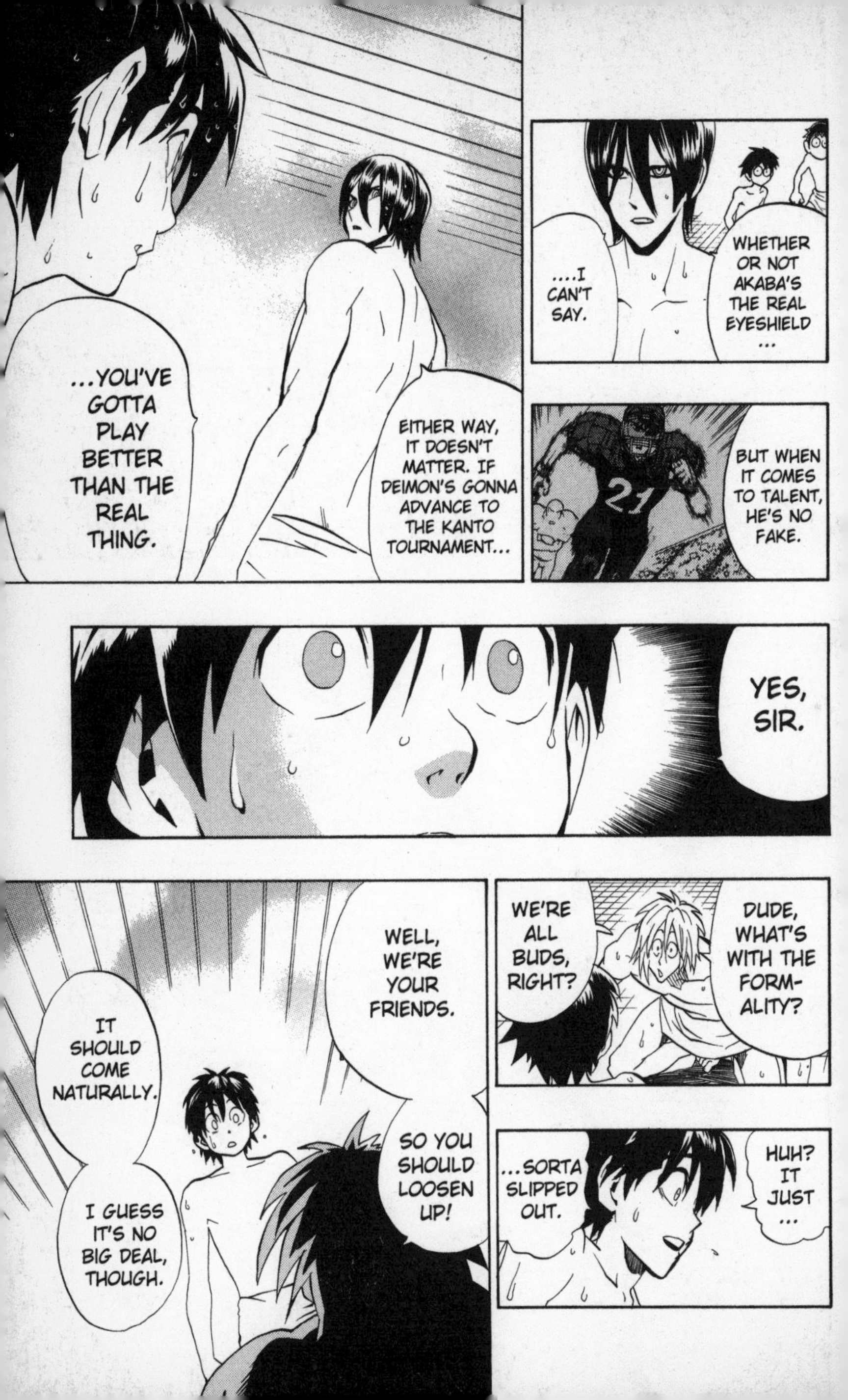
WHETHER OR NOT AKABA'S THE REAL EYESHIELD...
....I CAN'T SAY.
BUT WHEN IT COMES TO TALENT, HE'S NO FAKE.
EITHER WAY, IT DOESN'T MATTER. IF DEIMON'S GONNA ADVANCE TO THE KANTO TOURNAMENT...
...YOU'VE GOTTA PLAY BETTER THAN THE REAL THING.
YES, SIR.
DUDE, WHAT'S WITH THE FORMALITY?
WE'RE ALL BUDS, RIGHT?
HUH? IT JUST...
...SORTA SLIPPED OUT.
WELL, WE'RE YOUR FRIENDS.
SO YOU SHOULD LOOSEN UP!
IT SHOULD COME NATURALLY.
I GUESS IT'S NO BIG DEAL, THOUGH.

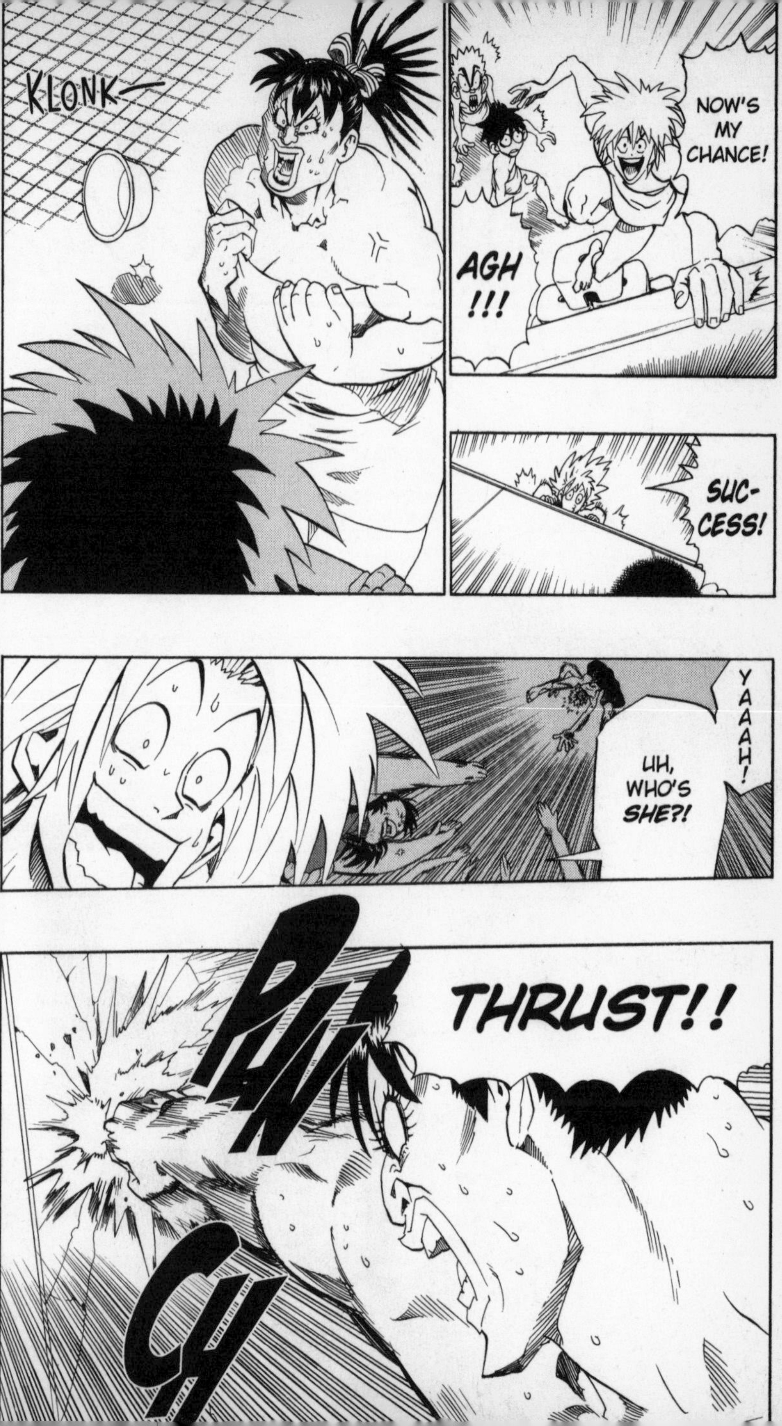
NOW'S MY CHANCE!
AGH !!!
SUC-CESS!
KLONK
YAAAAH!
UH, WHO'S SHE?!
THRUST!!

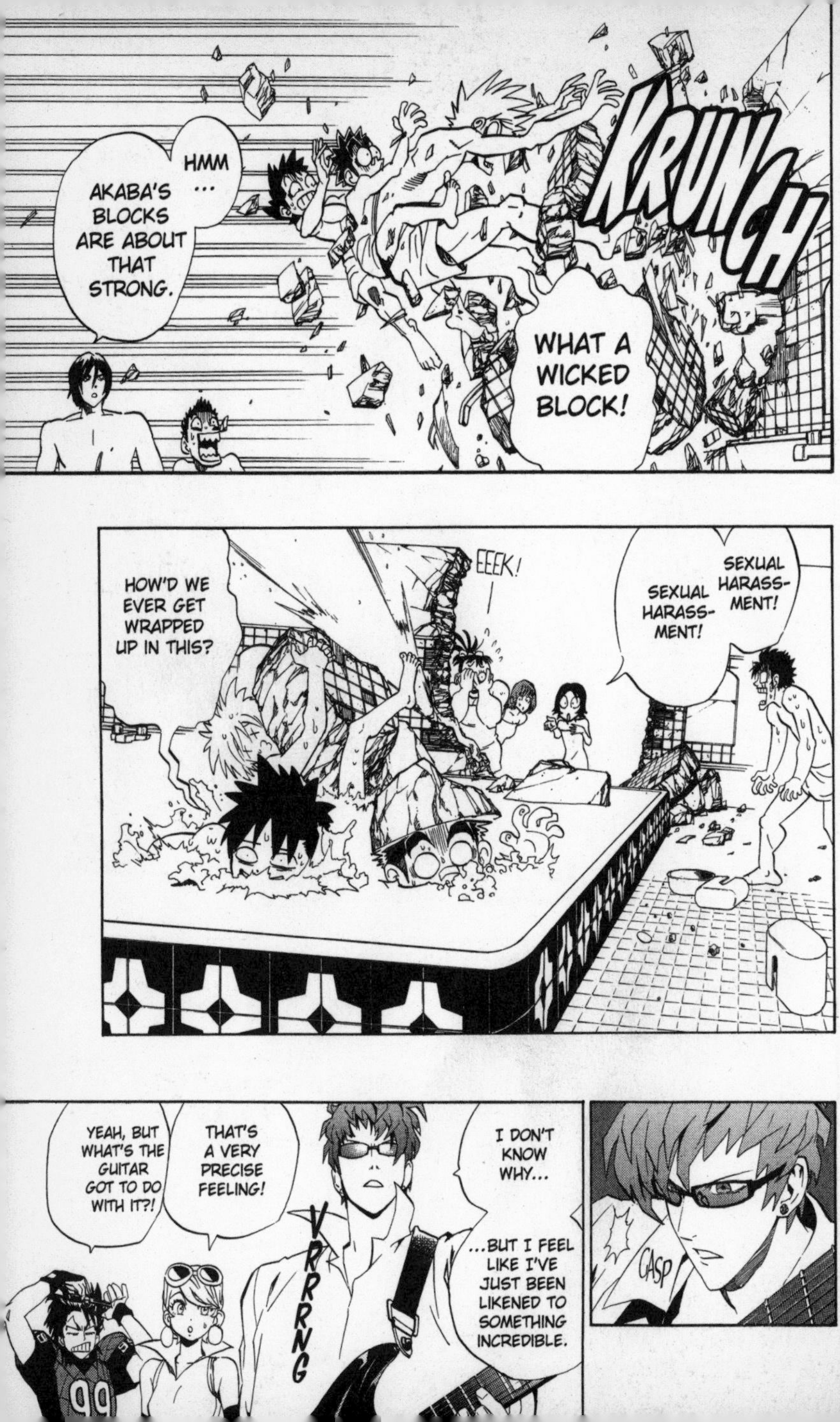
KRUNCH
WHAT A WICKED BLOCK!
HMM...
AKABA'S BLOCKS ARE ABOUT THAT STRONG.
SEXUAL HARASS-MENT!
SEXUAL HARASS-MENT!
EEEK!
HOW'D WE EVER GET WRAPPED UP IN THIS?
GASP
I DON'T KNOW WHY...
...BUT I FEEL LIKE I'VE JUST BEEN LIKENED TO SOMETHING INCREDIBLE.
VRRRNG
THAT'S A VERY PRECISE FEELING!
YEAH, BUT WHAT'S THE GUITAR GOT TO DO WITH IT?!

Kotaro Sasaki

KOTARO SASAKI

KICK SHOCK

1. Kotaro Sasaki's Theme Song
"KICK SHOCK"

Lyrics / Composition / Vocals: The Principal

KICK the boredom,
sprain an ankle,
get SHOCKED

KICK an empty can,
beer spills out,
get SHOCKED

KICK a rock, hit a yakuza, get SHOT

Coolly burn to cinders,
don't mind the heat
KICK the ball through the uprights,
HAT TRICK

PRIVATE·DATA

Family Members: Father, mother,
  older sister

Favorite Food: Meat

Favorite Animal: Dogs (because
  of their devotion)

Personal Hero: Elvis Presley

Most Important Thing in Life:
  Passion

Most Important Thing in Football:
  The kicking team

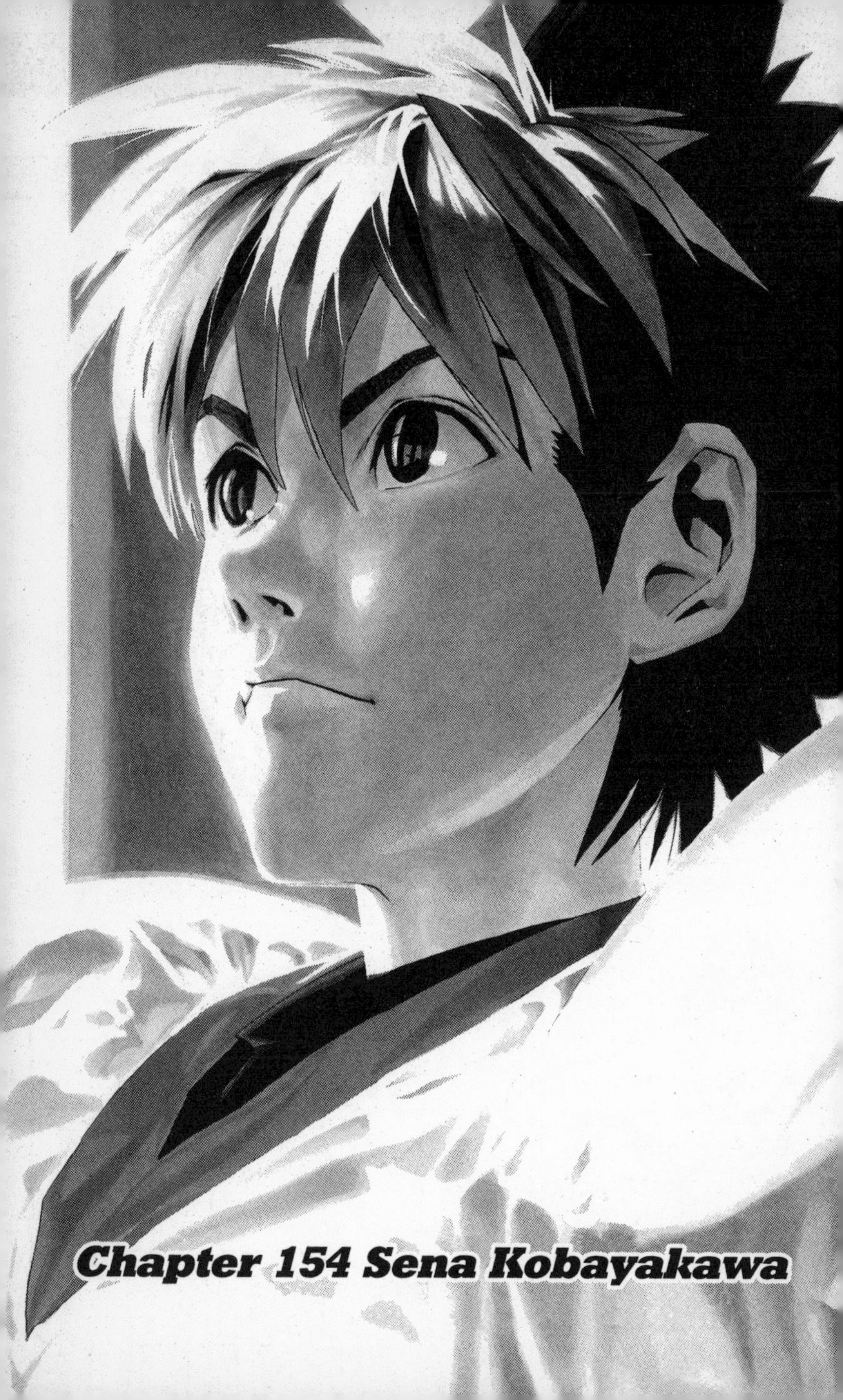

Chapter 154 Sena Kobayakawa

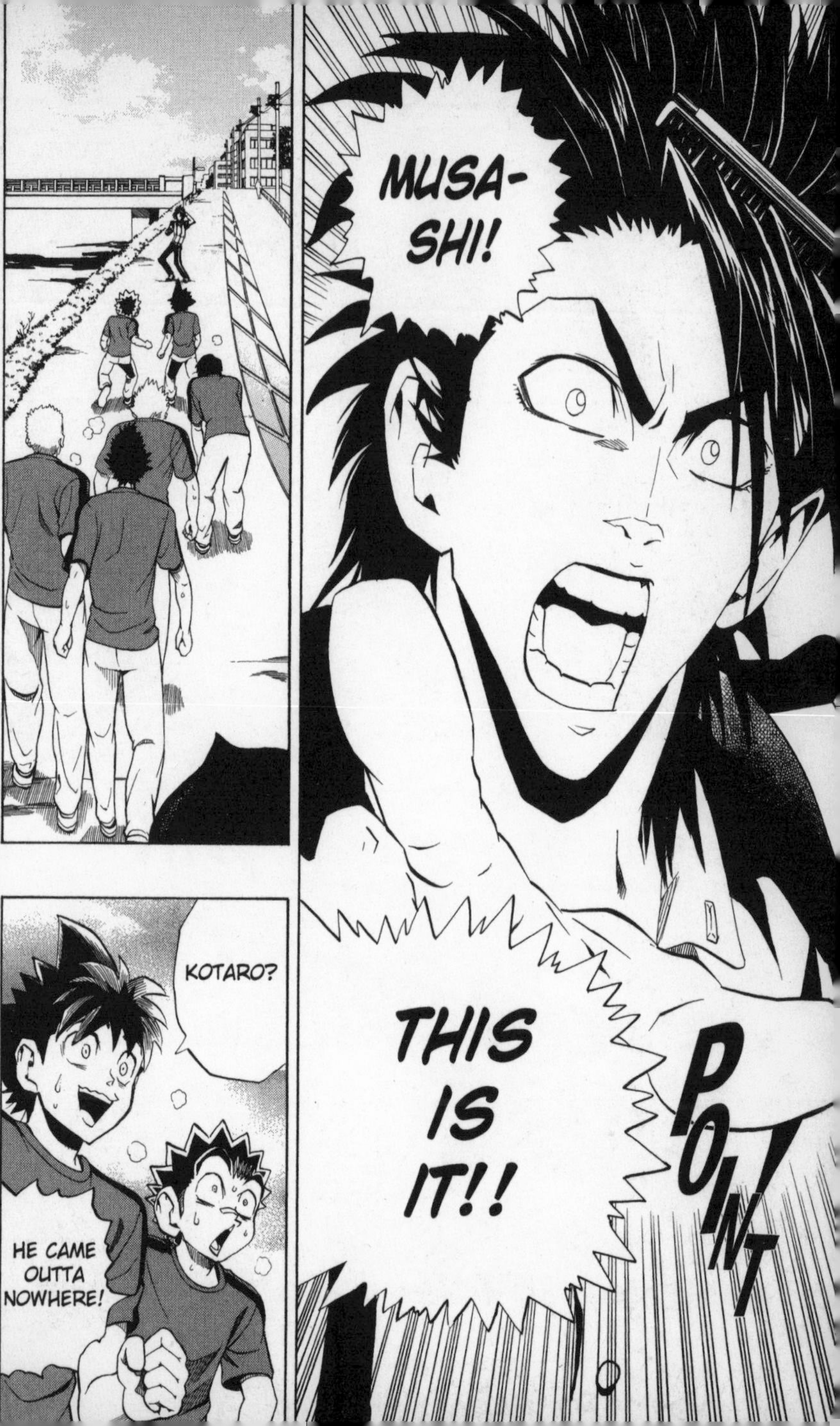
MUSA-SHI!
THIS IS IT!!
POINT
KOTARO?
HE CAME OUTTA NOWHERE!

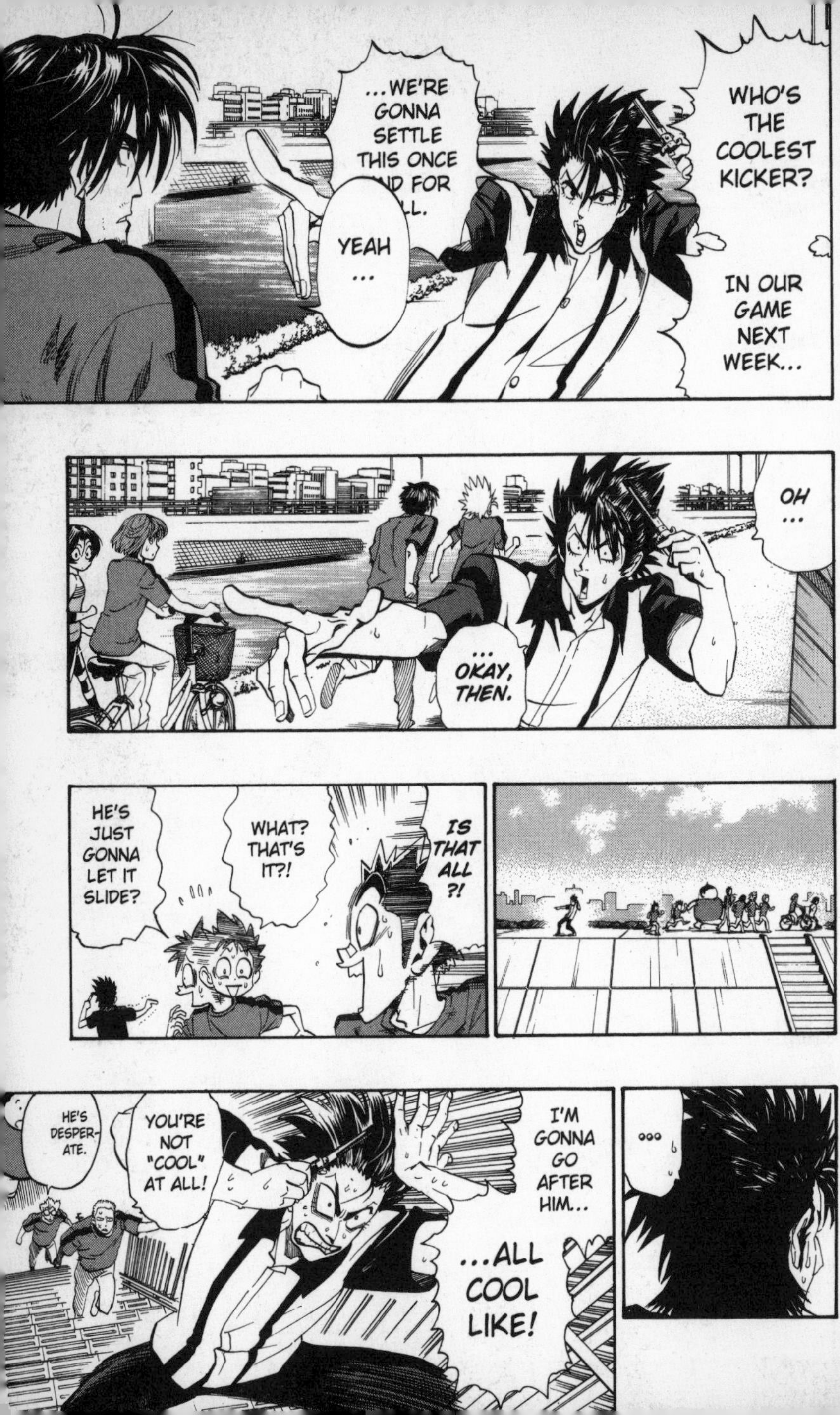
WHO'S THE COOLEST KICKER?
IN OUR GAME NEXT WEEK...
...WE'RE GONNA SETTLE THIS ONCE ND FOR LL.
YEAH ...
OH ...
... OKAY, THEN.
IS THAT ALL ?!
WHAT? THAT'S IT?!
HE'S JUST GONNA LET IT SLIDE?
...
I'M GONNA GO AFTER HIM...
...ALL COOL LIKE!
YOU'RE NOT "COOL" AT ALL!
HE'S DESPERATE.

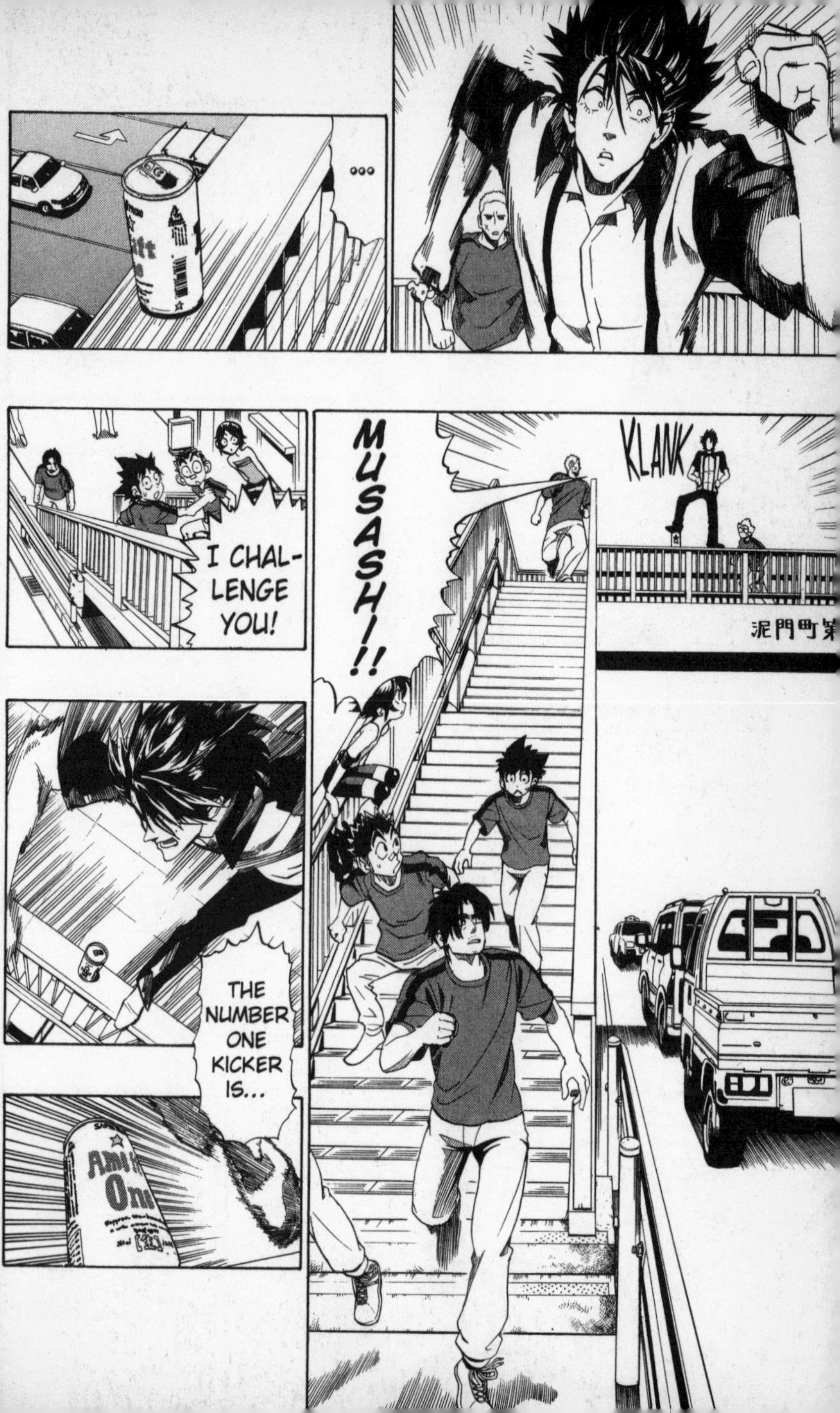
...
KLANK
MUSASHI!!
泥門町第
I CHAL-
LENGE
YOU!
THE NUMBER ONE KICKER IS...

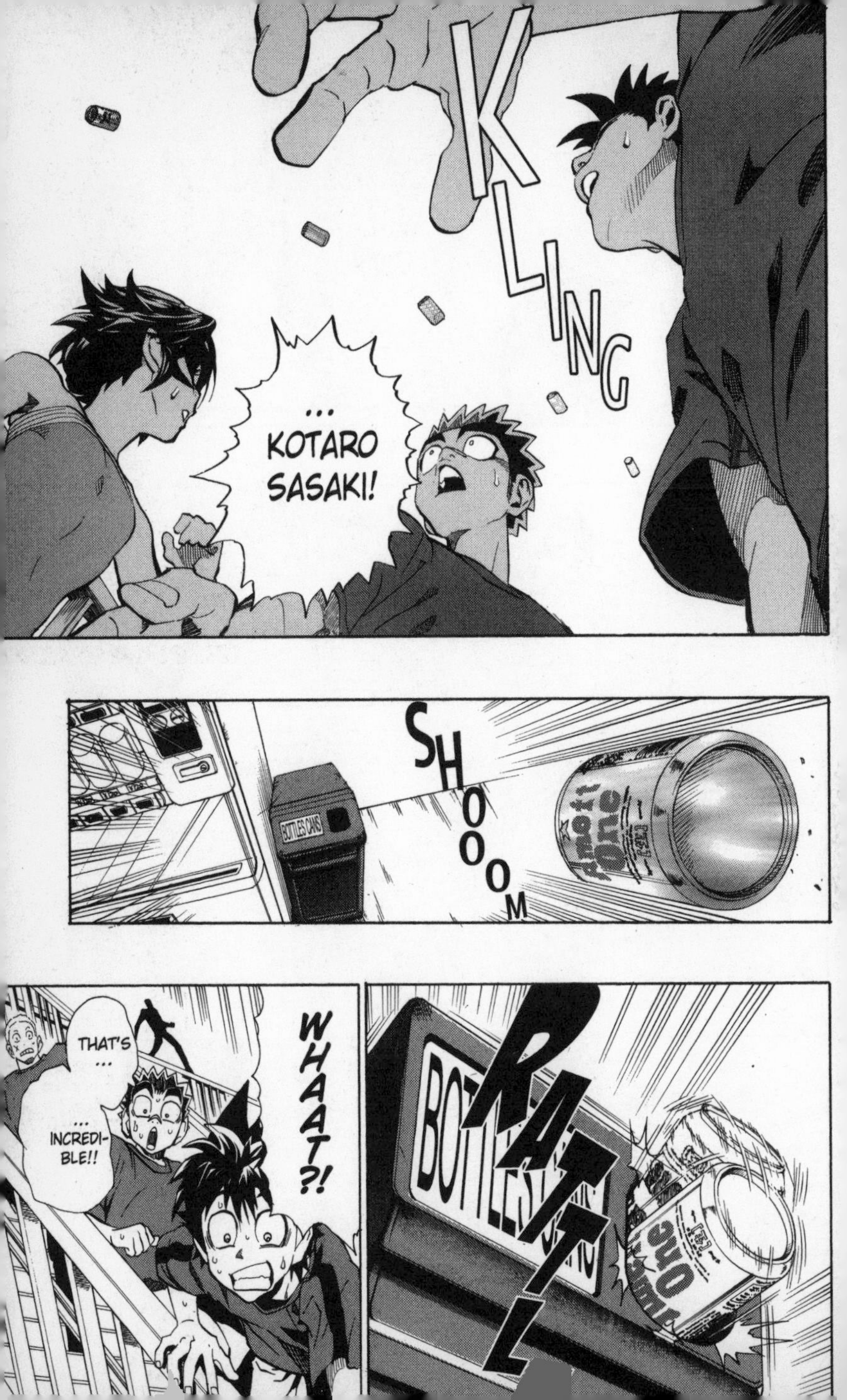
KLING
... KOTARO SASAKI!
SHOOOM
BOTTLES CANS
RATTL
WHAAAT?!
THAT'S ...
... INCREDIBLE!!

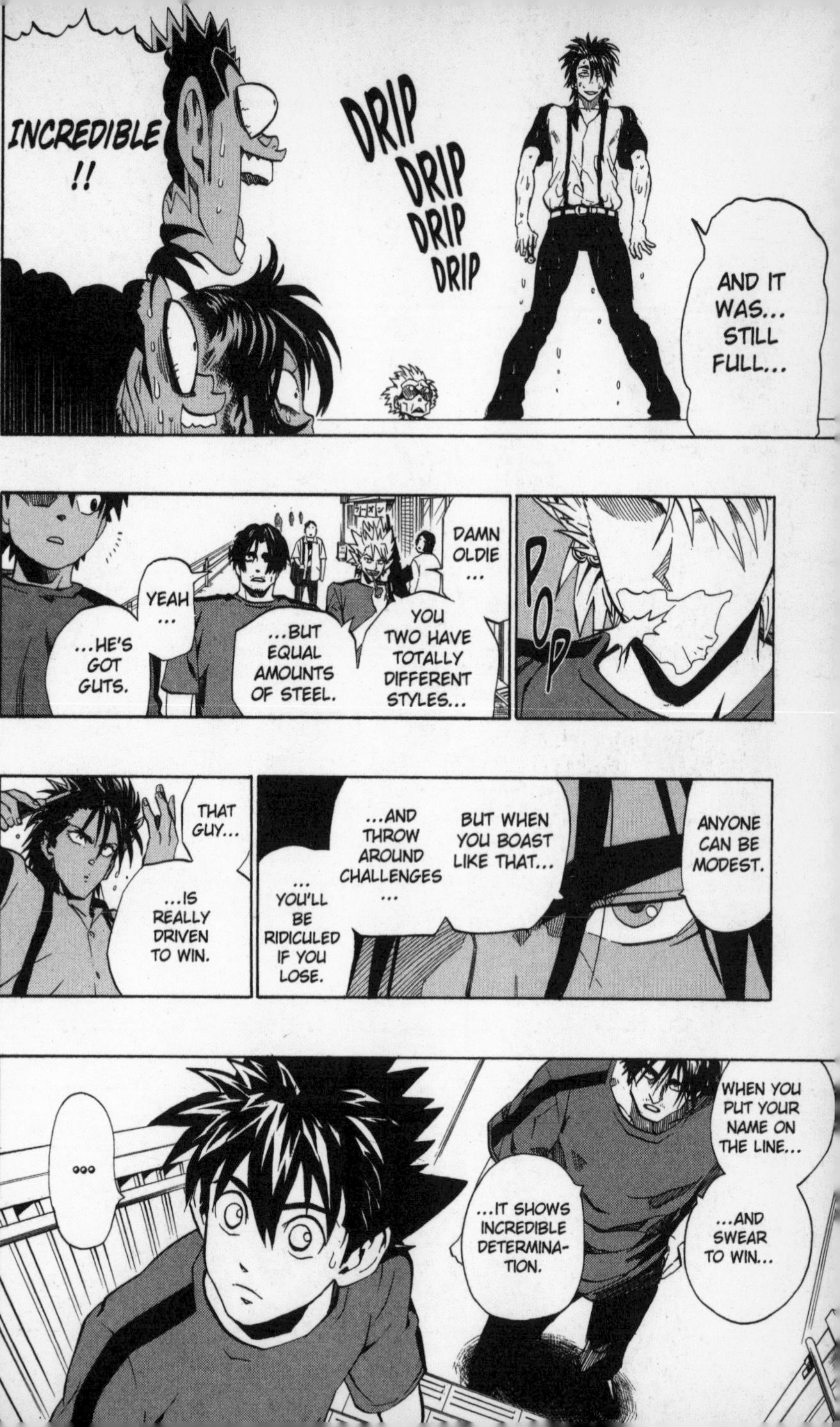
AND IT WAS... STILL FULL...
DRIP DRIP DRIP DRIP
INCREDIBLE !!
POP
DAMN OLDIE...
YOU TWO HAVE TOTALLY DIFFERENT STYLES...
...BUT EQUAL AMOUNTS OF STEEL.
YEAH...
...HE'S GOT GUTS.
ANYONE CAN BE MODEST.
BUT WHEN YOU BOAST LIKE THAT...
...AND THROW AROUND CHALLENGES...
...YOU'LL BE RIDICULED IF YOU LOSE.
THAT GUY...
...IS REALLY DRIVEN TO WIN.
WHEN YOU PUT YOUR NAME ON THE LINE...
...AND SWEAR TO WIN...
...IT SHOWS INCREDIBLE DETERMINATION.
...

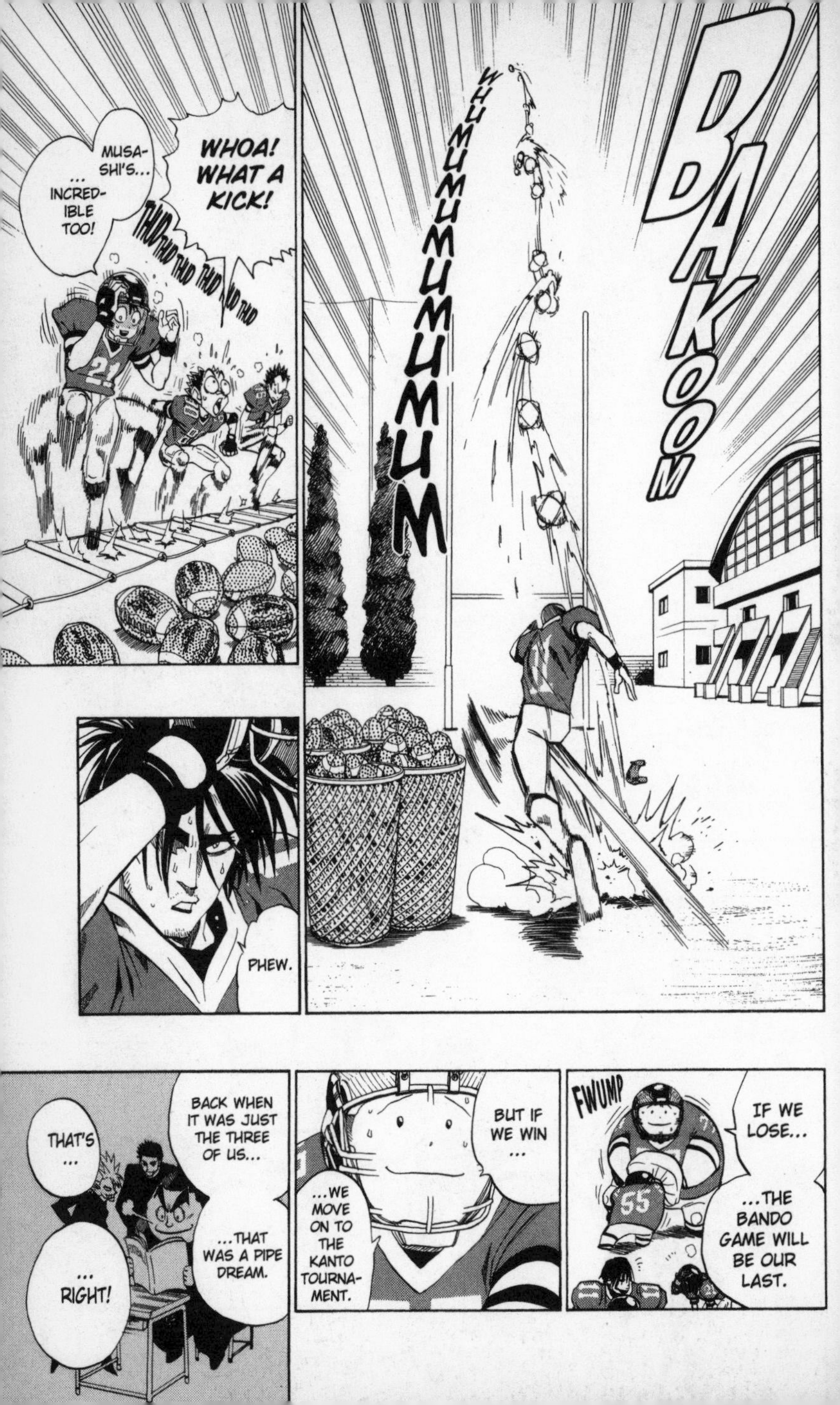
DAKOOOM
WHUMUMUMUMUMUMUM
WHOA! WHAT A KICK!
MUSA-SHI'S... ...INCRED-IBLE TOO!
THUD THUD THUD THUD THUD THUD
PHEW.
FWUMP
IF WE LOSE...
...THE BANDO GAME WILL BE OUR LAST.
BUT IF WE WIN...
...WE MOVE ON TO THE KANTO TOURNA-MENT.
BACK WHEN IT WAS JUST THE THREE OF US...
...THAT WAS A PIPE DREAM.
THAT'S...
...RIGHT!

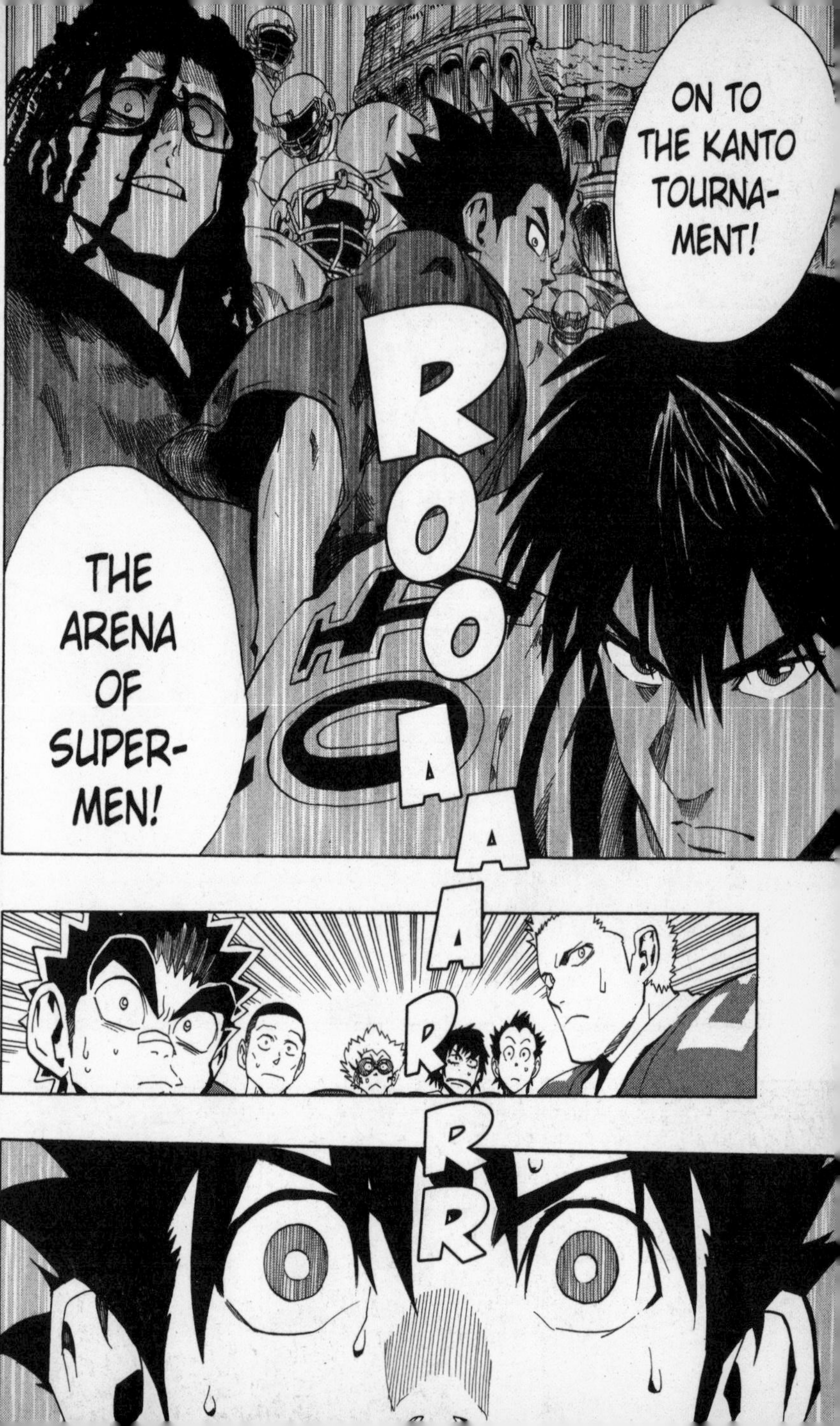
ON TO THE KANTO TOURNAMENT!
THE ARENA OF SUPERMEN!
ROOAAARRR

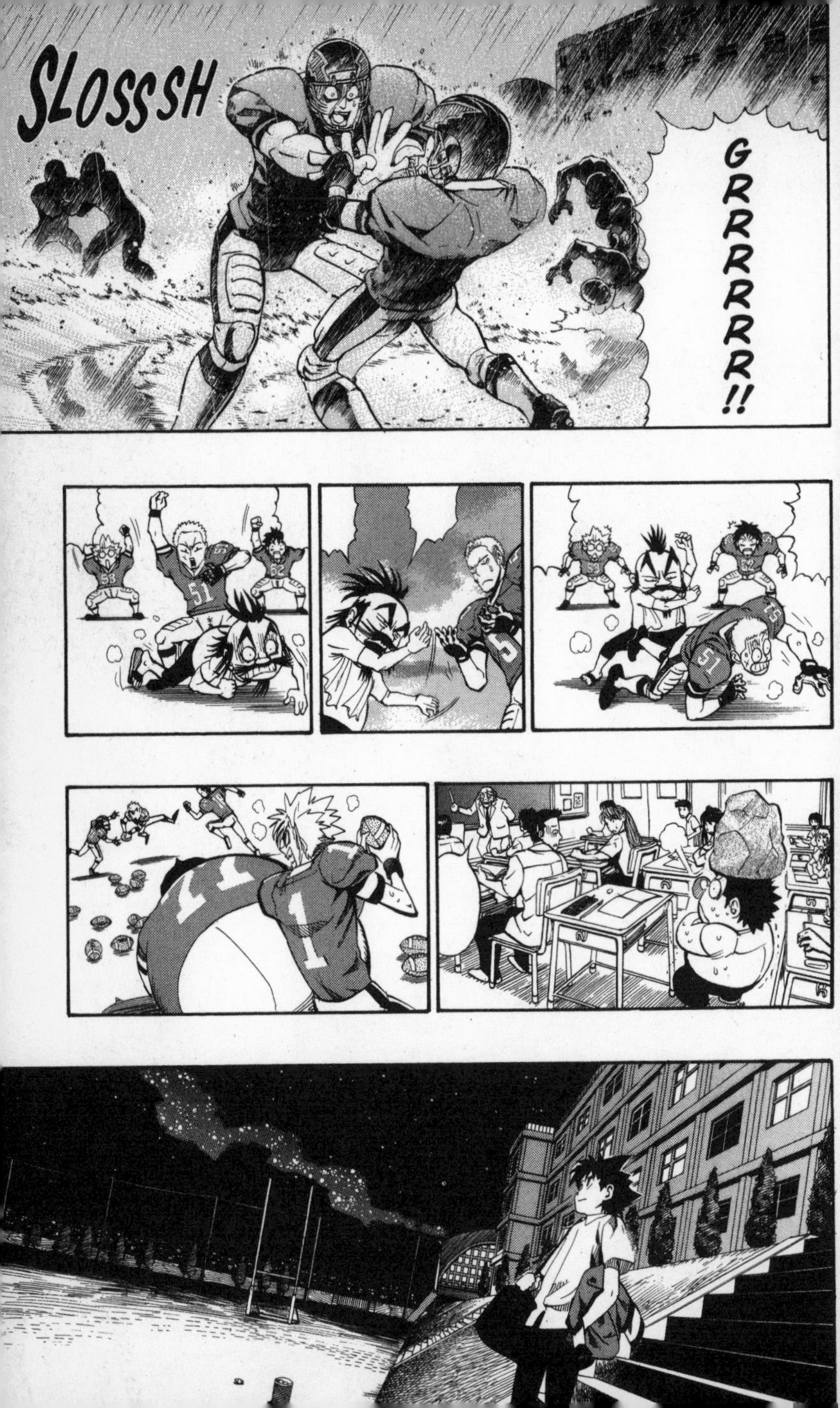
GRRRRRR!!
SLOSSSH

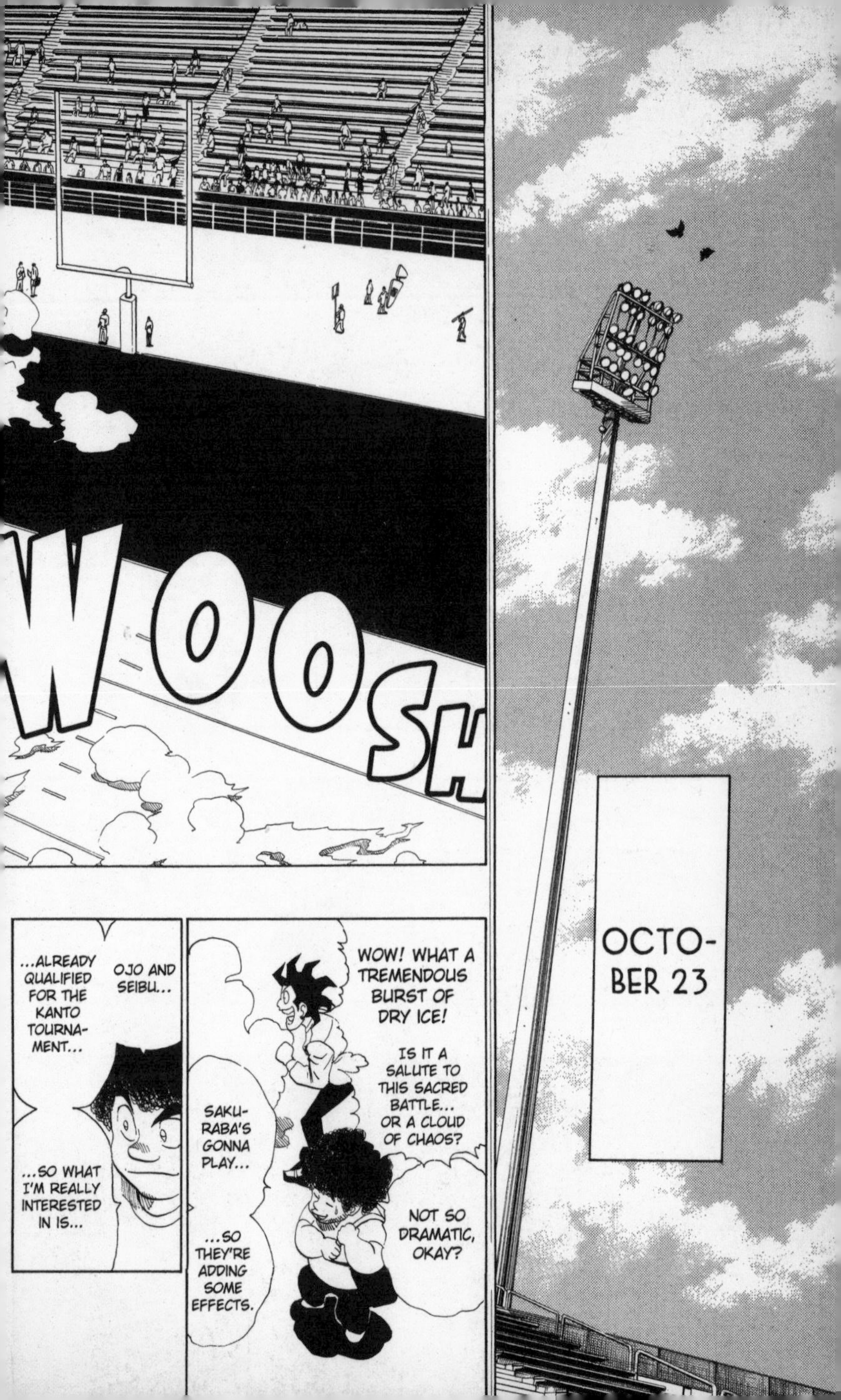
OCTOBER 23
WOOSH
WOW! WHAT A TREMENDOUS BURST OF DRY ICE!
IS IT A SALUTE TO THIS SACRED BATTLE... OR A CLOUD OF CHAOS?
SAKURABA'S GONNA PLAY...
NOT SO DRAMATIC, OKAY?
...SO THEY'RE ADDING SOME EFFECTS.
OJO AND SEIBU...
...ALREADY QUALIFIED FOR THE KANTO TOURNAMENT...
...SO WHAT I'M REALLY INTERESTED IN IS...

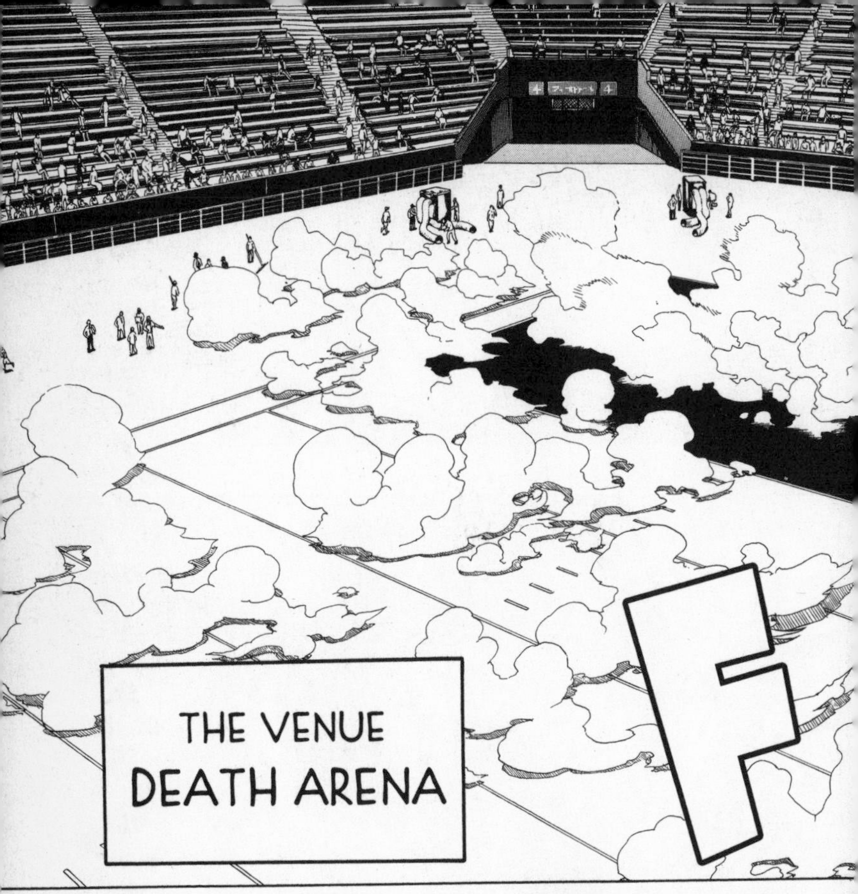
THE VENUE
DEATH ARENA
F

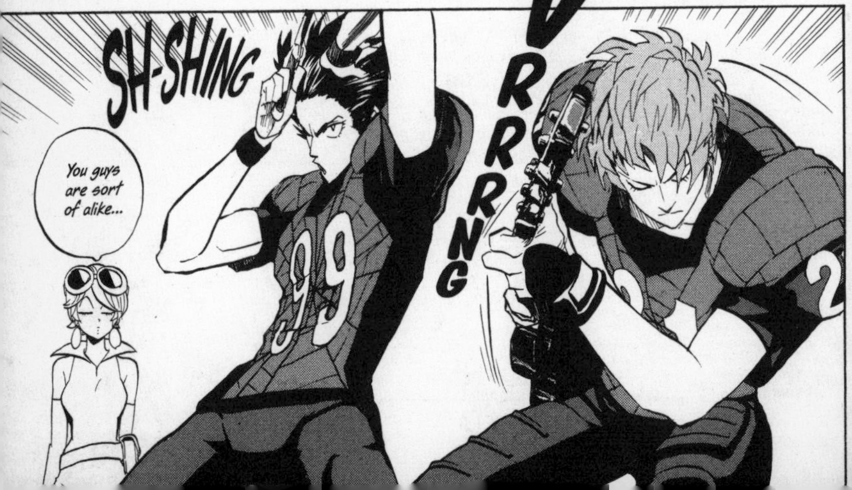
VRRRRRNG
SH-SHING
You guys are sort of alike...

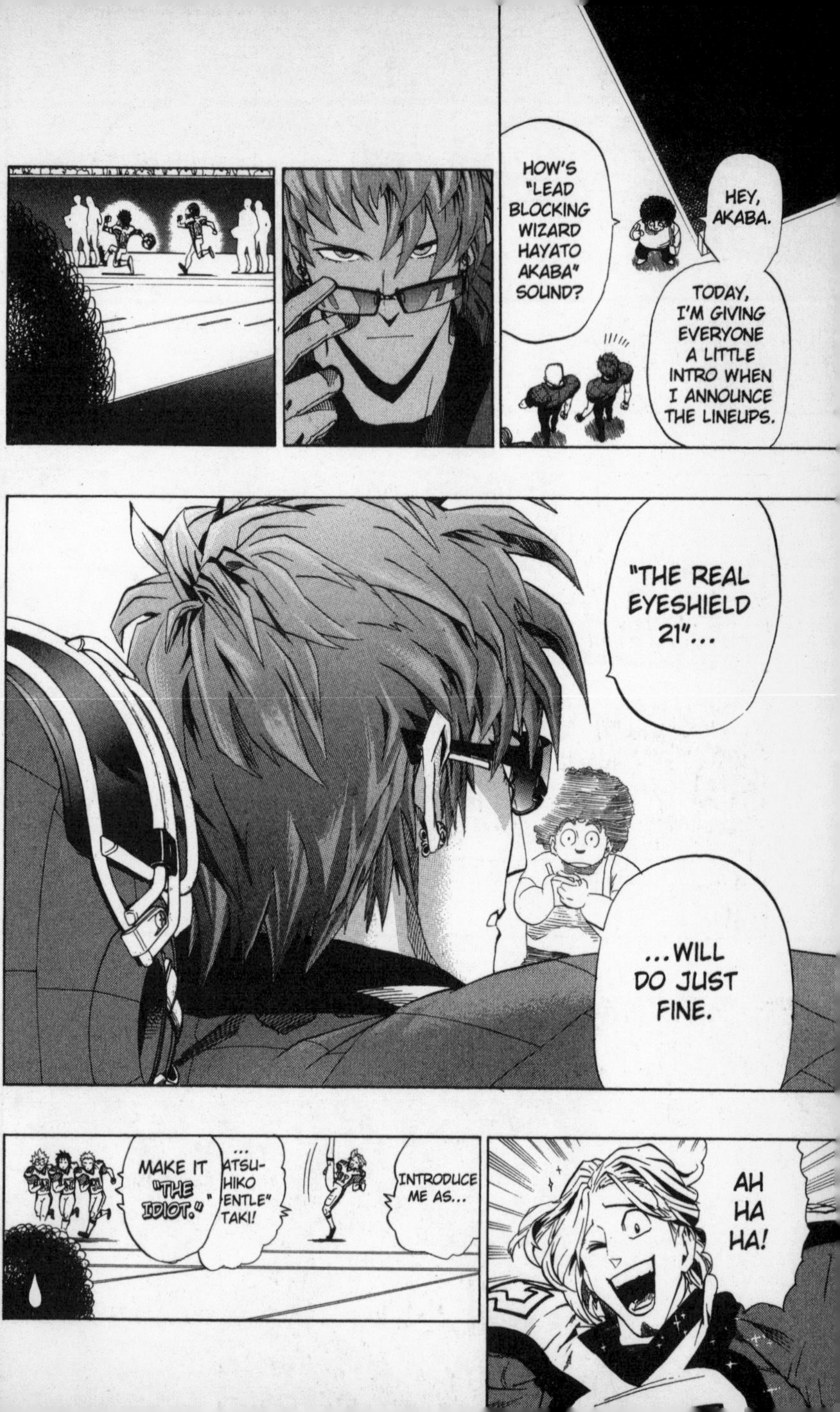
HEY, AKABA.
TODAY, I'M GIVING EVERYONE A LITTLE INTRO WHEN I ANNOUNCE THE LINEUPS.
HOW'S "LEAD BLOCKING WIZARD HAYATO AKABA" SOUND?
"THE REAL EYESHIELD 21"...
...WILL DO JUST FINE.
AH HA HA!
INTRODUCE ME AS...
...ATSU-HIKO ENTLE" TAKI!
MAKE IT "THE IDIOT."

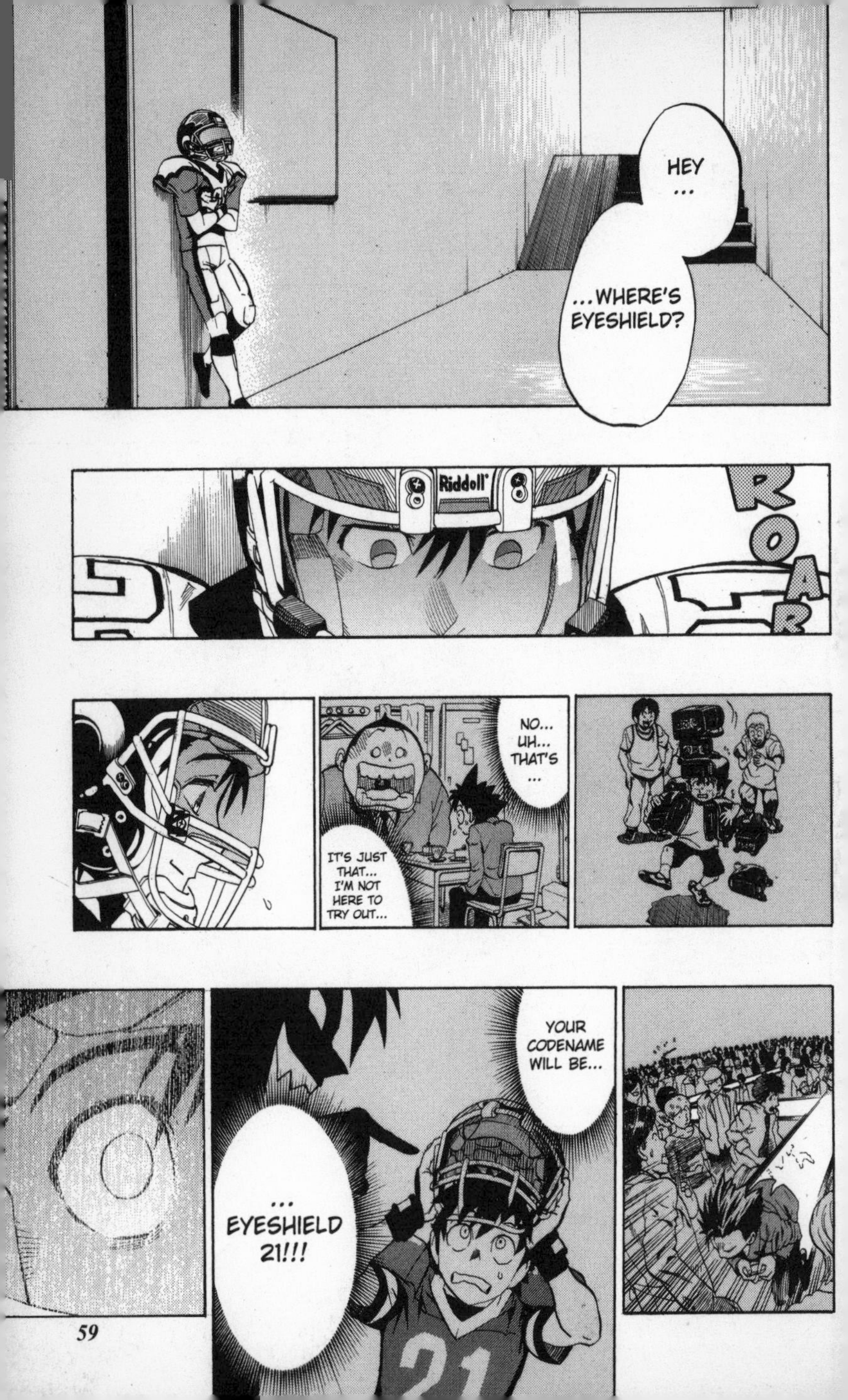
HEY...
...WHERE'S EYESHIELD?
ROAR
NO... UH... THAT'S...
IT'S JUST THAT... I'M NOT HERE TO TRY OUT...
YOUR CODENAME WILL BE...
...EYESHIELD 21!!!

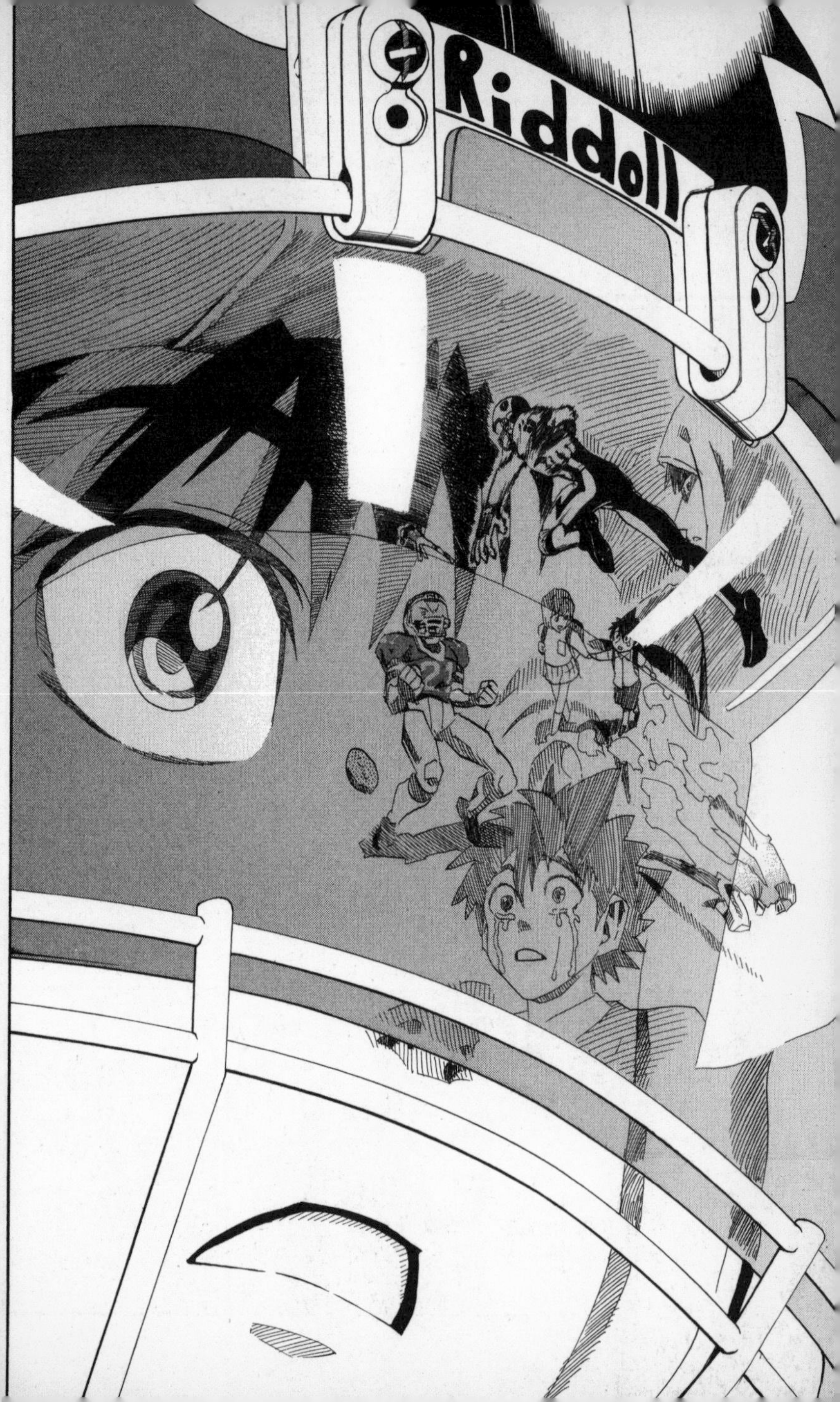
Riddoll

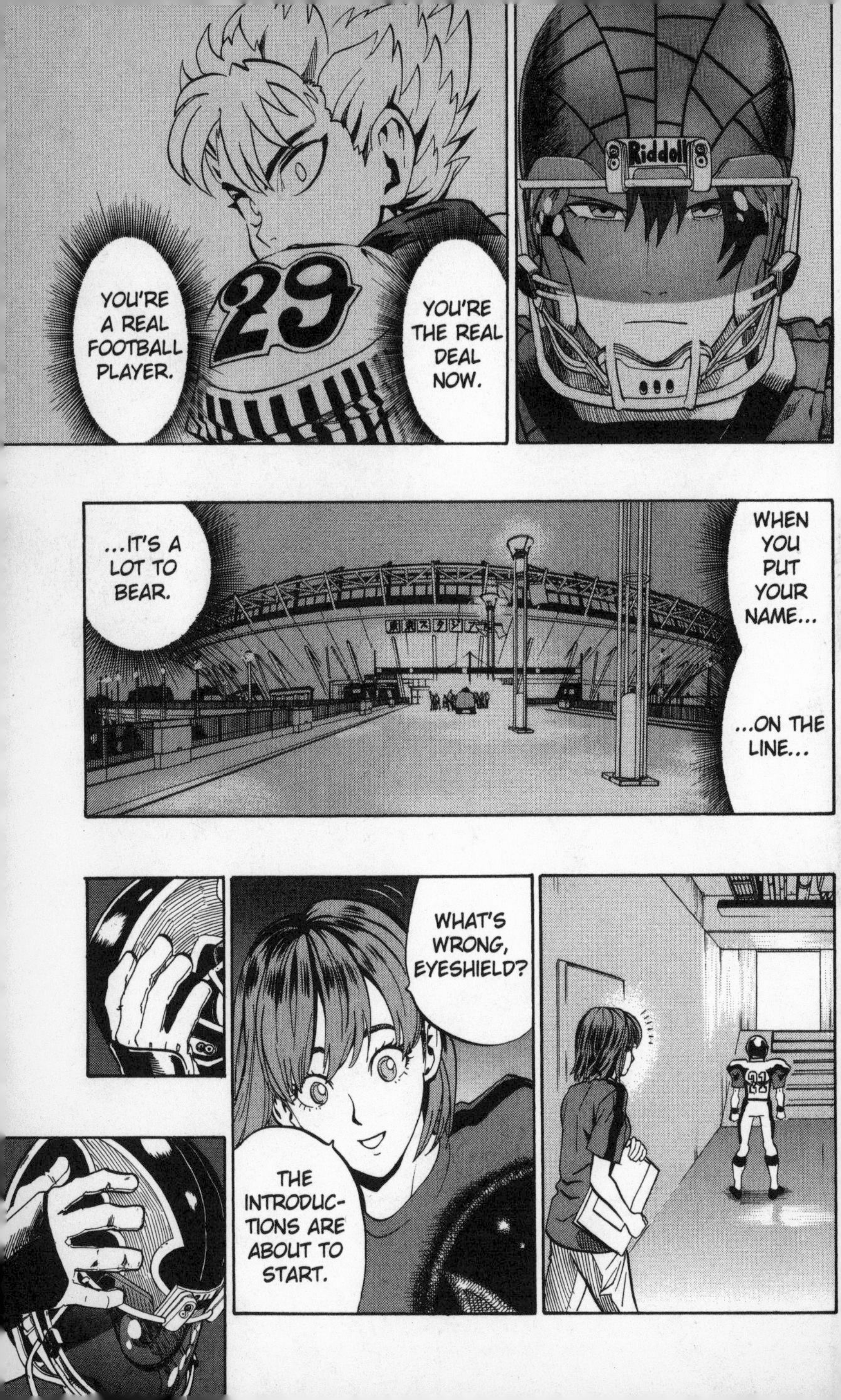
YOU'RE THE REAL DEAL NOW.
YOU'RE A REAL FOOTBALL PLAYER.
WHEN YOU PUT YOUR NAME...
...ON THE LINE...
...IT'S A LOT TO BEAR.
WHAT'S WRONG, EYESHIELD?
THE INTRODUCTIONS ARE ABOUT TO START.

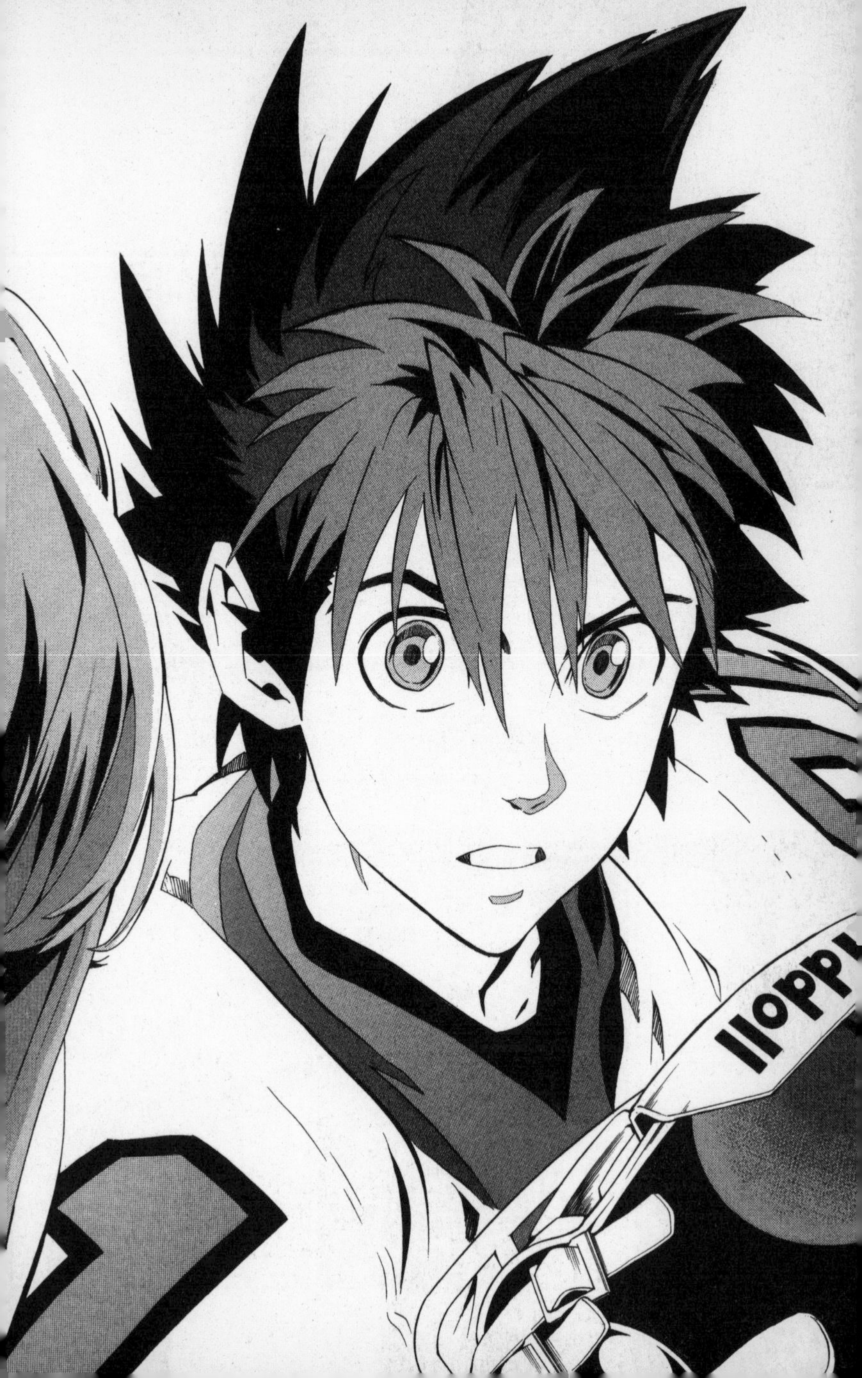

SE...

...NA...?

...TOO DANGEROUS...

...FOR YOU.

DADONK

WHAT'RE YOU DOING, SENA?

FOOT-BALL'S...

I'M SORRY, BUT I COULDN'T TELL YOU, MAMORI.

I'VE GOTTA GO...

...BECAUSE I'M...

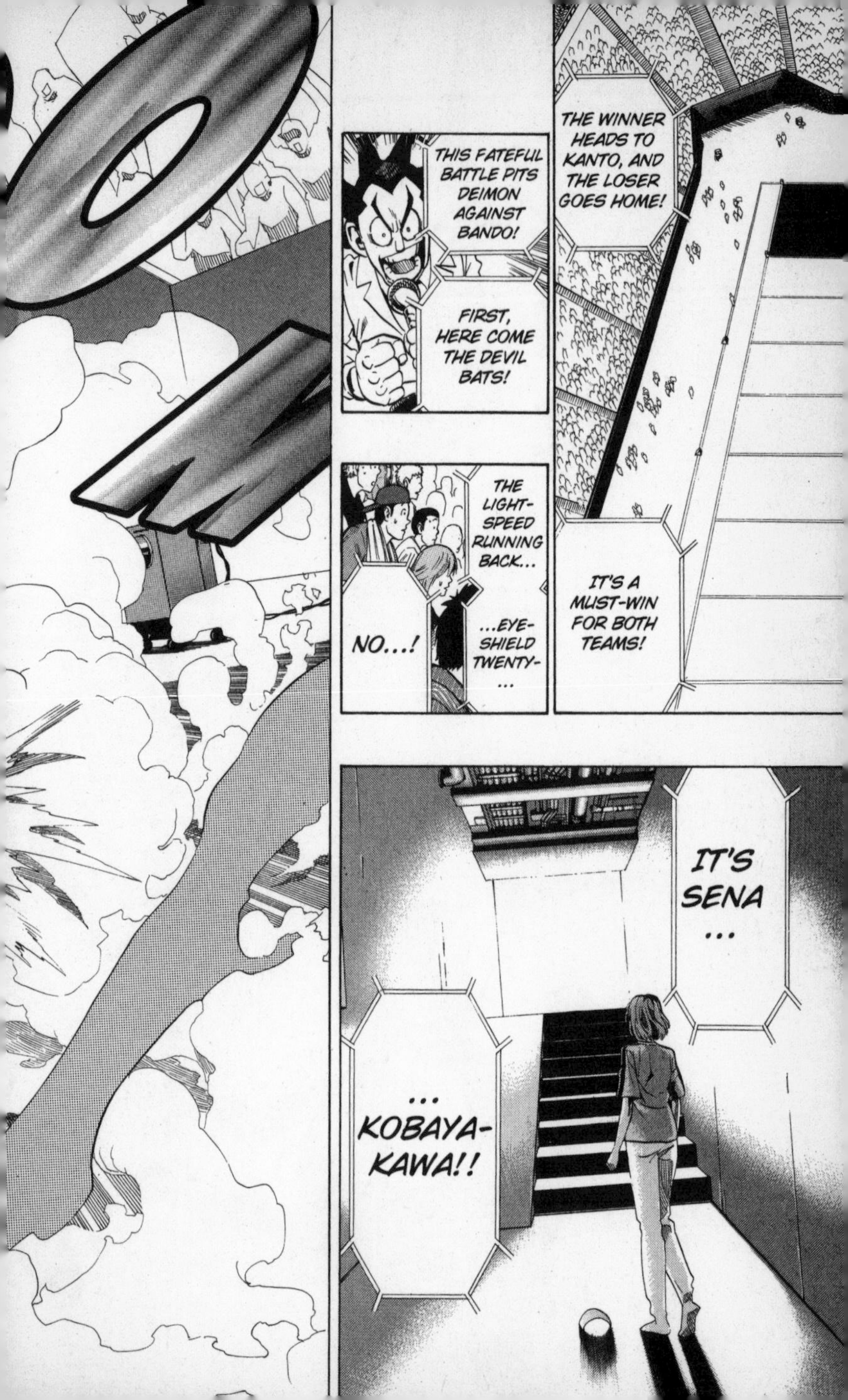
THE WINNER HEADS TO KANTO, AND THE LOSER GOES HOME!
IT'S A MUST-WIN FOR BOTH TEAMS!
THIS FATEFUL BATTLE PITS DEIMON AGAINST BANDO!
FIRST, HERE COME THE DEVIL BATS!
THE LIGHT-SPEED RUNNING BACK...
...EYE-SHIELD TWENTY-...
NO...!
IT'S SENA...
...KOBAYA-KAWA!!

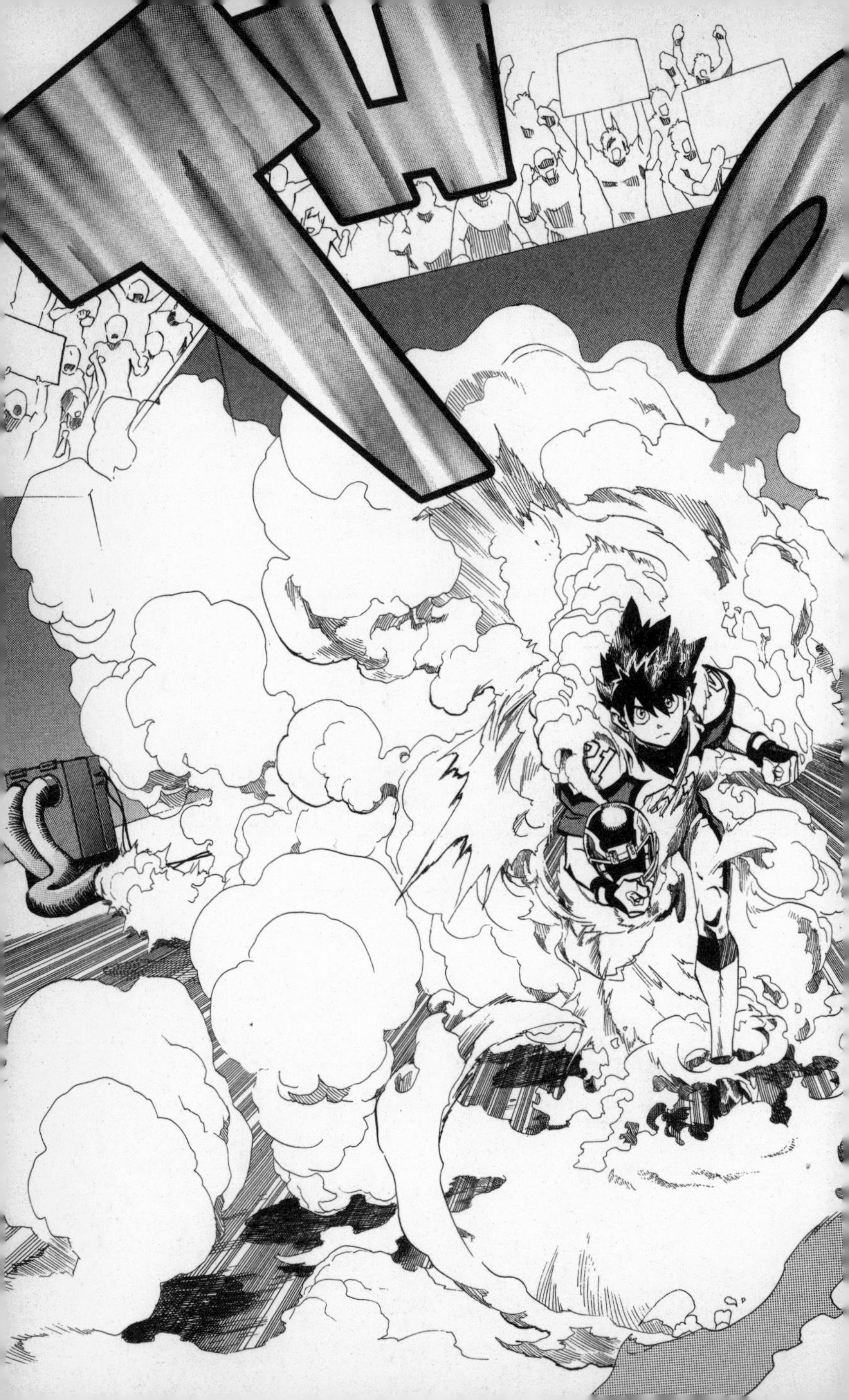
THO

V-Bowl

Extra down 04

Spring Music

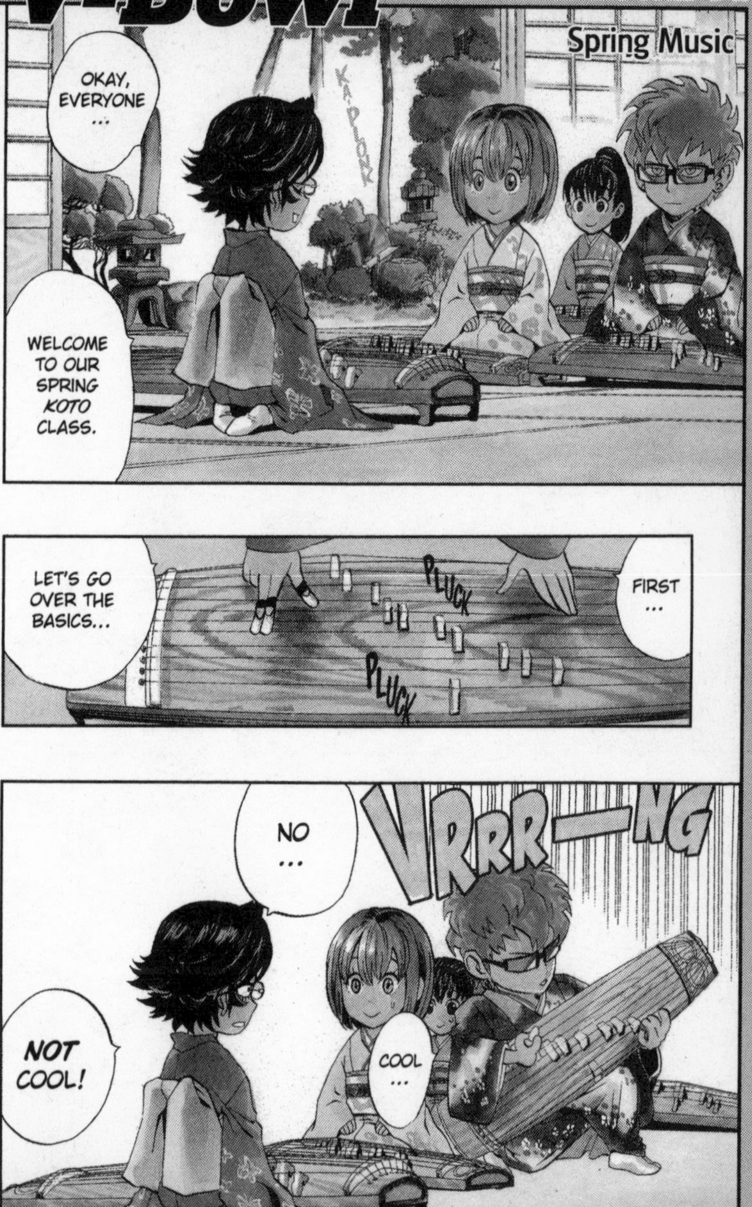
KA-PLONK
OKAY, EVERYONE ...
WELCOME TO OUR SPRING KOTO CLASS.
FIRST ...
PLUCK
PLUCK
LET'S GO OVER THE BASICS...
VRRR—NG
NO ...
COOL ...
NOT COOL!

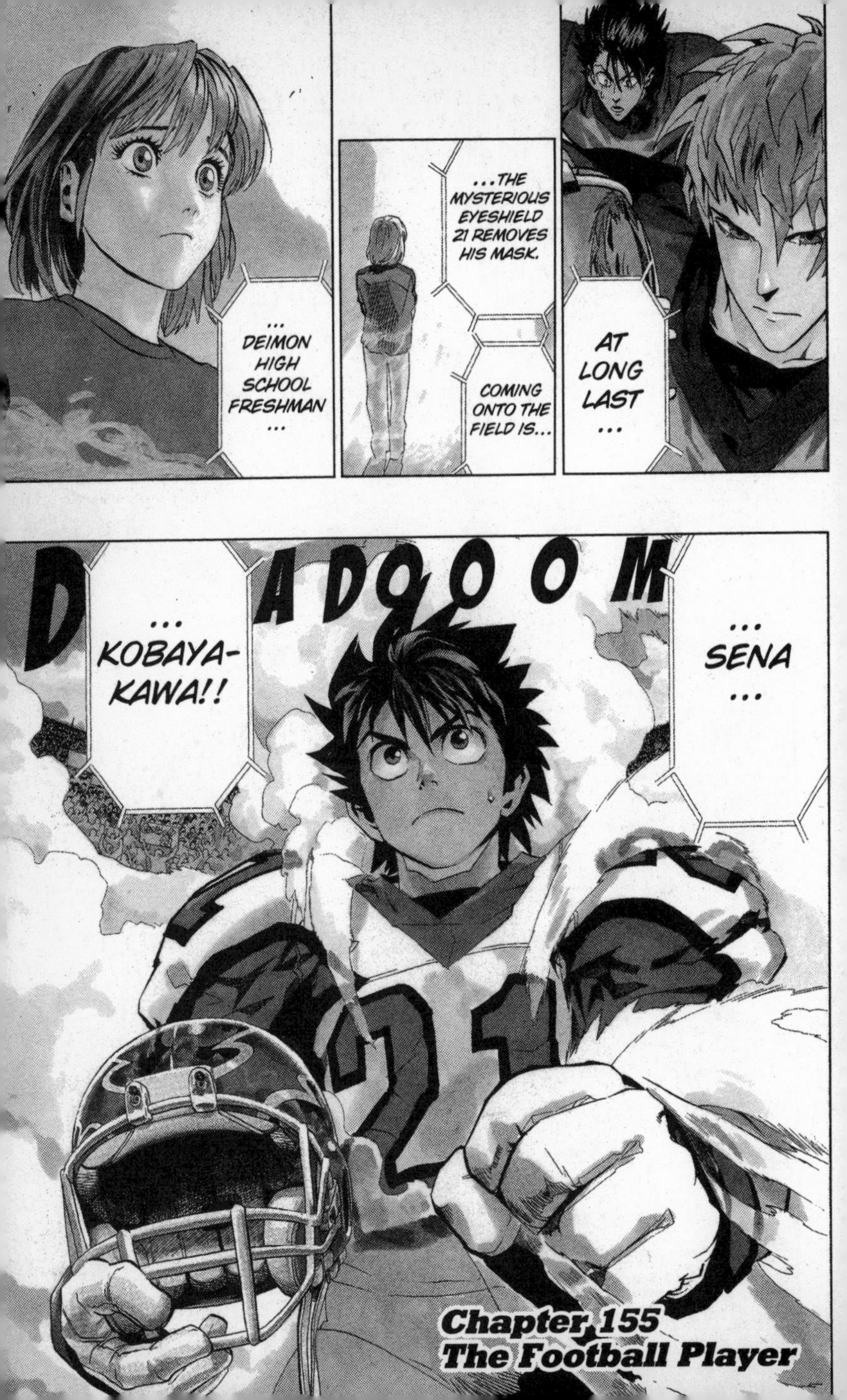
AT LONG LAST ...
...THE MYSTERIOUS EYESHIELD 21 REMOVES HIS MASK.
COMING ONTO THE FIELD IS...
... DEIMON HIGH SCHOOL FRESHMAN ...
DADOOOM
... SENA ...
... KOBAYA-KAWA!!

Chapter 155 The Football Player

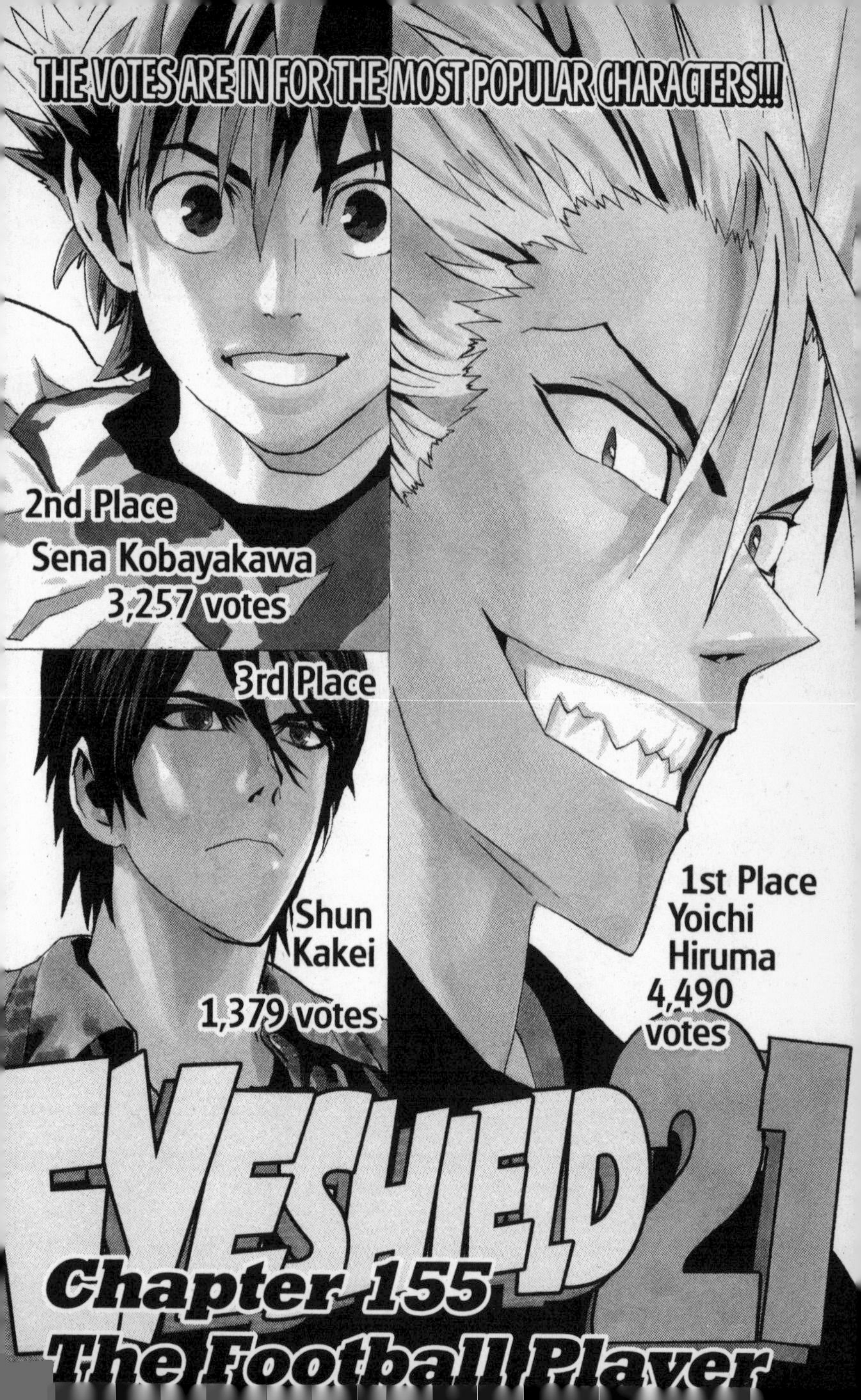
THE VOTES ARE IN FOR THE MOST POPULAR CHARACTERS!!!
1st Place
Yoichi Hiruma
4,490 votes
2nd Place
Sena Kobayakawa
3,257 votes
3rd Place
Shun Kakei
1,379 votes
Chapter 155
The Football Player

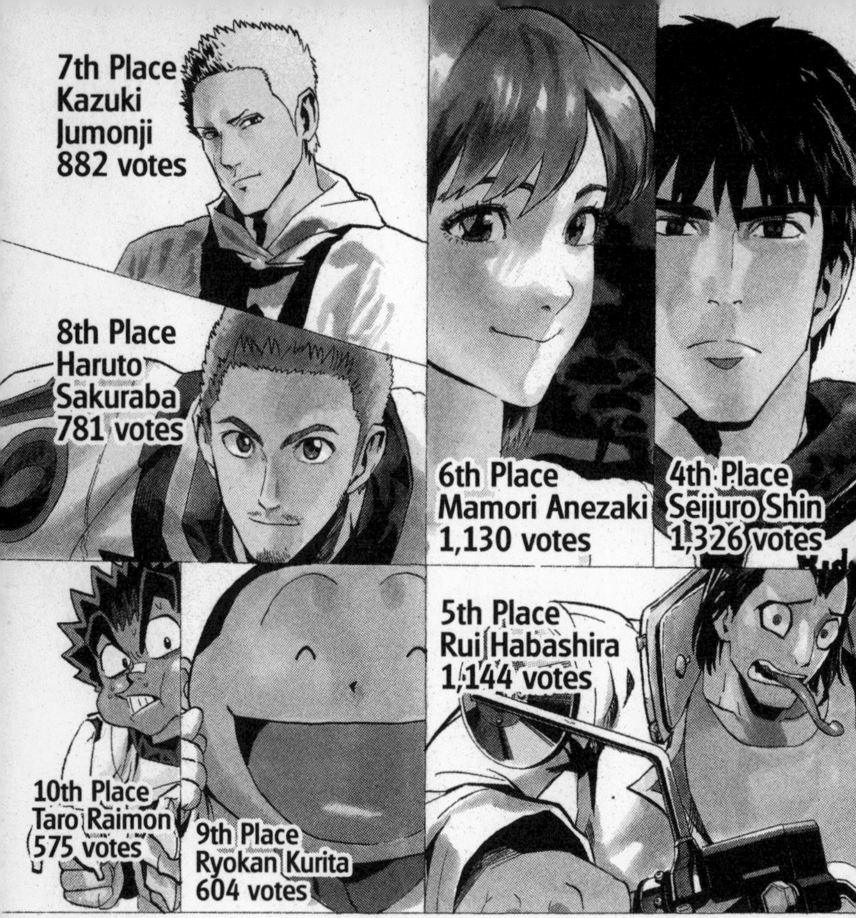
4th Place
Seijuro Shin
1,326 votes
6th Place
Mamori Anezaki
1,130 votes
7th Place
Kazuki
Jumonji
882 votes
8th Place
Haruto
Sakuraba
781 votes
5th Place
Rui Habashira
1,144 votes
9th Place
Ryokan Kurita
604 votes
10th Place
Taro Raimon
575 votes

20,311 Votes Were Cast!! A Big Thanks to All Who Voted!!

The rest of the results are below!!

11th Place	Kengo Mizumachi	530 votes	16th Place	Manabu Yukimitsu	214 Votes
12th Place	Gen Takekura	407 votes	17th Place	Daikichi Komusubi	208 votes
13th Place	Cerberus	383 votes	18th Place	Riku Kaitani	200 votes
14th Place	The Kid	345 votes	19th Place	Koji Kuroki	191 votes
15th Place	Suzuna Taki	271 votes	20th Place	Unsui Kongo	156 votes

Others with Votes

Tetsuo Ishimaru, Natsuhiko Taki, The Devil Bat, Hiroshi Ohira, Hiroshi Onishi, Ichiro Takami, Jo Tetsuma, Agon Kongo, Koharu Wakana, Shozo Togano, The Kongo Brothers, Megu Tsuyumine, Kotaro Sasaki, Homer, Ikkyu Hosokawa, Piggyberus, The Gonzalez Brothers, The Hah Brothers…

Fell from
9th place
to 21st.

It's okay,
it's okay...

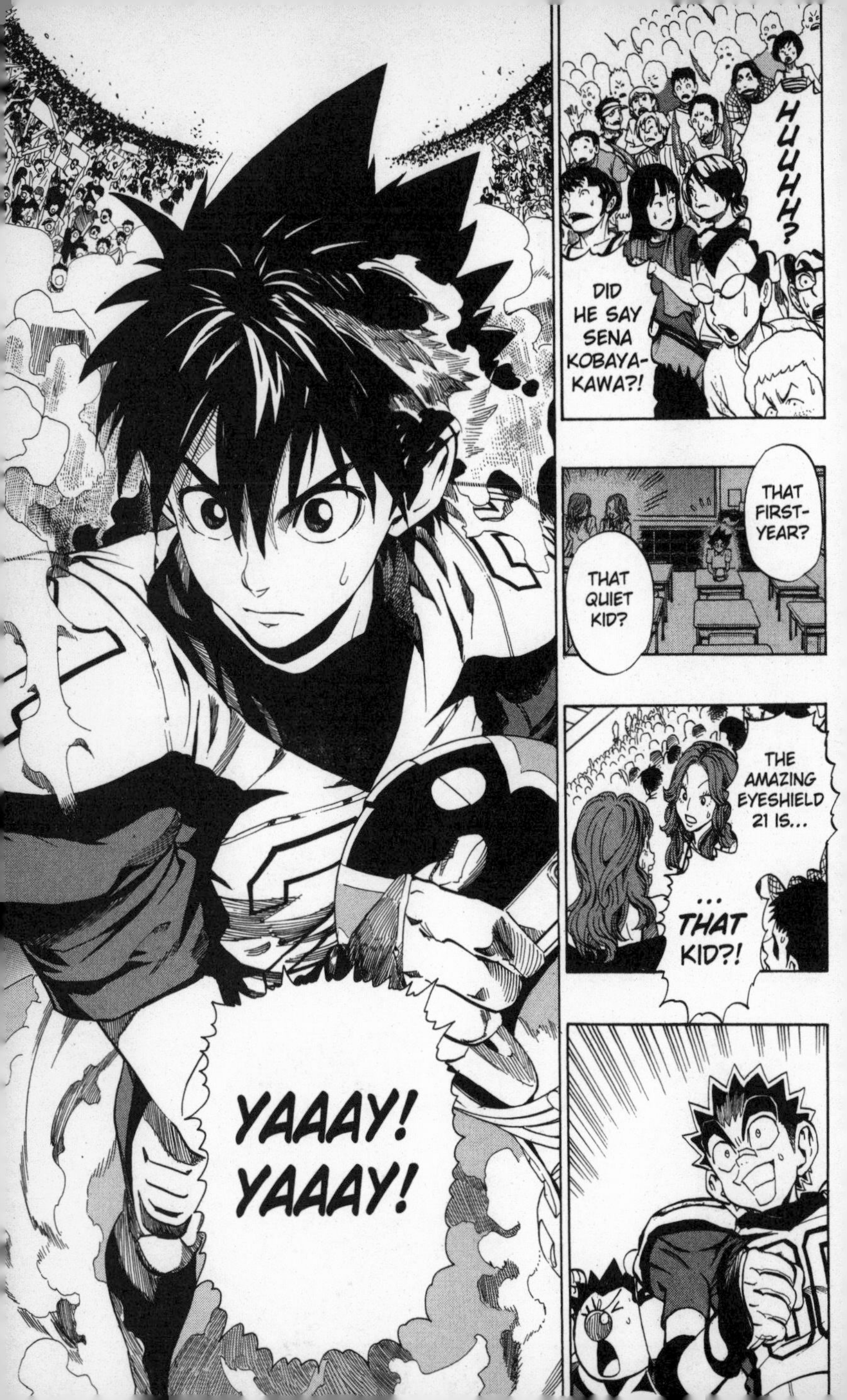
HUUHHH?
DID HE SAY SENA KOBAYA-KAWA?!
THAT FIRST-YEAR?
THAT QUIET KID?
THE AMAZING EYESHIELD 21 IS...
... THAT KID?!
YAAAY! YAAAY!

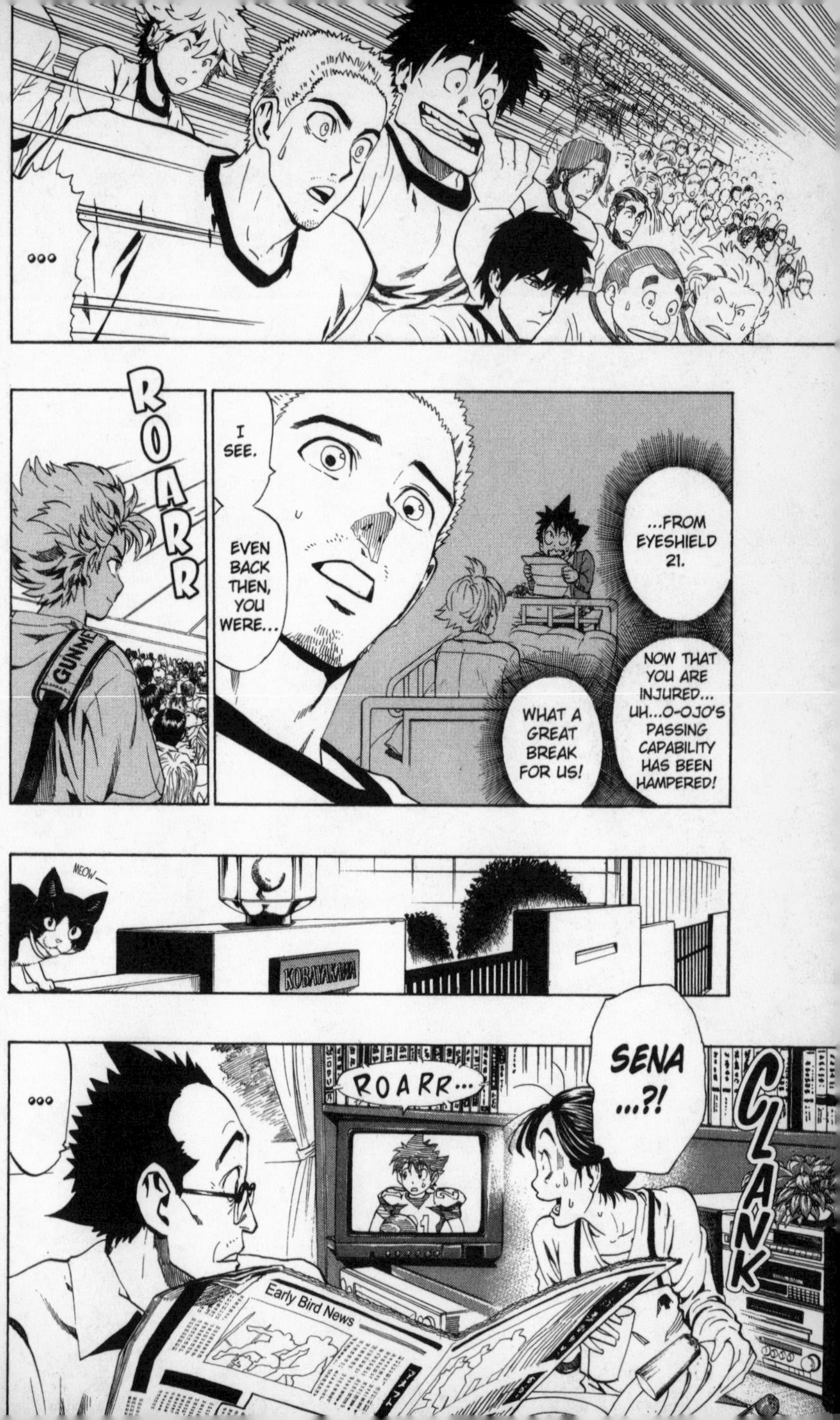

...
...FROM EYESHIELD 21.
NOW THAT YOU ARE INJURED... UH...O-OJO'S PASSING CAPABILITY HAS BEEN HAMPERED!
WHAT A GREAT BREAK FOR US!
I SEE.
EVEN BACK THEN, YOU WERE...
ROARR
GUNME
KOBAYAKAWA
MEOW
CLANK
SENA ...?!
ROARR...
...
Early Bird News

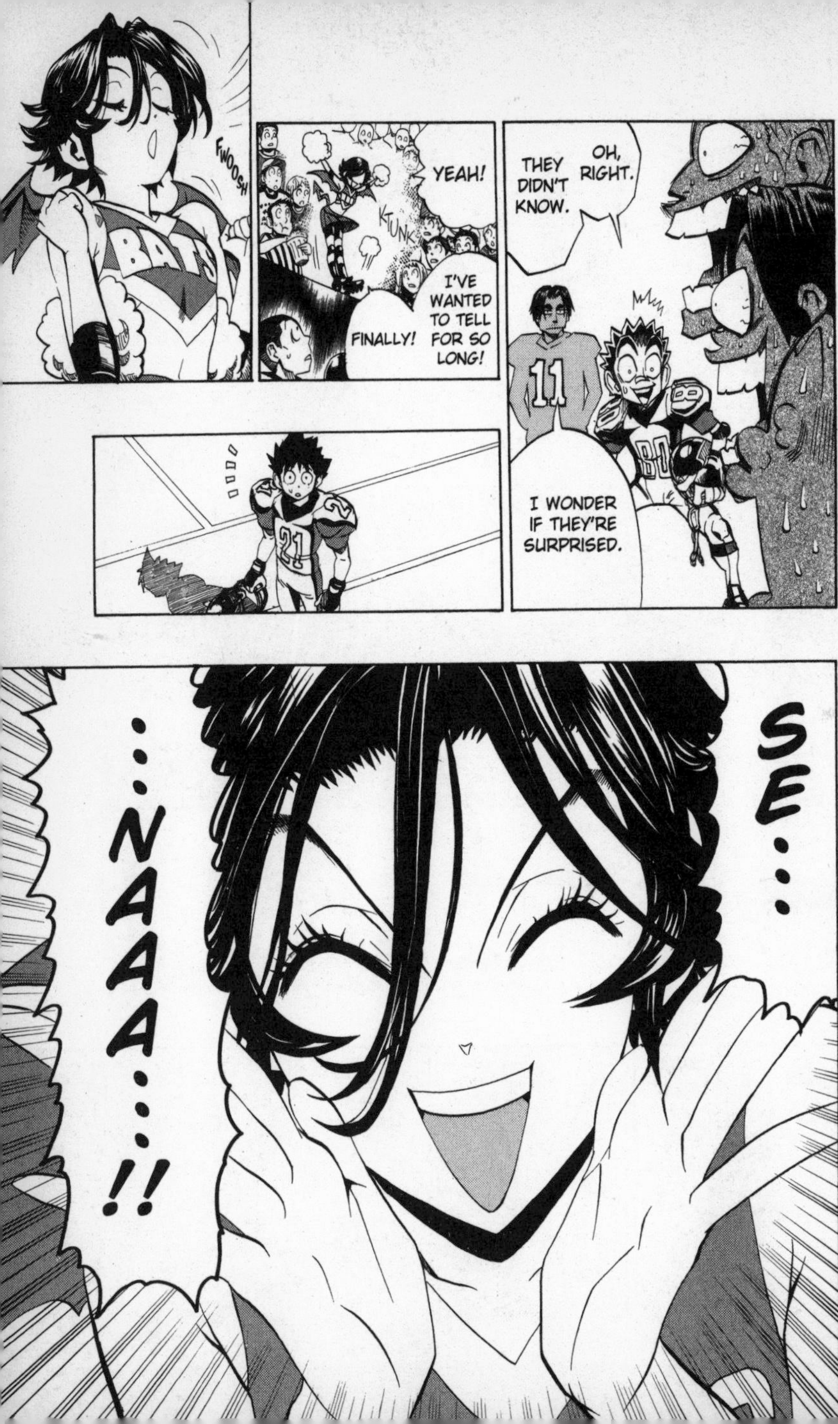
OH, RIGHT.
THEY DIDN'T KNOW.
I WONDER IF THEY'RE SURPRISED.
YEAH!
KTUNK
I'VE WANTED TO TELL FOR SO LONG!
FINALLY!
FWOOSH
SE...
...NAAA...!!

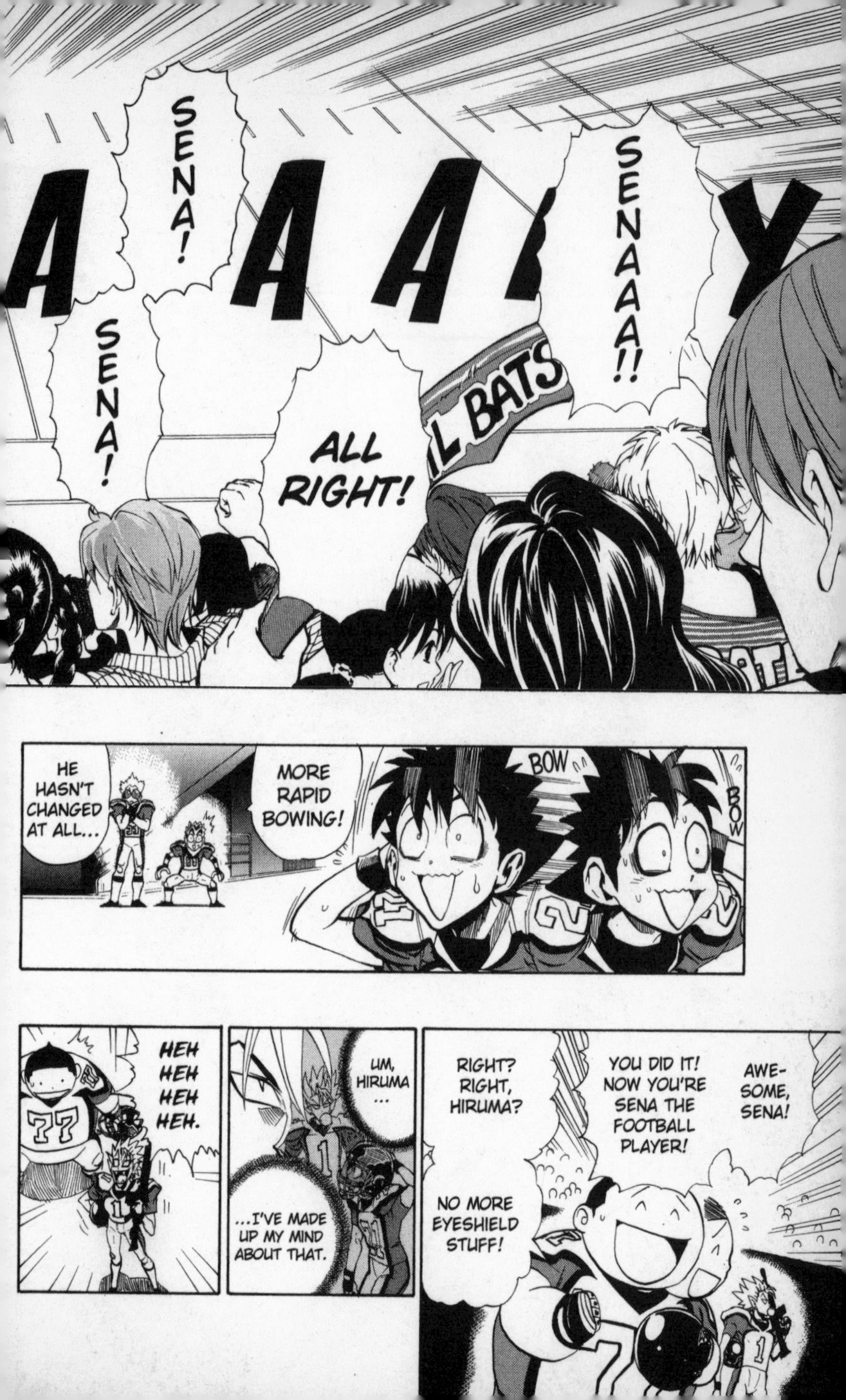
AAAAY
SENAAAA!!
SENA!
ALL RIGHT!
SENA!
L BATS
BOW
BOW
MORE RAPID BOWING!
HE HASN'T CHANGED AT ALL...
AWE-SOME, SENA!
YOU DID IT! NOW YOU'RE SENA THE FOOTBALL PLAYER!
RIGHT? RIGHT, HIRUMA?
NO MORE EYESHIELD STUFF!
UM, HIRUMA...
...I'VE MADE UP MY MIND ABOUT THAT.
HEH HEH HEH HEH.

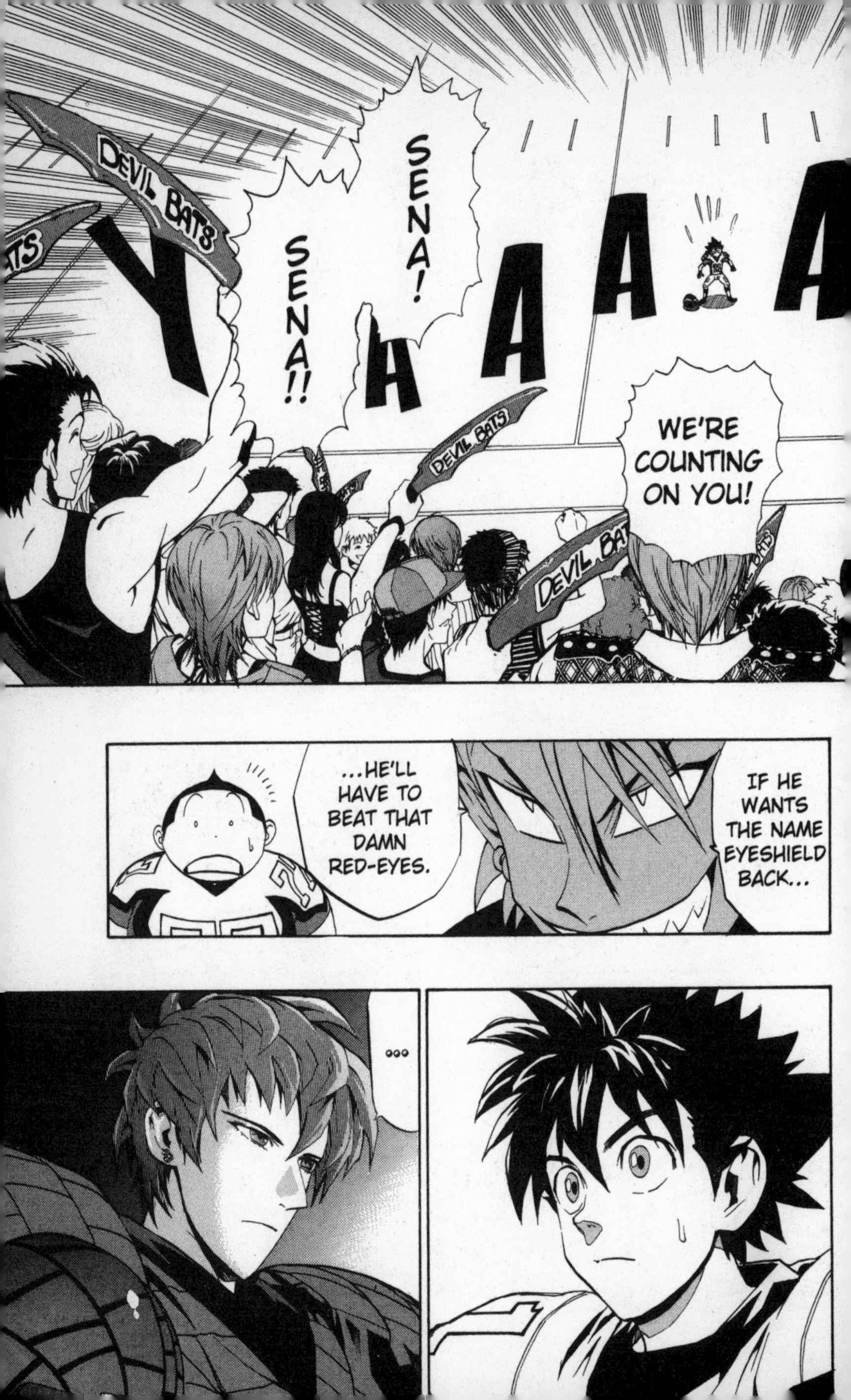
WE'RE COUNTING ON YOU!
SENA!
SENA!!
YAAAAA
DEVIL BATS
DEVIL BATS
DEVIL BATS
IF HE WANTS THE NAME EYESHIELD BACK...
...HE'LL HAVE TO BEAT THAT DAMN RED-EYES.
...

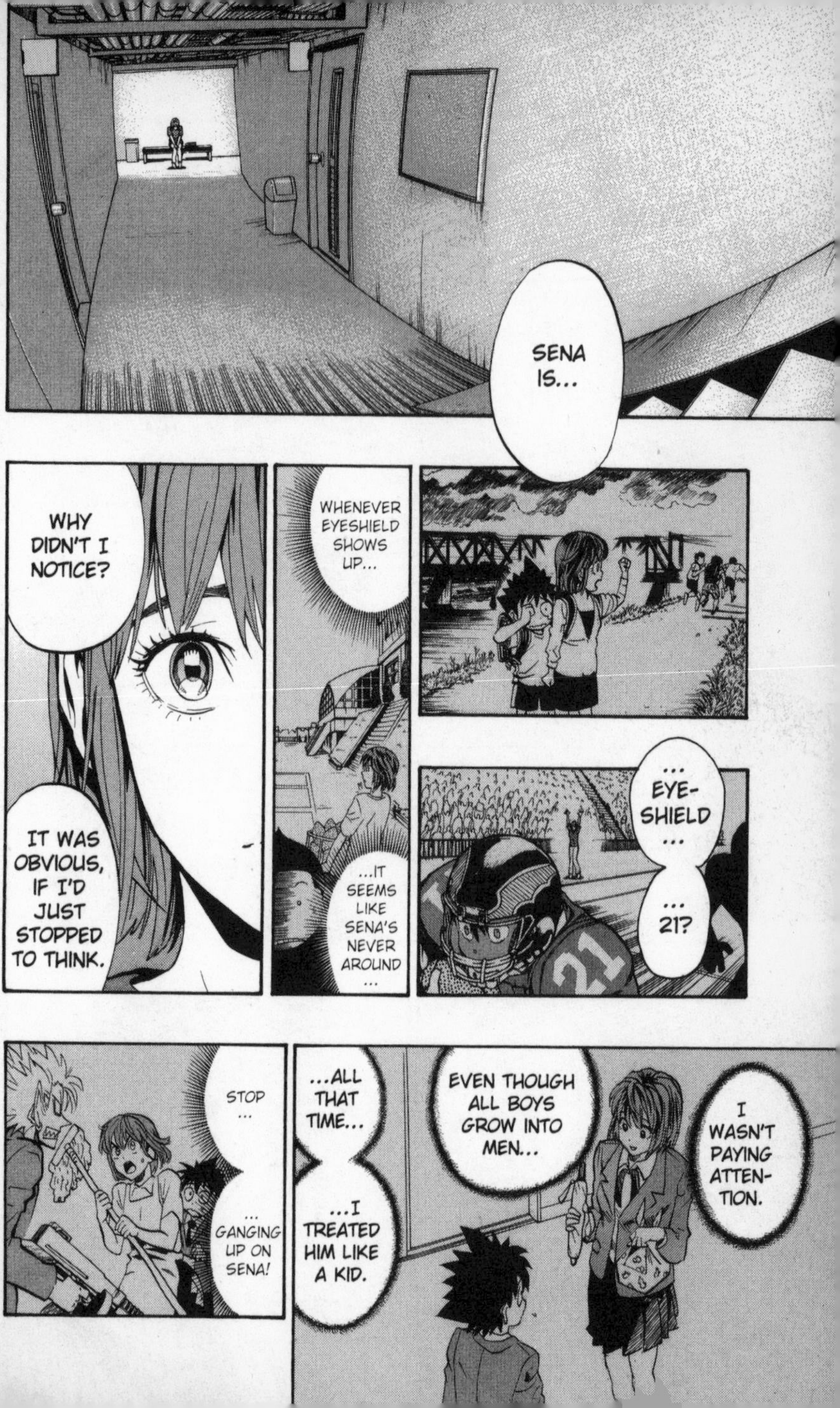
SENA IS...
...EYE-SHIELD...
...21?
WHENEVER EYESHIELD SHOWS UP...
...IT SEEMS LIKE SENA'S NEVER AROUND...
WHY DIDN'T I NOTICE?
IT WAS OBVIOUS, IF I'D JUST STOPPED TO THINK.
I WASN'T PAYING ATTEN-TION.
EVEN THOUGH ALL BOYS GROW INTO MEN...
...ALL THAT TIME...
...I TREATED HIM LIKE A KID.
STOP...
...GANGING UP ON SENA!

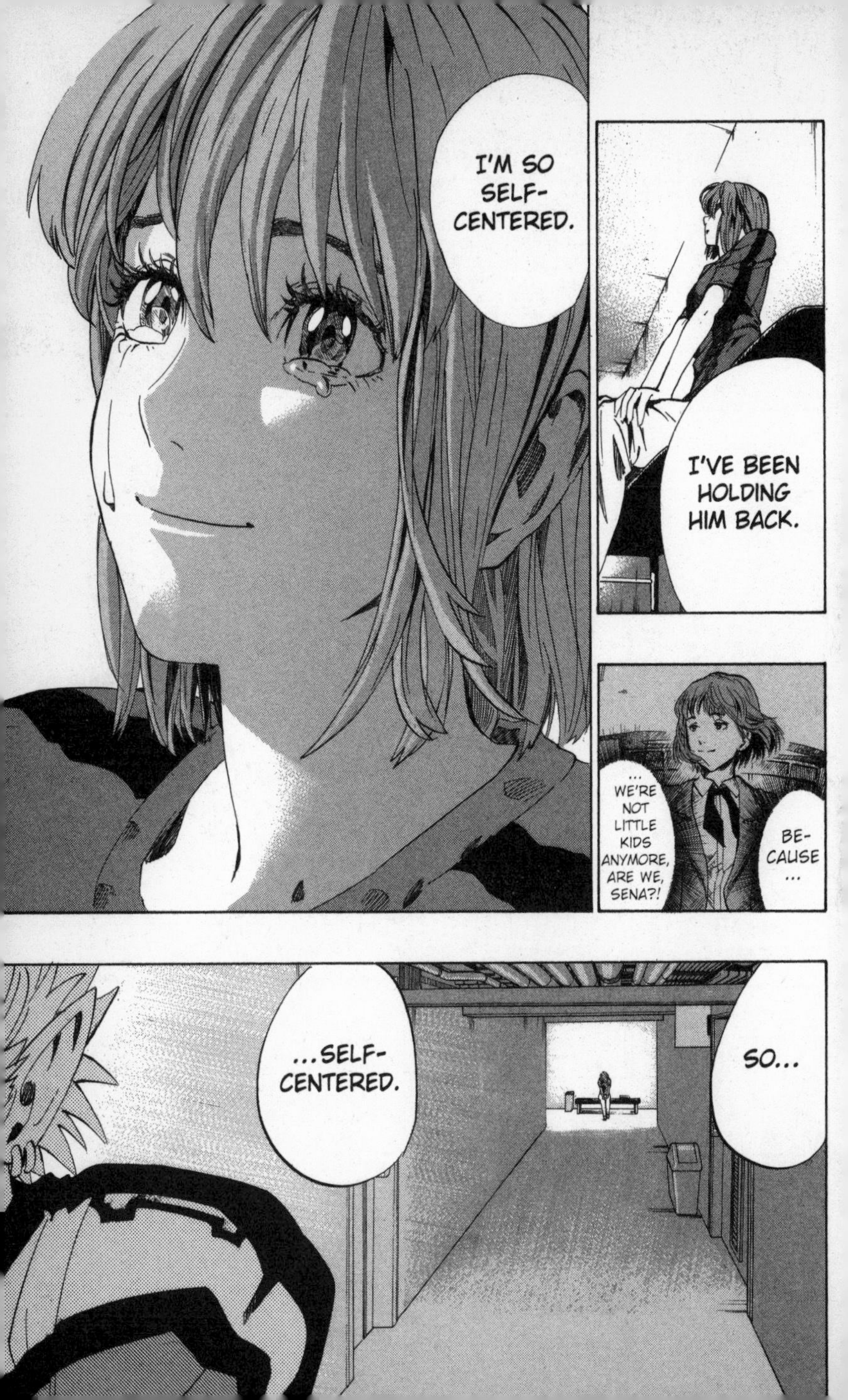
I'VE BEEN HOLDING HIM BACK.
BE-CAUSE ...
... WE'RE NOT LITTLE KIDS ANYMORE, ARE WE, SENA?!
I'M SO SELF-CENTERED.
SO...
...SELF-CENTERED.

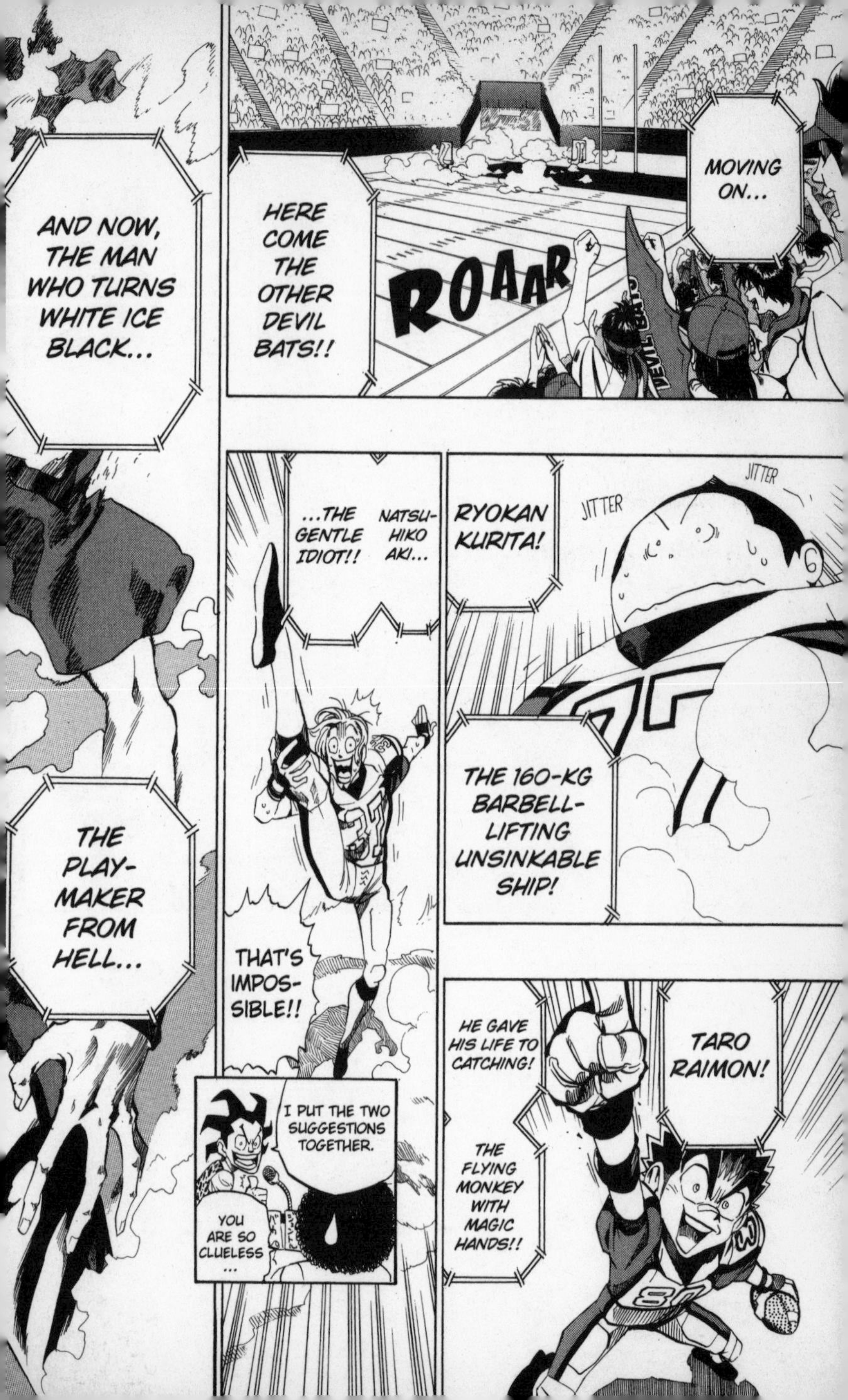
MOVING ON...
HERE COME THE OTHER DEVIL BATS!!
ROAAR
DEVIL BATS
RYOKAN KURITA!
JITTER
JITTER
THE 160-KG BARBELL-LIFTING UNSINKABLE SHIP!
TARO RAIMON!
HE GAVE HIS LIFE TO CATCHING!
THE FLYING MONKEY WITH MAGIC HANDS!!
NATSUHIKO AKI...
...THE GENTLE IDIOT!!
THAT'S IMPOSSIBLE!!
I PUT THE TWO SUGGESTIONS TOGETHER.
YOU ARE SO CLUELESS ...
AND NOW, THE MAN WHO TURNS WHITE ICE BLACK...
THE PLAYMAKER FROM HELL...

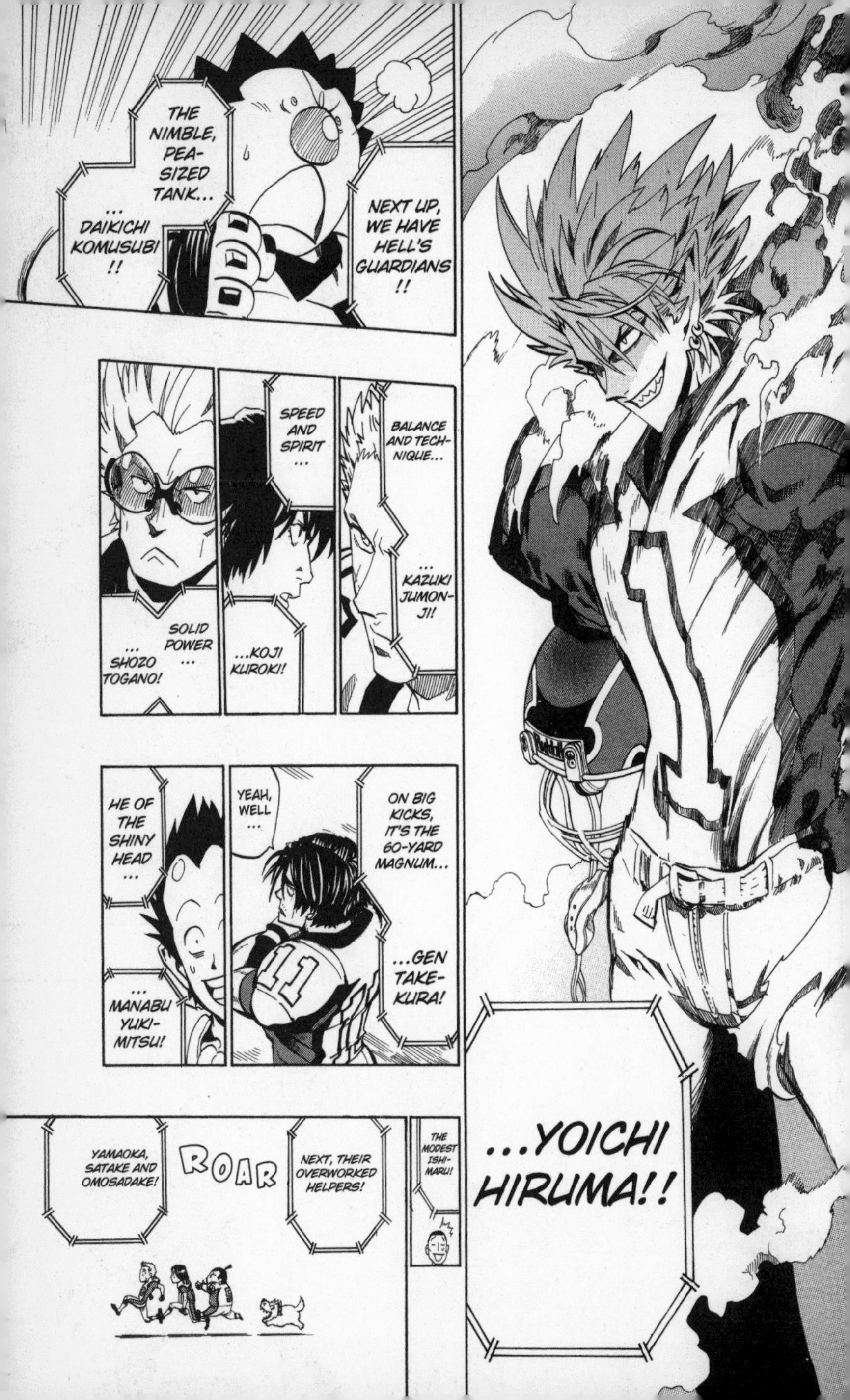
...YOICHI HIRUMA!!
NEXT UP, WE HAVE HELL'S GUARDIANS!!
THE NIMBLE, PEA-SIZED TANK...
...DAIKICHI KOMUSUBI!!
BALANCE AND TECHNIQUE...
...KAZUKI JUMONJI!
SPEED AND SPIRIT...
...KOJI KUROKI!
SOLID POWER...
...SHOZO TOGANO!
ON BIG KICKS, IT'S THE 60-YARD MAGNUM...
...GEN TAKEKURA!
YEAH, WELL...
HE OF THE SHINY HEAD...
...MANABU YUKIMITSU!
THE MODEST ISHIMARU!
NEXT, THEIR OVERWORKED HELPERS!
ROAR
YAMAOKA, SATAKE AND OMOSADAKE!

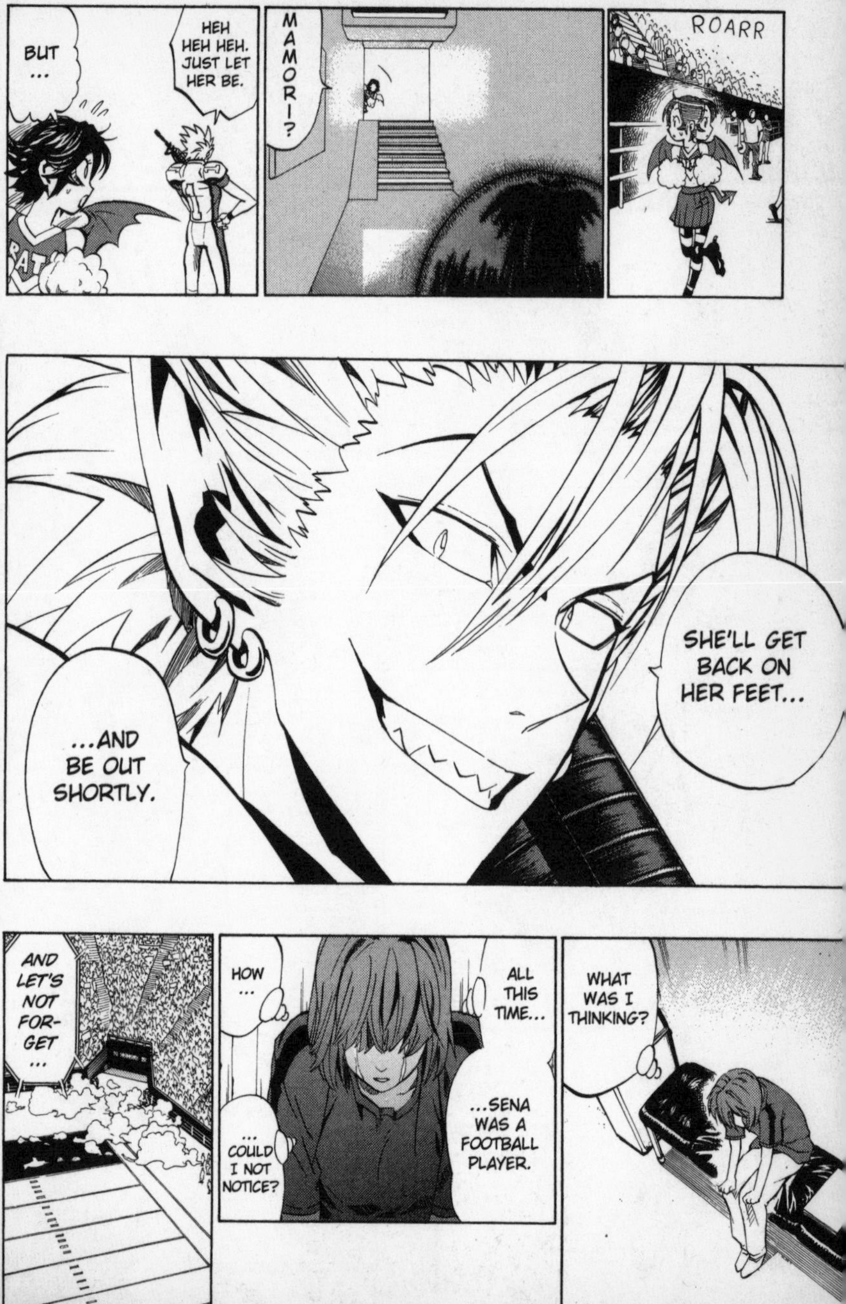
ROARR
MAMORI-?
HEH HEH HEH. JUST LET HER BE.
BUT ...
SHE'LL GET BACK ON HER FEET...
...AND BE OUT SHORTLY.
WHAT WAS I THINKING?
ALL THIS TIME...
HOW ...
...SENA WAS A FOOTBALL PLAYER.
... COULD I NOT NOTICE?
AND LET'S NOT FOR-GET ...

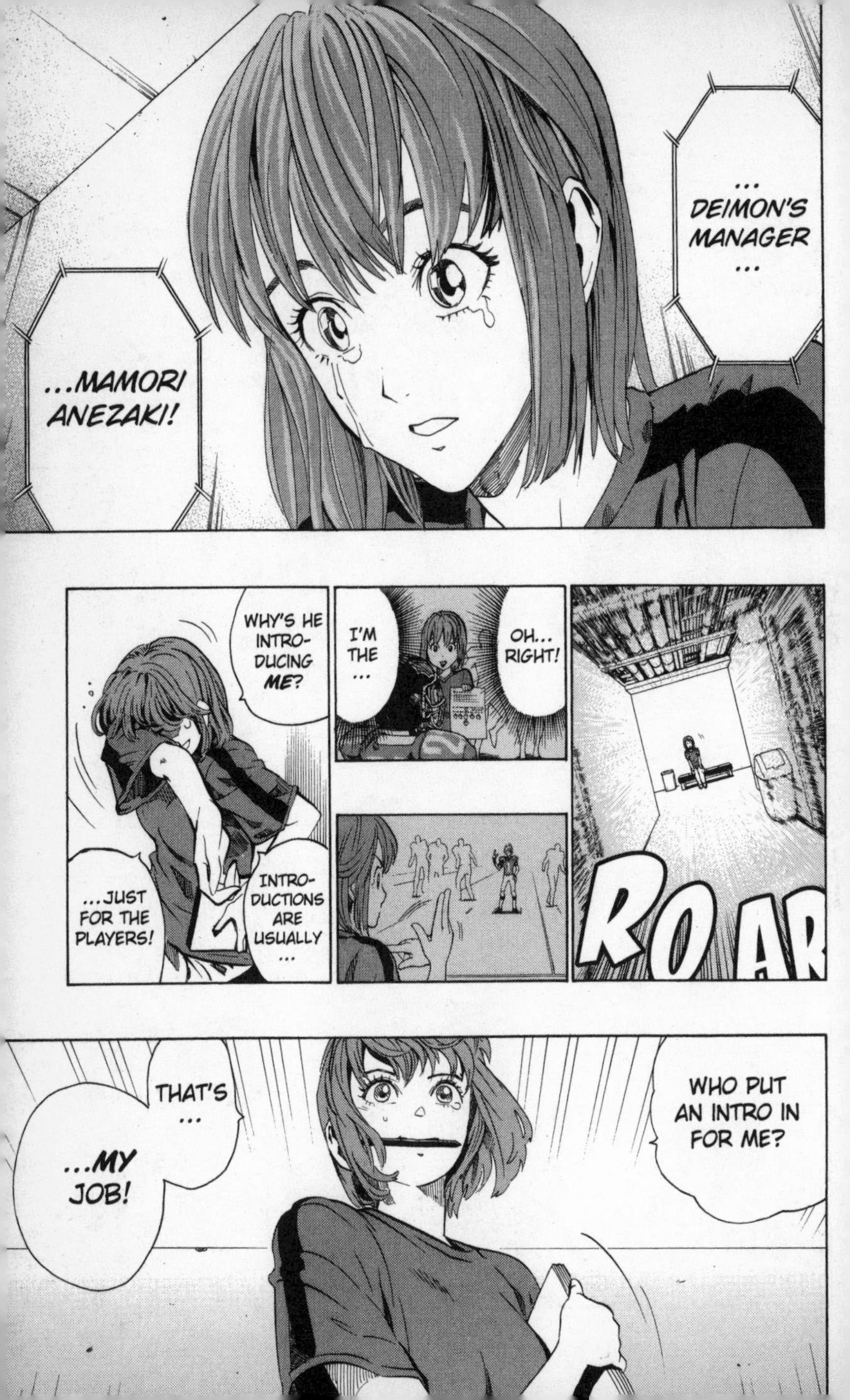
...DEIMON'S MANAGER...
...MAMORI ANEZAKI!
ROAR
OH... RIGHT!
I'M THE...
WHY'S HE INTRODUCING ME?
INTRODUCTIONS ARE USUALLY...
...JUST FOR THE PLAYERS!
WHO PUT AN INTRO IN FOR ME?
THAT'S...
...MY JOB!

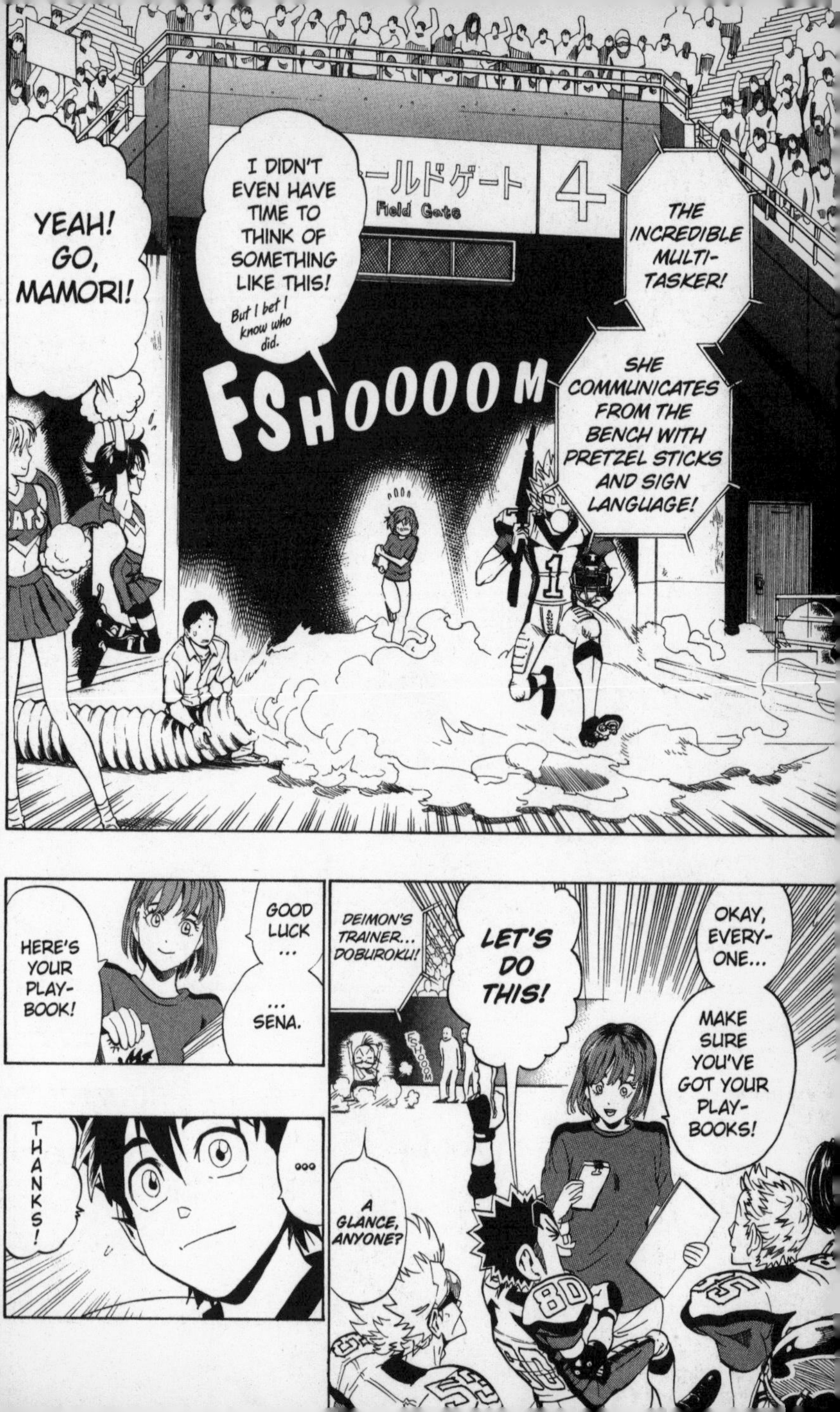
THE INCREDIBLE MULTI-TASKER!
SHE COMMUNICATES FROM THE BENCH WITH PRETZEL STICKS AND SIGN LANGUAGE!
4
ールドゲート
Field Gate
I DIDN'T EVEN HAVE TIME TO THINK OF SOMETHING LIKE THIS!
But I bet I know who did.
FSHOOOOM
YEAH! GO, MAMORI!
OKAY, EVERY-ONE...
MAKE SURE YOU'VE GOT YOUR PLAY-BOOKS!
LET'S DO THIS!
DEIMON'S TRAINER... DOBUROKU!
FSHOOOM
...
A GLANCE, ANYONE?
GOOD LUCK ...
HERE'S YOUR PLAY-BOOK!
... SENA.
THANKS!

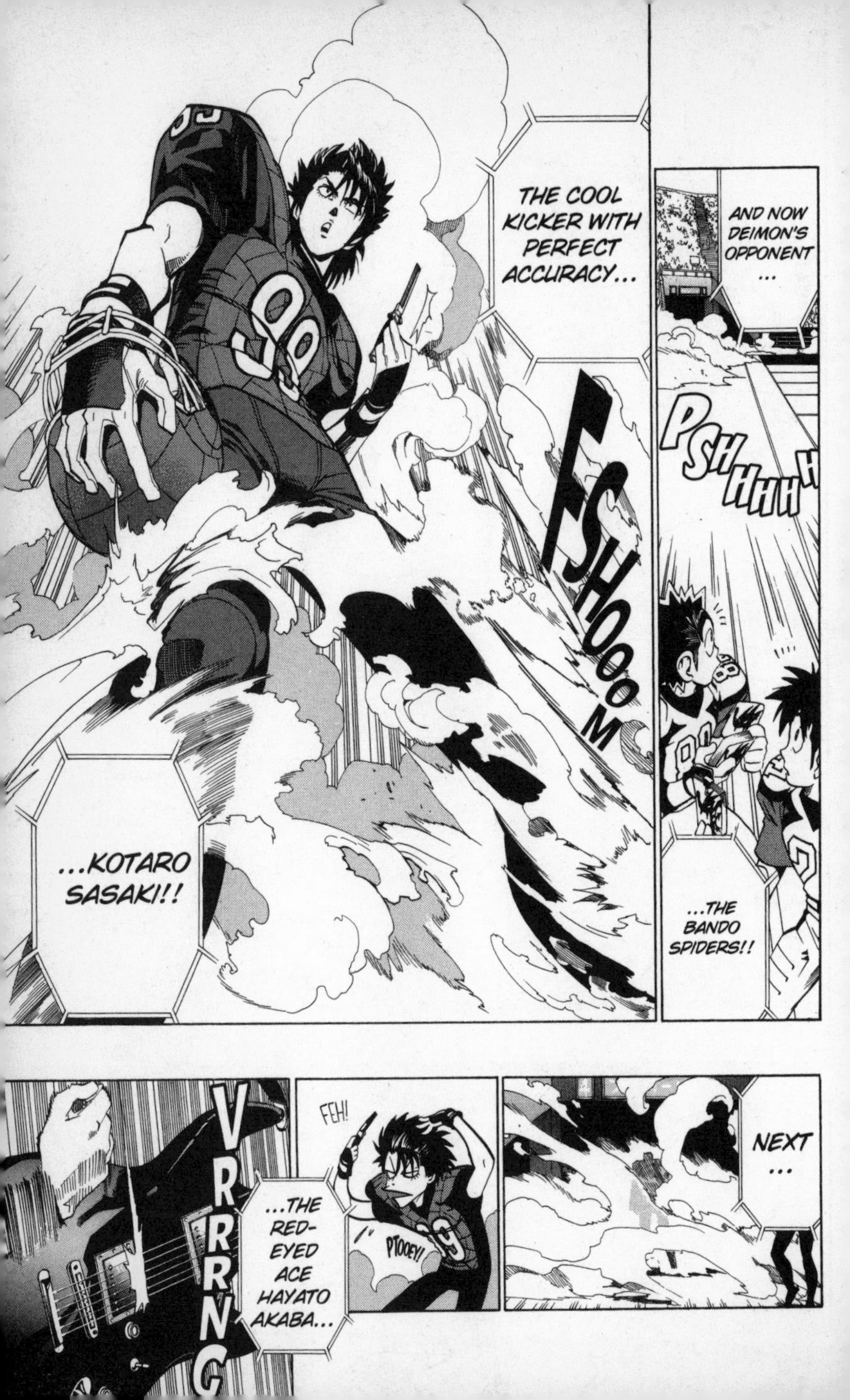
AND NOW DEIMON'S OPPONENT ...
PSHHHHH
...THE BANDO SPIDERS!!
THE COOL KICKER WITH PERFECT ACCURACY...
FSHOOOOM
...KOTARO SASAKI!!
NEXT ...
FEH!
PTOOEY!
...THE RED-EYED ACE HAYATO AKABA...
VRRNG

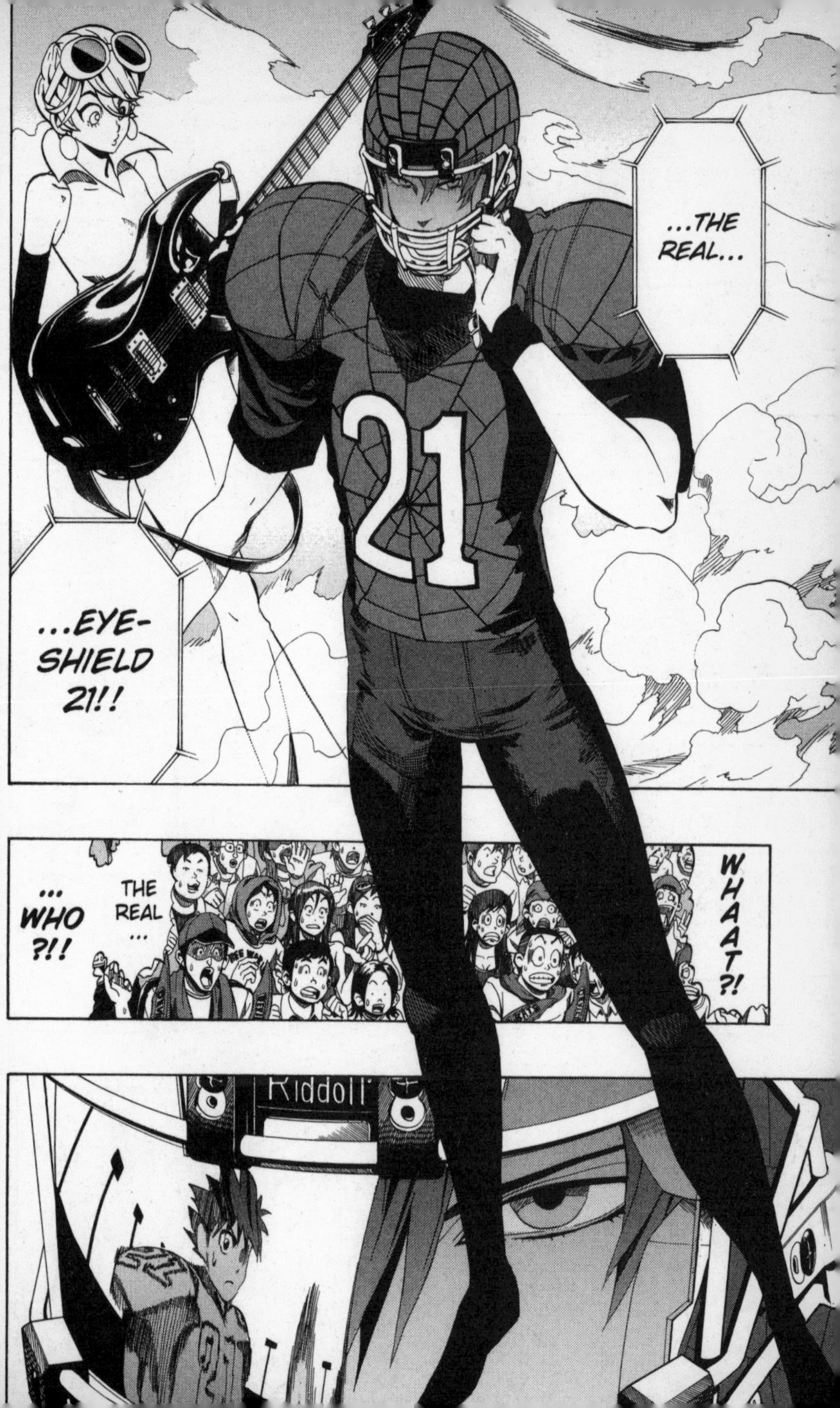
...THE REAL...
...EYE-SHIELD 21!!
WHAAT?!
THE REAL...
...WHO?!!

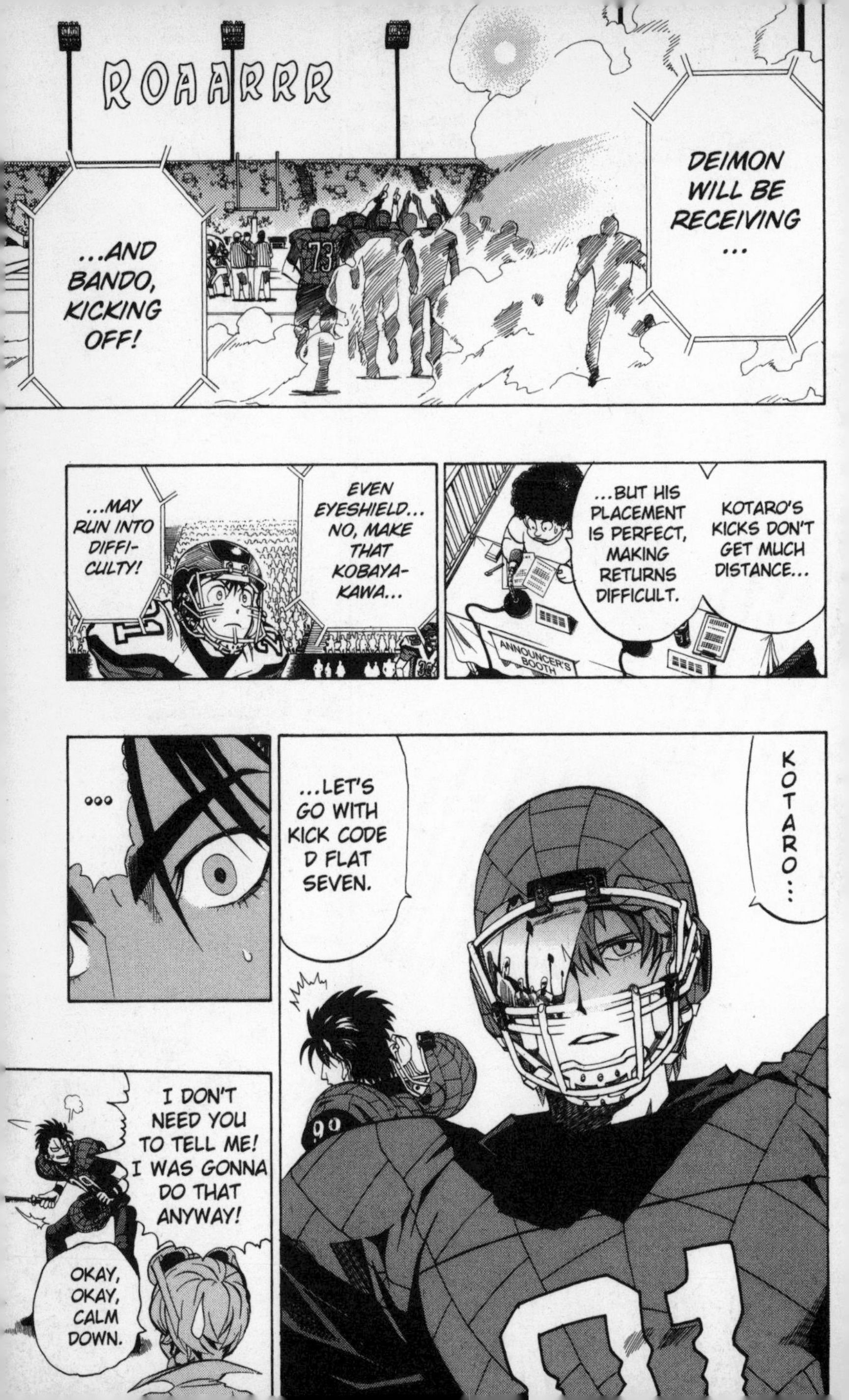

ROAARRR
DEIMON WILL BE RECEIVING...
...AND BANDO, KICKING OFF!
KOTARO'S KICKS DON'T GET MUCH DISTANCE...
...BUT HIS PLACEMENT IS PERFECT, MAKING RETURNS DIFFICULT.
ANNOUNCER'S BOOTH
EVEN EYESHIELD... NO, MAKE THAT KOBAYAKAWA...
...MAY RUN INTO DIFFICULTY!
KOTARO...
...LET'S GO WITH KICK CODE D FLAT SEVEN.
...
I DON'T NEED YOU TO TELL ME! I WAS GONNA DO THAT ANYWAY!
OKAY, OKAY, CALM DOWN.

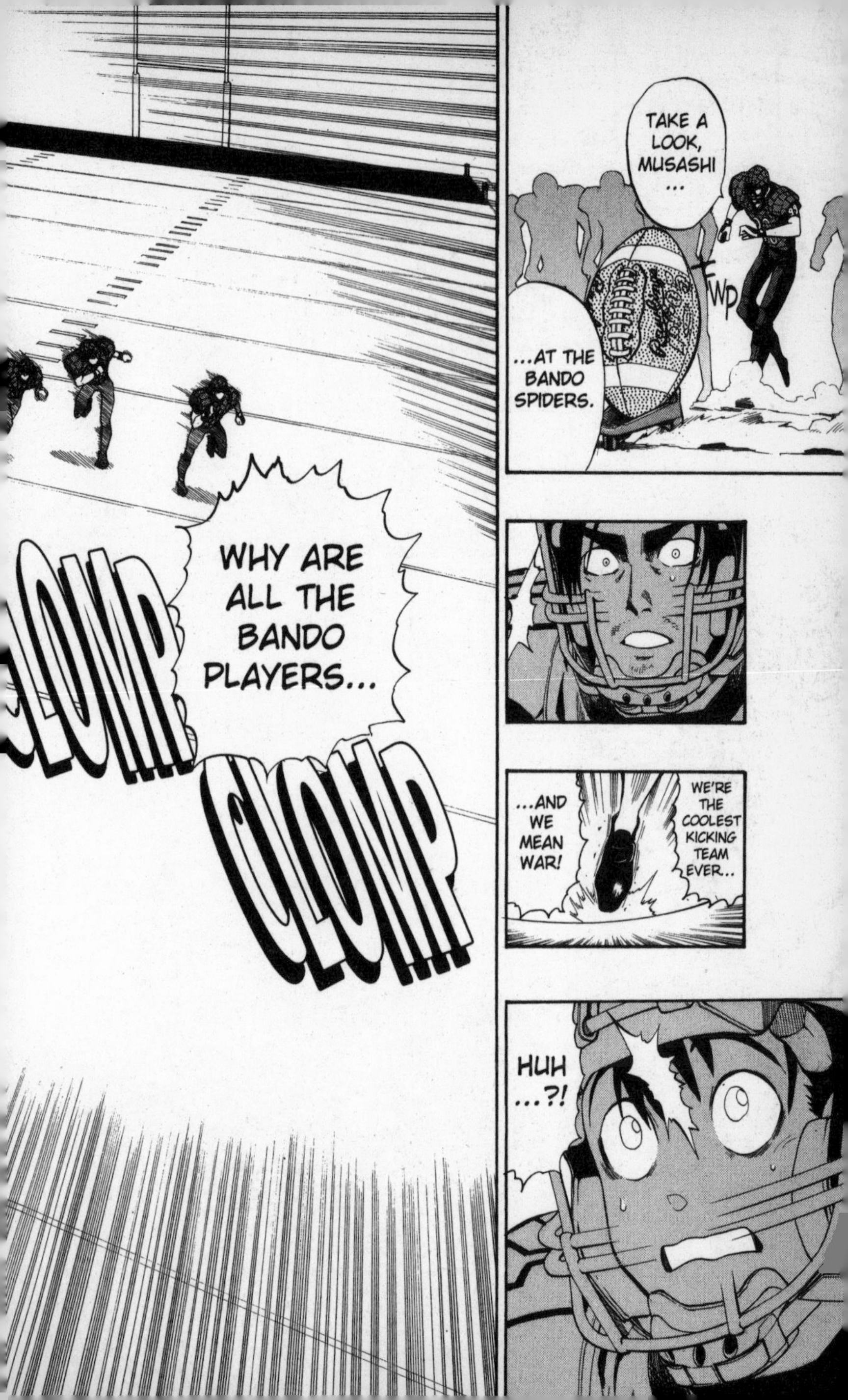
TAKE A LOOK, MUSASHI ...
FWP
...AT THE BANDO SPIDERS.
WE'RE THE COOLEST KICKING TEAM EVER...
...AND WE MEAN WAR!
HUH ...?!
WHY ARE ALL THE BANDO PLAYERS...
CLOMP
CLOMP

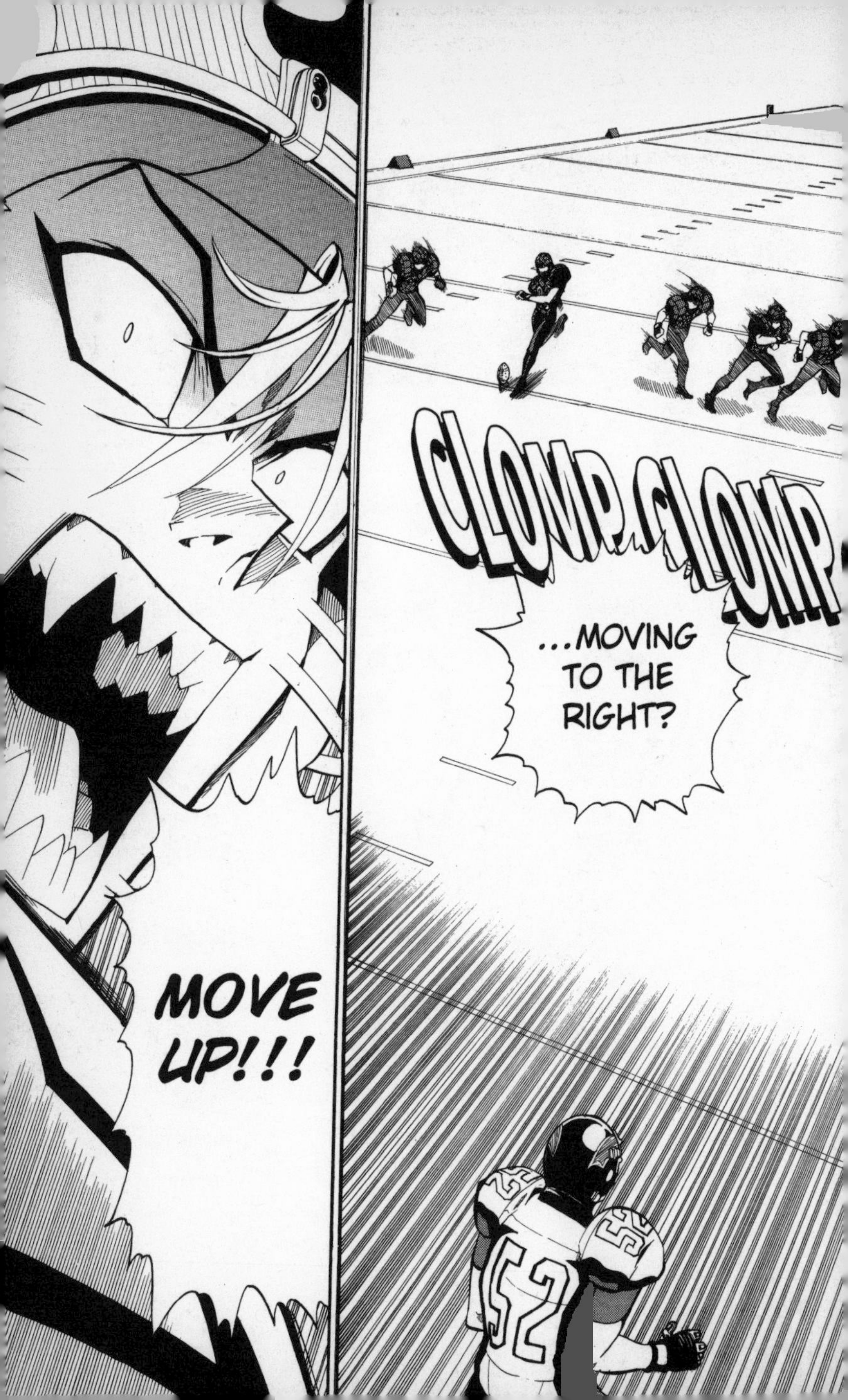
CLOMP CLOMP
...MOVING TO THE RIGHT?
MOVE UP!!!

Eyeshield 21 Survey Corner

Devil Bat 021

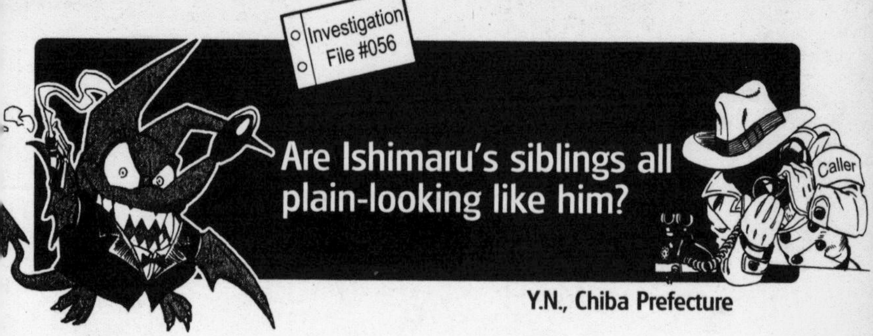
Investigation File #056
Are Ishimaru's siblings all plain-looking like him?
Caller

Y.N., Chiba Prefecture

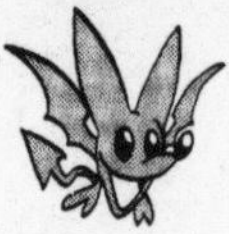

HIYA! HERE'RE ALL OF ISHIMARU'S BROTHERS AND SISTERS!

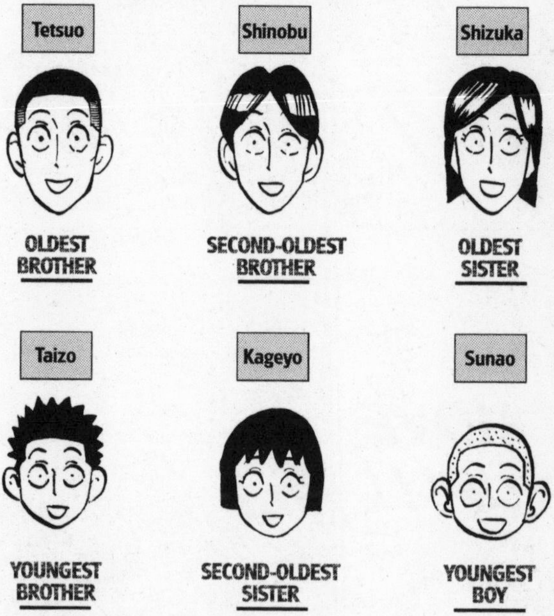
Tetsuo
Shinobu
Shizuka
OLDEST BROTHER
SECOND-OLDEST BROTHER
OLDEST SISTER
Taizo
Kageyo
Sunao
YOUNGEST BROTHER
SECOND-OLDEST SISTER
YOUNGEST BOY

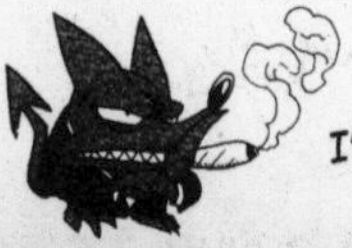

I'LL LET *YOU* DECIDE!

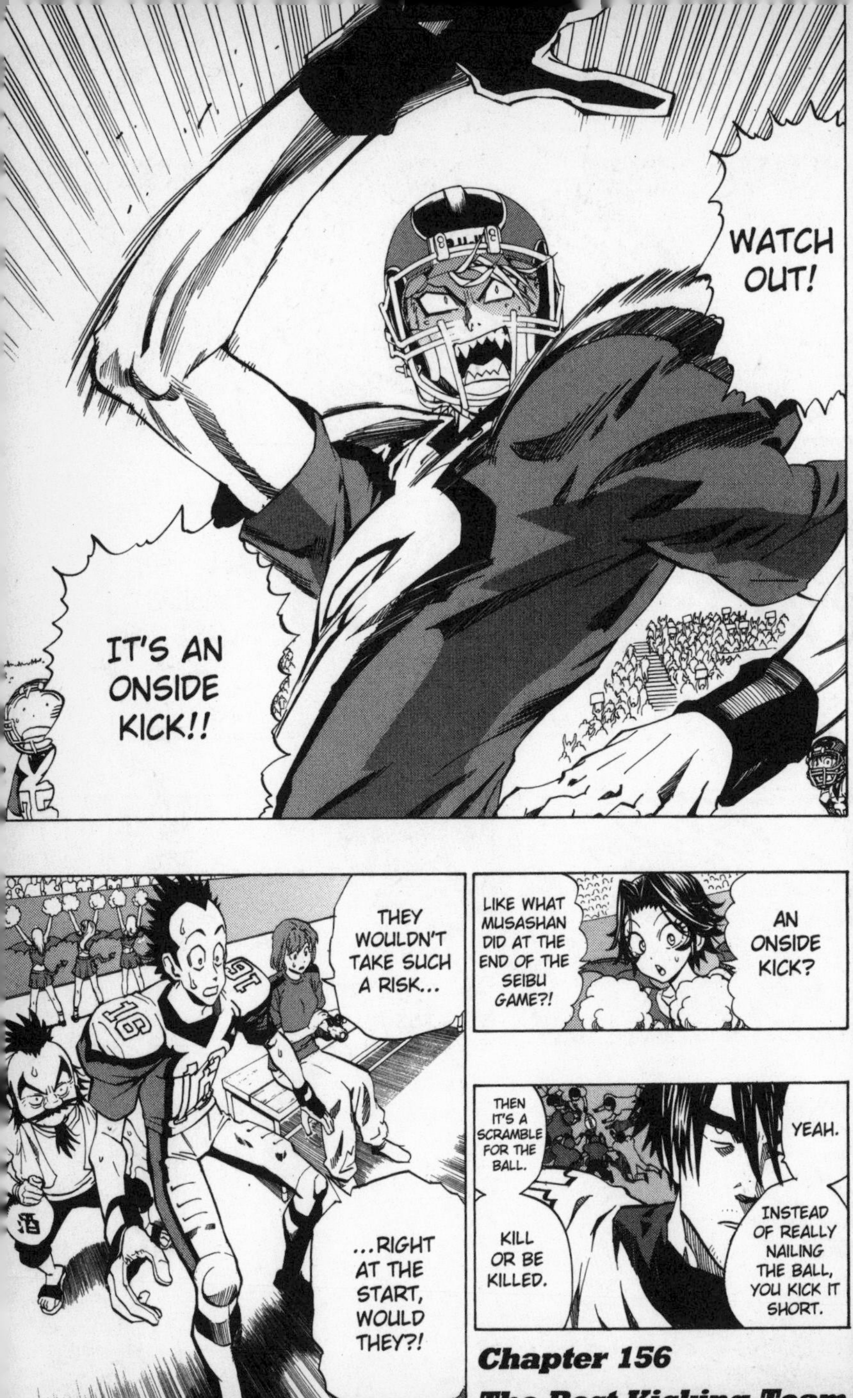
WATCH OUT!
IT'S AN ONSIDE KICK!!
AN ONSIDE KICK?
LIKE WHAT MUSASHAN DID AT THE END OF THE SEIBU GAME?!
YEAH.
INSTEAD OF REALLY NAILING THE BALL, YOU KICK IT SHORT.
THEN IT'S A SCRAMBLE FOR THE BALL.
KILL OR BE KILLED.
THEY WOULDN'T TAKE SUCH A RISK...
...RIGHT AT THE START, WOULD THEY?!

Chapter 156
The Best Kicking Team

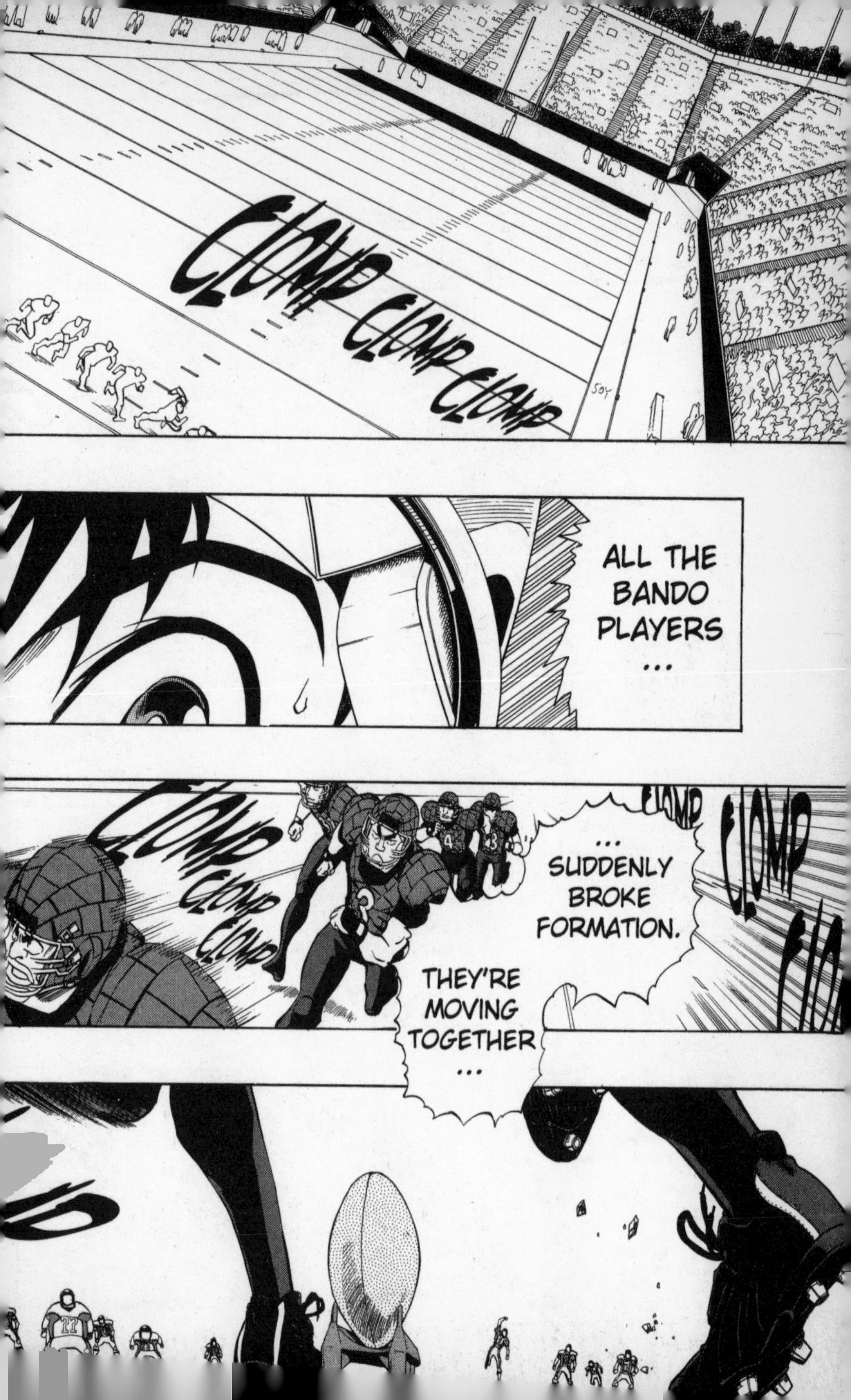
CLOMP CLOMP CLOMP
ALL THE BANDO PLAYERS ...
CLOMP
CLOMP
... SUDDENLY BROKE FORMATION.
CLOMP CLOMP CLOMP
THEY'RE MOVING TOGETHER ...

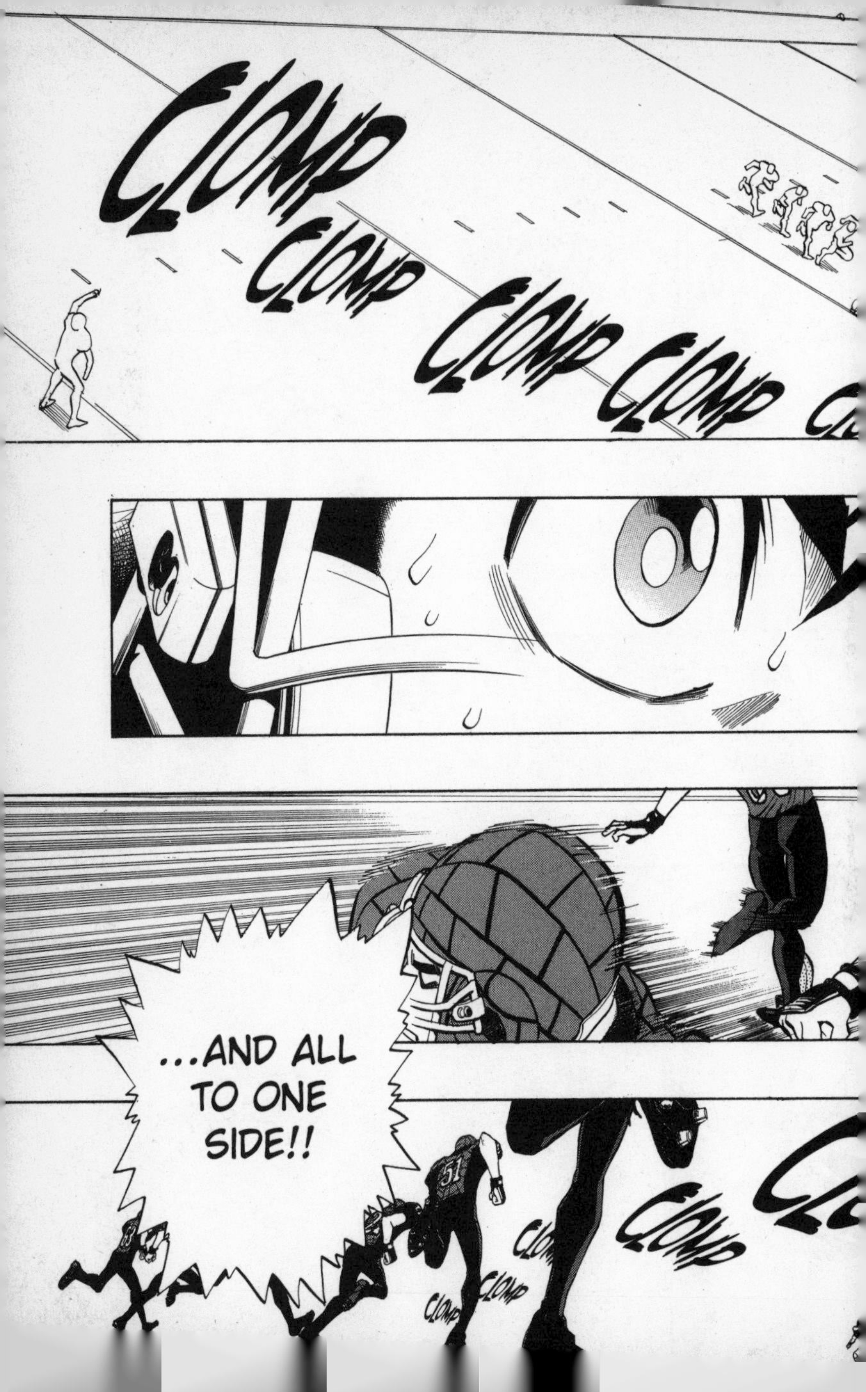
CLOMP
CLOMP
CLOMP
CLOMP
...AND ALL TO ONE SIDE!!
CLOMP
CLOMP
CLOMP
CLOMP

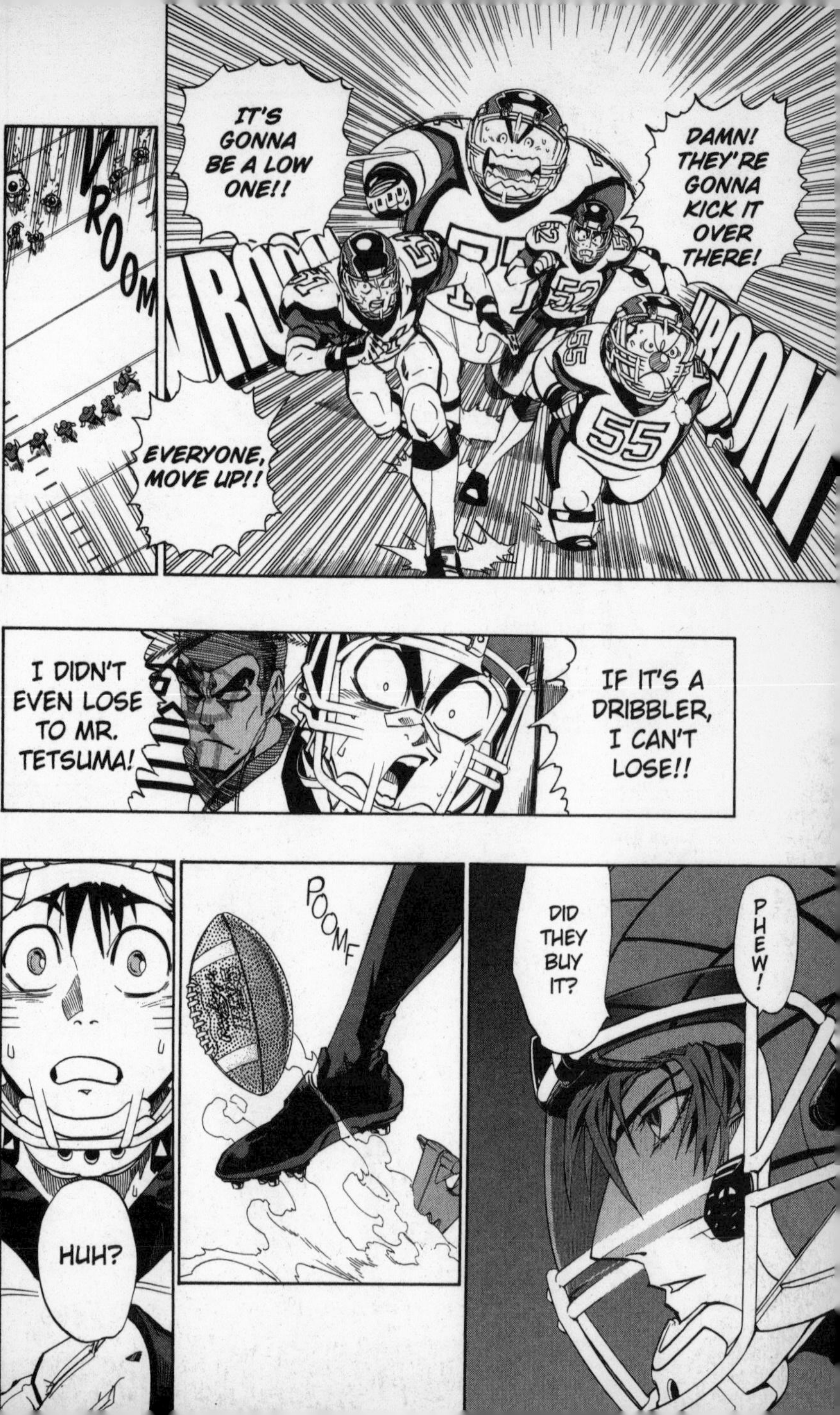
DAMN! THEY'RE GONNA KICK IT OVER THERE!
IT'S GONNA BE A LOW ONE!!
VROOM
VROOM
EVERYONE, MOVE UP!!
VROOM
IF IT'S A DRIBBLER, I CAN'T LOSE!!
I DIDN'T EVEN LOSE TO MR. TETSUMA!
PHEW!
DID THEY BUY IT?
POOMF
HUH?

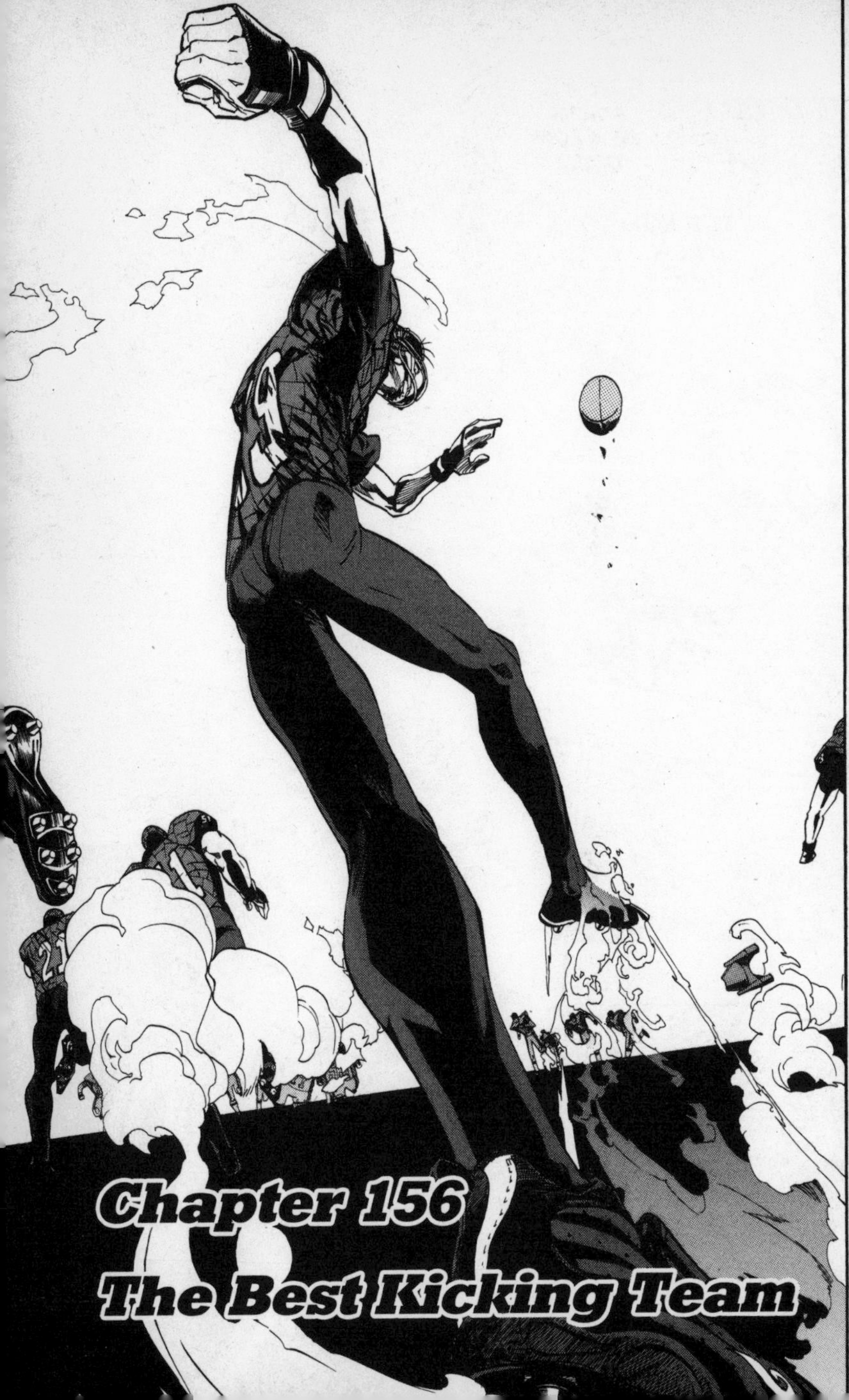
Chapter 156
The Best Kicking Team

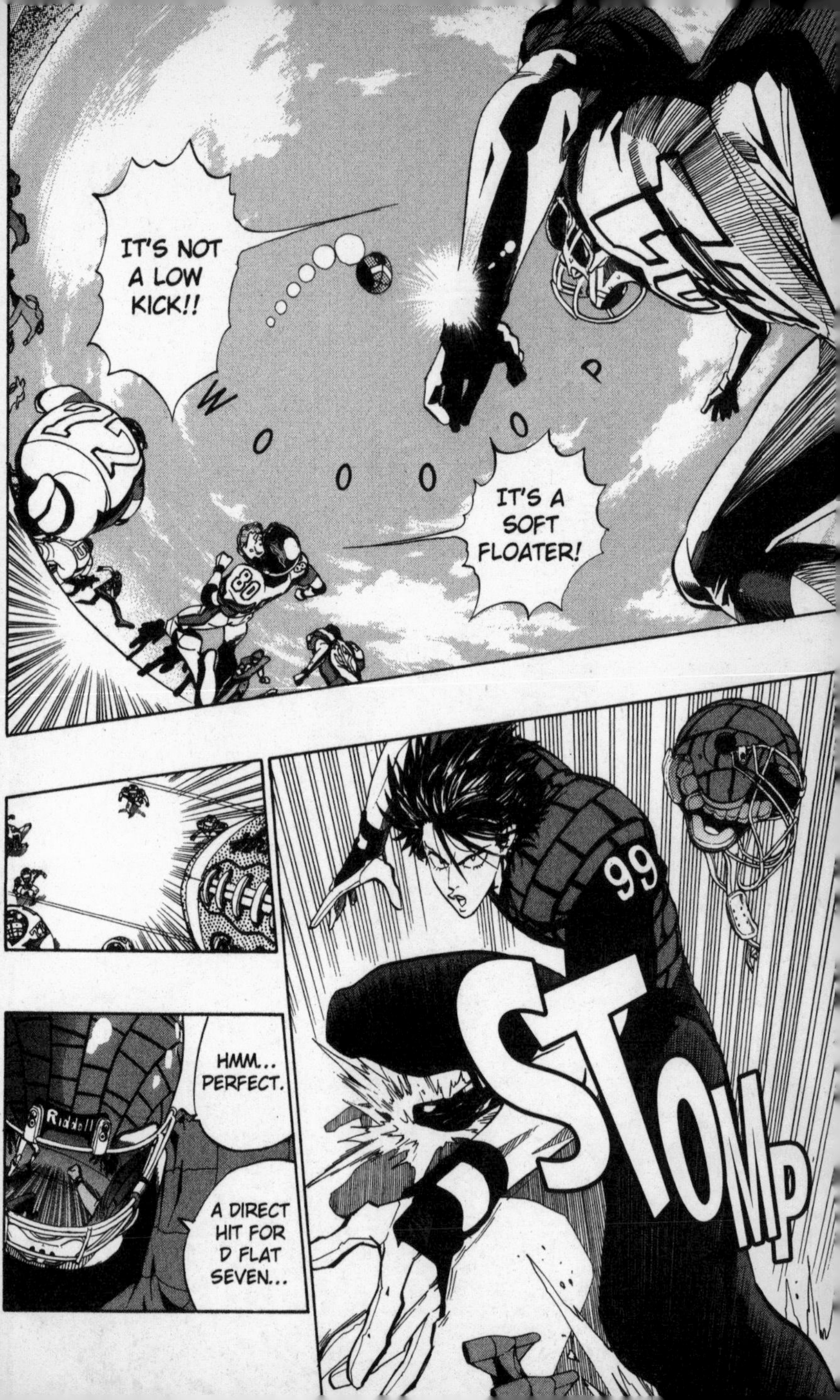
IT'S NOT A LOW KICK!!
WOOOOOP
IT'S A SOFT FLOATER!
STOMP
HMM... PERFECT.
A DIRECT HIT FOR D FLAT SEVEN...

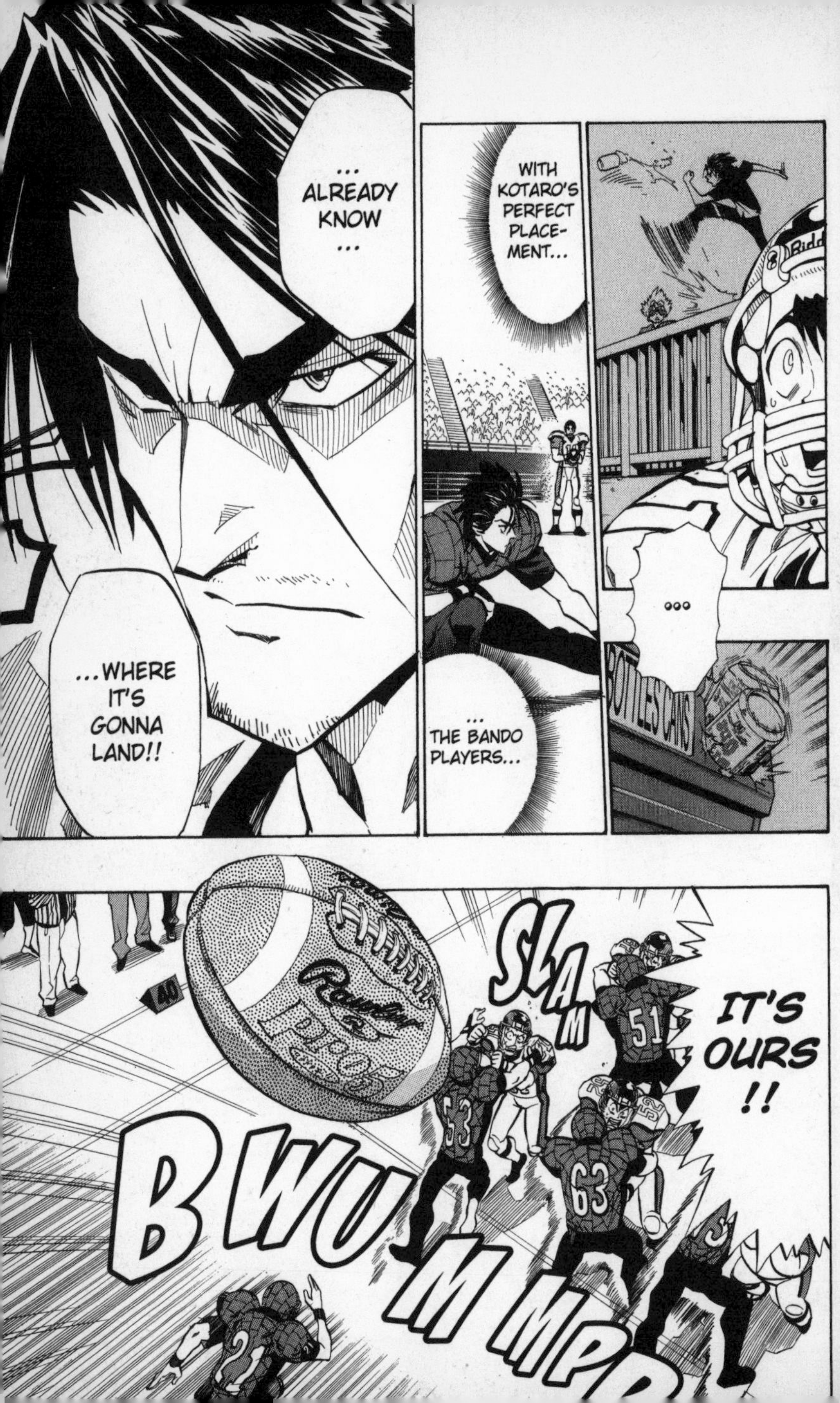
...
BOTTLES CANS
WITH KOTARO'S PERFECT PLACEMENT...
...THE BANDO PLAYERS...
...ALREADY KNOW...
...WHERE IT'S GONNA LAND!!
IT'S OURS!!
SLAM
BWUMMP

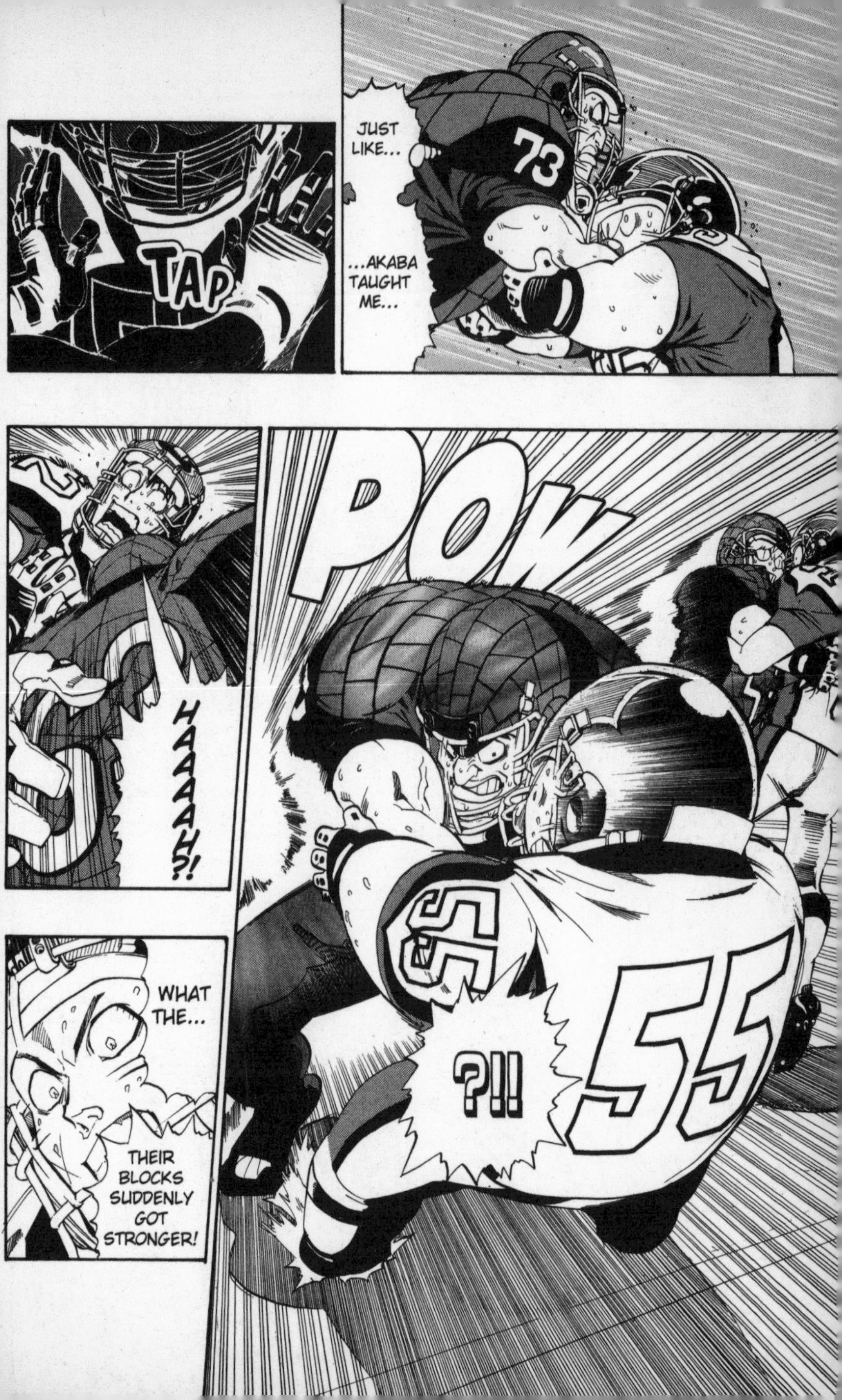
JUST LIKE...
...AKABA TAUGHT ME...
TAP
POW
?!!
HAAAAAH?!
WHAT THE...
THEIR BLOCKS SUDDENLY GOT STRONGER!

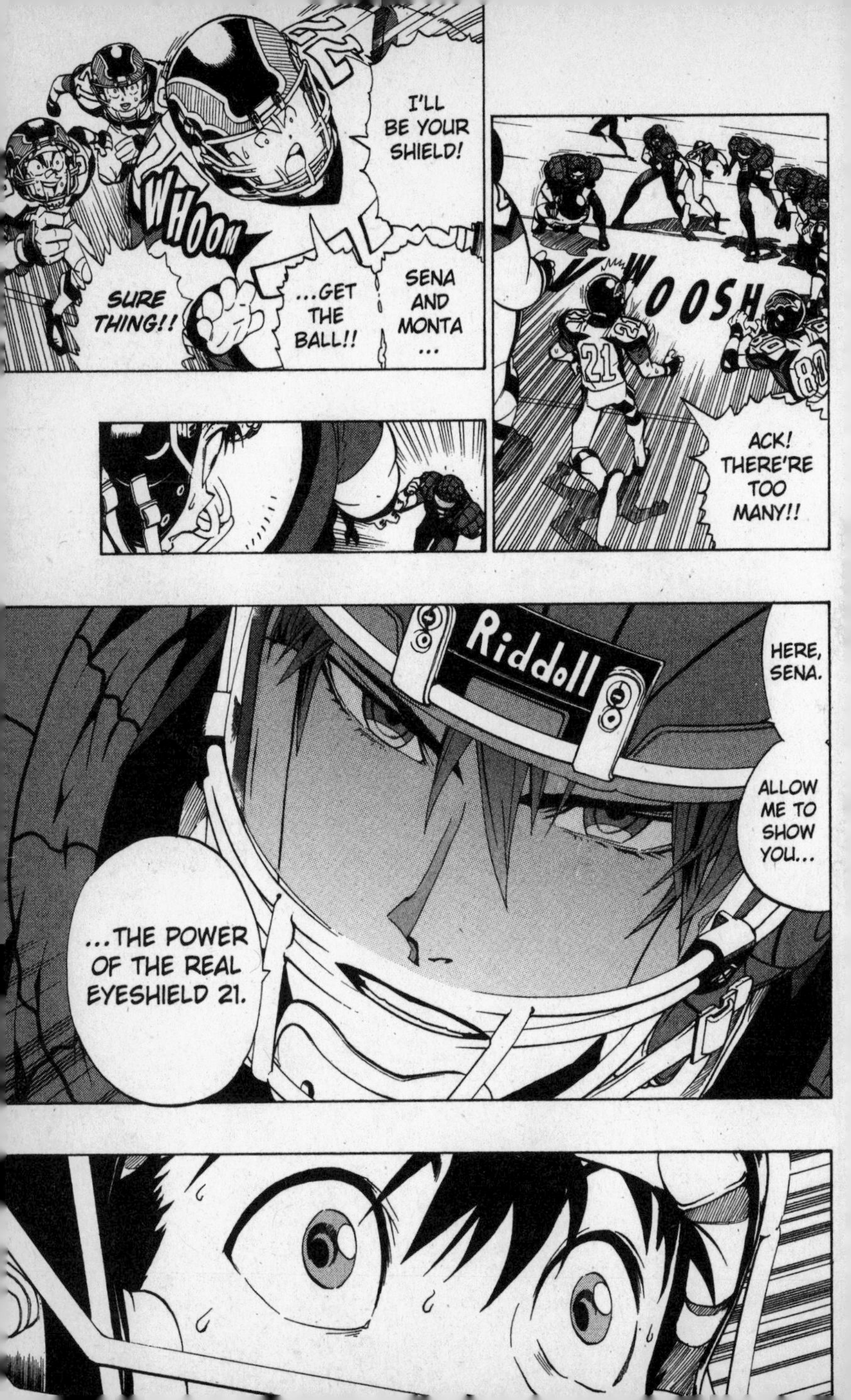
I'LL BE YOUR SHIELD!
WHOOM
SENA AND MONTA ...
...GET THE BALL!!
SURE THING!!
WOOSH
ACK! THERE'RE TOO MANY!!
Riddoll
HERE, SENA.
ALLOW ME TO SHOW YOU...
...THE POWER OF THE REAL EYESHIELD 21.

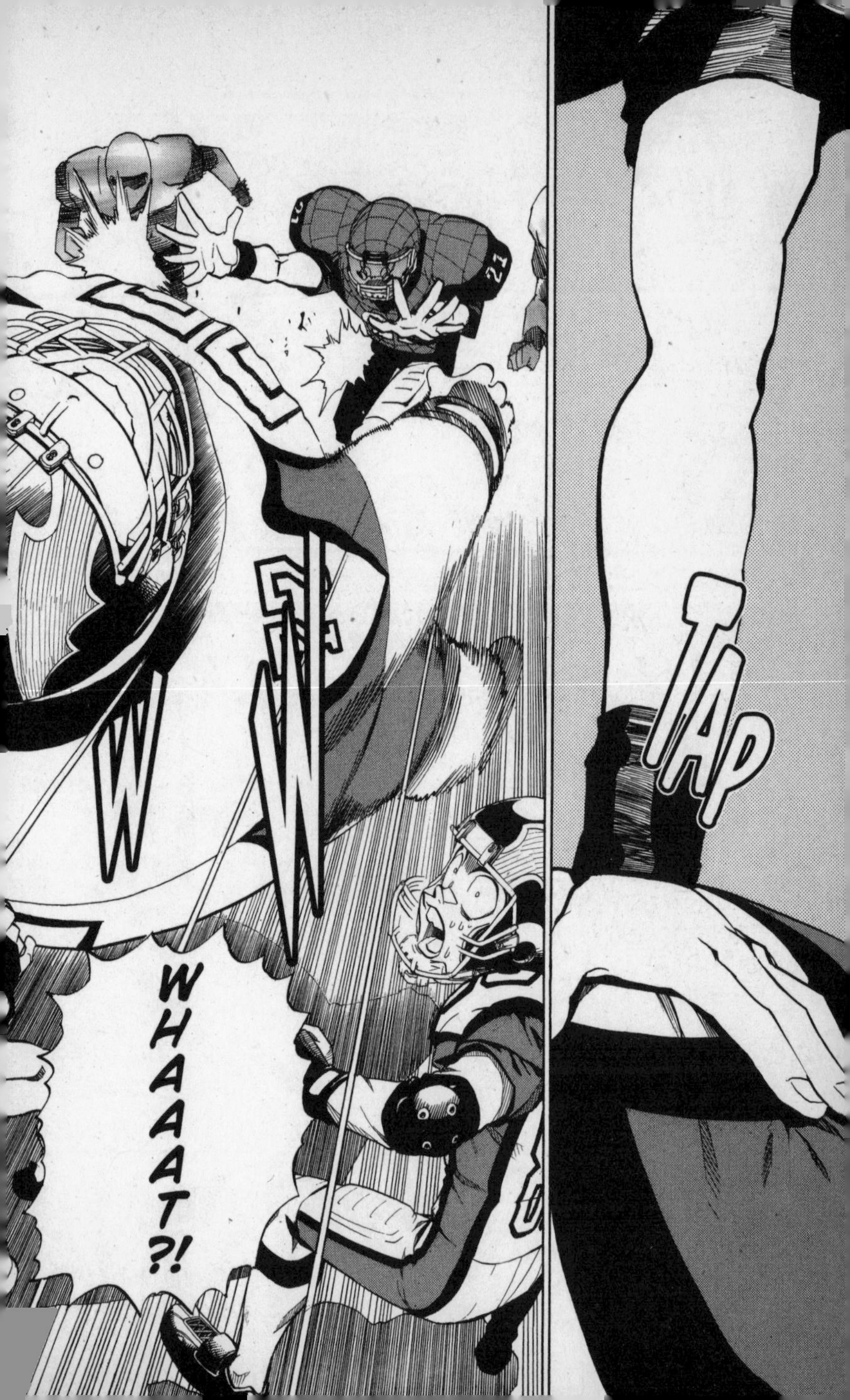
TAP
WHAAAAT?!

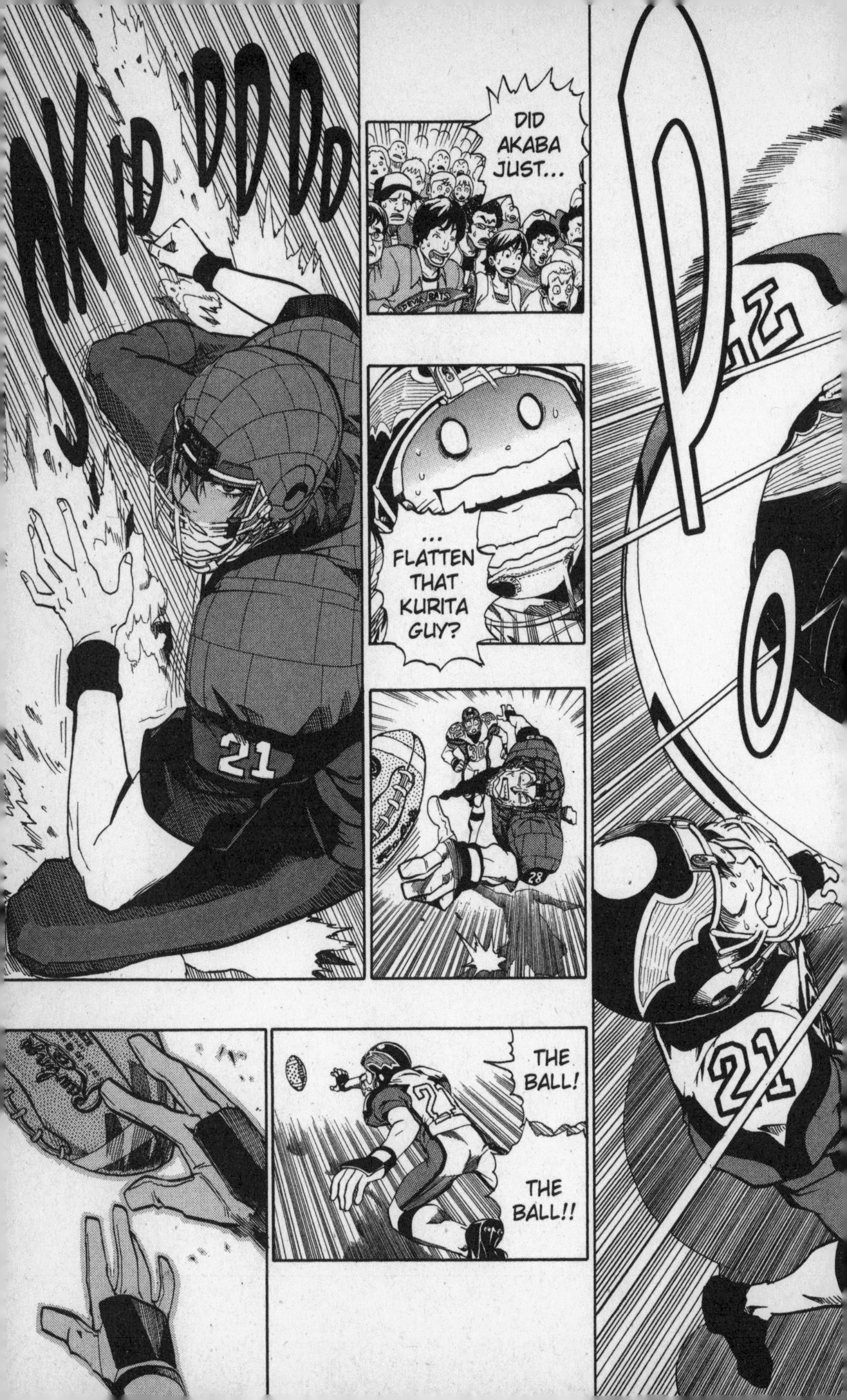
DID AKABA JUST...
... FLATTEN THAT KURITA GUY?
SKIDDDDD
THE BALL!
THE BALL!!

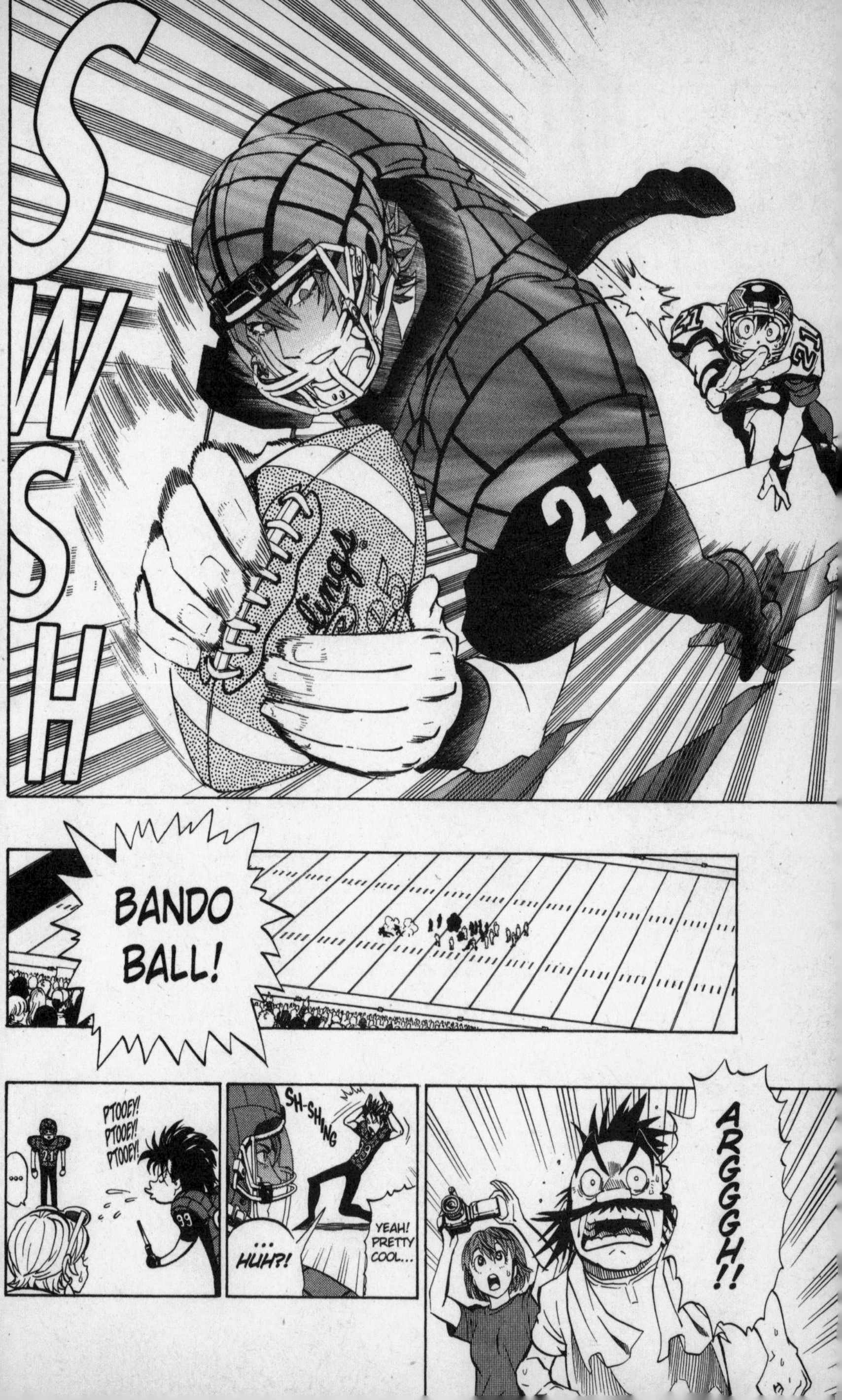
SWSH
BANDO BALL!
ARGGGH!!
SH-SHING
YEAH! PRETTY COOL...
... HUH?!
PTOOEY! PTOOEY! PTOOEY!
...

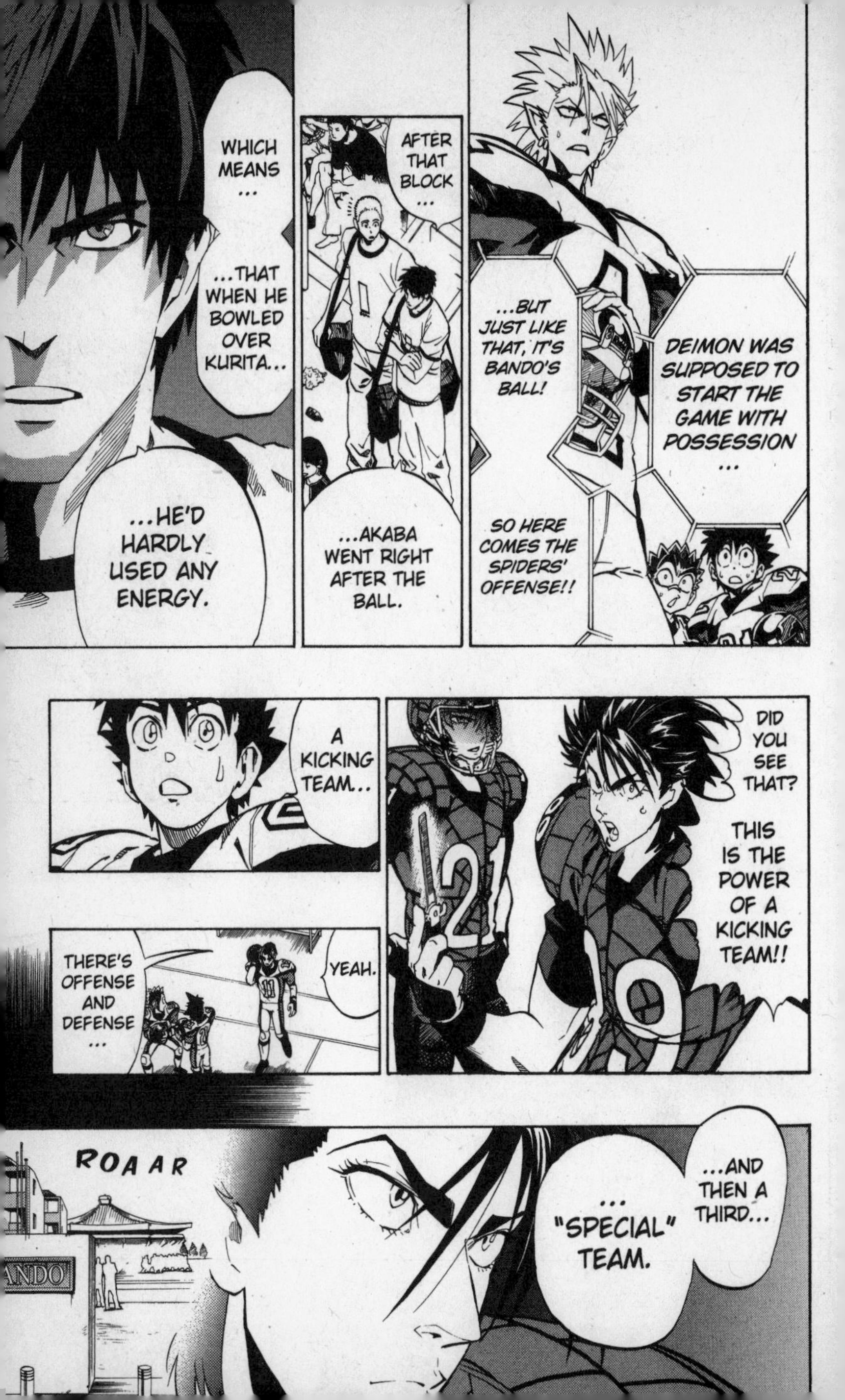
DEIMON WAS SUPPOSED TO START THE GAME WITH POSSESSION ...
...BUT JUST LIKE THAT, IT'S BANDO'S BALL!
SO HERE COMES THE SPIDERS' OFFENSE!!
AFTER THAT BLOCK ...
...AKABA WENT RIGHT AFTER THE BALL.
WHICH MEANS ...
...THAT WHEN HE BOWLED OVER KURITA...
...HE'D HARDLY USED ANY ENERGY.
DID YOU SEE THAT?
THIS IS THE POWER OF A KICKING TEAM!!
A KICKING TEAM...
YEAH.
THERE'S OFFENSE AND DEFENSE ...
...AND THEN A THIRD...
... "SPECIAL" TEAM.
ROAAR

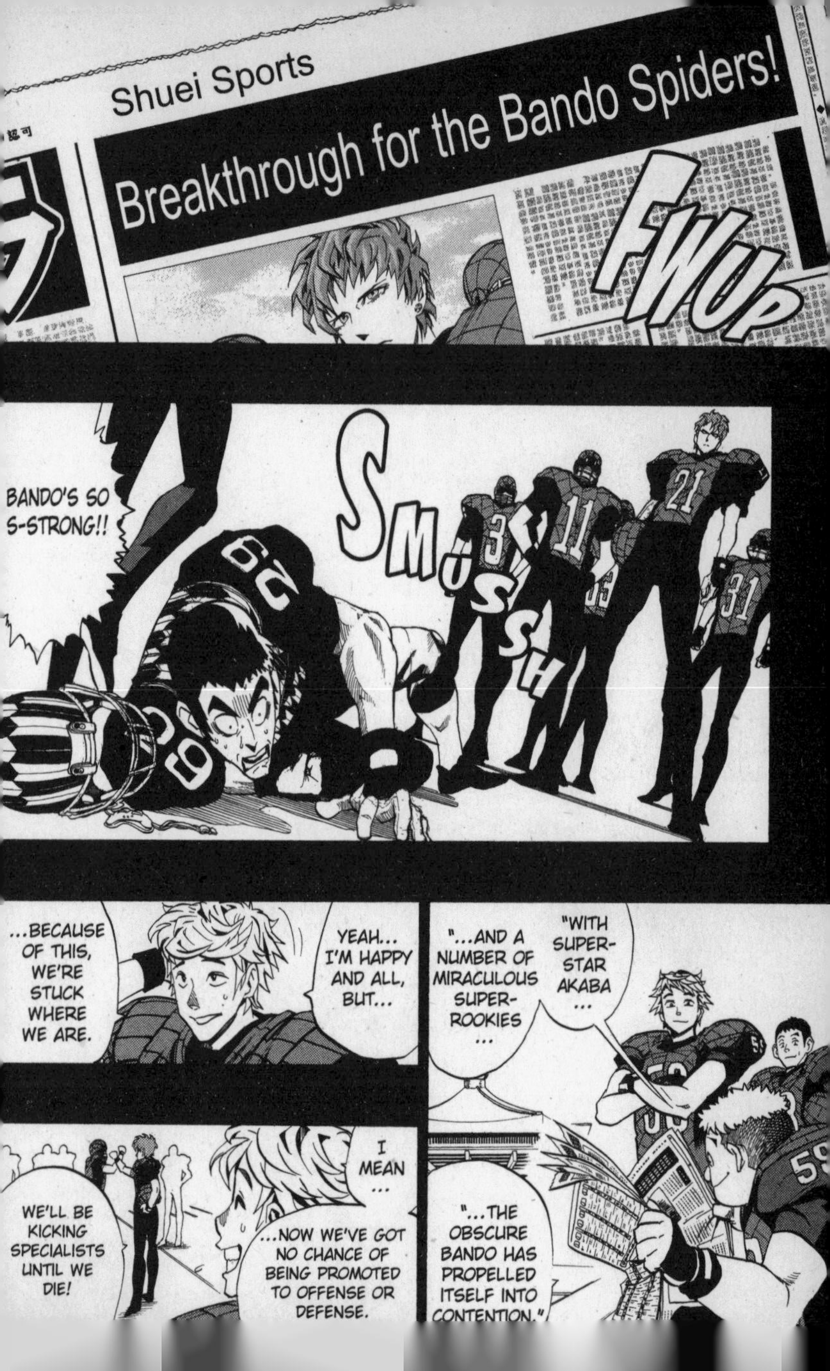

Shuei Sports
Breakthrough for the Bando Spiders!
FWUP
SMUSSH
BANDO'S SO S-STRONG!!
"WITH SUPER-STAR AKABA ...
"...AND A NUMBER OF MIRACULOUS SUPER-ROOKIES ...
"...THE OBSCURE BANDO HAS PROPELLED ITSELF INTO CONTENTION."
YEAH... I'M HAPPY AND ALL, BUT...
...BECAUSE OF THIS, WE'RE STUCK WHERE WE ARE.
I MEAN ...
...NOW WE'VE GOT NO CHANCE OF BEING PROMOTED TO OFFENSE OR DEFENSE.
WE'LL BE KICKING SPECIALISTS UNTIL WE DIE!

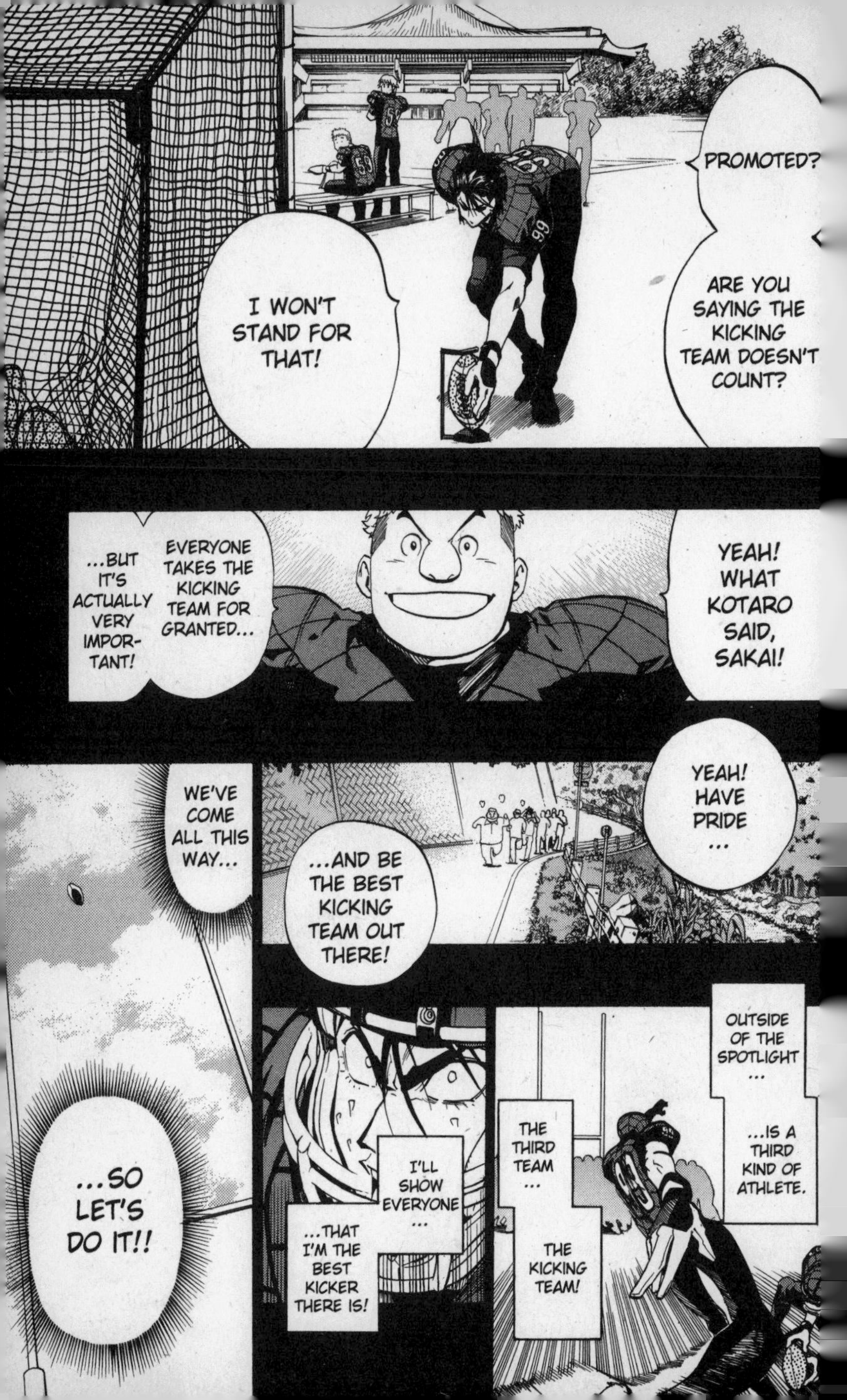
PROMOTED?
ARE YOU SAYING THE KICKING TEAM DOESN'T COUNT?
I WON'T STAND FOR THAT!
YEAH! WHAT KOTARO SAID, SAKAI!
EVERYONE TAKES THE KICKING TEAM FOR GRANTED...
...BUT IT'S ACTUALLY VERY IMPOR-TANT!
YEAH! HAVE PRIDE ...
...AND BE THE BEST KICKING TEAM OUT THERE!
OUTSIDE OF THE SPOTLIGHT ...
...IS A THIRD KIND OF ATHLETE.
THE THIRD TEAM ...
THE KICKING TEAM!
I'LL SHOW EVERYONE ...
...THAT I'M THE BEST KICKER THERE IS!
WE'VE COME ALL THIS WAY...
...SO LET'S DO IT!!

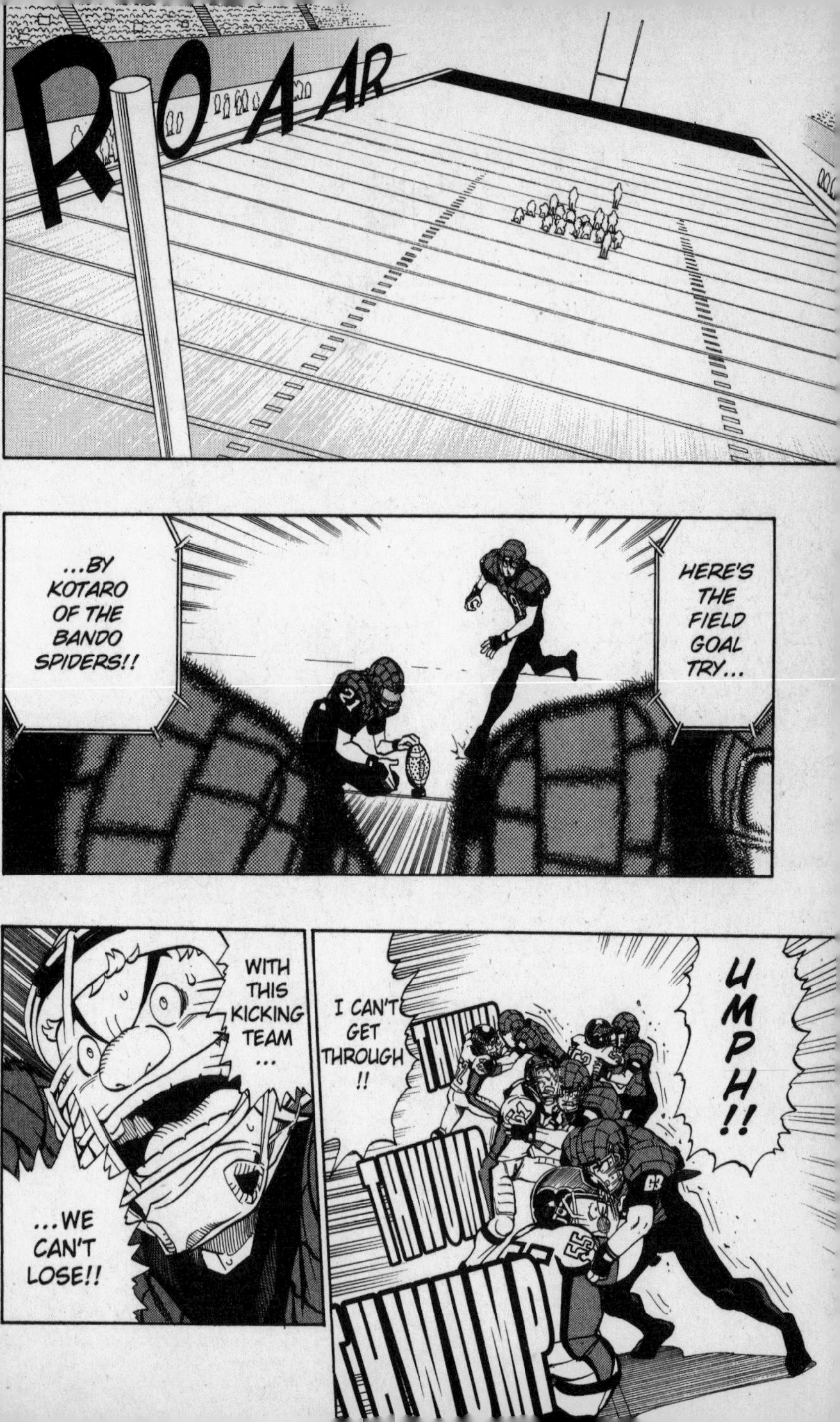
ROAAR
HERE'S THE FIELD GOAL TRY...
...BY KOTARO OF THE BANDO SPIDERS!!
UMPH!!
I CAN'T GET THROUGH!!
THWUMP
WITH THIS KICKING TEAM...
...WE CAN'T LOSE!!

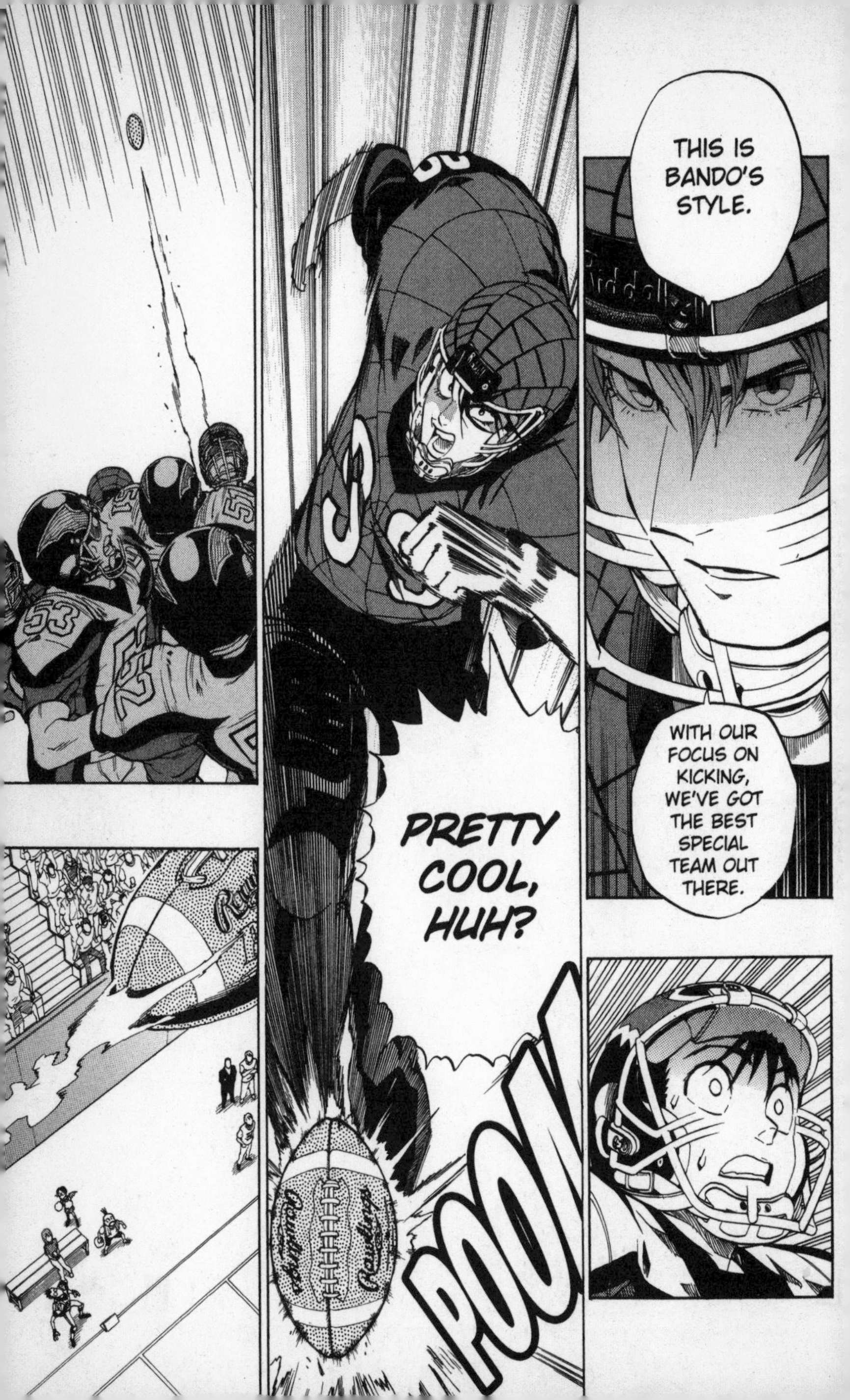
THIS IS BANDO'S STYLE.
WITH OUR FOCUS ON KICKING, WE'VE GOT THE BEST SPECIAL TEAM OUT THERE.
PRETTY COOL, HUH?

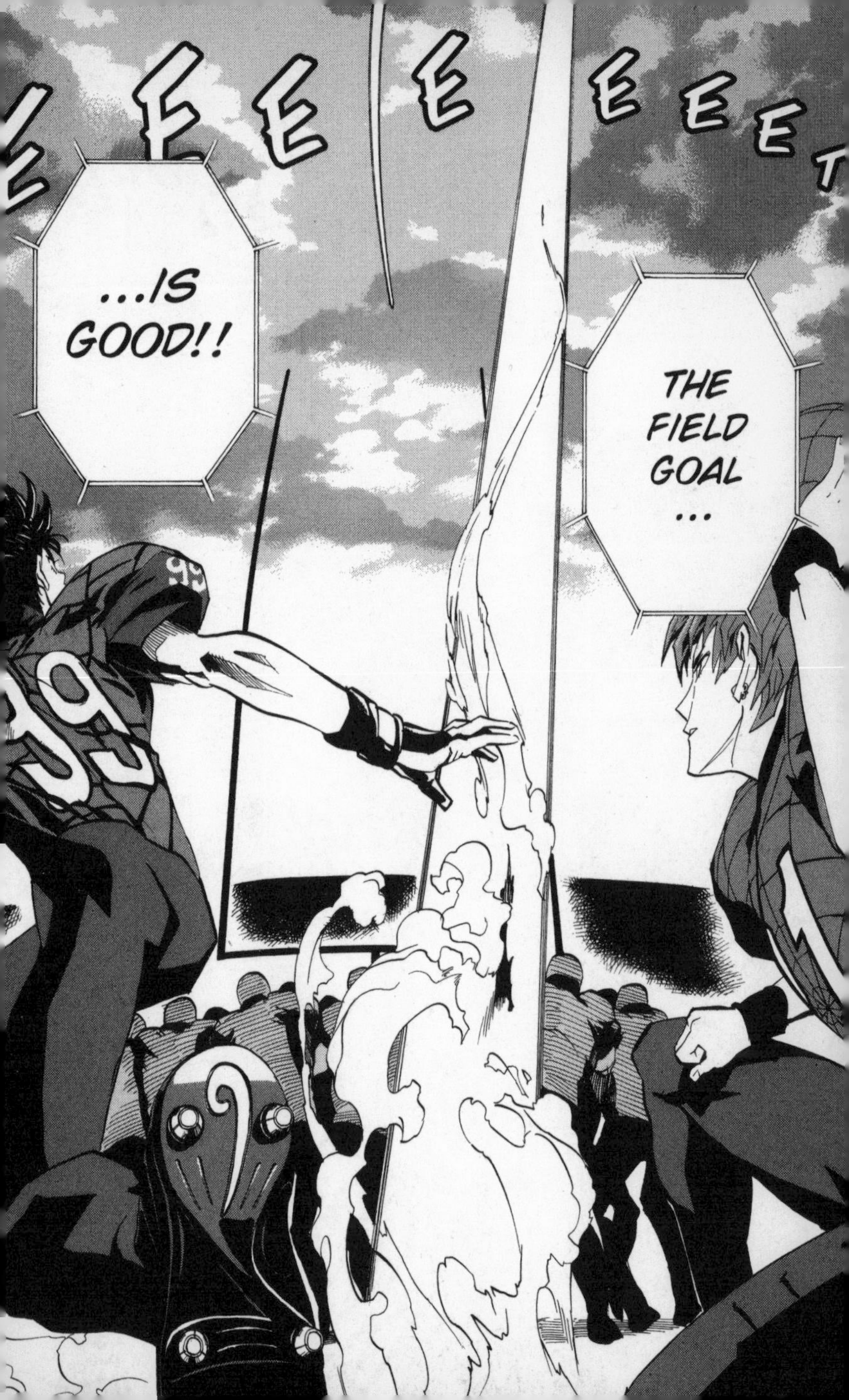
EEEEEEET
THE FIELD GOAL ...
...IS GOOD!!

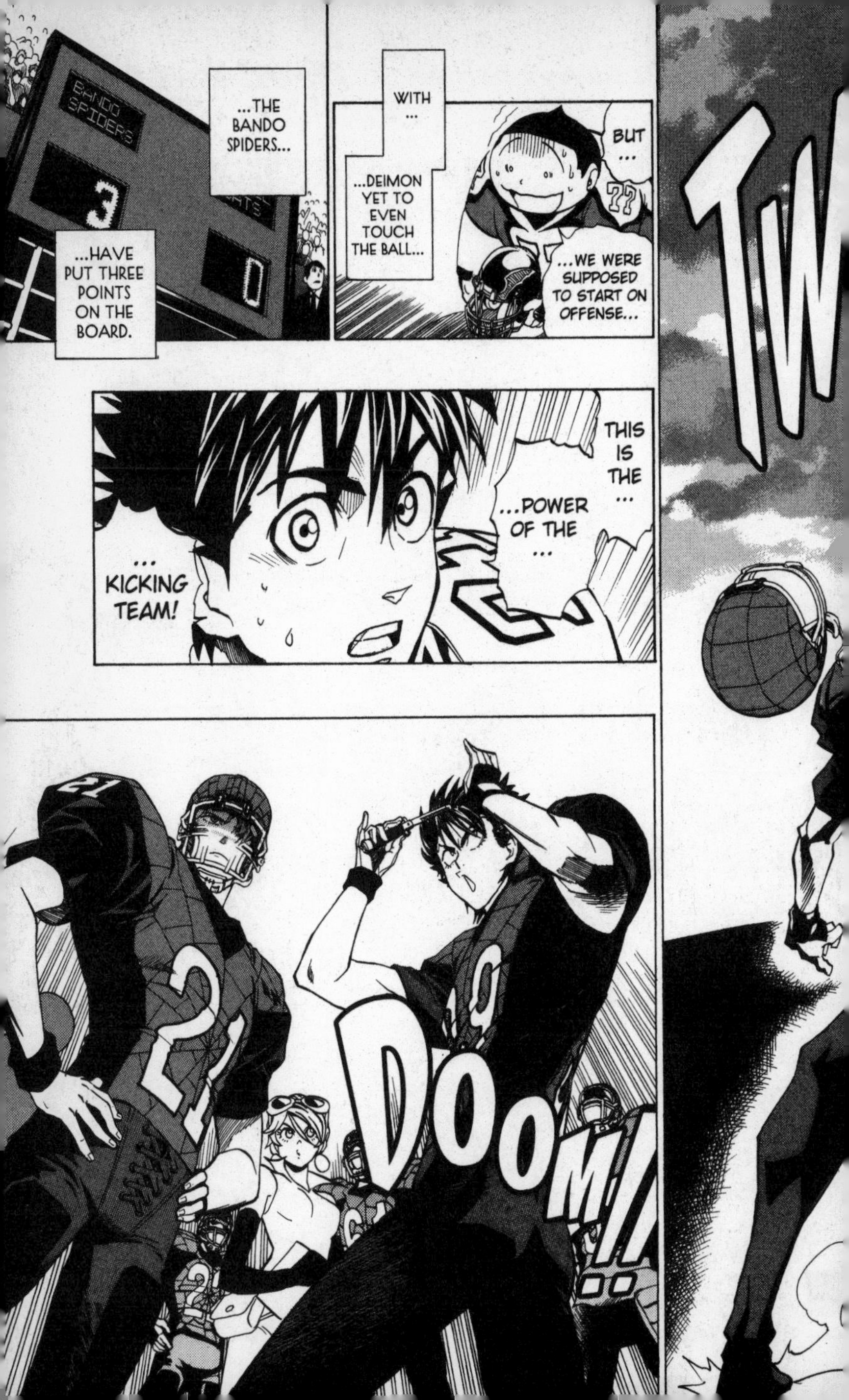
TW
WITH ...
...DEIMON YET TO EVEN TOUCH THE BALL...
BUT ...
...WE WERE SUPPOSED TO START ON OFFENSE...
BANDO SPIDERS
3
0
...THE BANDO SPIDERS...
...HAVE PUT THREE POINTS ON THE BOARD.
THIS IS THE ...
...POWER OF THE ...
... KICKING TEAM!
DOOM!!

Devil Bat 021

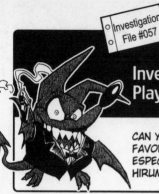

Investigation File #057

Investigate the Deimon Players' Favorite Books!!

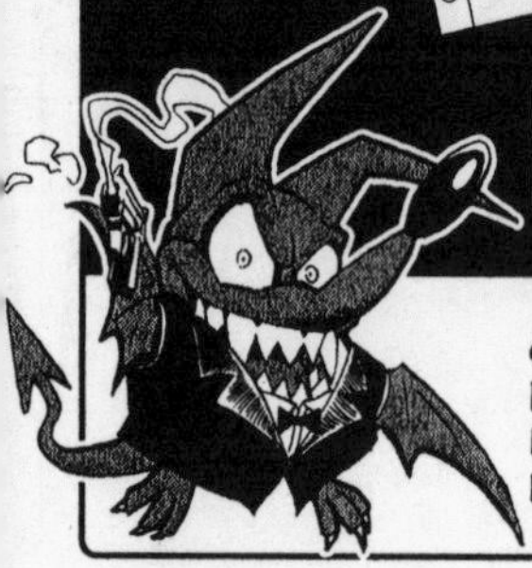

CAN YOU TELL ME EVERYONE'S FAVORITE THING TO READ? I'M ESPECIALLY INTERESTED IN HIRUMA'S.

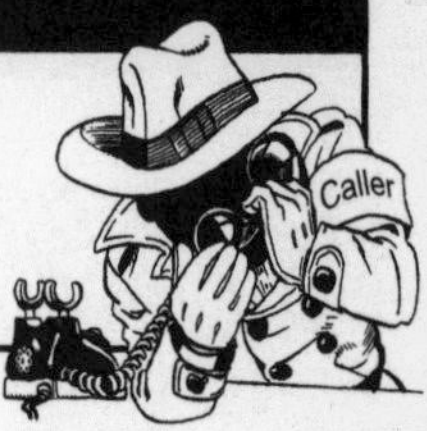
Caller

Bakukichi, Gifu Prefecture

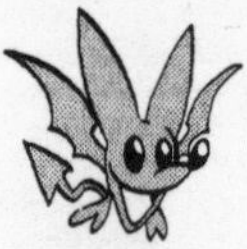

YAHA! AS USUAL, THAT'S A HUGE INVESTIGATION! I'M STARTING TO GET USED TO THIS!!

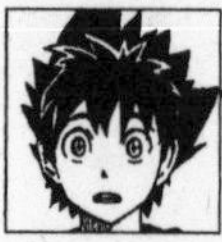
Sena
Jump

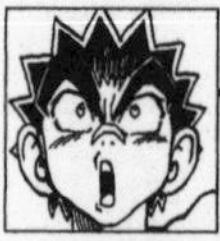
Monta
Journey to the West

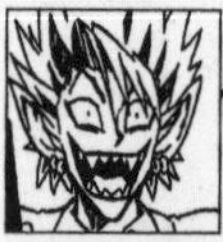
Hiruma
Skims all newspapers

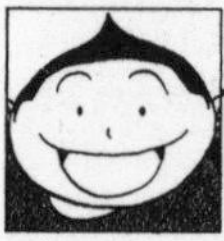
Kurita
Football Monthly

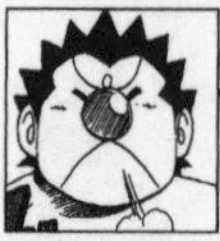
Komusubi
Fight

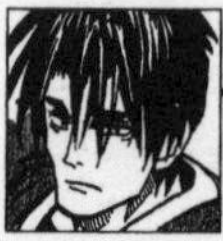
Musashi
The Carpenter's Friend

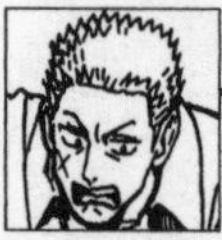
Jumonji
Mysteries

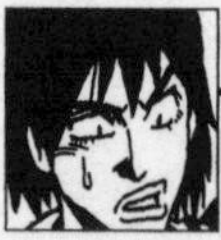
Kuroki
Famitsu

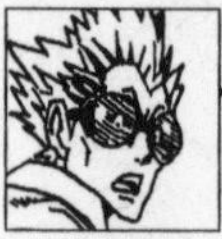
Togano
All shonen manga

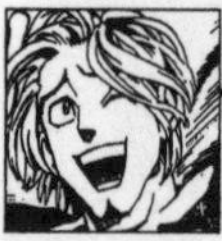
Taki
Celebrity mags

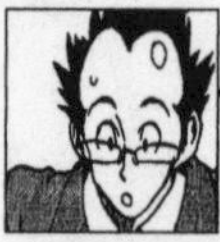
Yukimitsu
Study guides

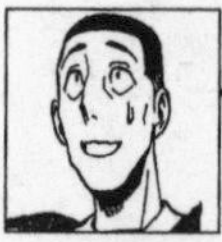
Ishimaru
The infozine ads

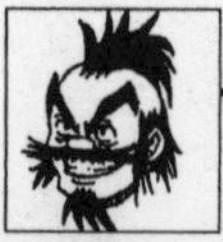
Doburoku
Japanese Enka Weekly
(comes with a CD)

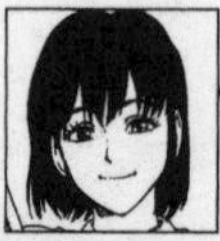
Mamori
All kinds of novels

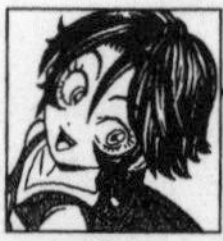
Suzuna
Tokyo Walker

Chapter 157

The Spider's Web

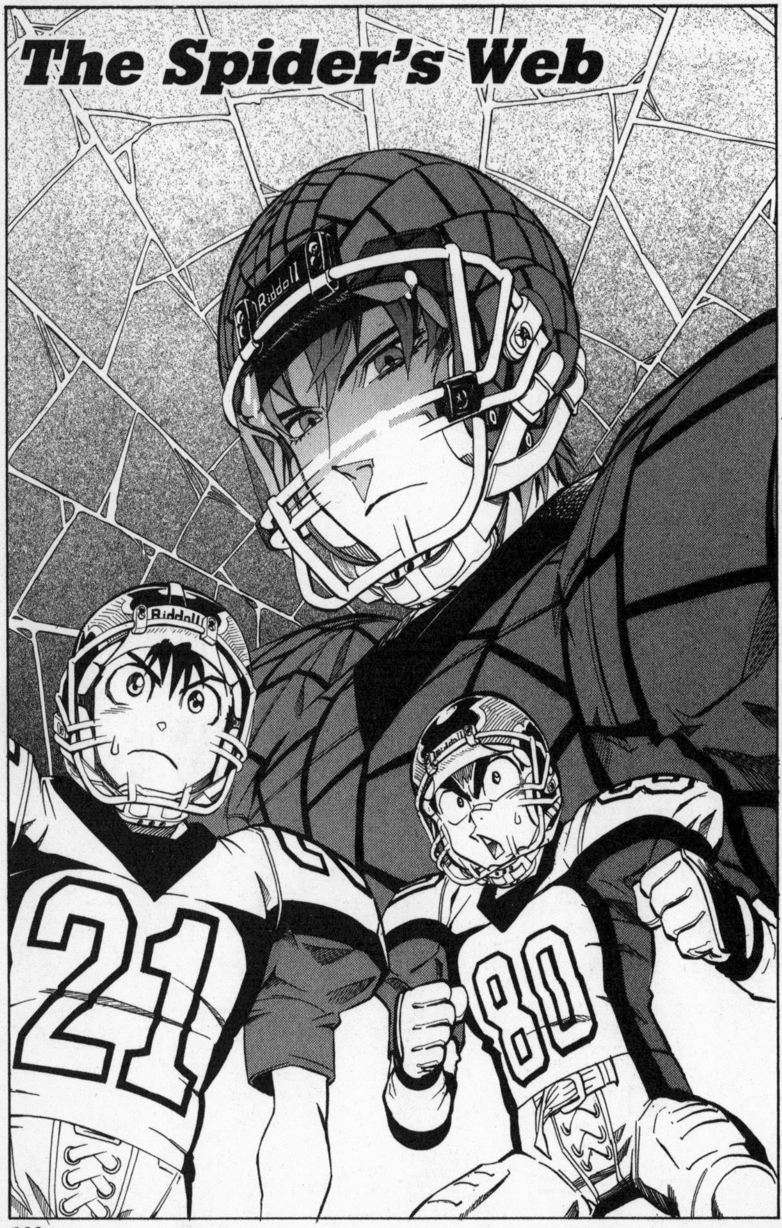

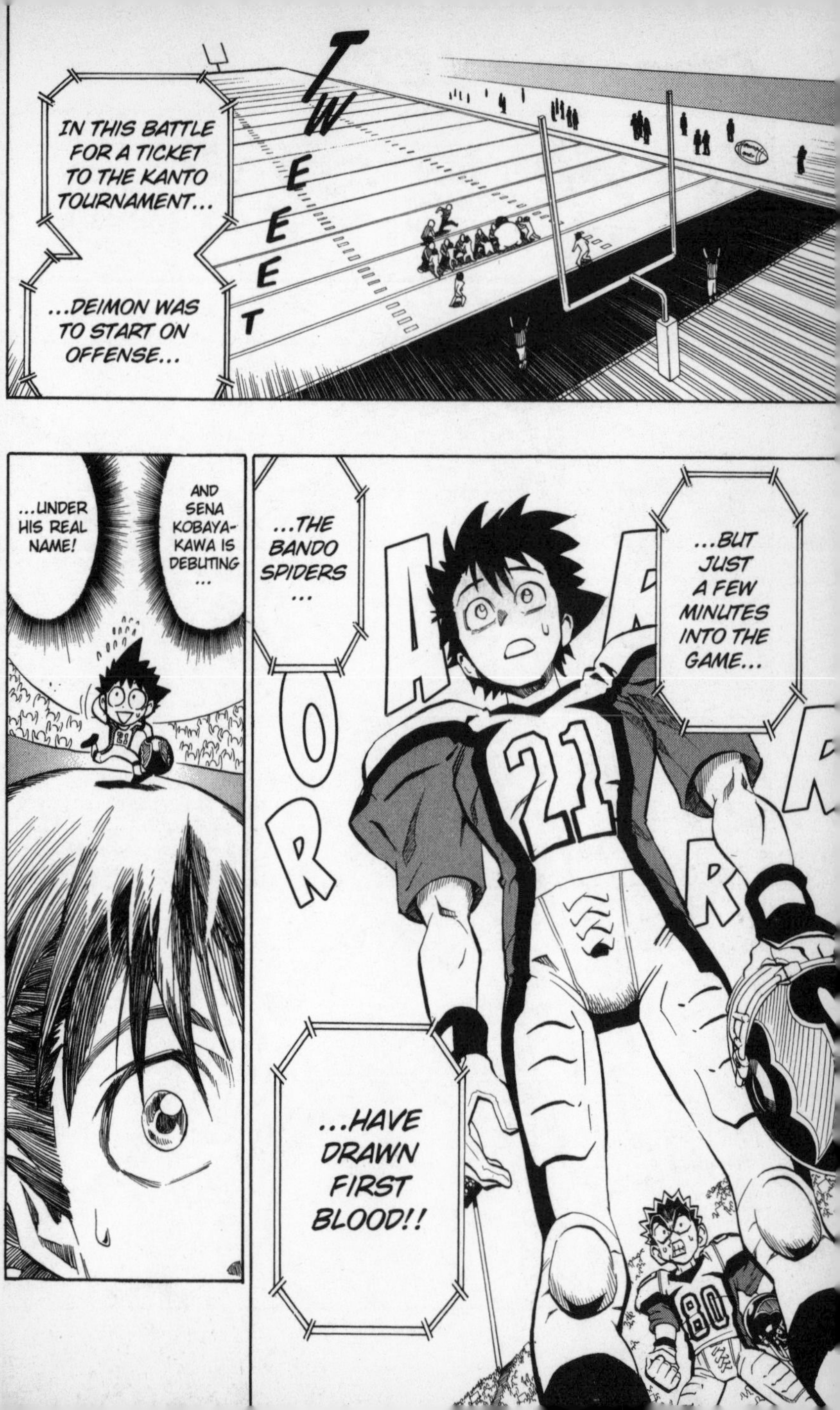

IN THIS BATTLE FOR A TICKET TO THE KANTO TOURNAMENT...
...DEIMON WAS TO START ON OFFENSE...
TWEEEET
...BUT JUST A FEW MINUTES INTO THE GAME...
...THE BANDO SPIDERS...
ROAR
...HAVE DRAWN FIRST BLOOD!!
AND SENA KOBAYAKAWA IS DEBUTING...
...UNDER HIS REAL NAME!

READ THIS WAY

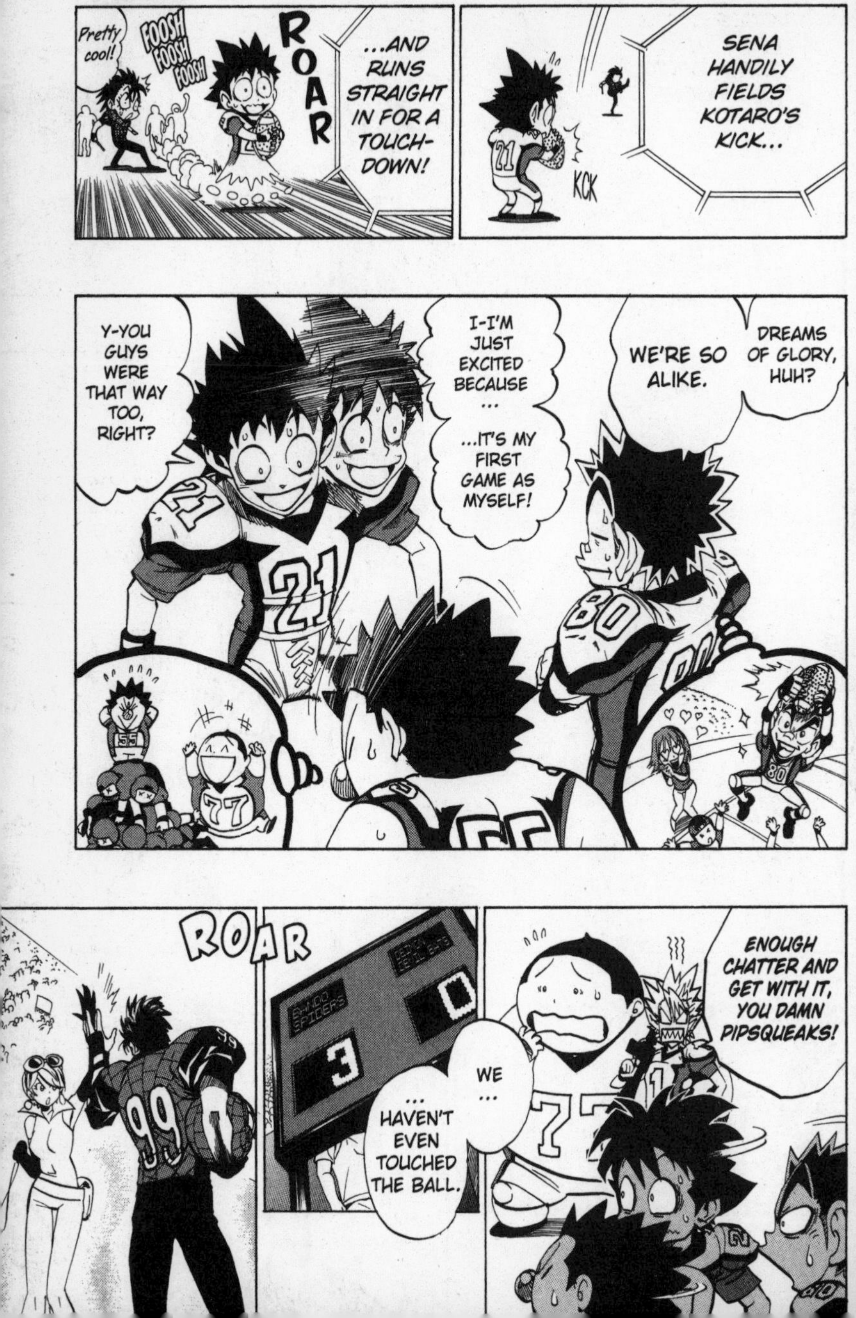
SENA HANDILY FIELDS KOTARO'S KICK...
KCK
...AND RUNS STRAIGHT IN FOR A TOUCH-DOWN!
ROAR
FOOSH FOOSH FOOSH
Pretty cool!
DREAMS OF GLORY, HUH?
WE'RE SO ALIKE.
I-I'M JUST EXCITED BECAUSE ...
...IT'S MY FIRST GAME AS MYSELF!
Y-YOU GUYS WERE THAT WAY TOO, RIGHT?
ENOUGH CHATTER AND GET WITH IT, YOU DAMN PIPSQUEAKS!
WE ...
... HAVEN'T EVEN TOUCHED THE BALL.
3
0
ROAR

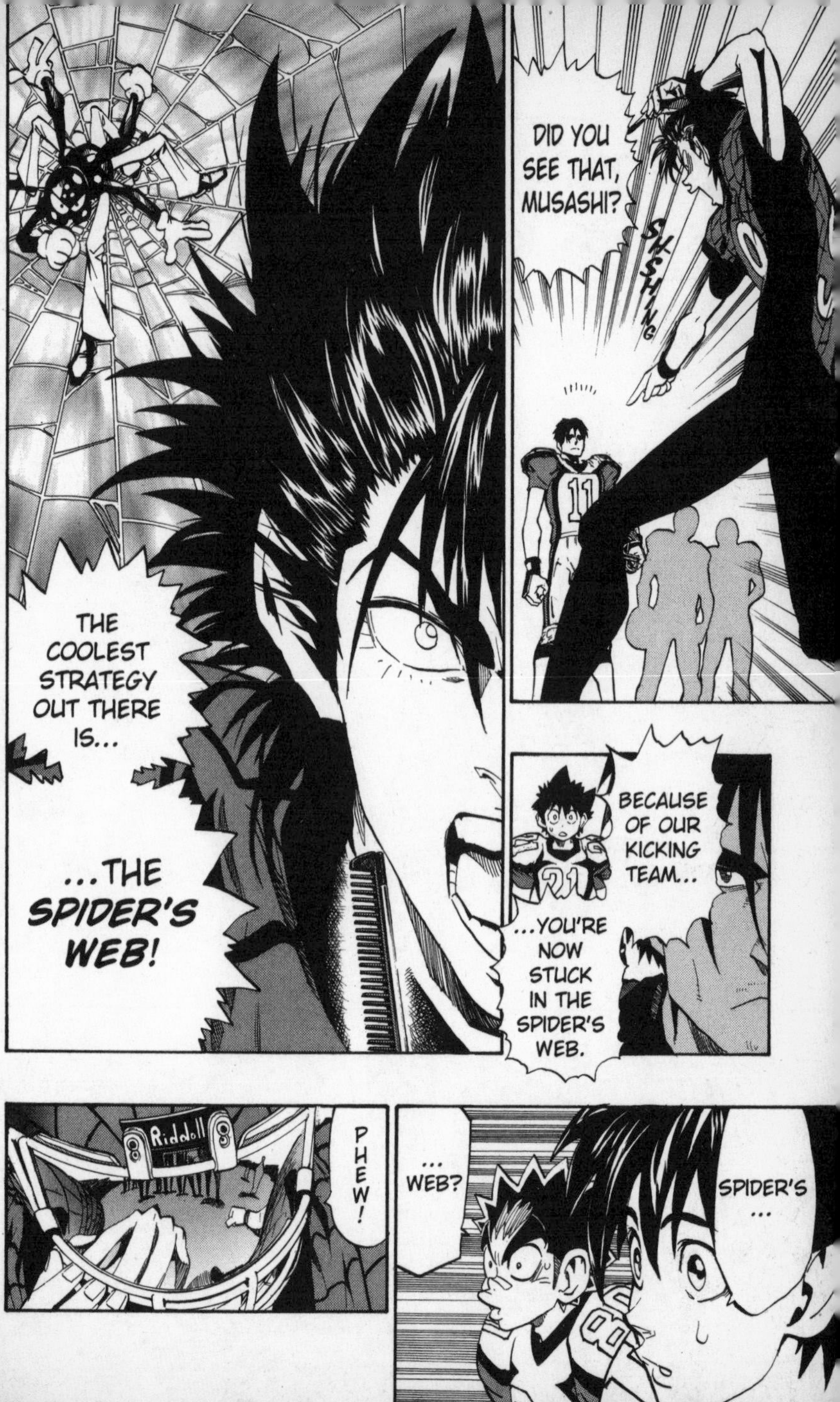
DID YOU SEE THAT, MUSASHI?
SHSHING
BECAUSE OF OUR KICKING TEAM...
...YOU'RE NOW STUCK IN THE SPIDER'S WEB.
THE COOLEST STRATEGY OUT THERE IS...
...THE SPIDER'S WEB!
SPIDER'S ...
... WEB?
PHEW!
Riddell

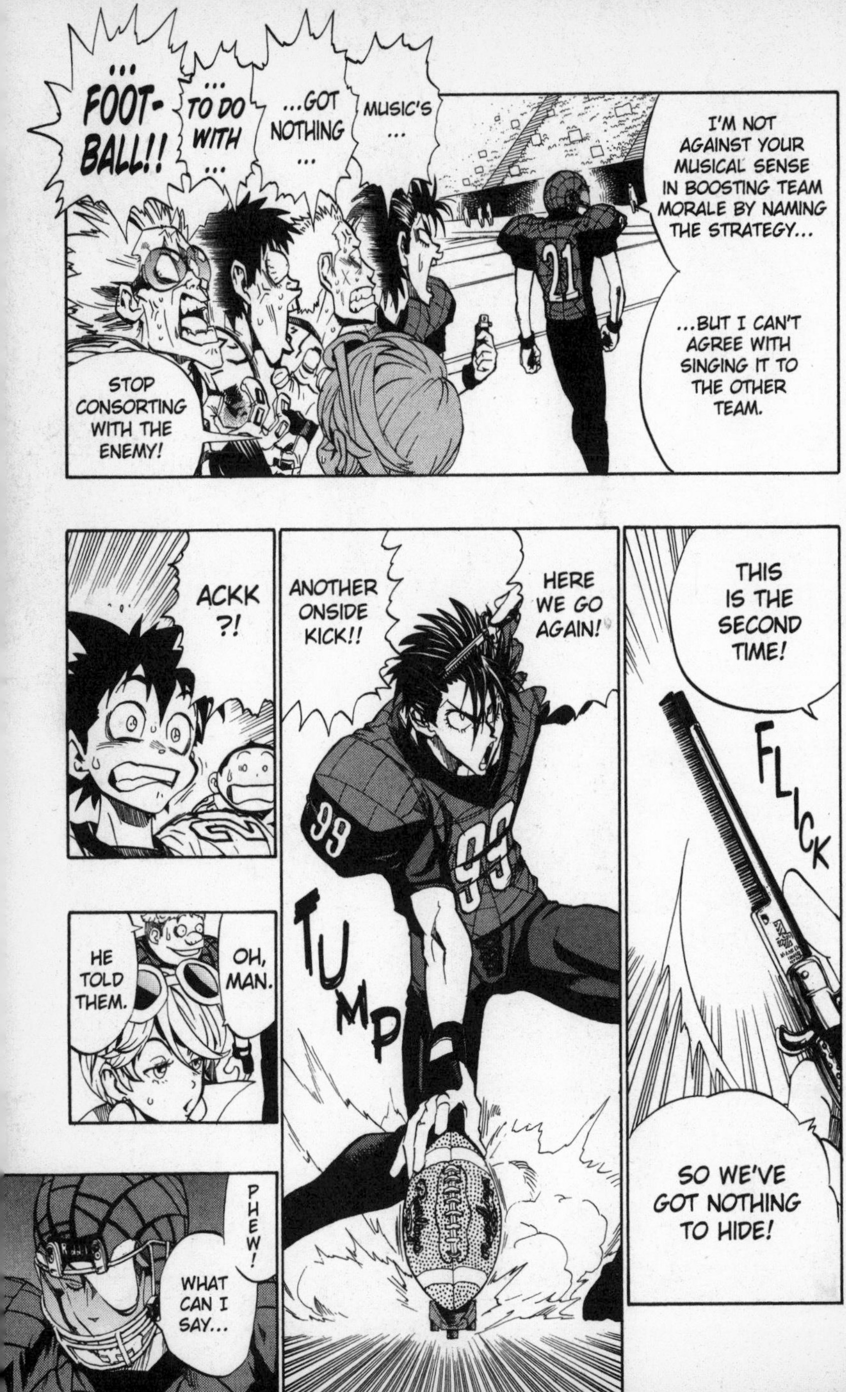
I'M NOT AGAINST YOUR MUSICAL SENSE IN BOOSTING TEAM MORALE BY NAMING THE STRATEGY...
...BUT I CAN'T AGREE WITH SINGING IT TO THE OTHER TEAM.
MUSIC'S ...
...GOT NOTHING ...
... TO DO WITH ...
... FOOT-BALL!!
STOP CONSORTING WITH THE ENEMY!
THIS IS THE SECOND TIME!
FLICK
SO WE'VE GOT NOTHING TO HIDE!
HERE WE GO AGAIN!
ANOTHER ONSIDE KICK!!
TUMP
ACKK ?!
OH, MAN.
HE TOLD THEM.
PHEW!
WHAT CAN I SAY...

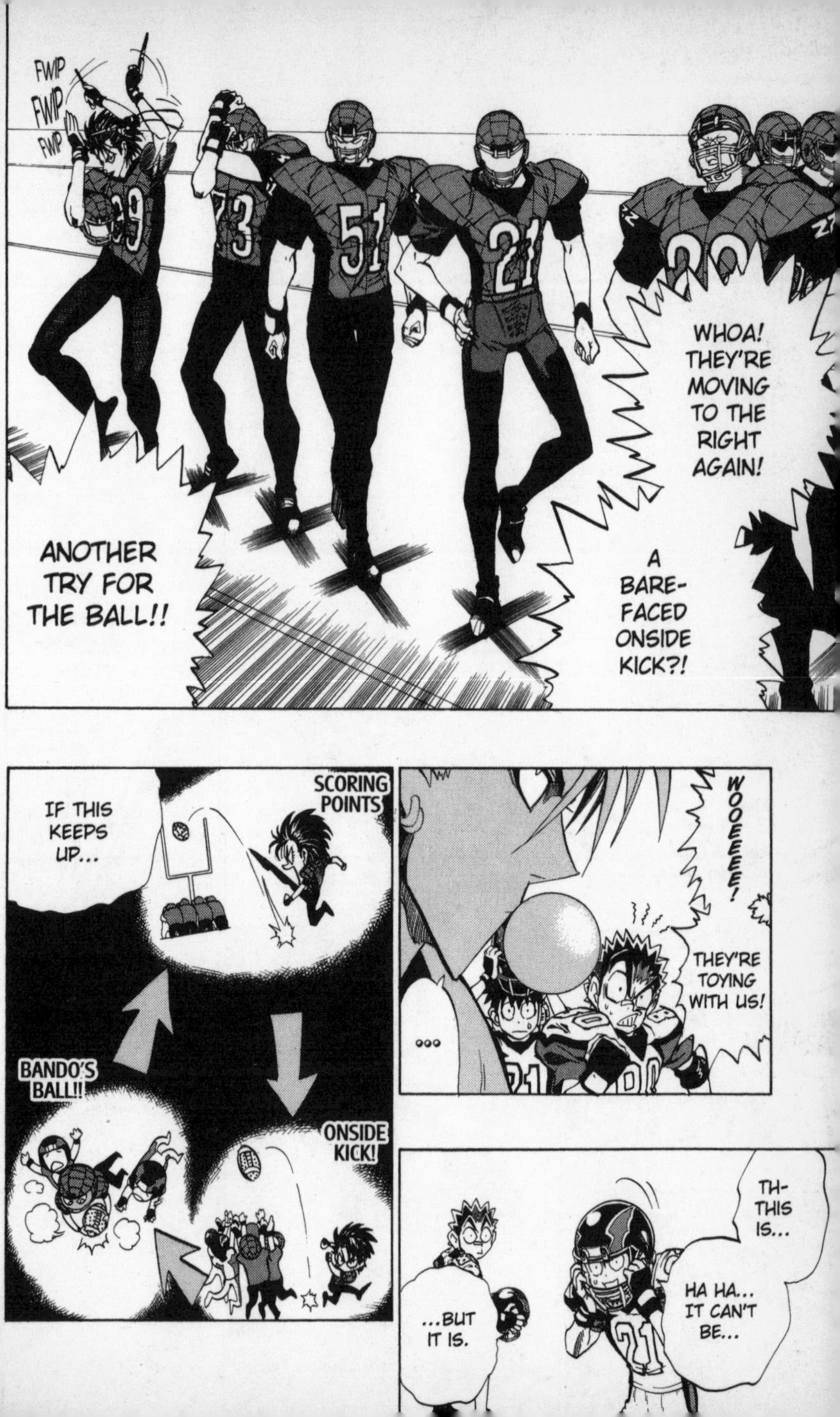
WHOA! THEY'RE MOVING TO THE RIGHT AGAIN!
A BARE-FACED ONSIDE KICK?!
FWIP FWIP FWIP
ANOTHER TRY FOR THE BALL!!
WOOEEEEE!
THEY'RE TOYING WITH US!
...
TH-THIS IS...
HA HA... IT CAN'T BE...
...BUT IT IS.
SCORING POINTS
IF THIS KEEPS UP...
ONSIDE KICK!
BANDO'S BALL!!

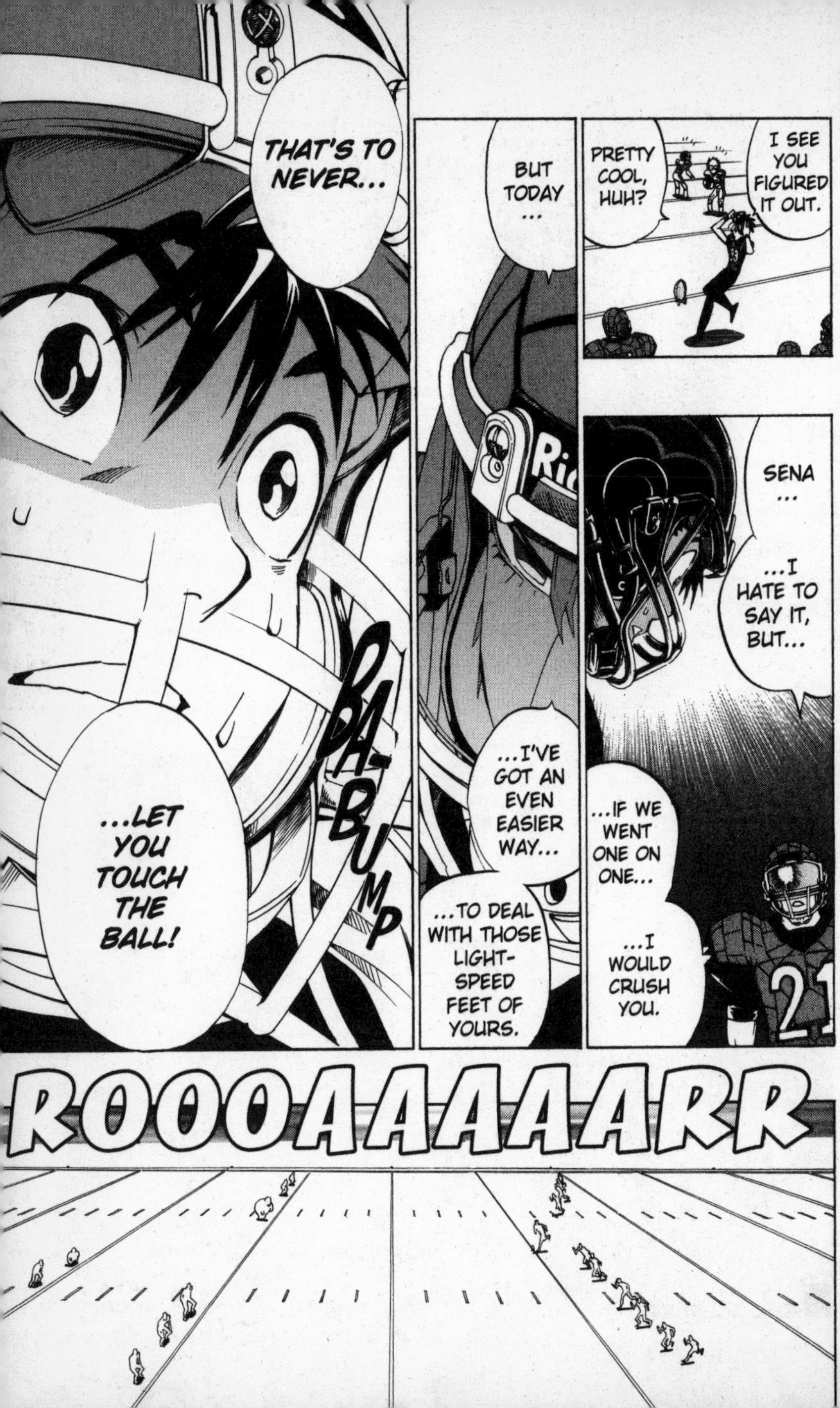
I SEE YOU FIGURED IT OUT.
PRETTY COOL, HUH?
SENA...
...I HATE TO SAY IT, BUT...
...IF WE WENT ONE ON ONE...
...I WOULD CRUSH YOU.
BUT TODAY...
...I'VE GOT AN EVEN EASIER WAY...
...TO DEAL WITH THOSE LIGHT-SPEED FEET OF YOURS.
THAT'S TO NEVER...
...LET YOU TOUCH THE BALL!
BA-BUMP
ROOOAAAAAARR

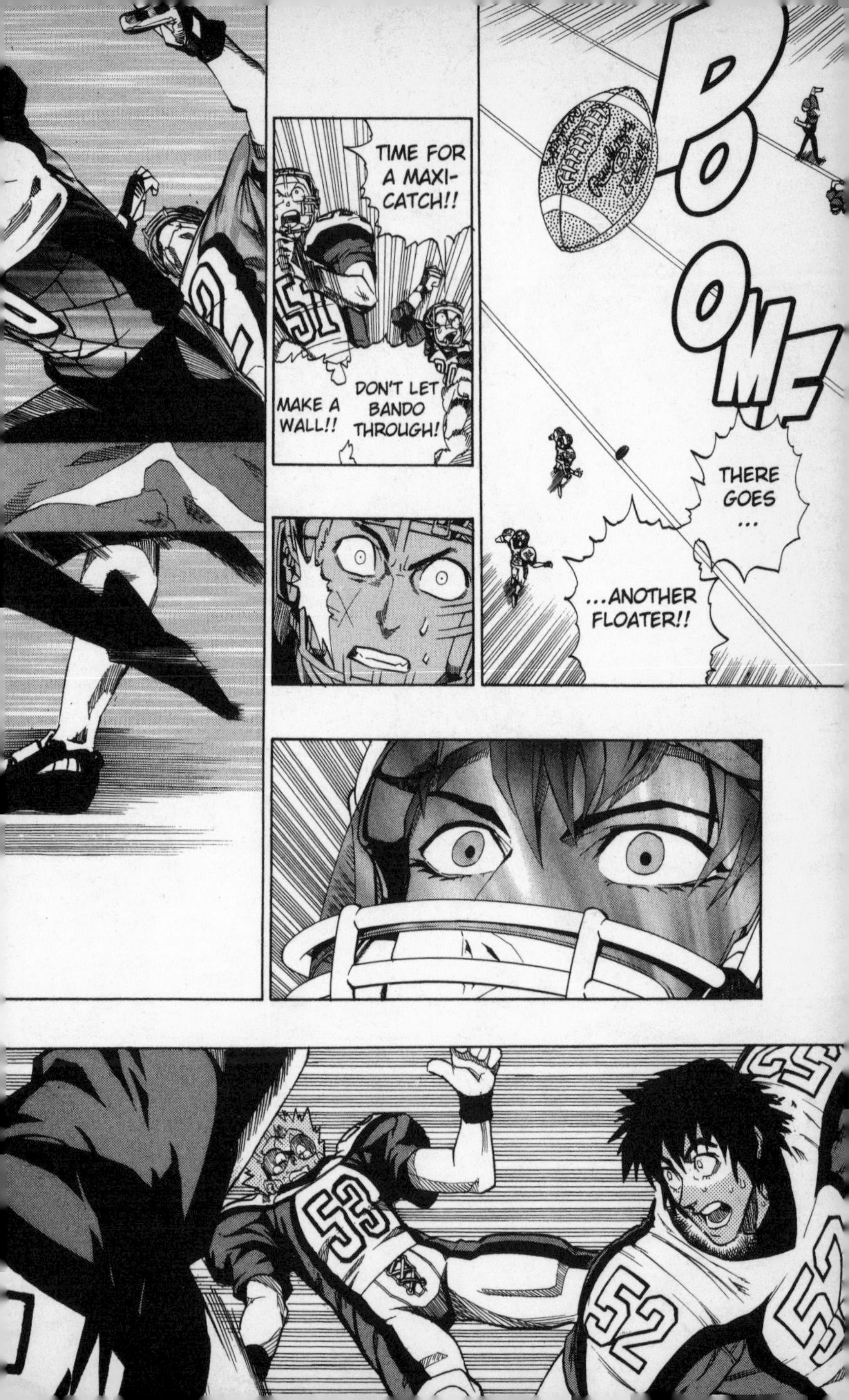
THERE GOES ...
...ANOTHER FLOATER!!
TIME FOR A MAXI-CATCH!!
DON'T LET BANDO THROUGH!
MAKE A WALL!!

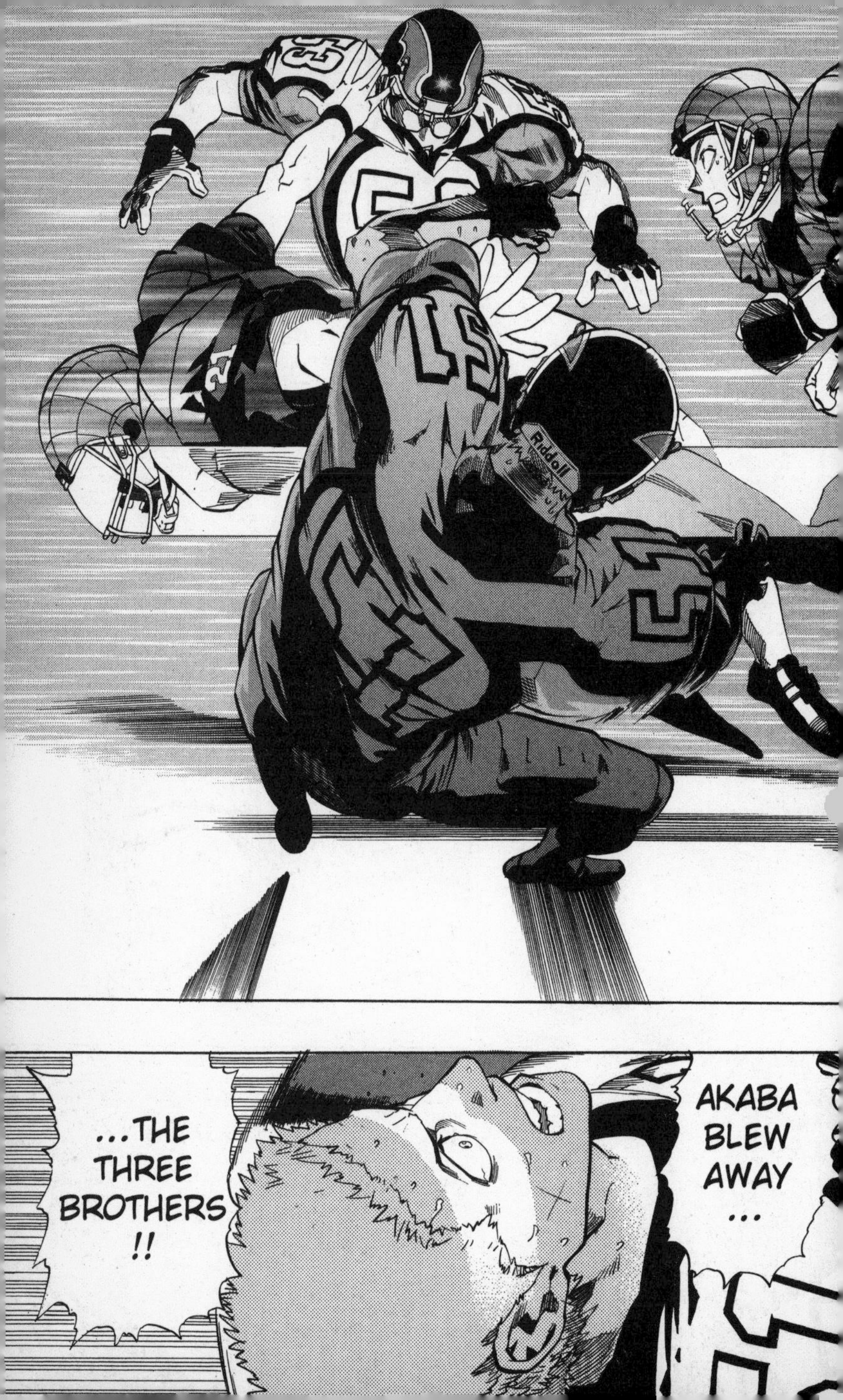
AKABA BLEW AWAY...
...THE THREE BROTHERS!!

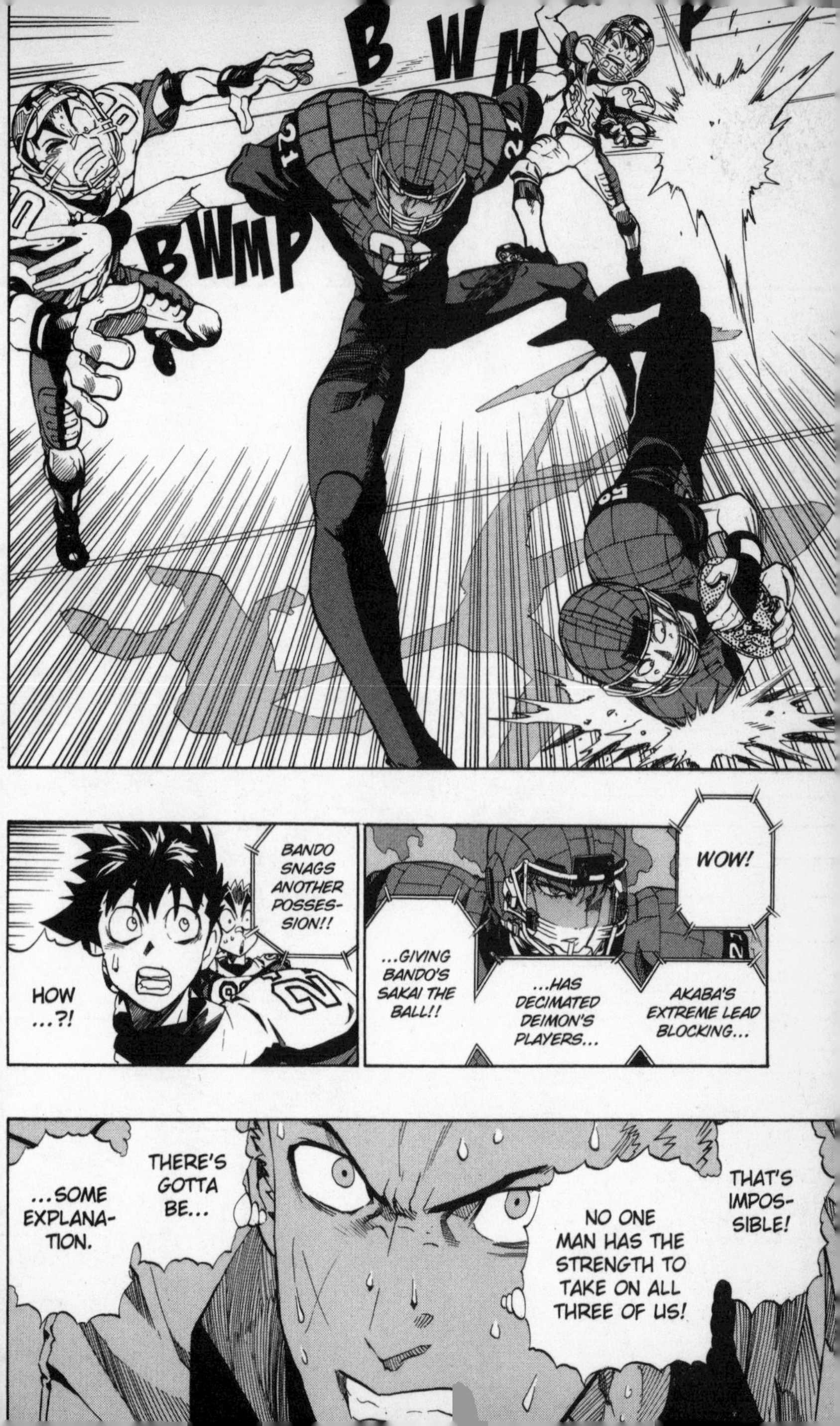
B W M
BWMP
WOW!
AKABA'S EXTREME LEAD BLOCKING...
...HAS DECIMATED DEIMON'S PLAYERS...
...GIVING BANDO'S SAKAI THE BALL!!
BANDO SNAGS ANOTHER POSSESSION!!
HOW ...?!
THAT'S IMPOSSIBLE!
NO ONE MAN HAS THE STRENGTH TO TAKE ON ALL THREE OF US!
THERE'S GOTTA BE...
...SOME EXPLANATION.

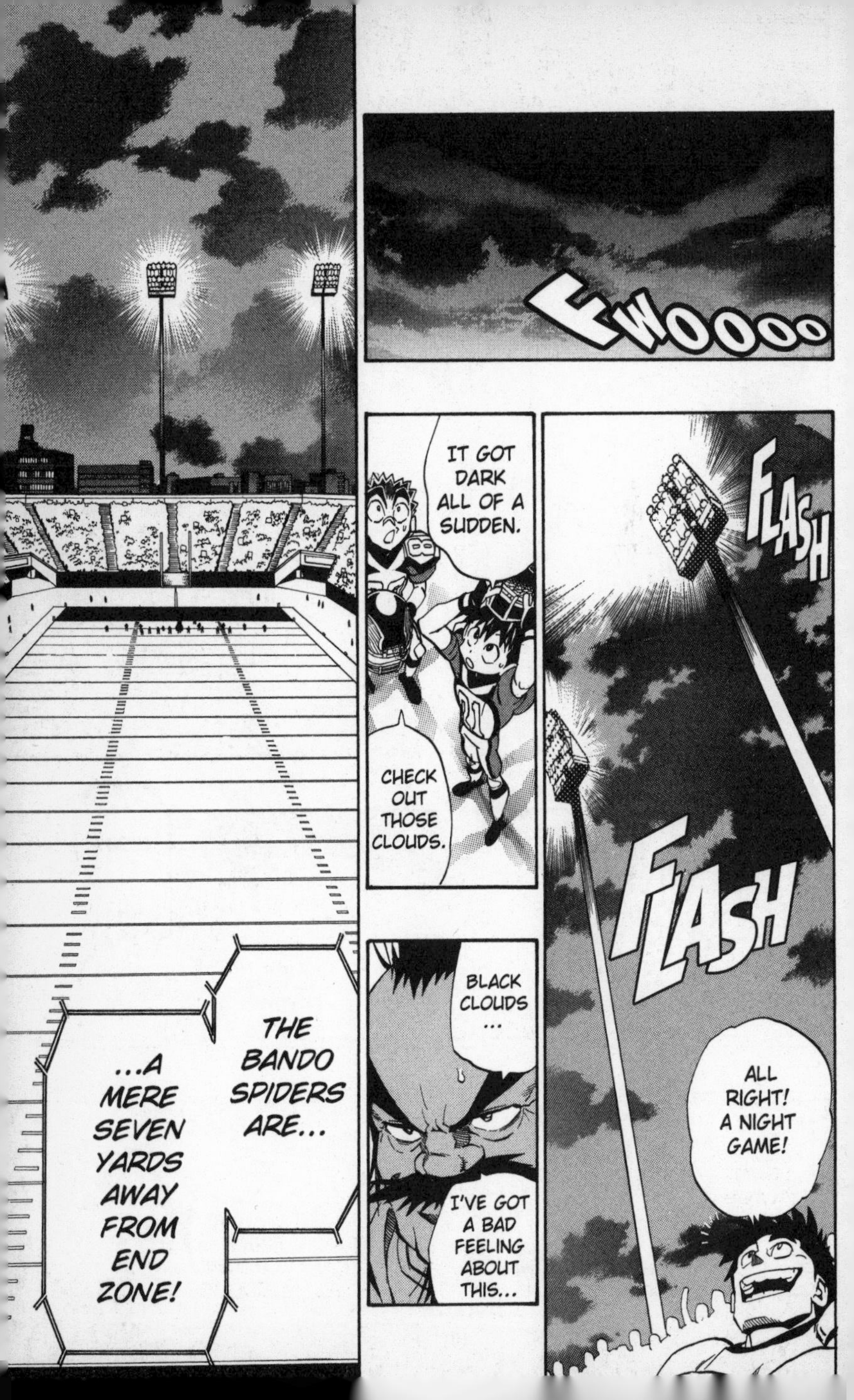
FWOOOO
FLASH
FLASH
ALL RIGHT! A NIGHT GAME!
IT GOT DARK ALL OF A SUDDEN.
CHECK OUT THOSE CLOUDS.
BLACK CLOUDS...
I'VE GOT A BAD FEELING ABOUT THIS...
THE BANDO SPIDERS ARE...
...A MERE SEVEN YARDS AWAY FROM END ZONE!

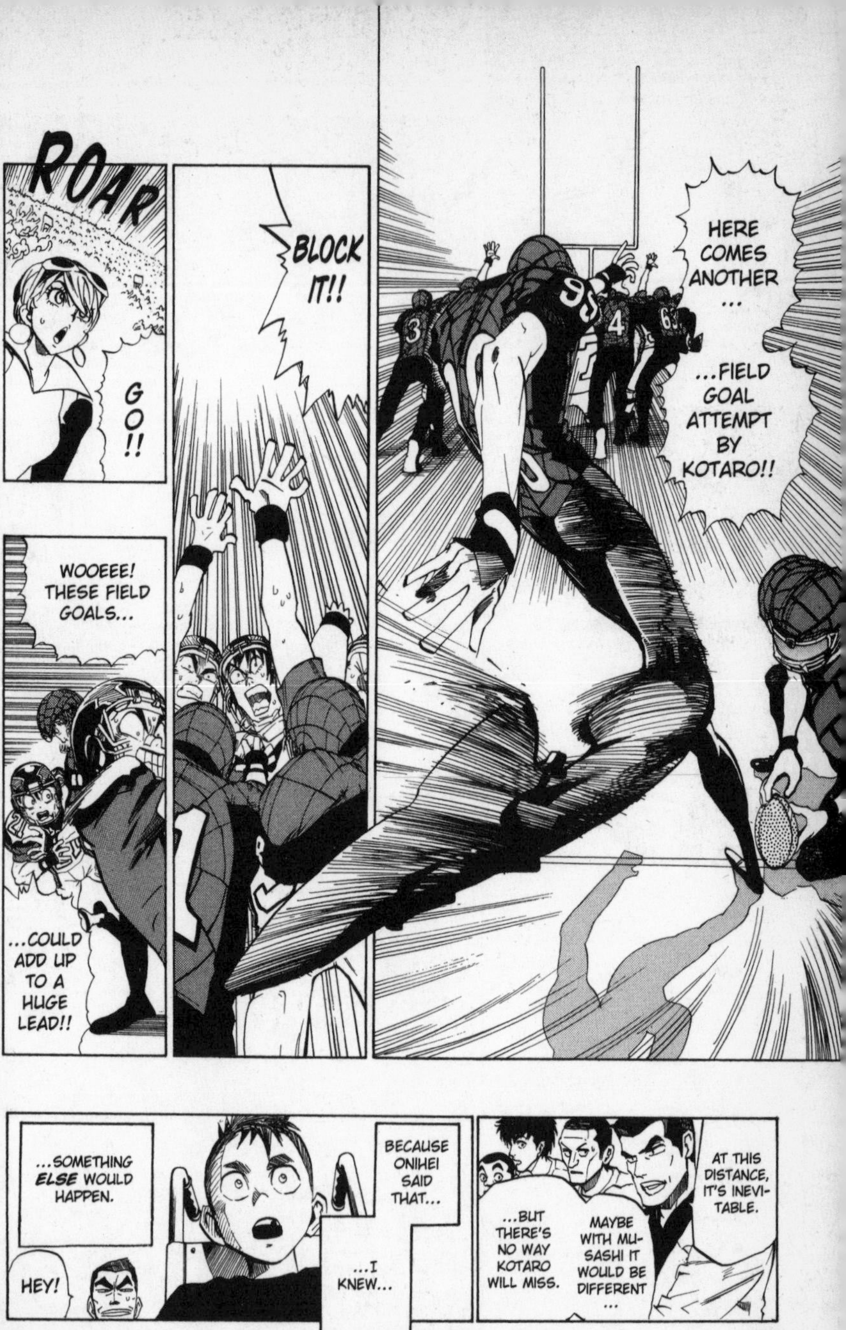
HERE COMES ANOTHER ...
...FIELD GOAL ATTEMPT BY KOTARO!!
BLOCK IT!!
ROAR
GO!!
WOOEEE! THESE FIELD GOALS...
...COULD ADD UP TO A HUGE LEAD!!
AT THIS DISTANCE, IT'S INEVI-TABLE.
MAYBE WITH MU-SASHI IT WOULD BE DIFFERENT ...
...BUT THERE'S NO WAY KOTARO WILL MISS.
BECAUSE ONIHEI SAID THAT...
...I KNEW...
...SOMETHING ELSE WOULD HAPPEN.
HEY!

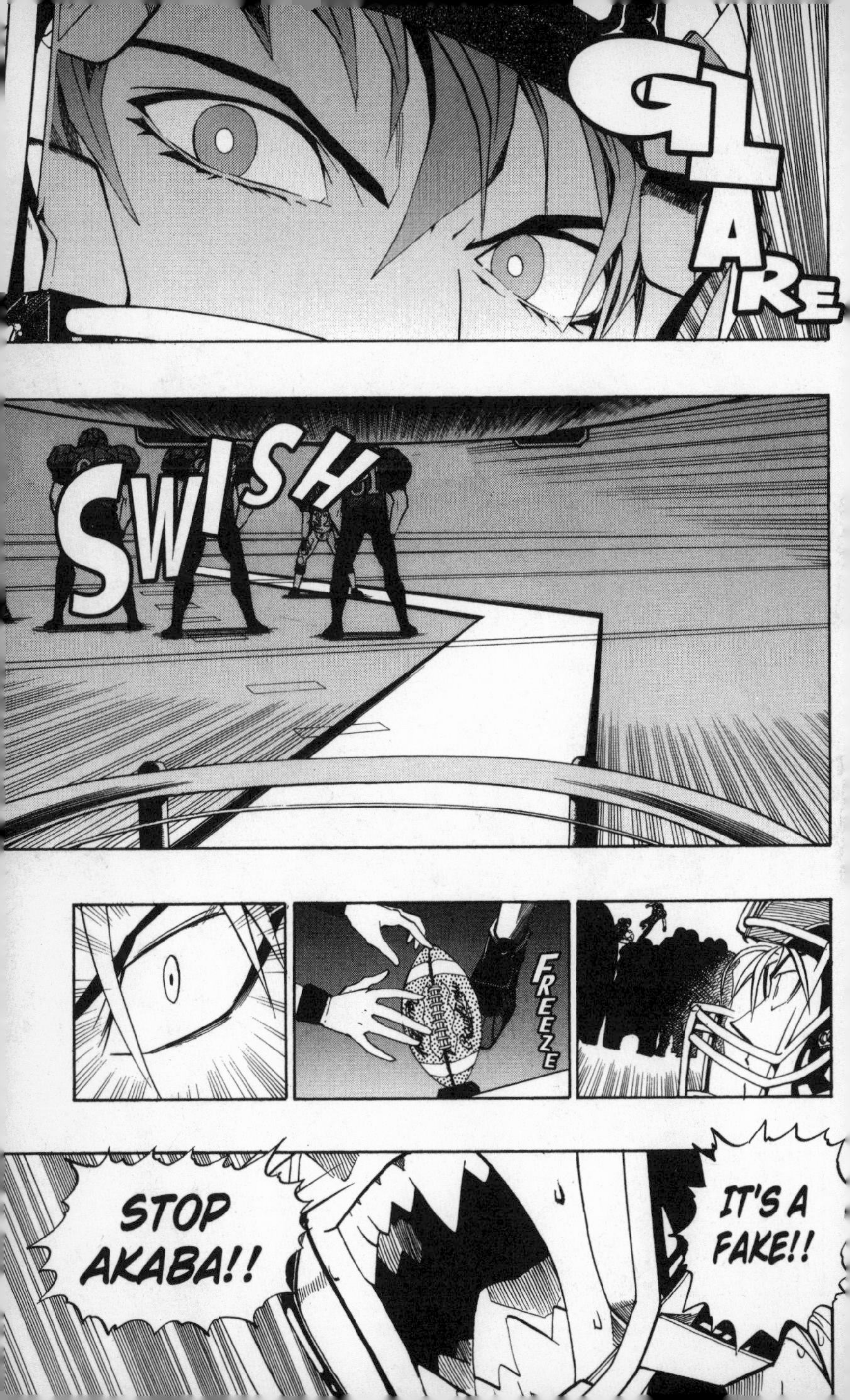
GLARE
SWISH
FREEZE
IT'S A FAKE!!
STOP AKABA!!

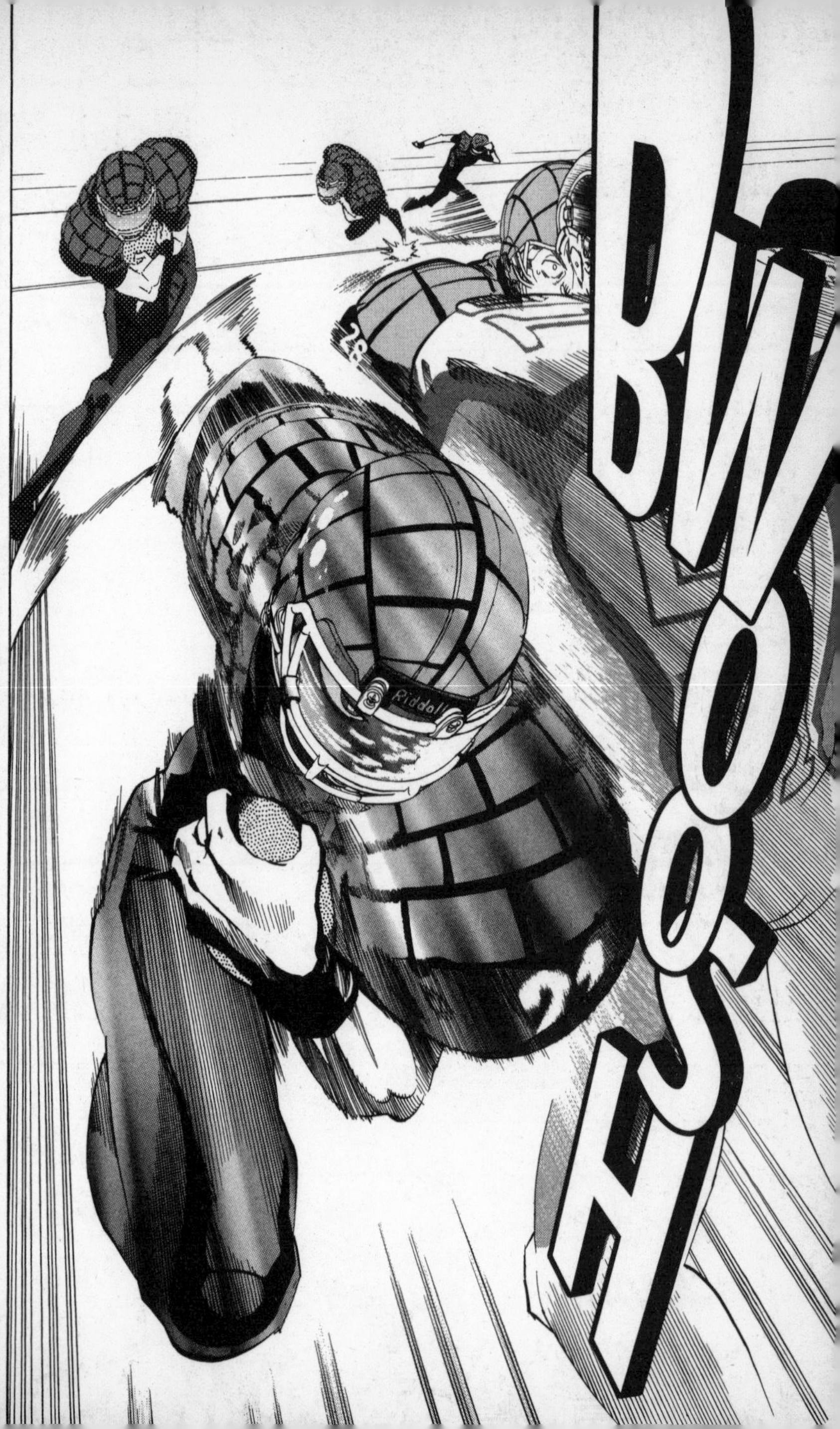
BWOOOSH

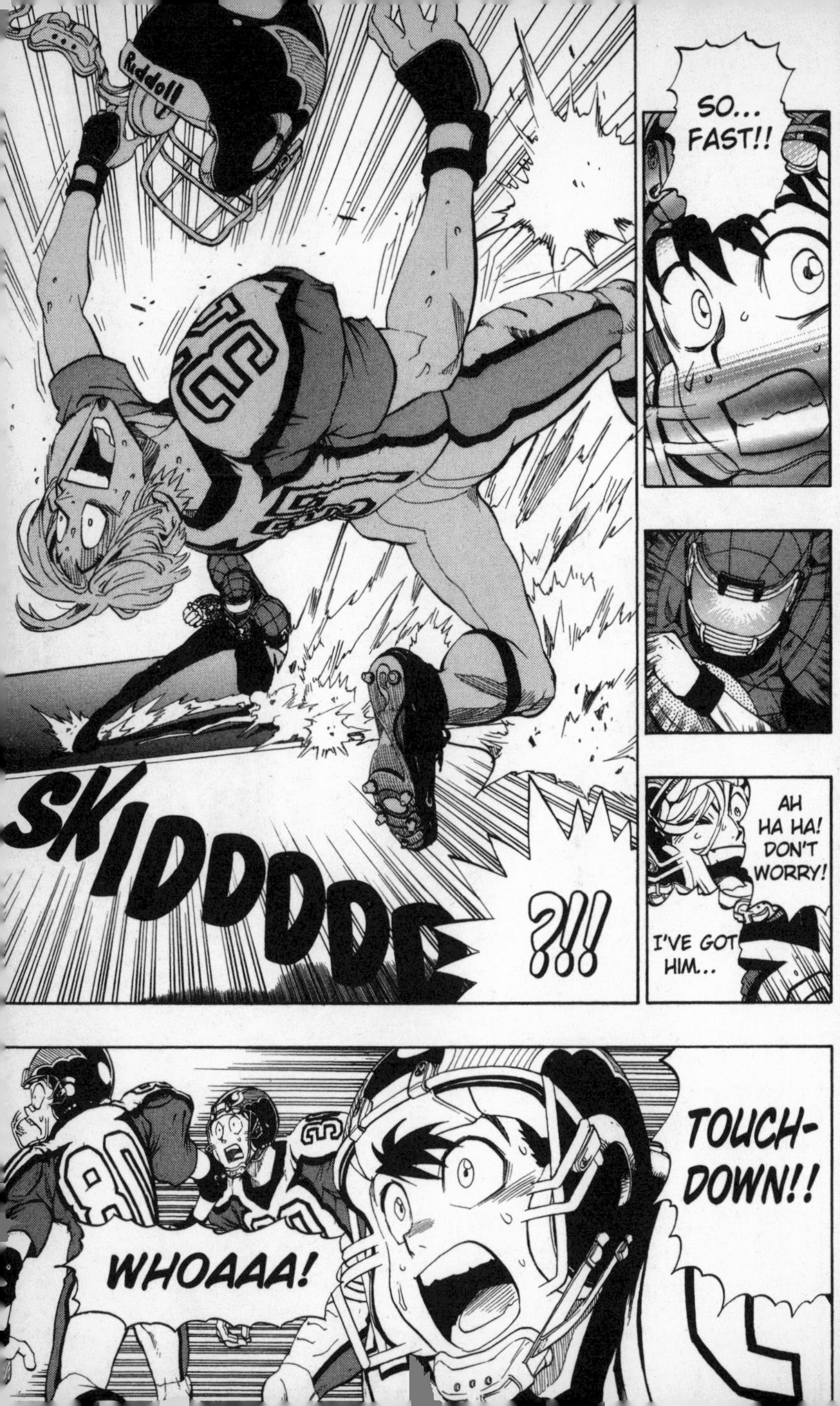
SO... FAST!!
AH HA HA! DON'T WORRY!
I'VE GOT HIM...
SKIDDDDE
?!!
TOUCH-DOWN!!
WHOAAA!

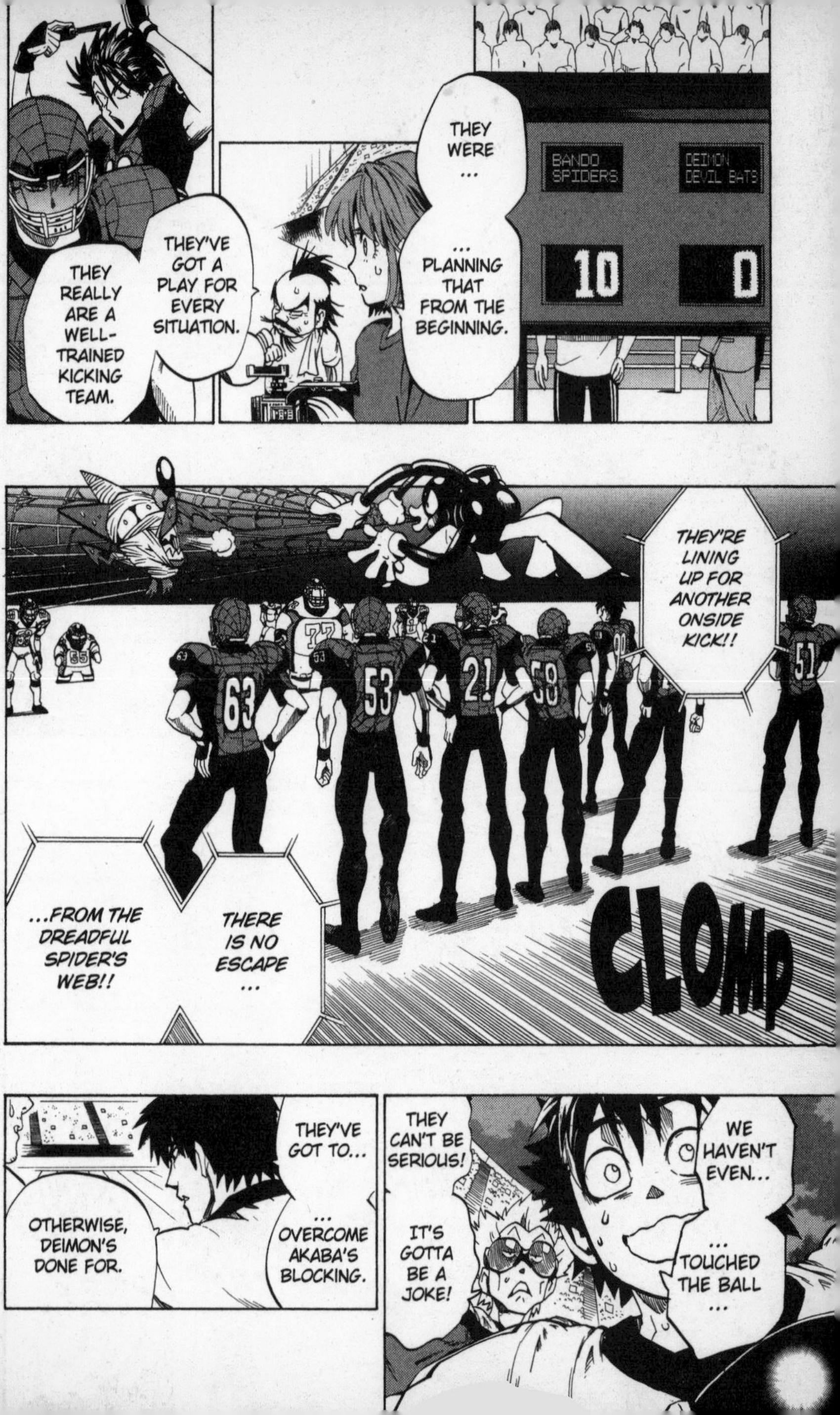
THEY WERE ...
... PLANNING THAT FROM THE BEGINNING.
BANDO SPIDERS
DEIMON DEVIL BATS
10
0
THEY'VE GOT A PLAY FOR EVERY SITUATION.
THEY REALLY ARE A WELL-TRAINED KICKING TEAM.
THEY'RE LINING UP FOR ANOTHER ONSIDE KICK!!
CLOMP
THERE IS NO ESCAPE ...
...FROM THE DREADFUL SPIDER'S WEB!!
WE HAVEN'T EVEN...
... TOUCHED THE BALL ...
THEY CAN'T BE SERIOUS!
IT'S GOTTA BE A JOKE!
THEY'VE GOT TO...
... OVERCOME AKABA'S BLOCKING.
OTHERWISE, DEIMON'S DONE FOR.

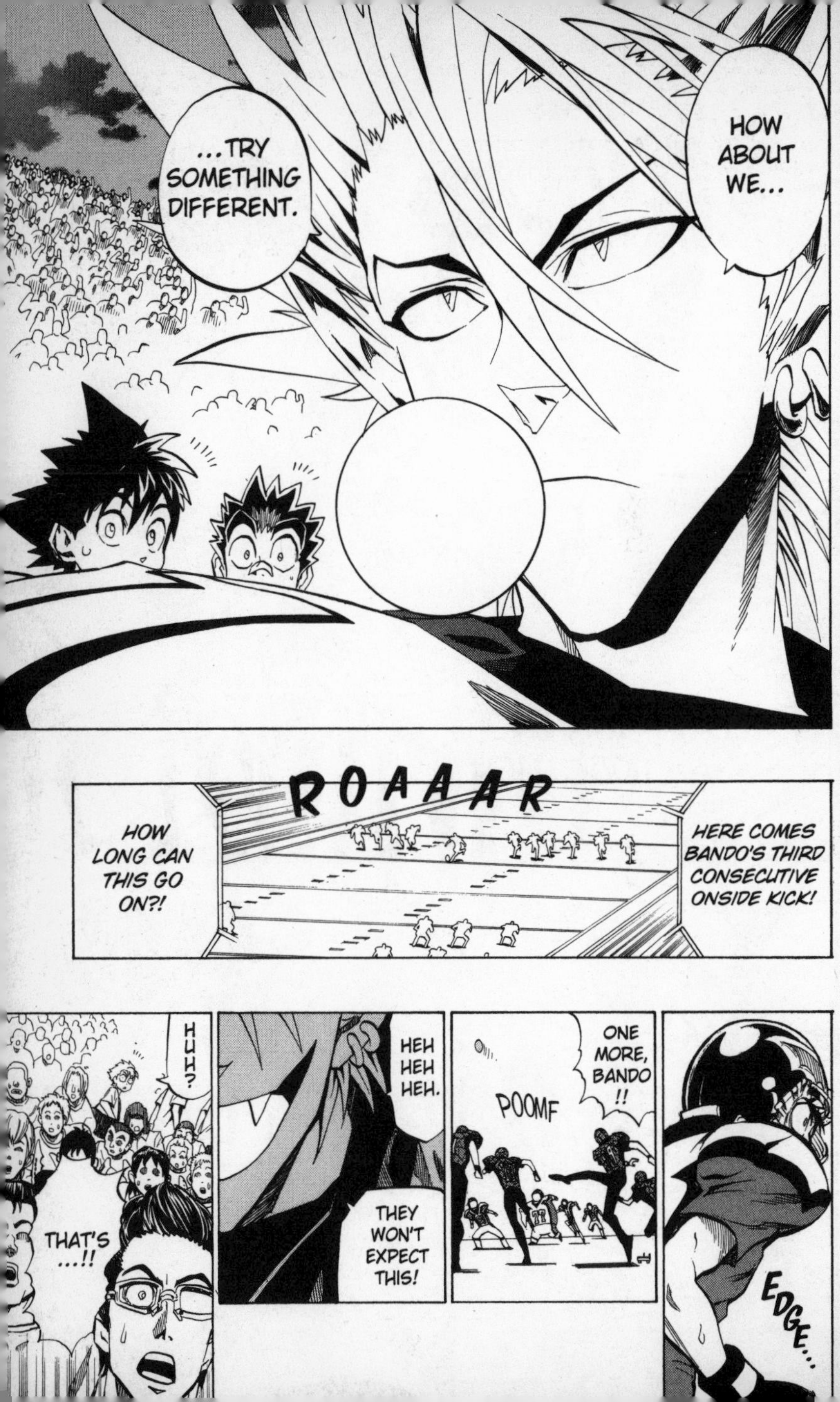
HOW ABOUT WE...
...TRY SOMETHING DIFFERENT.
ROAAAR
HERE COMES BANDO'S THIRD CONSECUTIVE ONSIDE KICK!
HOW LONG CAN THIS GO ON?!
EDGE...
ONE MORE, BANDO!!
POOMF
HEH HEH HEH.
THEY WON'T EXPECT THIS!
HUH?
THAT'S...!!

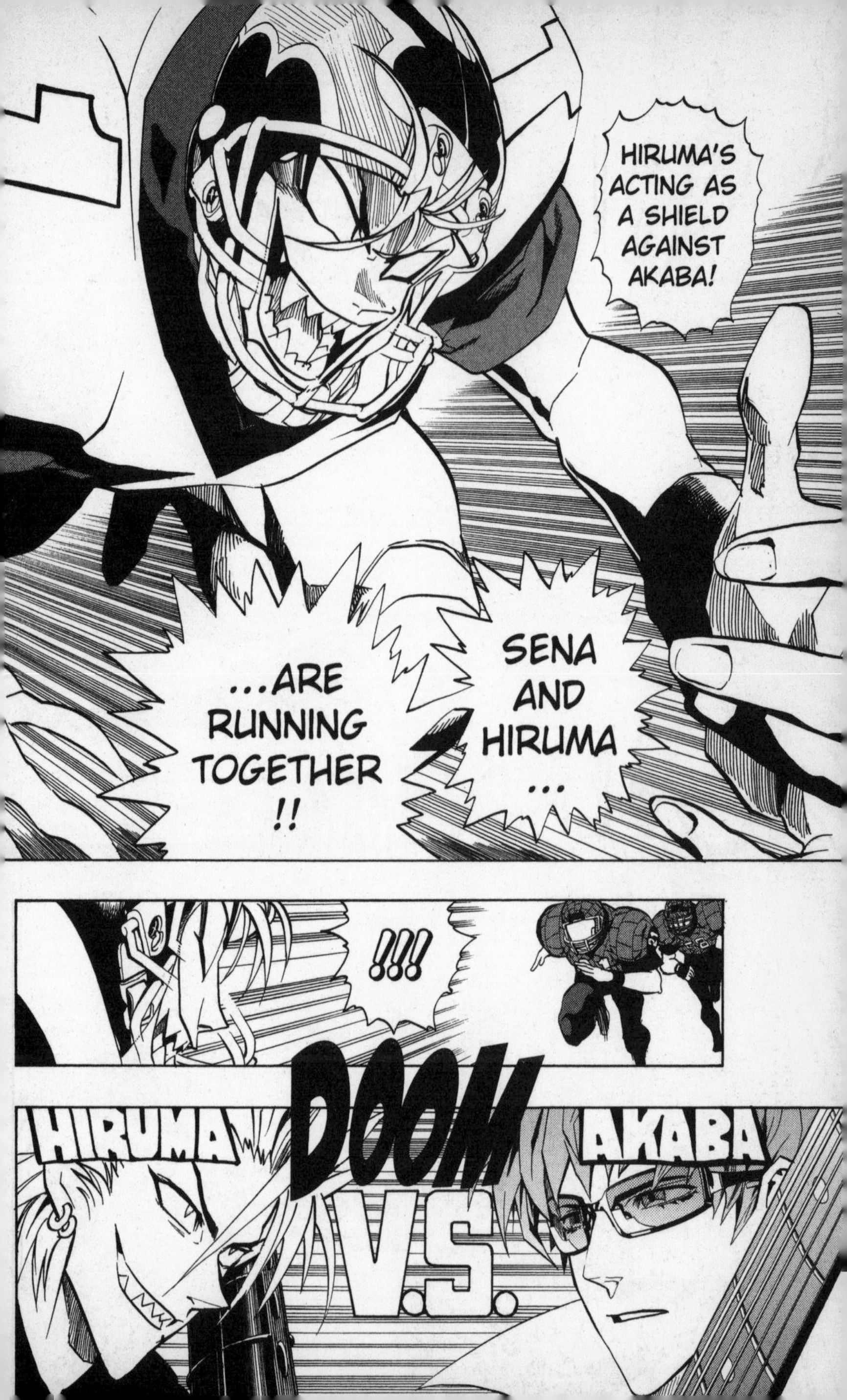
HIRUMA'S ACTING AS A SHIELD AGAINST AKABA!
SENA AND HIRUMA...
...ARE RUNNING TOGETHER!!
!!!
AKABA
DOOM
HIRUMA
V.S.

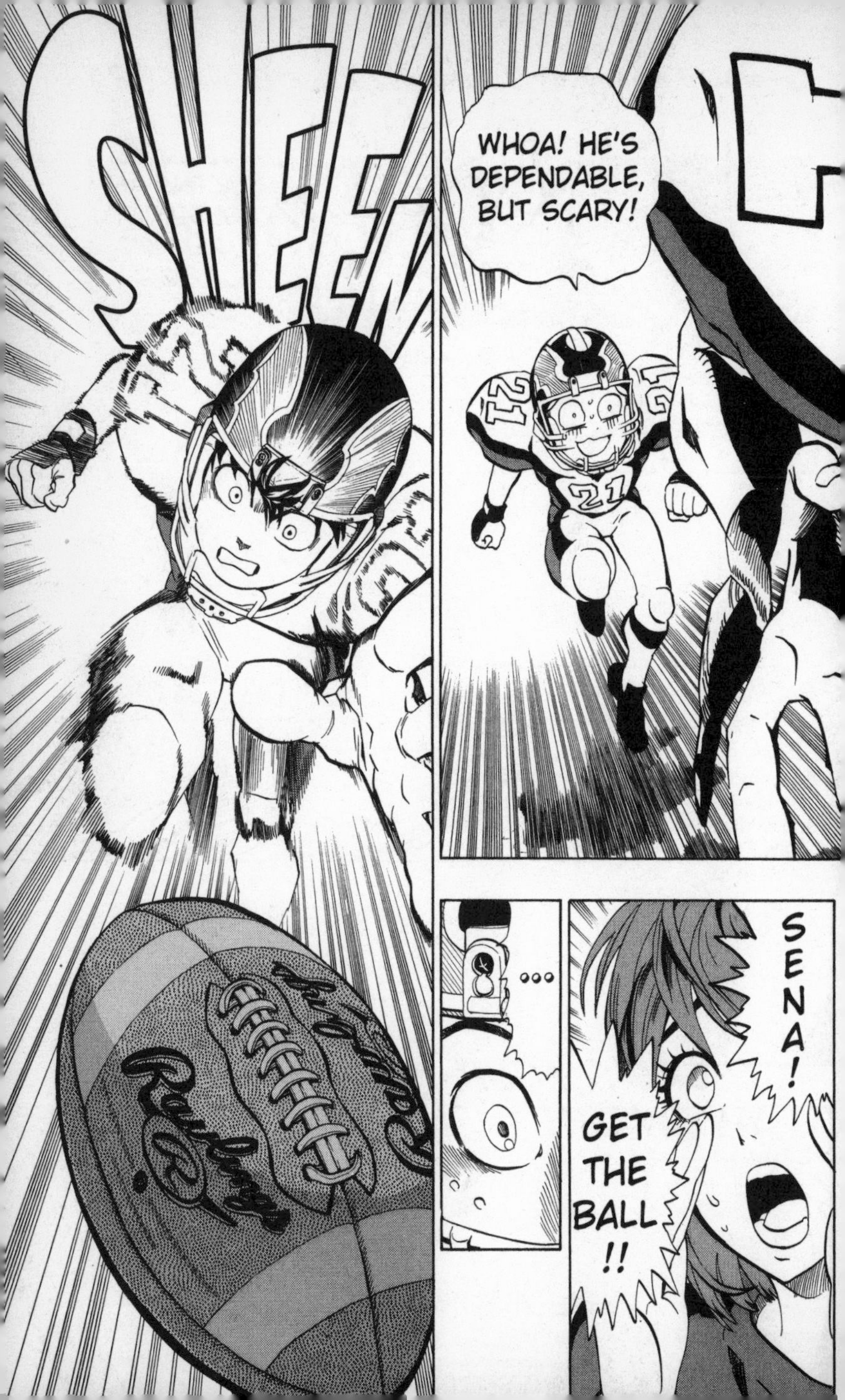
WHOA! HE'S DEPENDABLE, BUT SCARY!
SENA!
GET THE BALL!!
...
SHEE
Rawlings

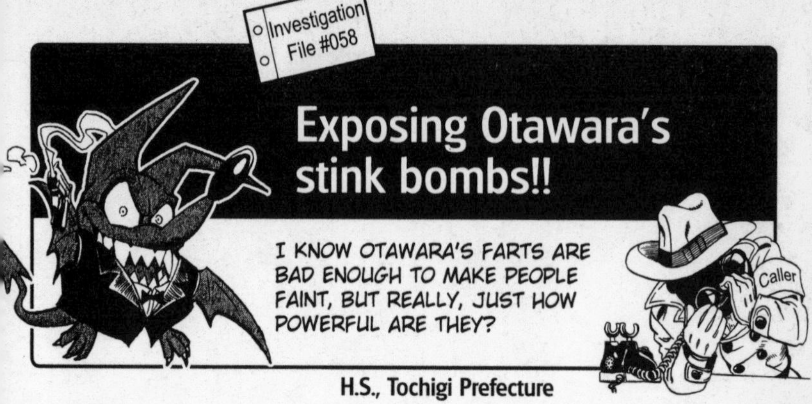
Investigation File #058
Exposing Otawara's stink bombs!!
I KNOW OTAWARA'S FARTS ARE BAD ENOUGH TO MAKE PEOPLE FAINT, BUT REALLY, JUST HOW POWERFUL ARE THEY?
Caller

H.S., Tochigi Prefecture

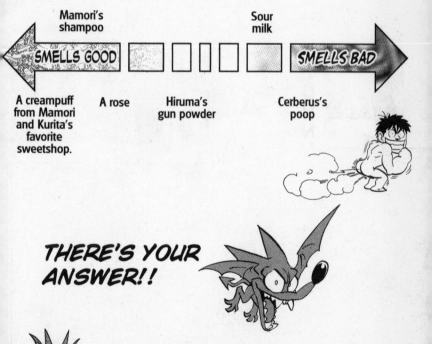

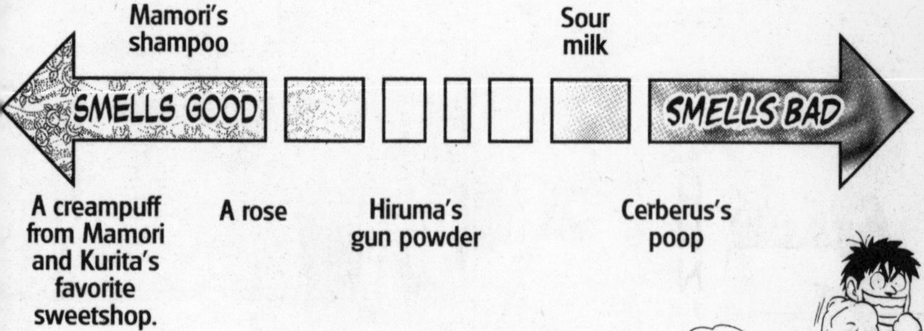
Mamori's shampoo
Sour milk
SMELLS GOOD
SMELLS BAD
A creampuff from Mamori and Kurita's favorite sweetshop.
A rose
Hiruma's gun powder
Cerberus's poop

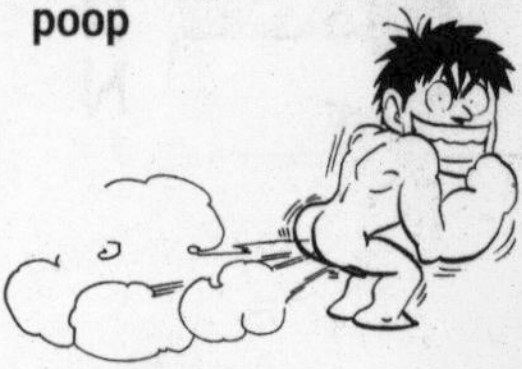

THERE'S YOUR ANSWER!!

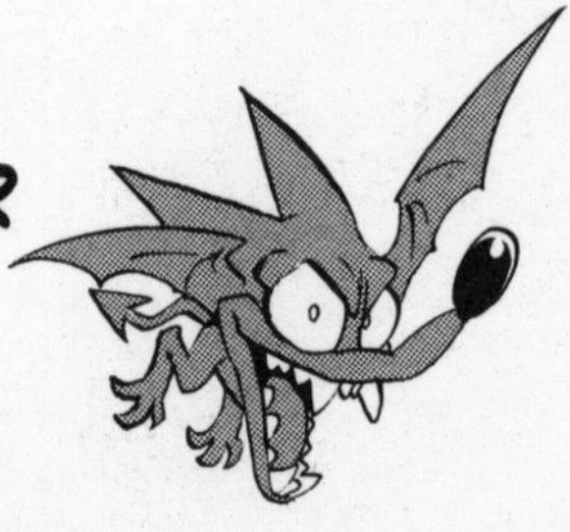

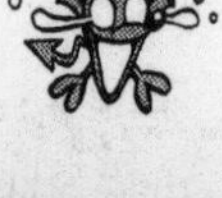

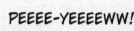

PEEEE-YEEEEWW!

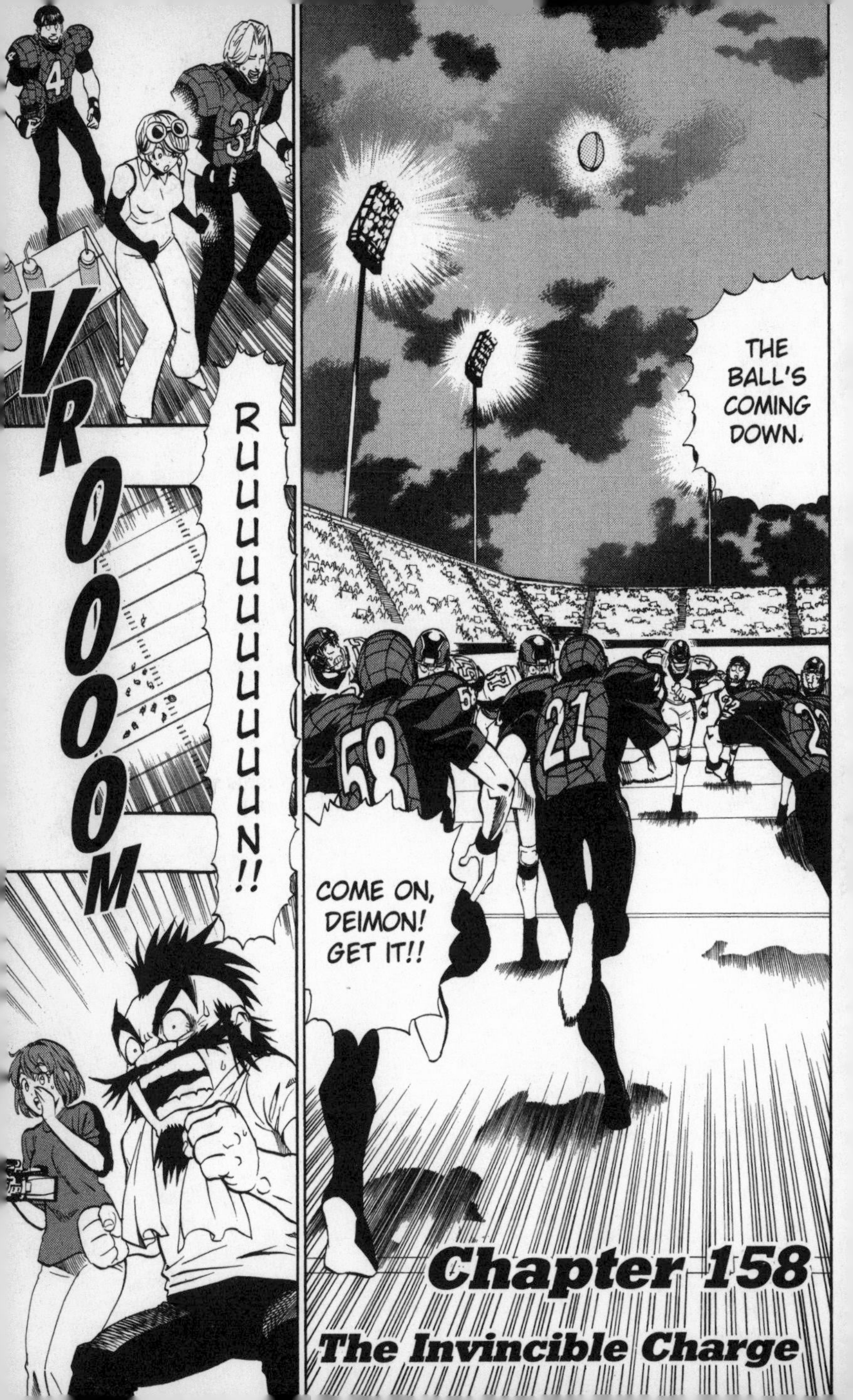
THE BALL'S COMING DOWN.
COME ON, DEIMON! GET IT!!
Chapter 158
The Invincible Charge
RUUUUUUUUUUN!!
VROOOOM

VROOOO

UH-OH! THIS COULD GET WILD!

DO

IT'S THEIR FIRST PAIRED RUN!

OM

SENA'S GOT A HIRUMA SHIELD!!

EVEN KURITA AND THE THREE BRO- THERS...

...WERE NO MATCH FOR HIM.

HIRUMA...

ACKK! HERE COMES AKABA!!

BWOOSH

SO HOW CAN HIRUMA...

...STOP HIM?

I'M SORRY, BUT YOU'RE NO MATCH FOR ME.

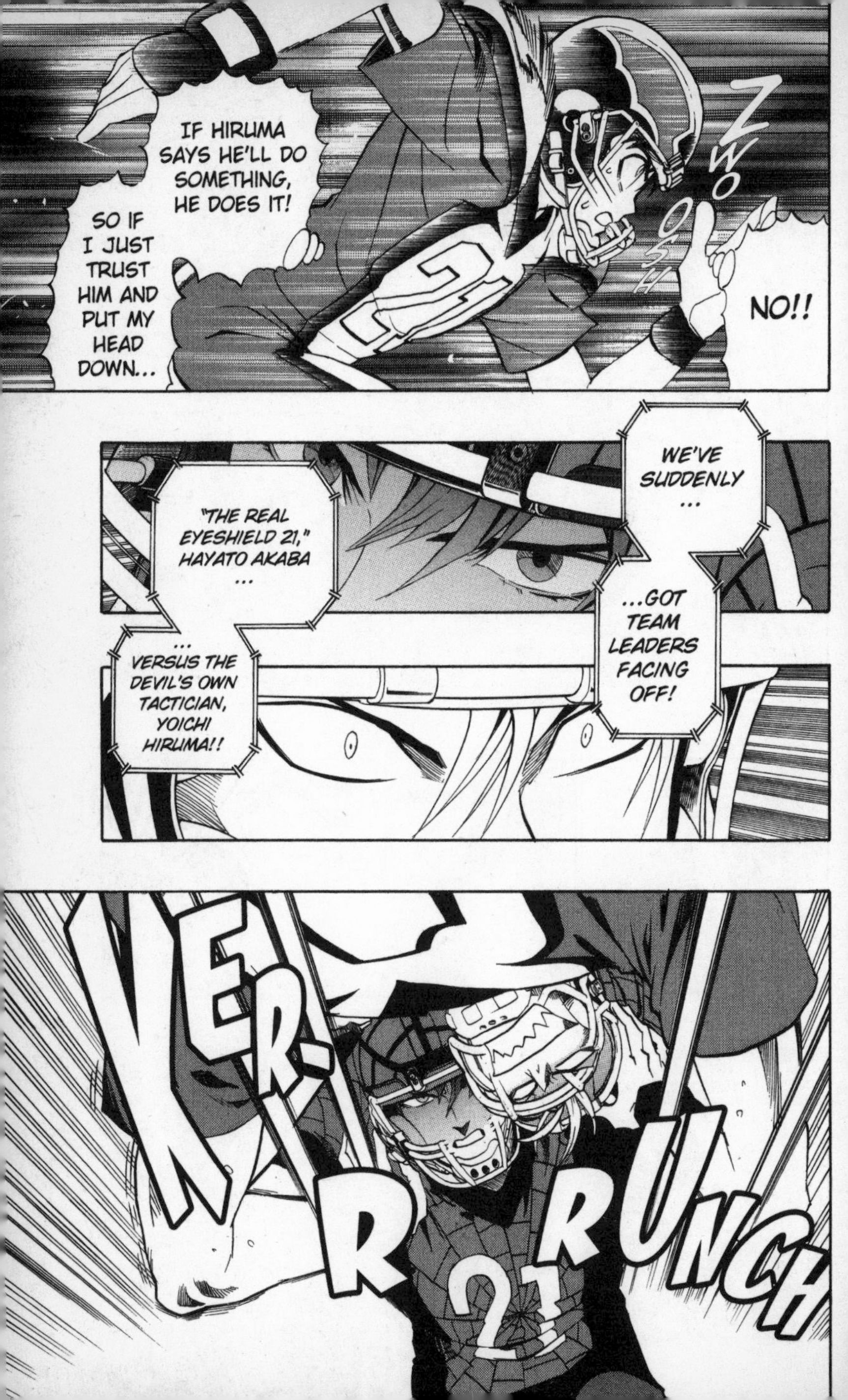
NO!!
ZWOOOSH
IF HIRUMA SAYS HE'LL DO SOMETHING, HE DOES IT!
SO IF I JUST TRUST HIM AND PUT MY HEAD DOWN...
WE'VE SUDDENLY...
...GOT TEAM LEADERS FACING OFF!
"THE REAL EYESHIELD 21," HAYATO AKABA...
...VERSUS THE DEVIL'S OWN TACTICIAN, YOICHI HIRUMA!!
KER-RRUNCH

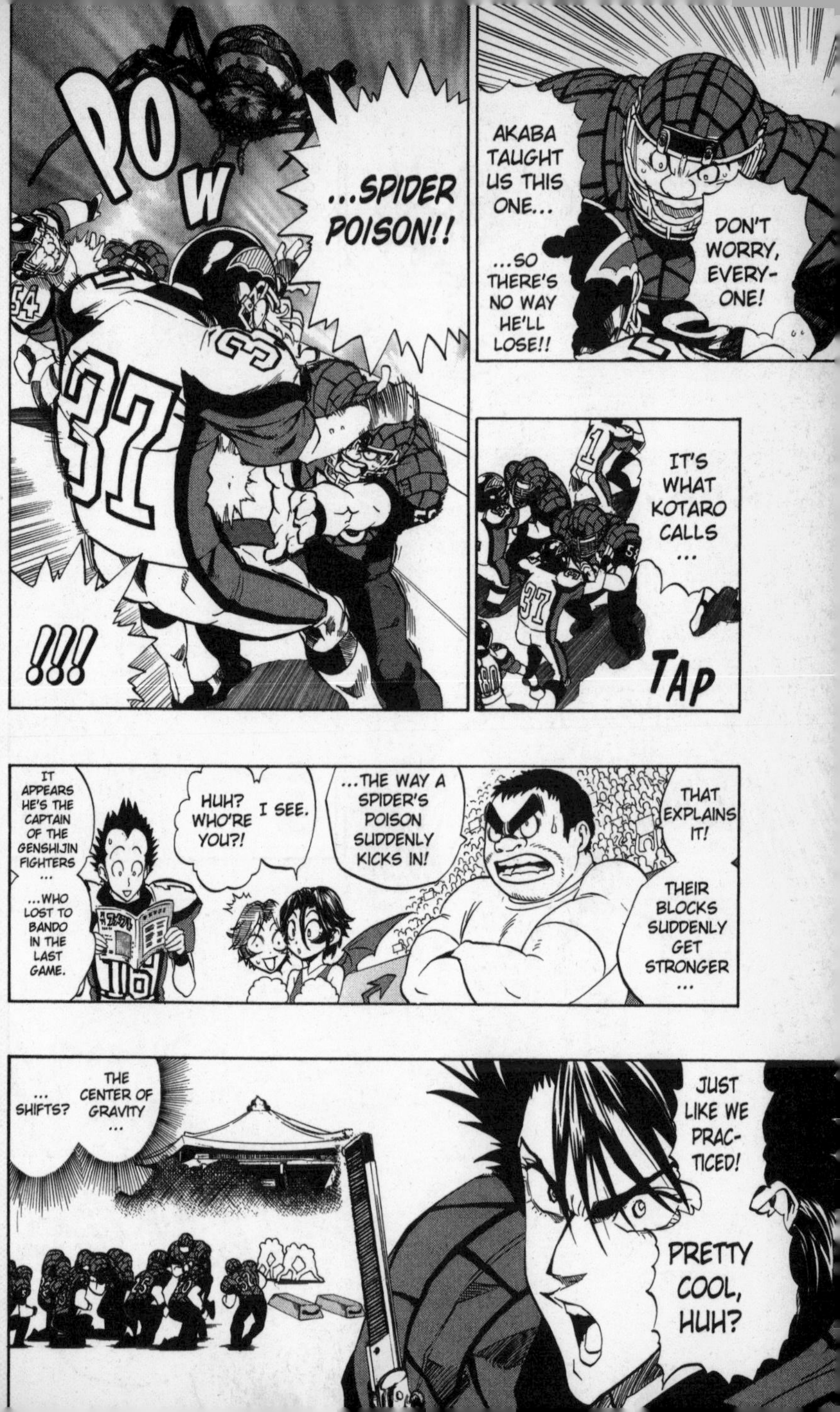
DON'T WORRY, EVERYONE!
AKABA TAUGHT US THIS ONE...
...SO THERE'S NO WAY HE'LL LOSE!!
IT'S WHAT KOTARO CALLS ...
TAP
POW
...SPIDER POISON!!
!!!
THAT EXPLAINS IT!
THEIR BLOCKS SUDDENLY GET STRONGER ...
...THE WAY A SPIDER'S POISON SUDDENLY KICKS IN!
I SEE.
HUH? WHO'RE YOU?!
IT APPEARS HE'S THE CAPTAIN OF THE GENSHIJIN FIGHTERS ...
...WHO LOST TO BANDO IN THE LAST GAME.
JUST LIKE WE PRAC-TICED!
PRETTY COOL, HUH?
THE CENTER OF GRAVITY ...
... SHIFTS?

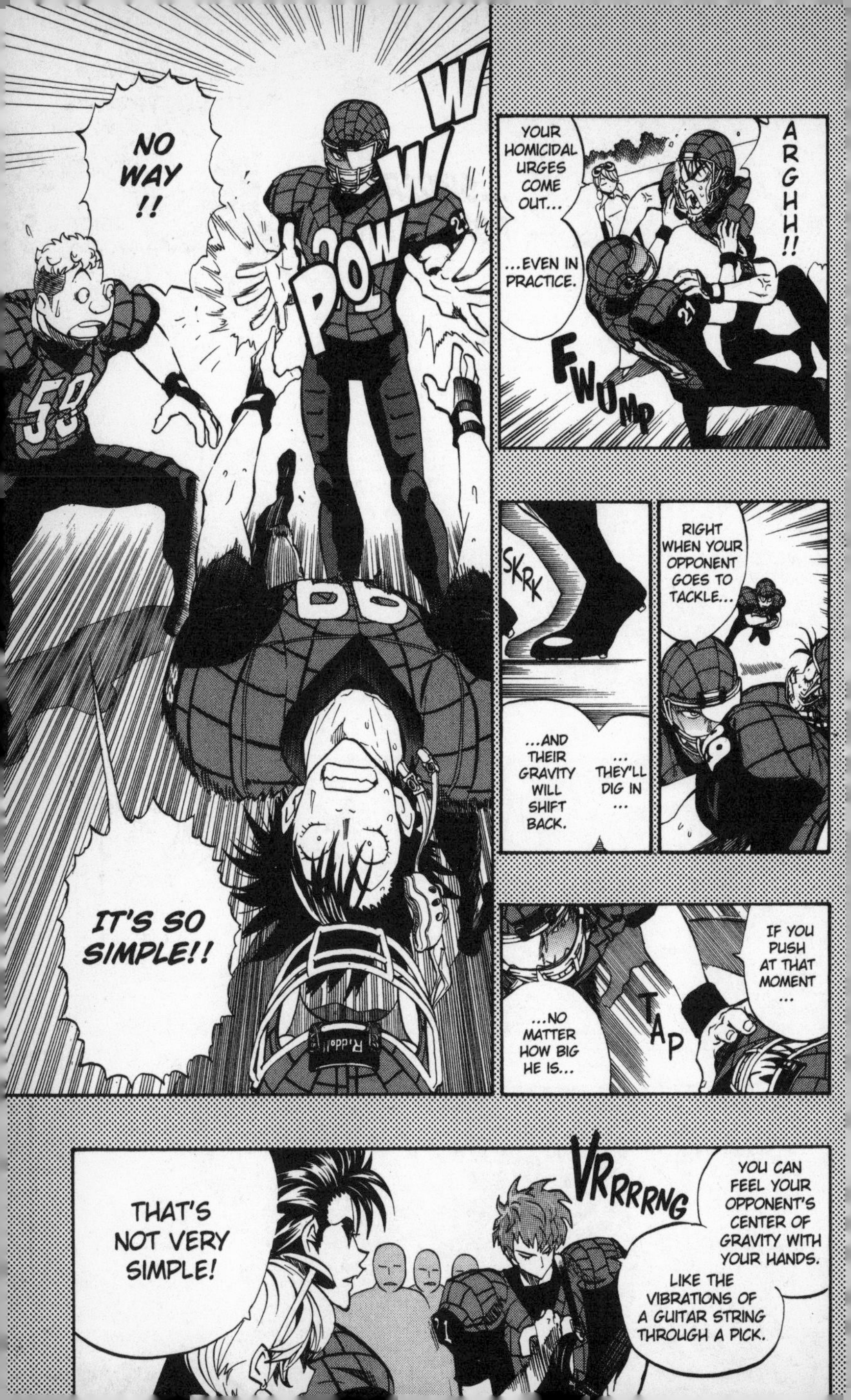
YOUR HOMICIDAL URGES COME OUT...
...EVEN IN PRACTICE.
ARGHH!!
FWUMP
NO WAY!!
POWWW
RIGHT WHEN YOUR OPPONENT GOES TO TACKLE...
...THEY'LL DIG IN...
...AND THEIR GRAVITY WILL SHIFT BACK.
SKRK
IF YOU PUSH AT THAT MOMENT...
...NO MATTER HOW BIG HE IS...
TAP
IT'S SO SIMPLE!!
YOU CAN FEEL YOUR OPPONENT'S CENTER OF GRAVITY WITH YOUR HANDS.
LIKE THE VIBRATIONS OF A GUITAR STRING THROUGH A PICK.
VRRRRNG
THAT'S NOT VERY SIMPLE!

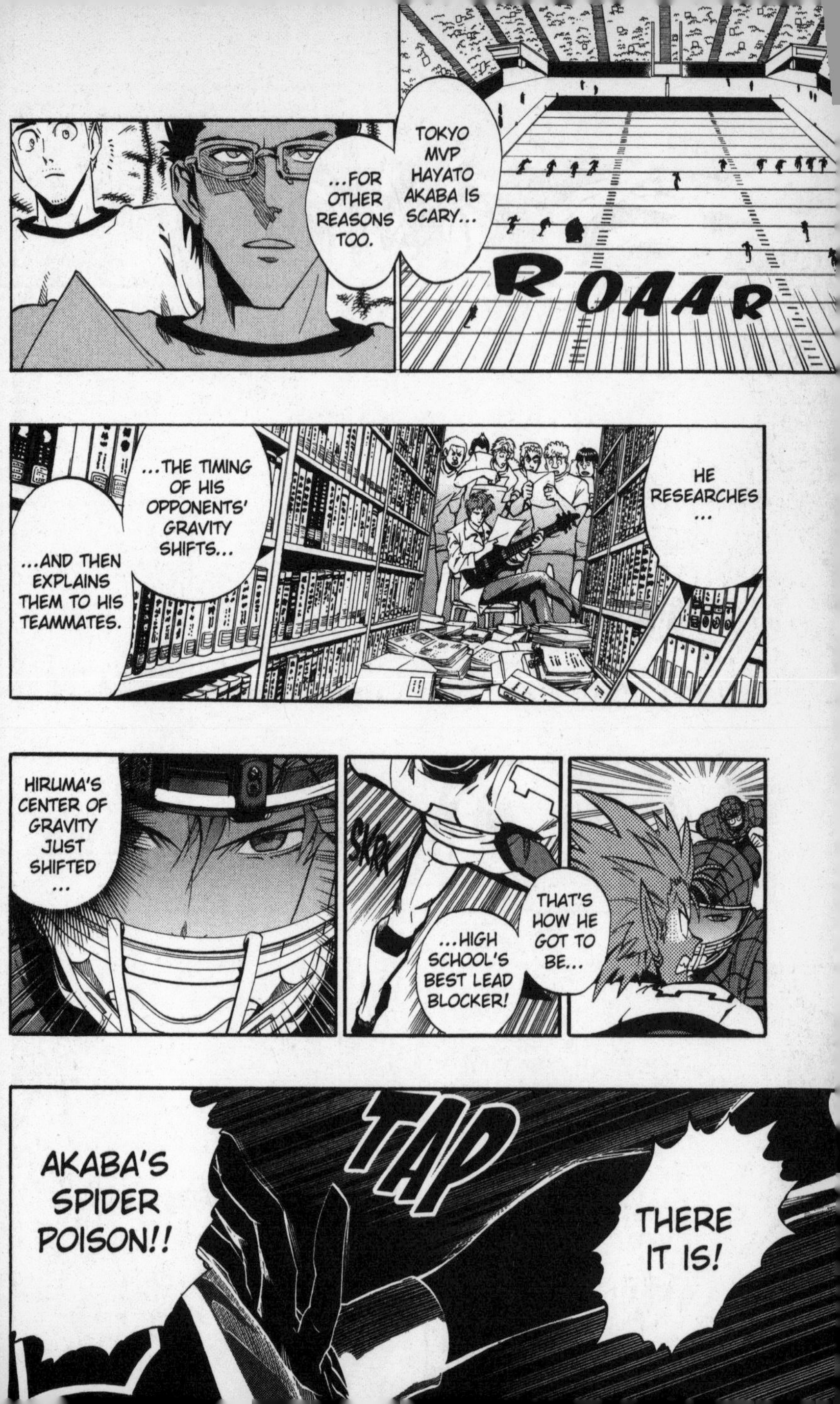
TOKYO MVP HAYATO AKABA IS SCARY...
ROAAR
...FOR OTHER REASONS TOO.
HE RESEARCHES ...
...THE TIMING OF HIS OPPONENTS' GRAVITY SHIFTS...
...AND THEN EXPLAINS THEM TO HIS TEAMMATES.
THAT'S HOW HE GOT TO BE...
...HIGH SCHOOL'S BEST LEAD BLOCKER!
HIRUMA'S CENTER OF GRAVITY JUST SHIFTED ...
THERE IT IS!
TAP
AKABA'S SPIDER POISON!!

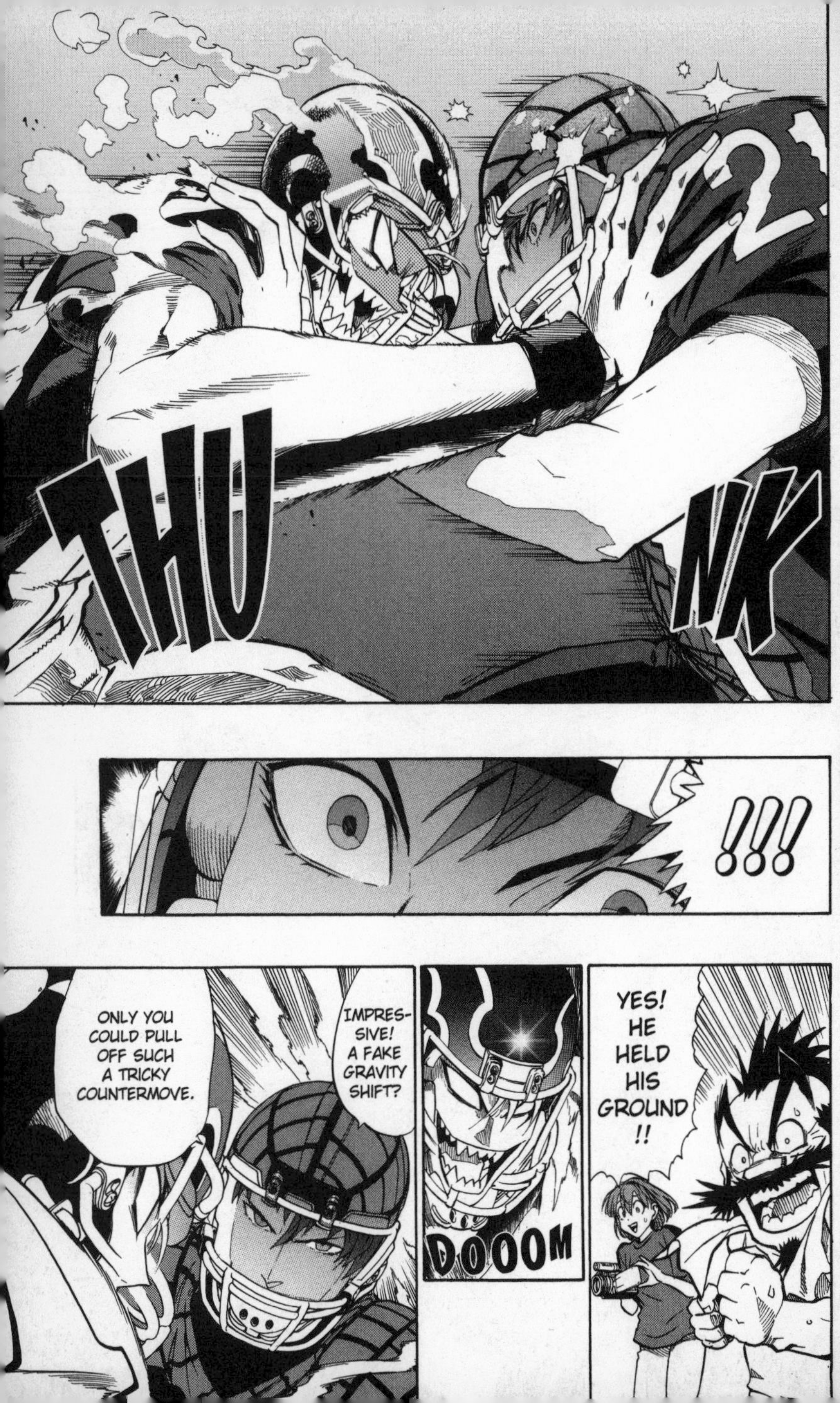
THUNK
!!!
YES! HE HELD HIS GROUND!!
DOOOM
IMPRES-SIVE! A FAKE GRAVITY SHIFT?
ONLY YOU COULD PULL OFF SUCH A TRICKY COUNTERMOVE.

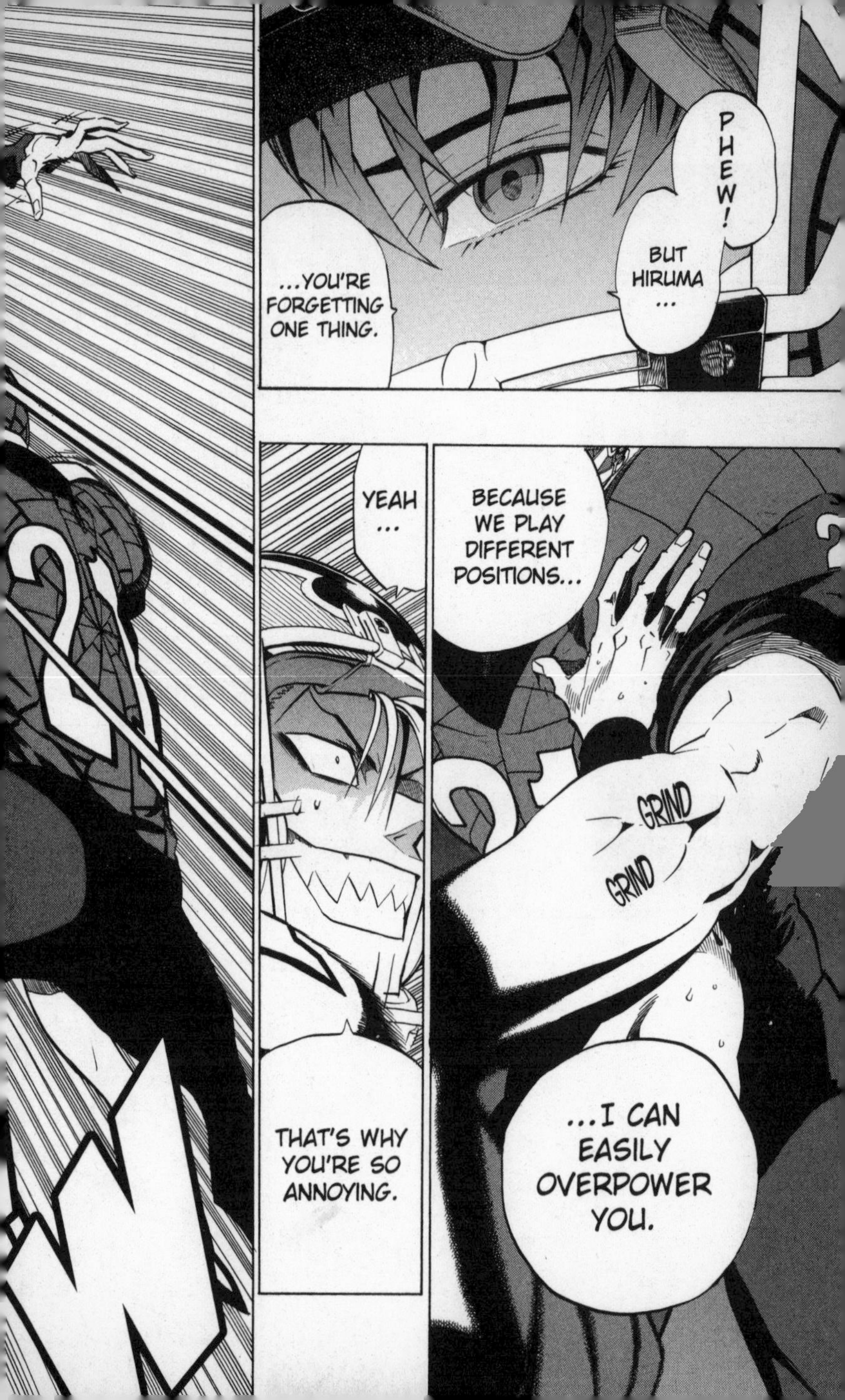
PHEW!
BUT HIRUMA...
...YOU'RE FORGETTING ONE THING.
BECAUSE WE PLAY DIFFERENT POSITIONS...
GRIND
GRIND
...I CAN EASILY OVERPOWER YOU.
YEAH...
THAT'S WHY YOU'RE SO ANNOYING.

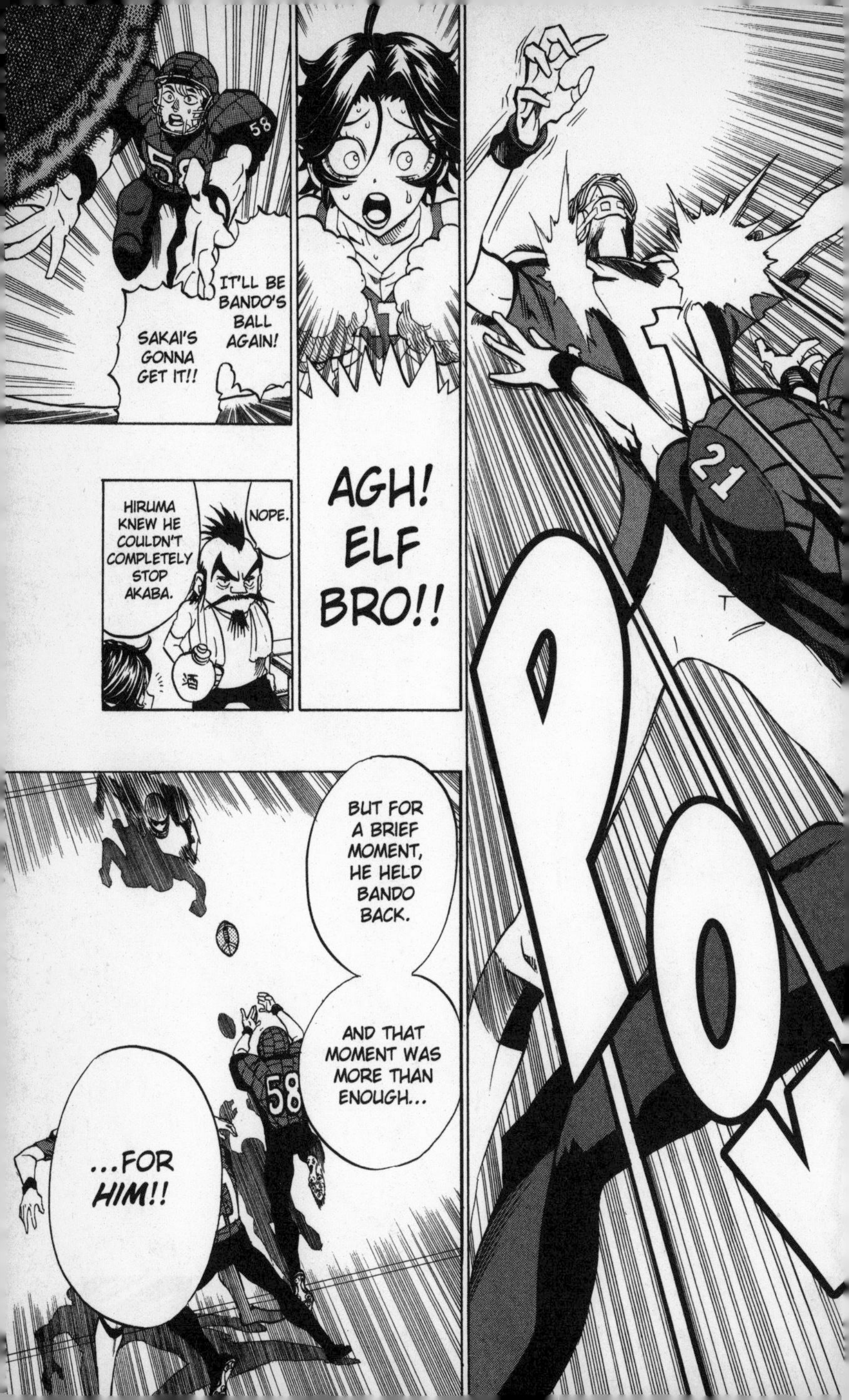
AGH! ELF BRO!!
IT'LL BE BANDO'S BALL AGAIN!
SAKAI'S GONNA GET IT!!
NOPE.
HIRUMA KNEW HE COULDN'T COMPLETELY STOP AKABA.
酒
BUT FOR A BRIEF MOMENT, HE HELD BANDO BACK.
AND THAT MOMENT WAS MORE THAN ENOUGH...
...FOR *HIM*!!

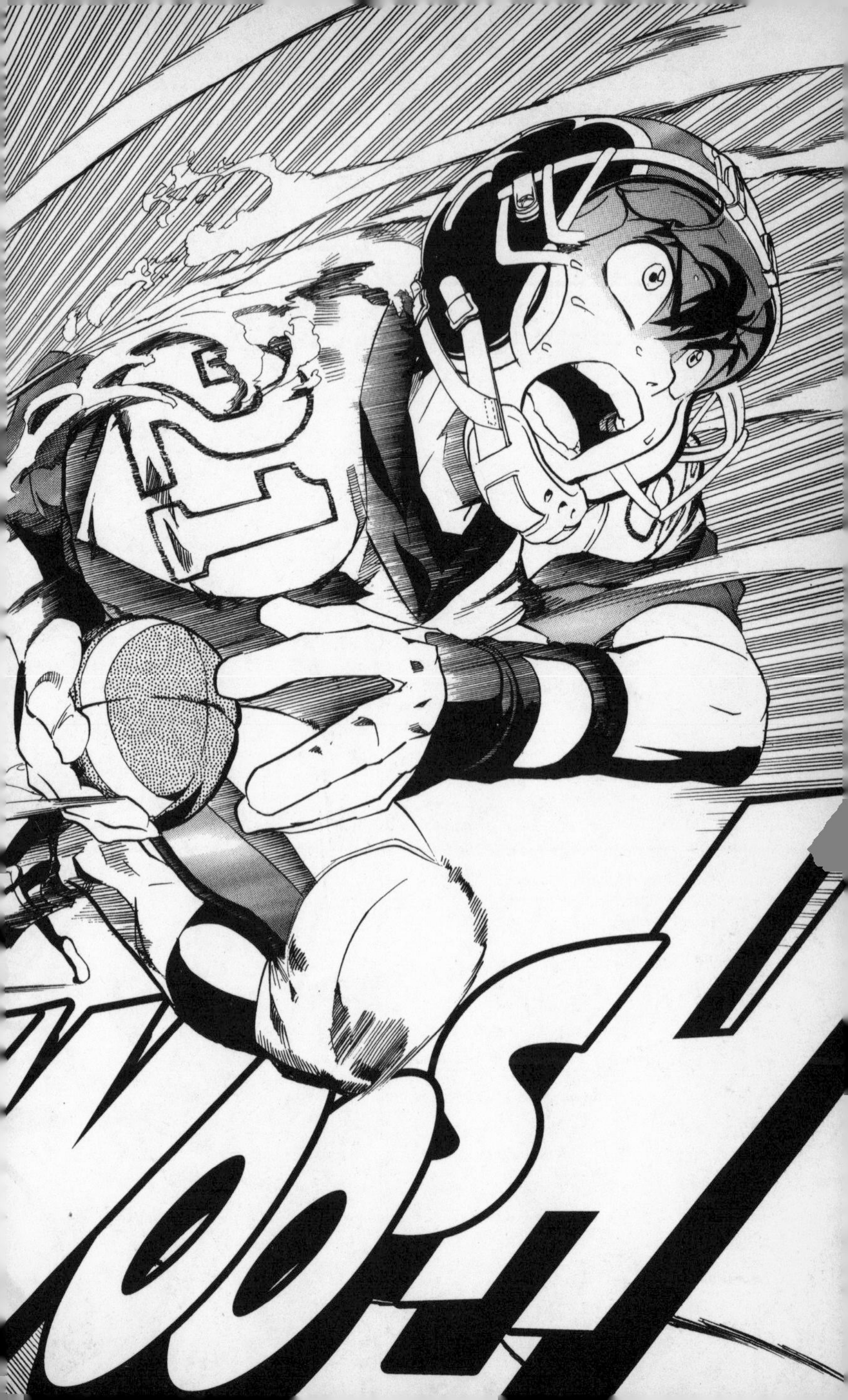
WOOSH!

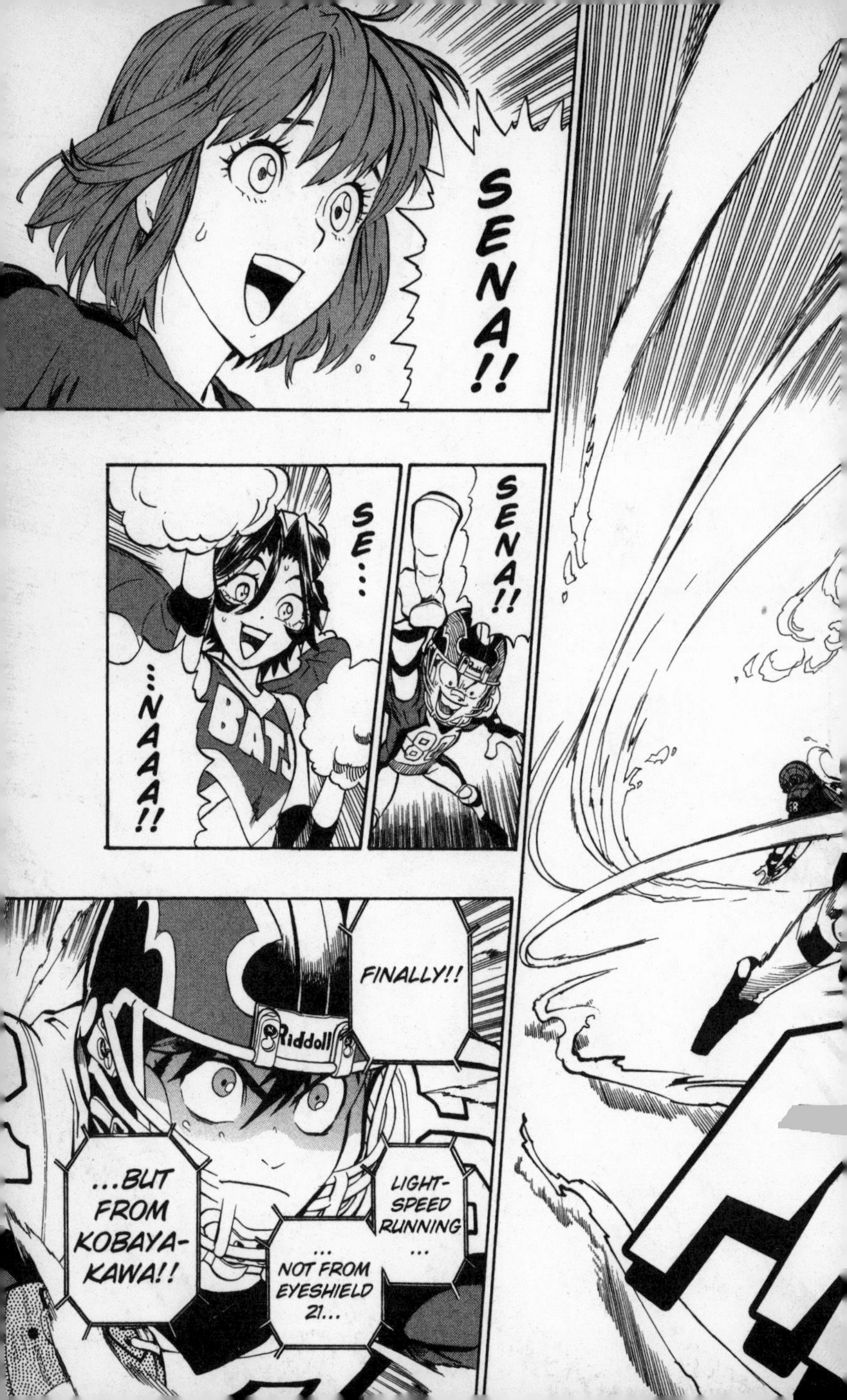
SENA!!
SENA!!
SE...
...NAAAA!!
FINALLY!!
LIGHT-SPEED RUNNING...
...NOT FROM EYESHIELD 21...
...BUT FROM KOBAYA-KAWA!!

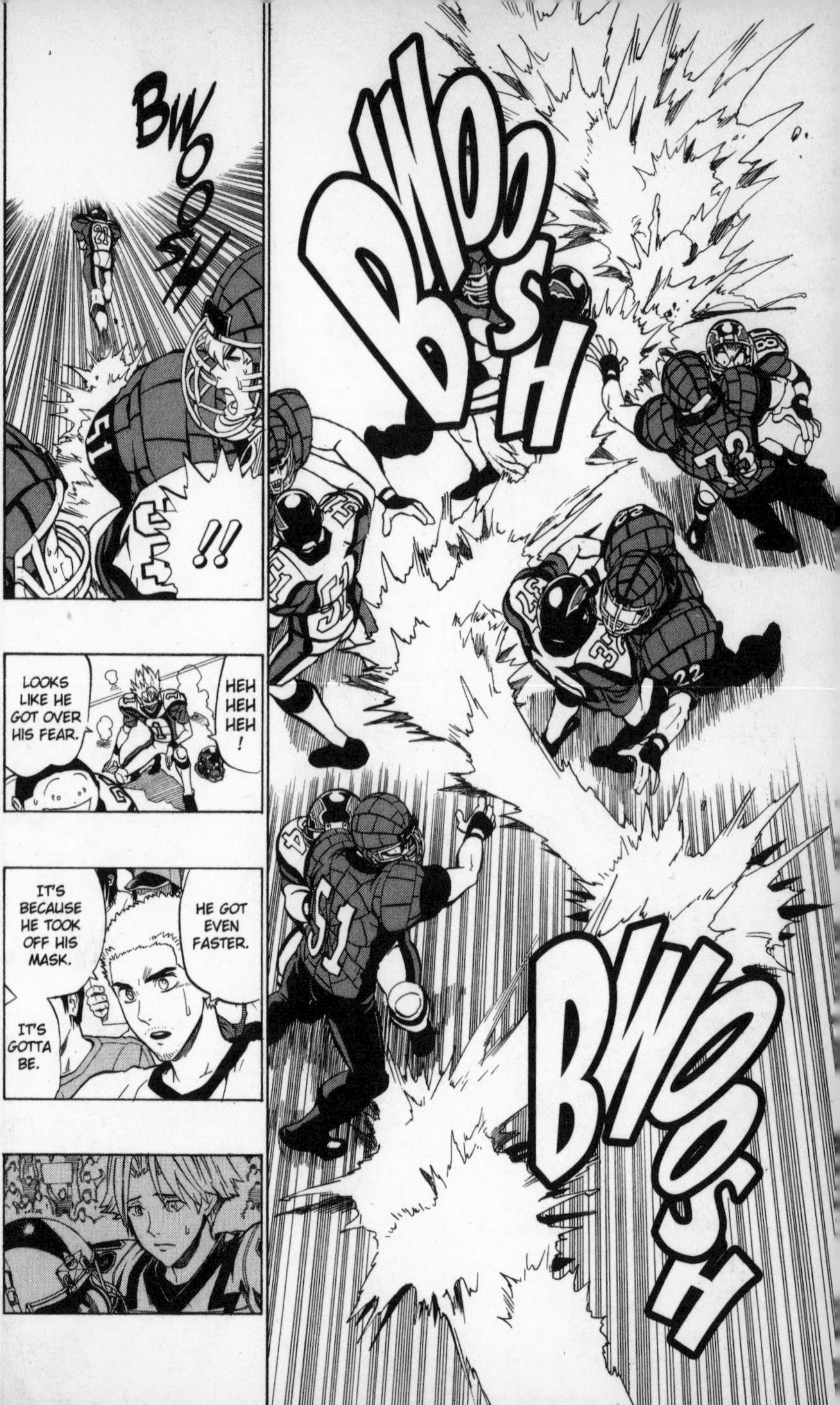
BWOOSH
BWOOSH
BWOOOSH
!!
HEH HEH HEH!
LOOKS LIKE HE GOT OVER HIS FEAR.
HE GOT EVEN FASTER.
IT'S BECAUSE HE TOOK OFF HIS MASK.
IT'S GOTTA BE.

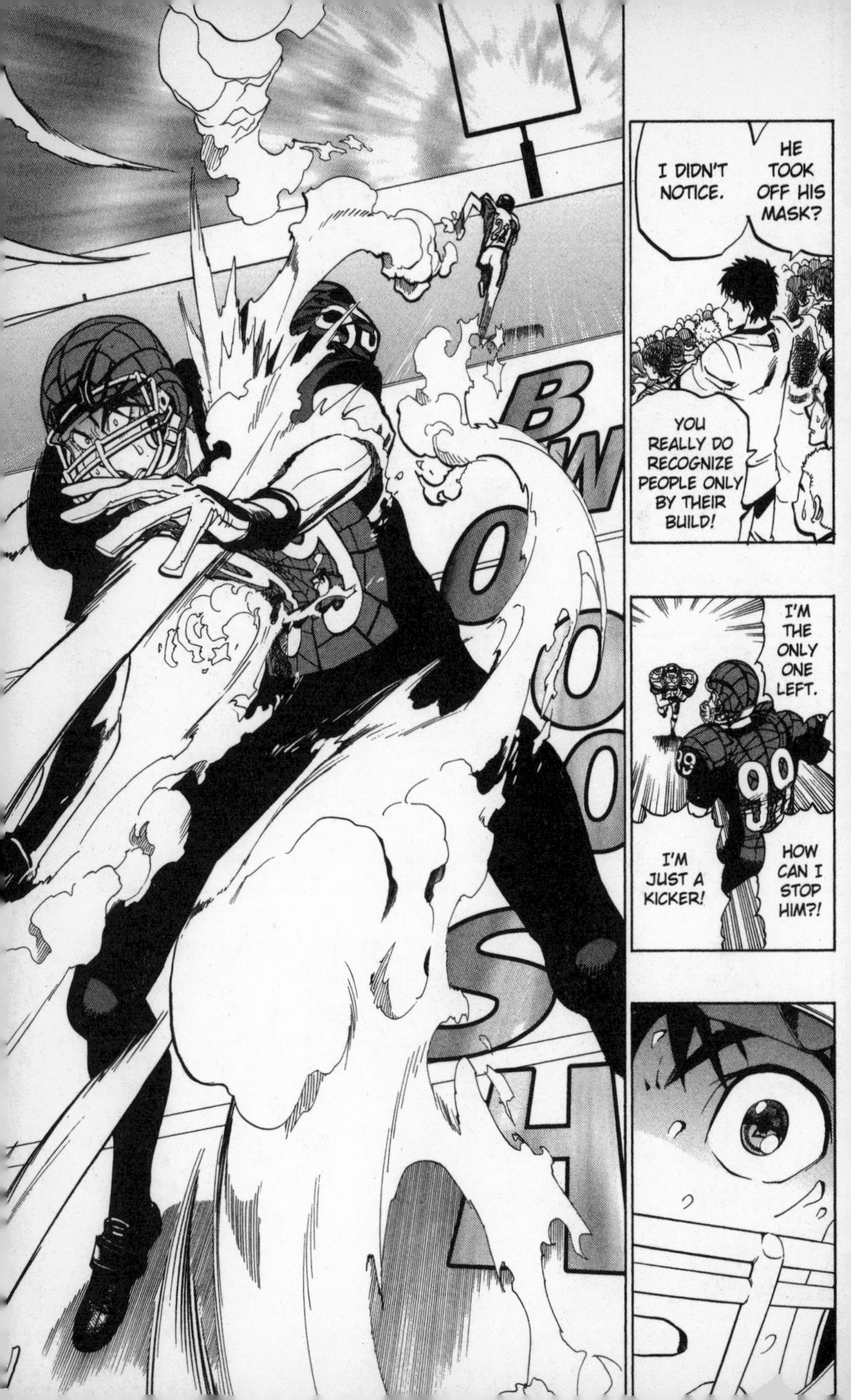
HE TOOK OFF HIS MASK?
I DIDN'T NOTICE.
YOU REALLY DO RECOGNIZE PEOPLE ONLY BY THEIR BUILD!
I'M THE ONLY ONE LEFT.
HOW CAN I STOP HIM?!
I'M JUST A KICKER!
BWOOOSH

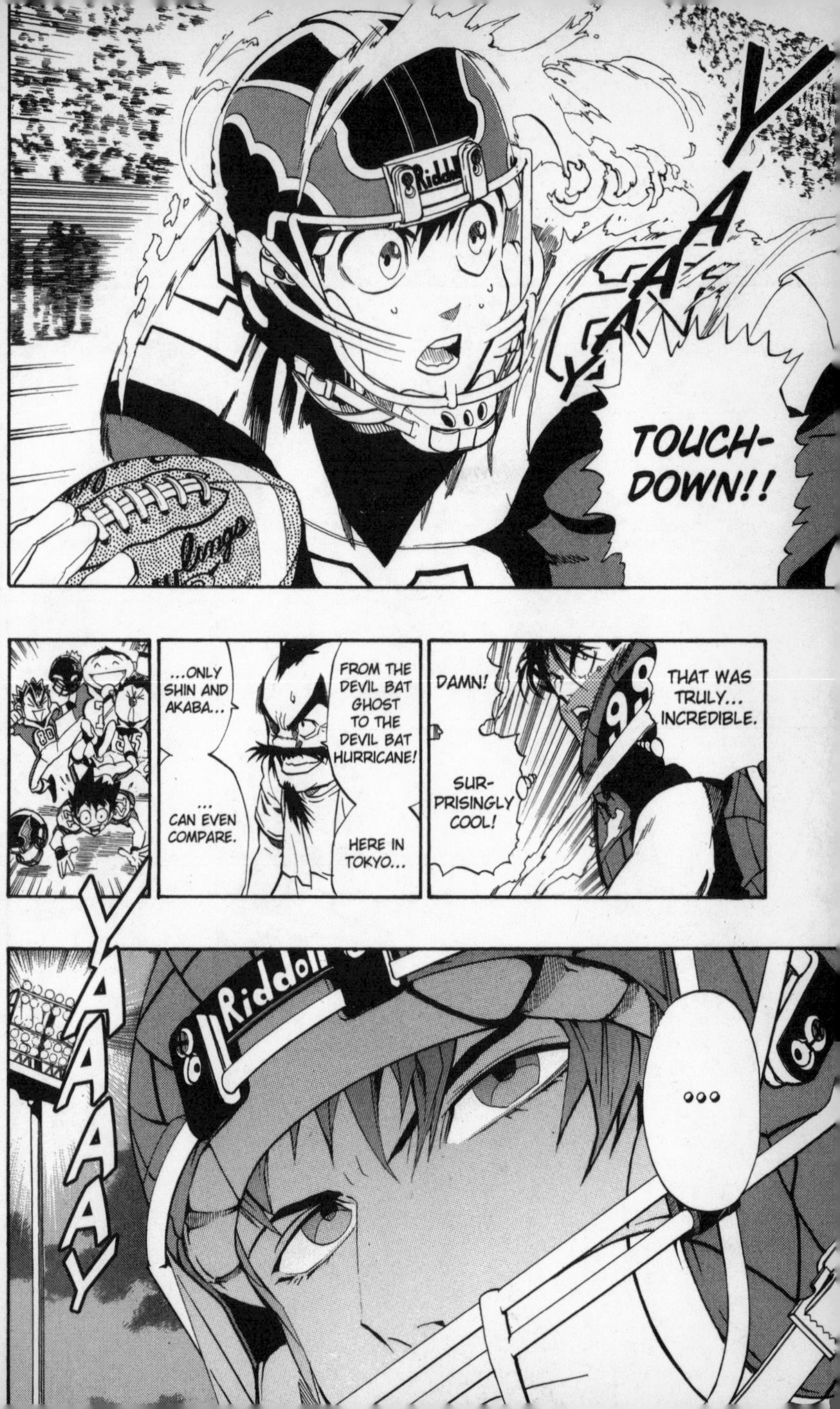
YAAAY
TOUCH-DOWN!!
THAT WAS TRULY... INCREDIBLE.
DAMN!
SUR-PRISINGLY COOL!
FROM THE DEVIL BAT GHOST TO THE DEVIL BAT HURRICANE!
HERE IN TOKYO...
...ONLY SHIN AND AKABA...
...CAN EVEN COMPARE.
...
YAAAAY

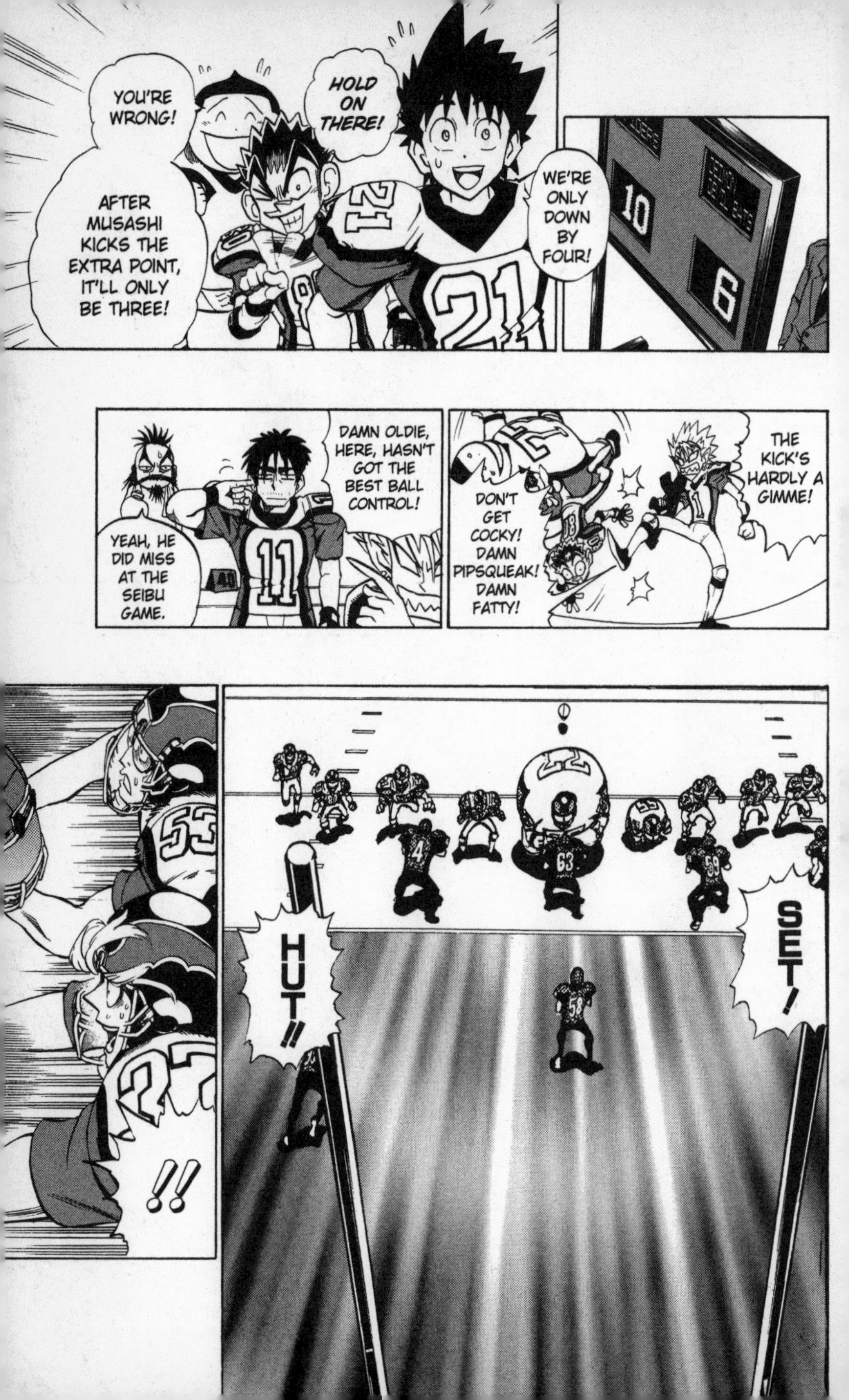
WE'RE ONLY DOWN BY FOUR!
HOLD ON THERE!
YOU'RE WRONG!
AFTER MUSASHI KICKS THE EXTRA POINT, IT'LL ONLY BE THREE!
10
6
THE KICK'S HARDLY A GIMME!
DON'T GET COCKY! DAMN PIPSQUEAK! DAMN FATTY!
DAMN OLDIE, HERE, HASN'T GOT THE BEST BALL CONTROL!
YEAH, HE DID MISS AT THE SEIBU GAME.
!
SET!
HUT!!
!!

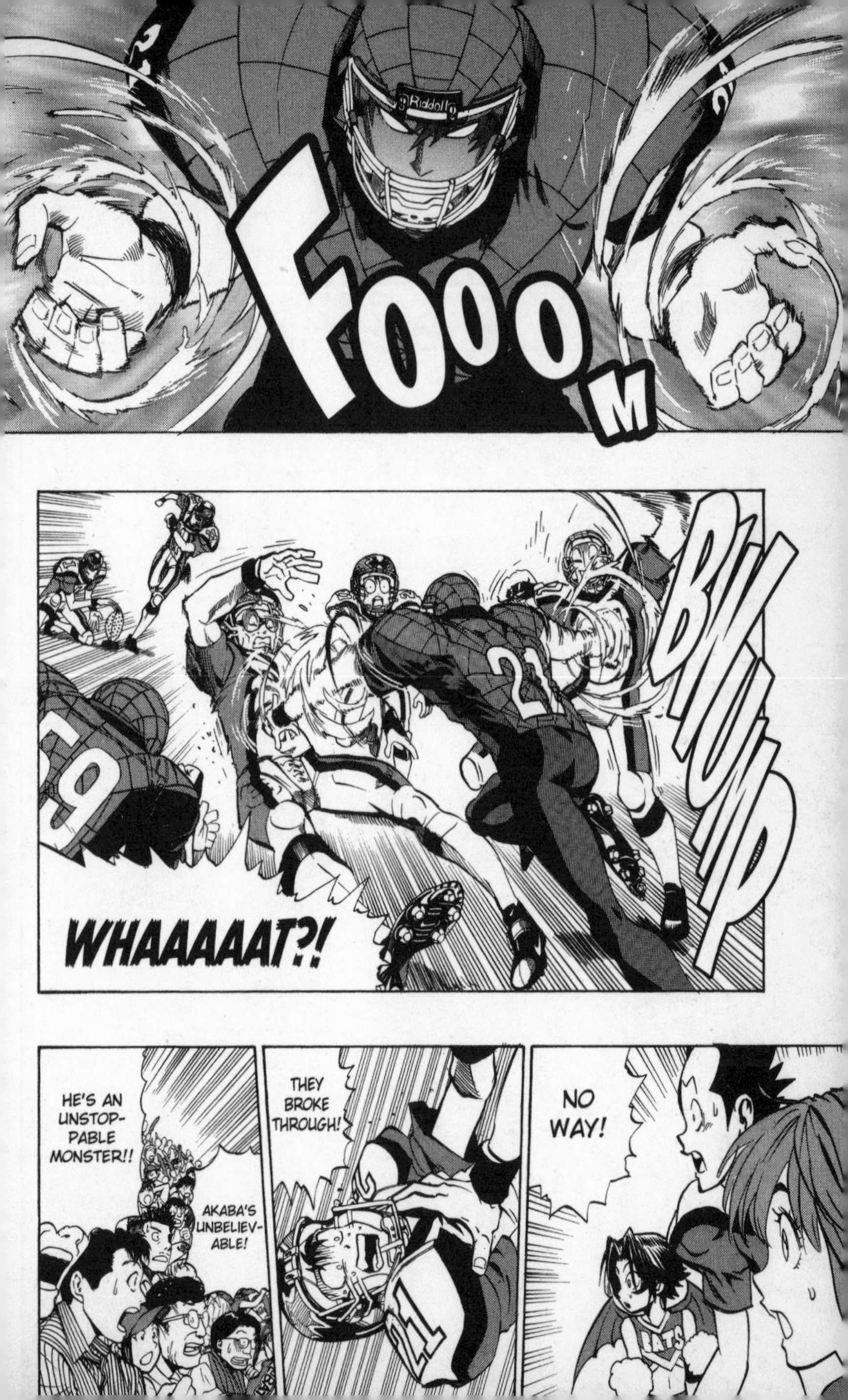
FOOOM
WHAAAAAT?!
NO WAY!
THEY BROKE THROUGH!
HE'S AN UNSTOP-PABLE MONSTER!!
AKABA'S UNBELIEV-ABLE!

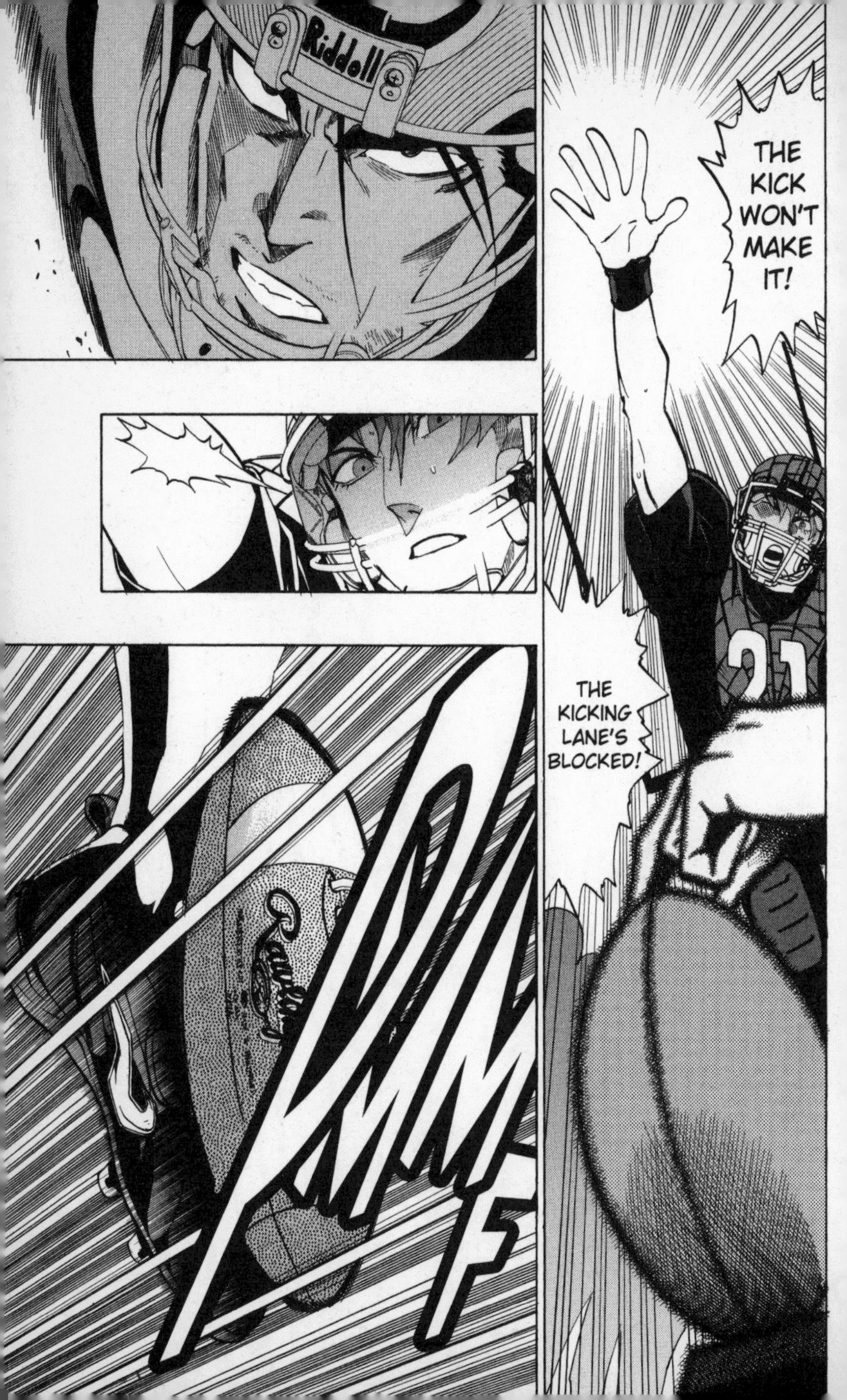
THE KICK WON'T MAKE IT!
THE KICKING LANE'S BLOCKED!
Riddell

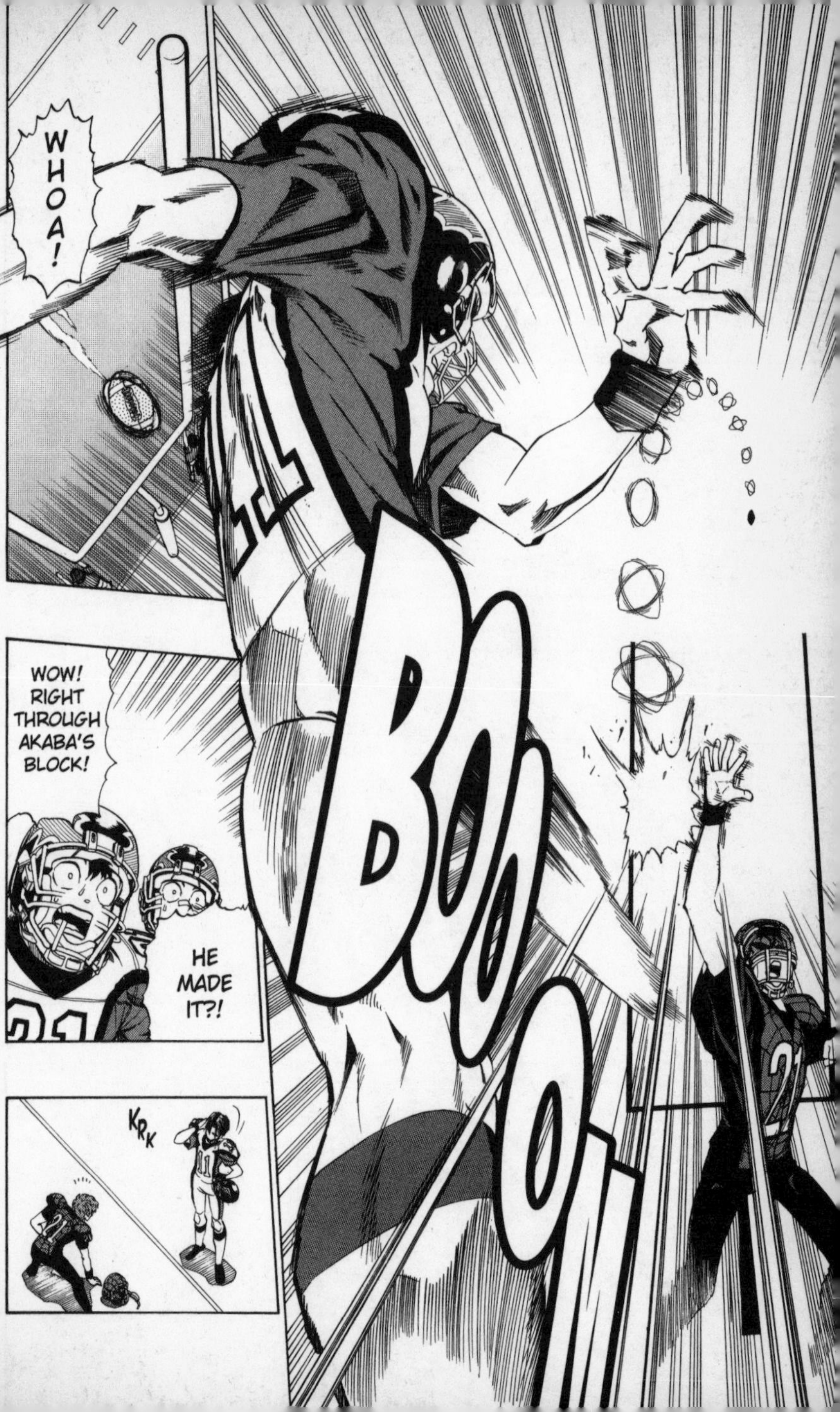
BOOO!!
WHOA!
WOW! RIGHT THROUGH AKABA'S BLOCK!
HE MADE IT?!
KRK

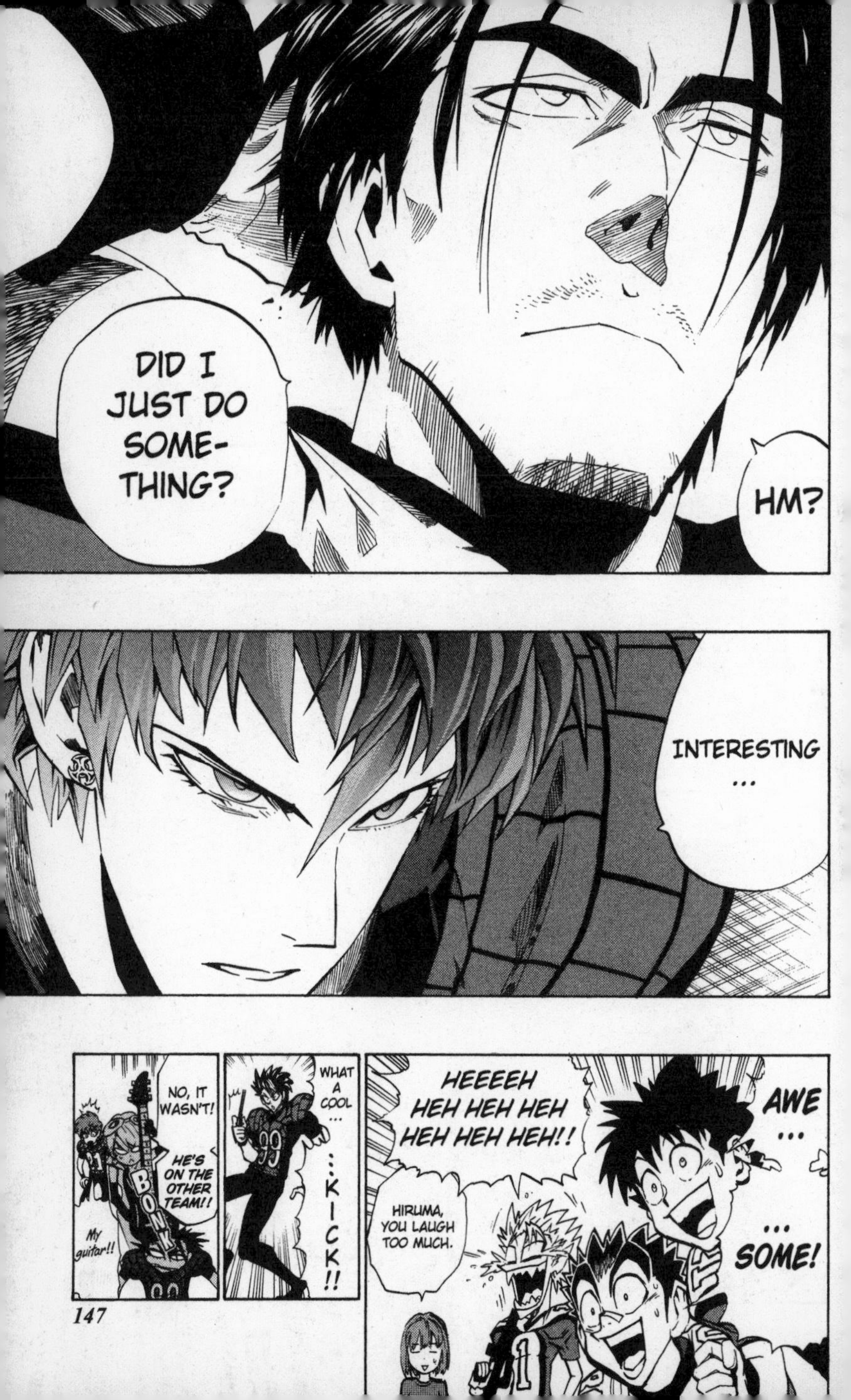
HM?
DID I JUST DO SOME-THING?
INTERESTING ...
AWE ... ... SOME!
HEEEEH HEH HEH HEH HEH HEH HEH!!
HIRUMA, YOU LAUGH TOO MUCH.
WHAT A COOL ...
...KICK!!
NO, IT WASN'T!
HE'S ON THE OTHER TEAM!!
BONK
My guitar!!

V-Bowl

Extra down 05

Cerberus on Skis

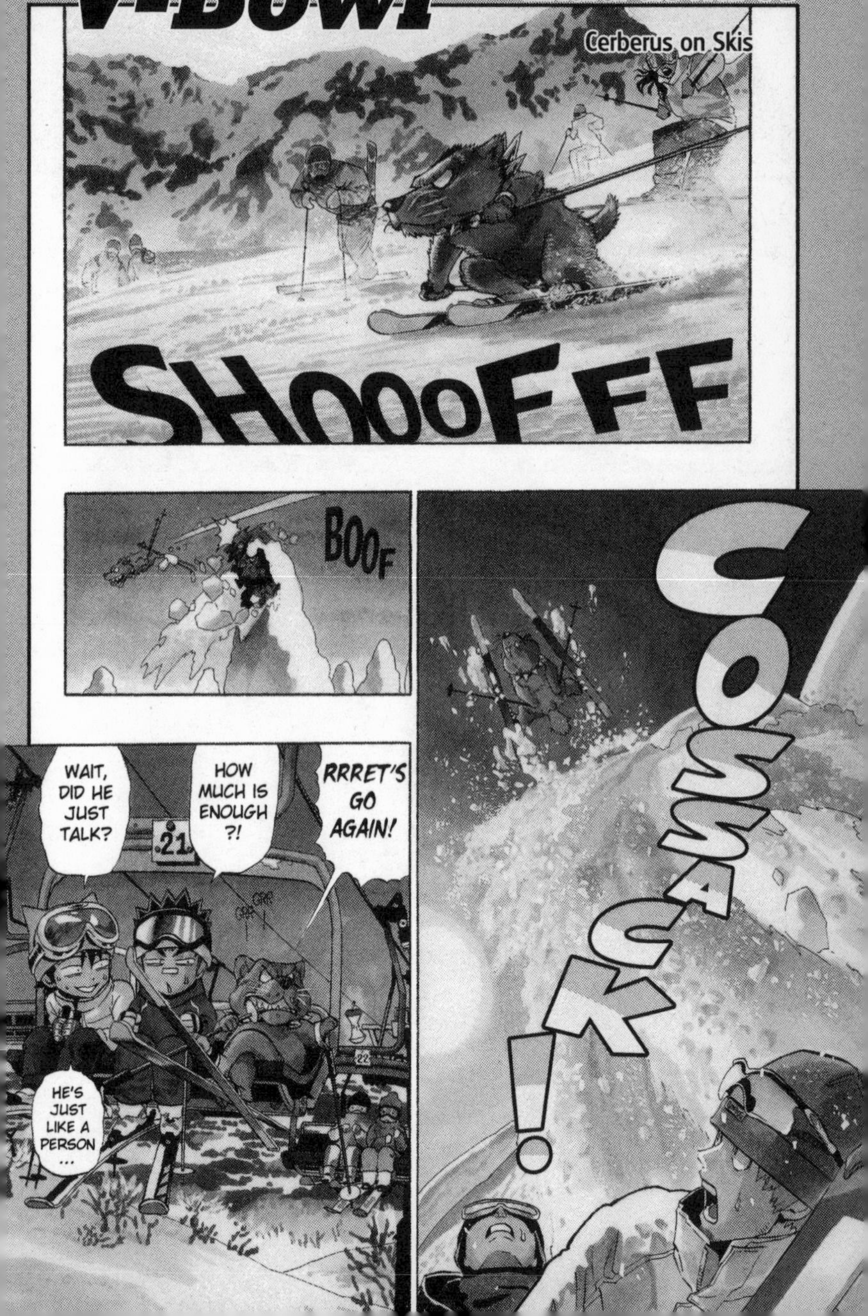
SHOOOFFF
COSSACK!
BOOF
RRRET'S GO AGAIN!
HOW MUCH IS ENOUGH?!
WAIT, DID HE JUST TALK?
HE'S JUST LIKE A PERSON...

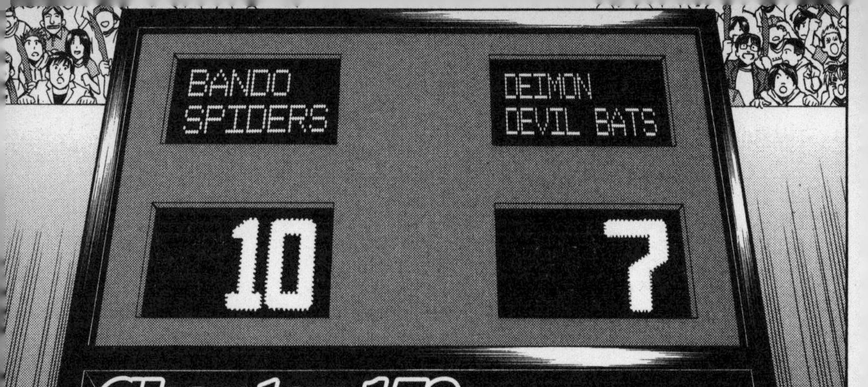
BANDO SPIDERS
DEIMON DEVIL BATS
10
7

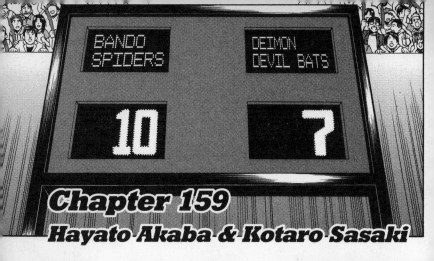

Chapter 159
Hayato Akaba & Kotaro Sasaki

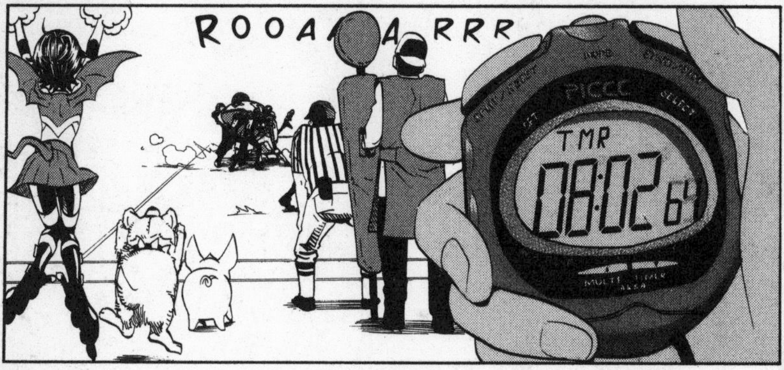
ROOA A RRR
TMR
08:02 64

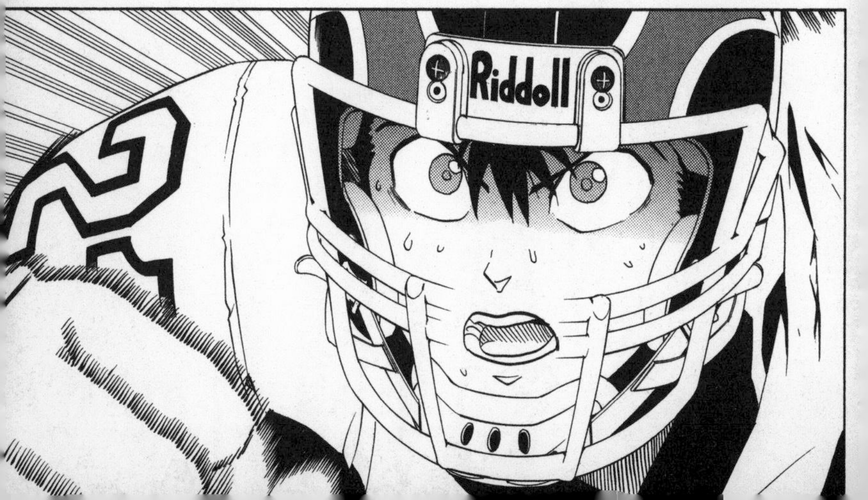
Riddoll

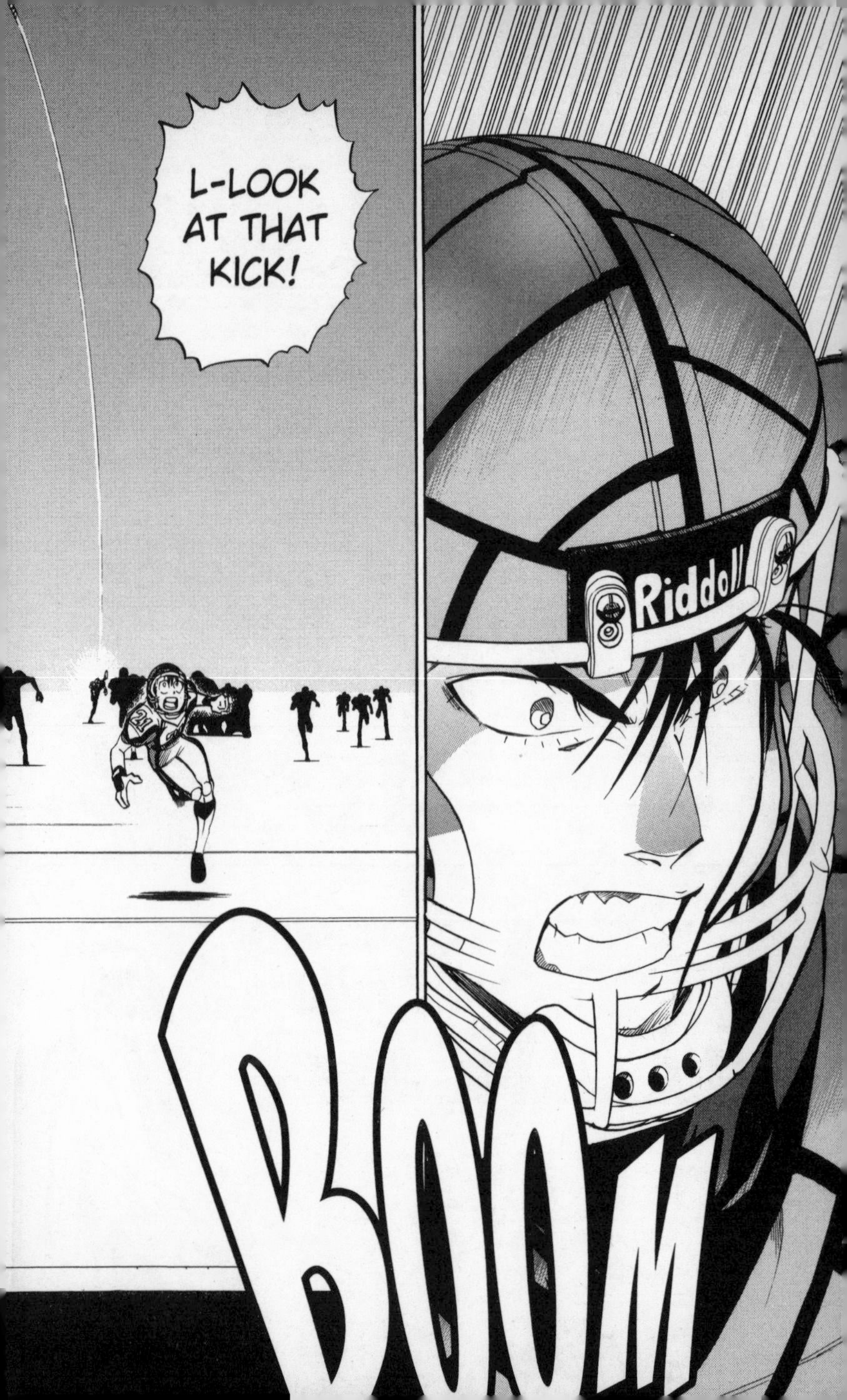
L-LOOK AT THAT KICK!
Riddoll
BOOM

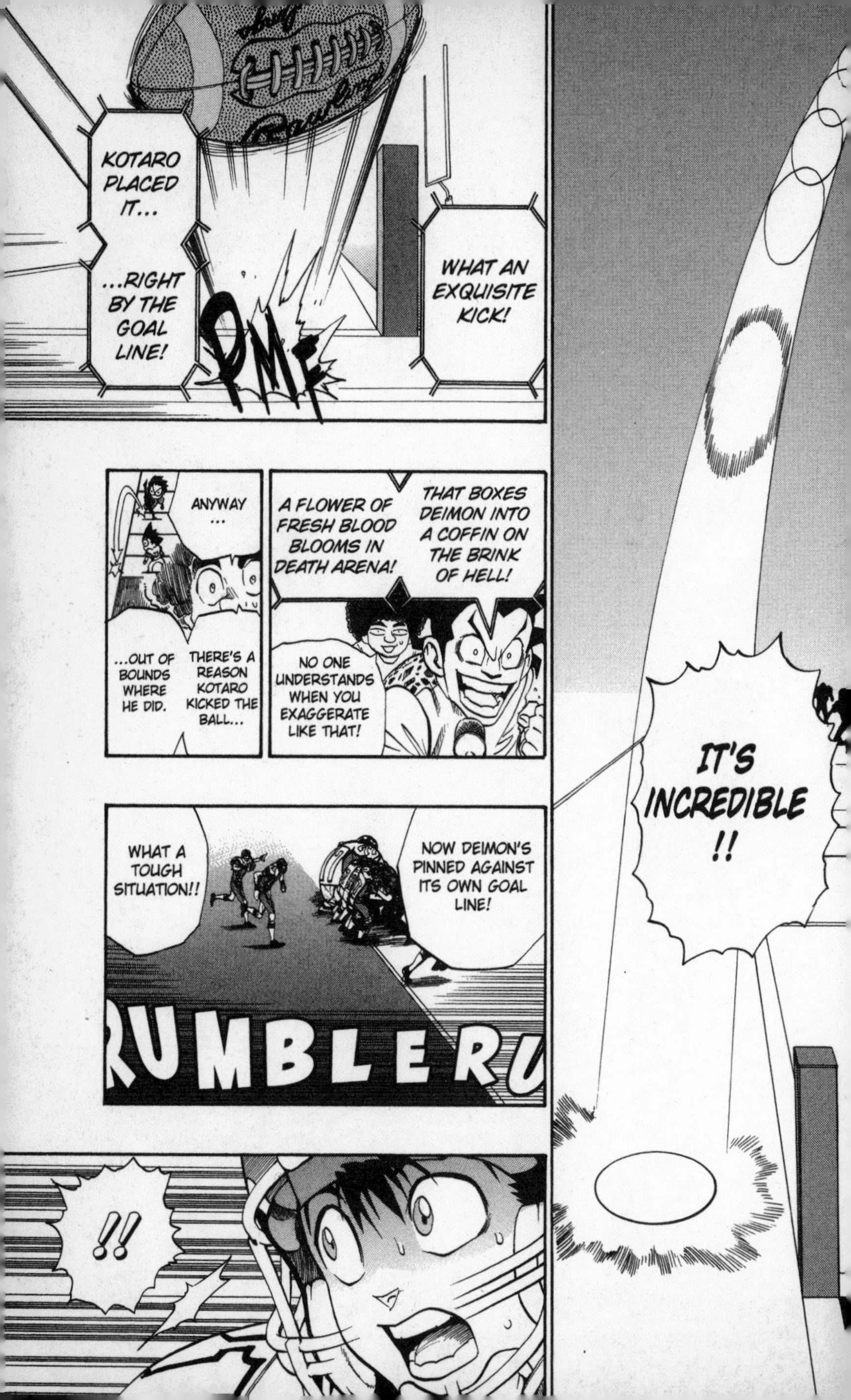
IT'S INCREDIBLE !!
WHAT AN EXQUISITE KICK!
KOTARO PLACED IT...
...RIGHT BY THE GOAL LINE!
PMF
THAT BOXES DEIMON INTO A COFFIN ON THE BRINK OF HELL!
A FLOWER OF FRESH BLOOD BLOOMS IN DEATH ARENA!
NO ONE UNDERSTANDS WHEN YOU EXAGGERATE LIKE THAT!
ANYWAY ...
THERE'S A REASON KOTARO KICKED THE BALL...
...OUT OF BOUNDS WHERE HE DID.
NOW DEIMON'S PINNED AGAINST ITS OWN GOAL LINE!
WHAT A TOUGH SITUATION!!
RUMBLERU
!!

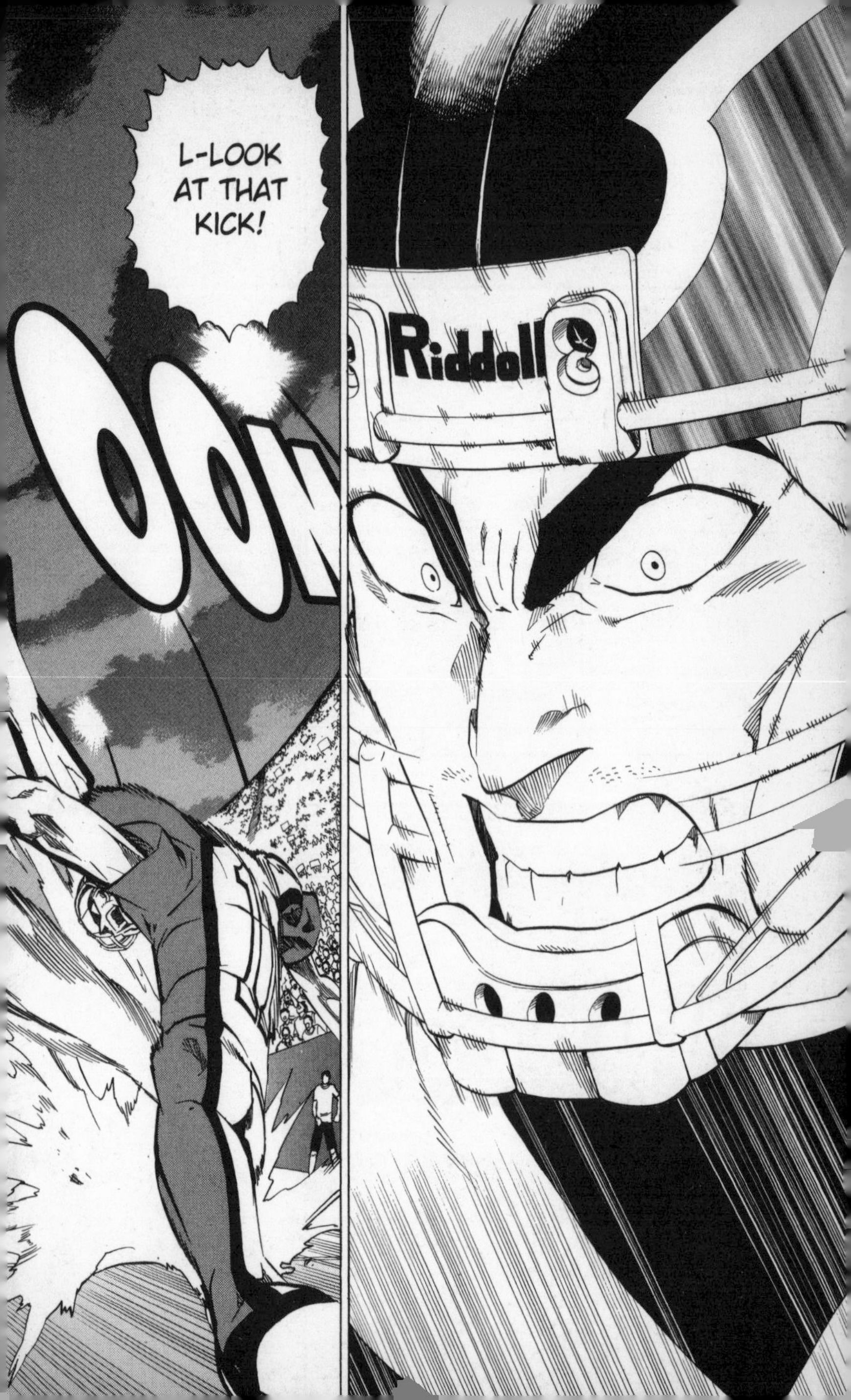
Riddoll
L-LOOK AT THAT KICK!

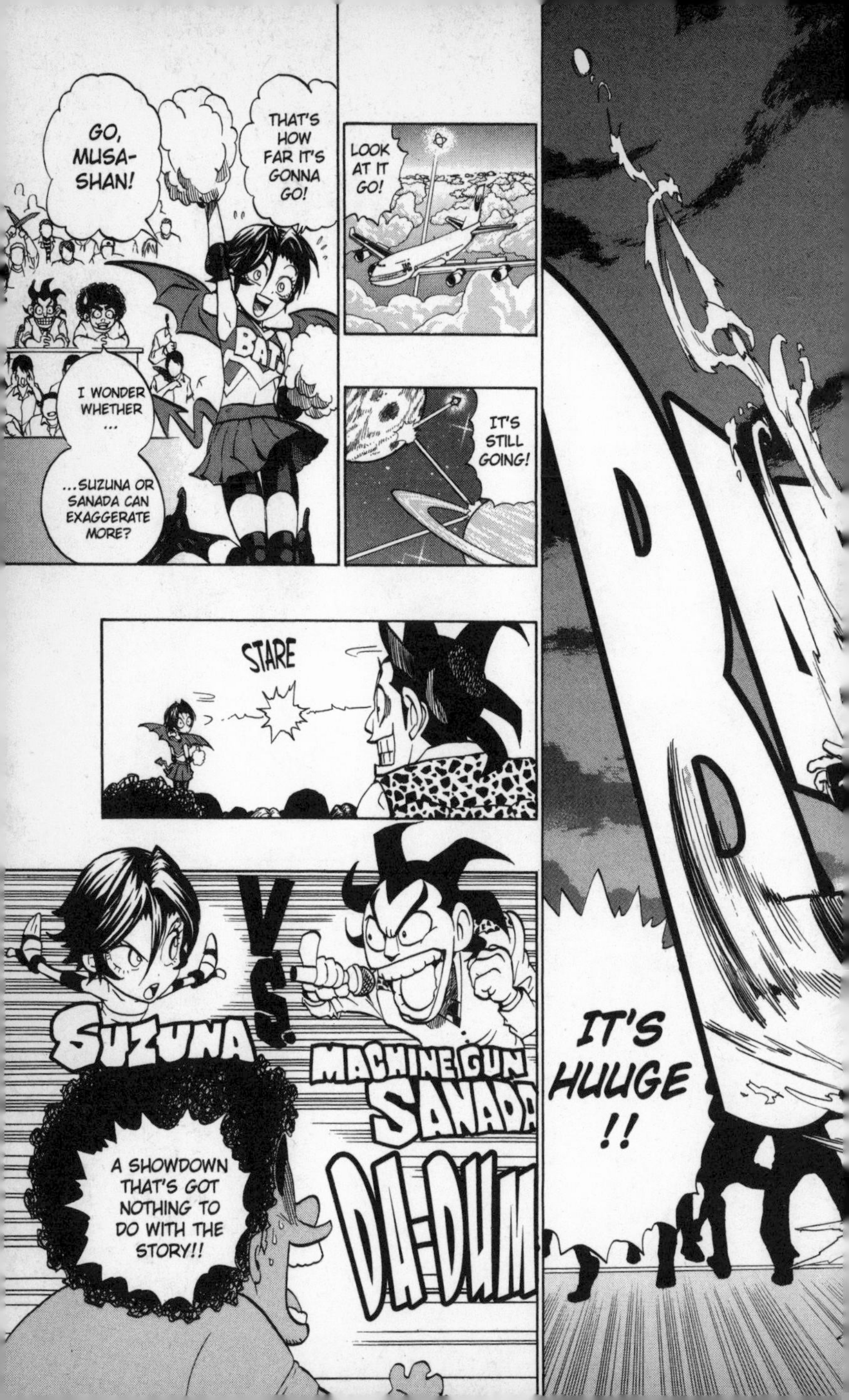
IT'S HUUGE !!
LOOK AT IT GO!
IT'S STILL GOING!
THAT'S HOW FAR IT'S GONNA GO!
GO, MUSA-SHAN!
I WONDER WHETHER ...
...SUZUNA OR SANADA CAN EXAGGERATE MORE?
STARE
MACHINE GUN SANADA
VS.
SUZUNA
DA-DUM
A SHOWDOWN THAT'S GOT NOTHING TO DO WITH THE STORY!!

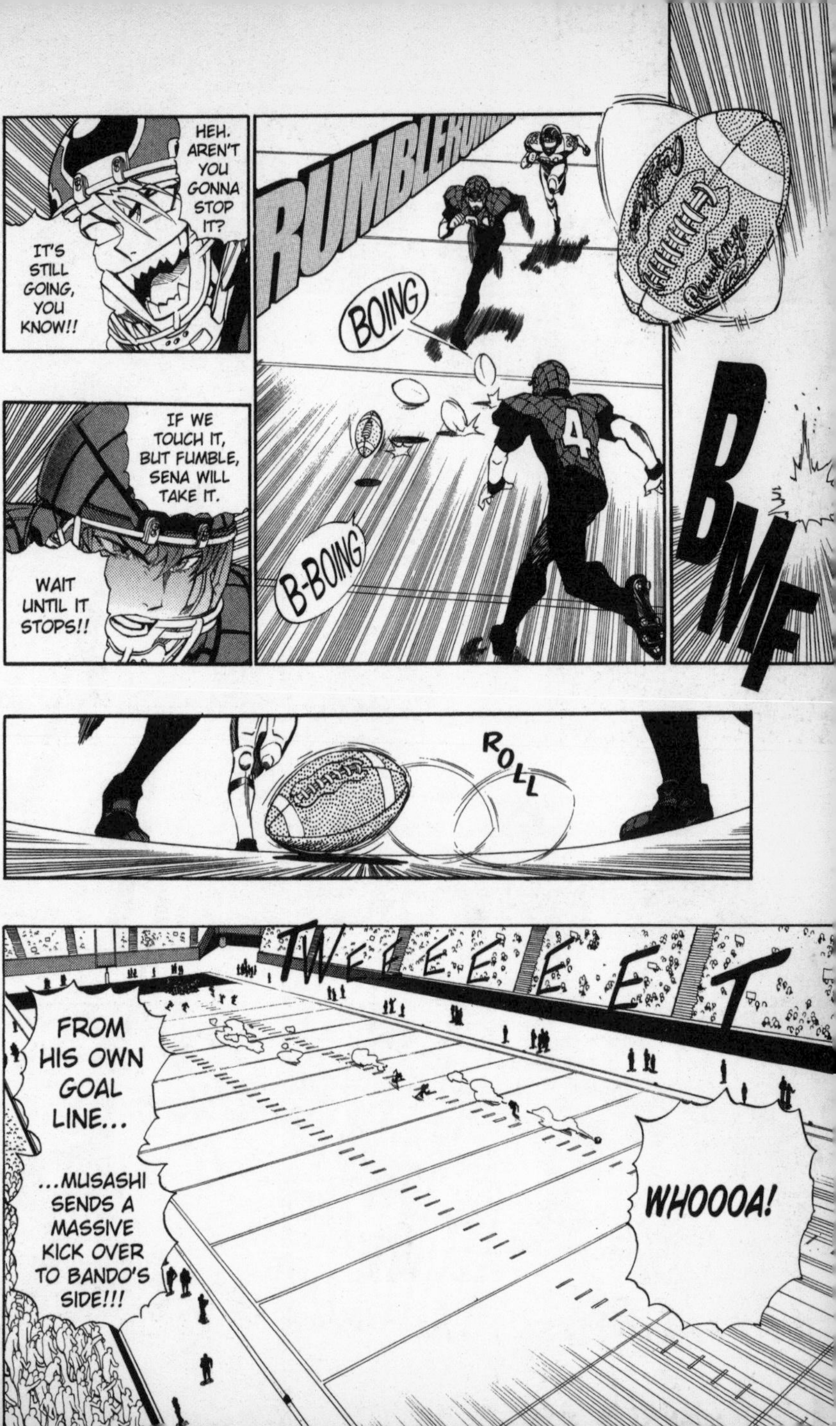

BMF
RUMBLERO
BOING
B-BOING
HEH. AREN'T YOU GONNA STOP IT?
IT'S STILL GOING, YOU KNOW!!
IF WE TOUCH IT, BUT FUMBLE, SENA WILL TAKE IT.
WAIT UNTIL IT STOPS!!
ROLL
TWEEEEEET
WHOOOA!
FROM HIS OWN GOAL LINE...
...MUSASHI SENDS A MASSIVE KICK OVER TO BANDO'S SIDE!!!

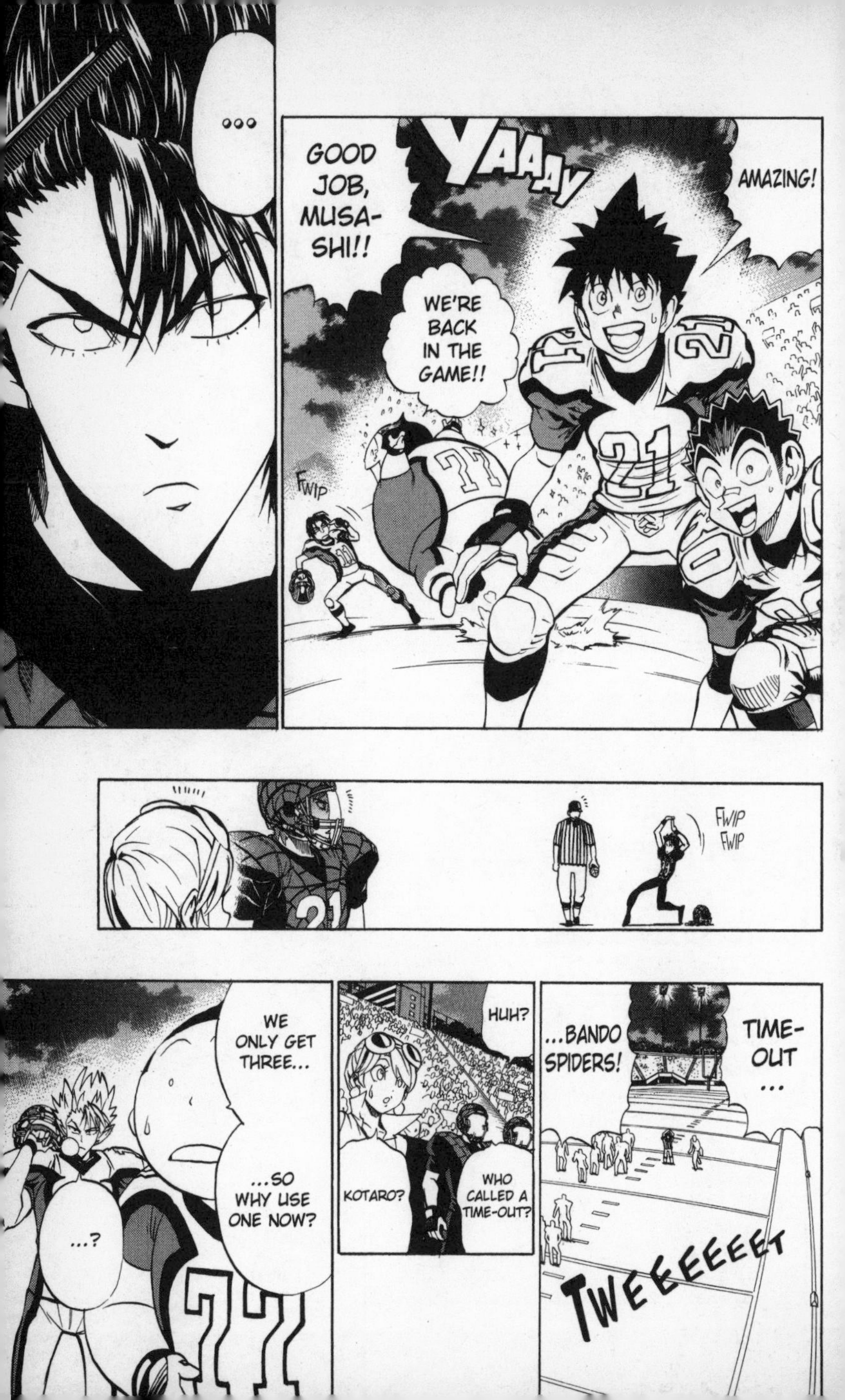
AMAZING!
YAAAAY
GOOD JOB, MUSASHI!!
WE'RE BACK IN THE GAME!!
FWIP
...
FWIP FWIP
TIME-OUT...
...BANDO SPIDERS!
TWEEEEEET
HUH?
WHO CALLED A TIME-OUT?
KOTARO?
WE ONLY GET THREE...
...SO WHY USE ONE NOW?
...?

ROARR

MUSASHI!

JUST LIKE I PROMISED...

...THIS GAME COMES DOWN TO OUR KICKING.

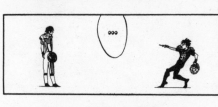

...

WITH THE KANTO TOURNAMENT AS PRIZE...

...LET'S SEE...

...WHO'S THE BEST KICKING TEAM EVER!!

DID YOU USE A TIME-OUT...

...JUST TO SAY THAT?!

HUUUHHHHH ~~~~ ?!

NO...

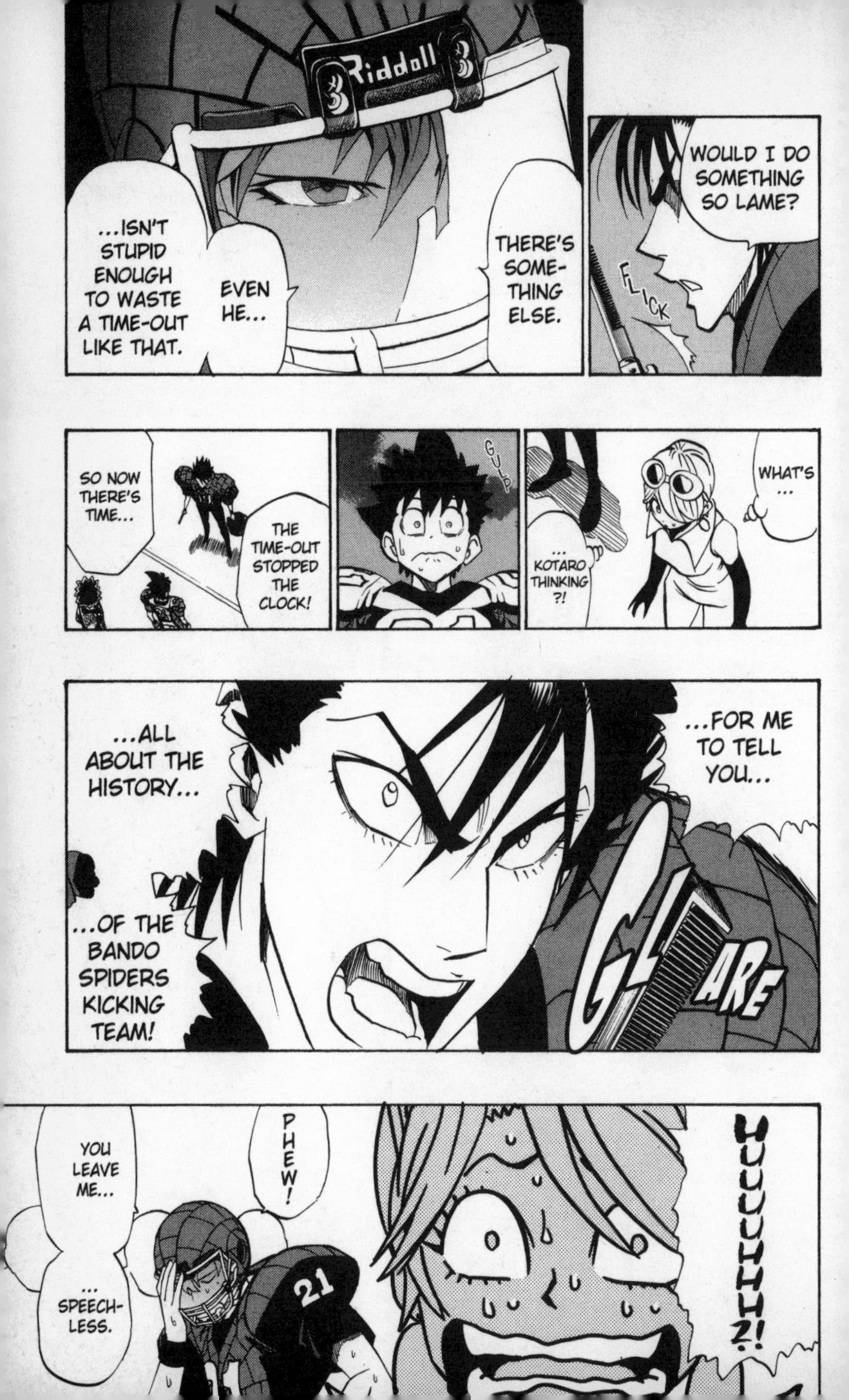
WOULD I DO SOMETHING SO LAME?
FLICK
Riddoll
THERE'S SOME-THING ELSE.
EVEN HE...
...ISN'T STUPID ENOUGH TO WASTE A TIME-OUT LIKE THAT.
WHAT'S ...
...KOTARO THINKING?!
GULP
THE TIME-OUT STOPPED THE CLOCK!
SO NOW THERE'S TIME...
...FOR ME TO TELL YOU...
...ALL ABOUT THE HISTORY...
GLARE
...OF THE BANDO SPIDERS KICKING TEAM!
HUUUUHHH?!
PHEW!
YOU LEAVE ME...
...SPEECH-LESS.
21

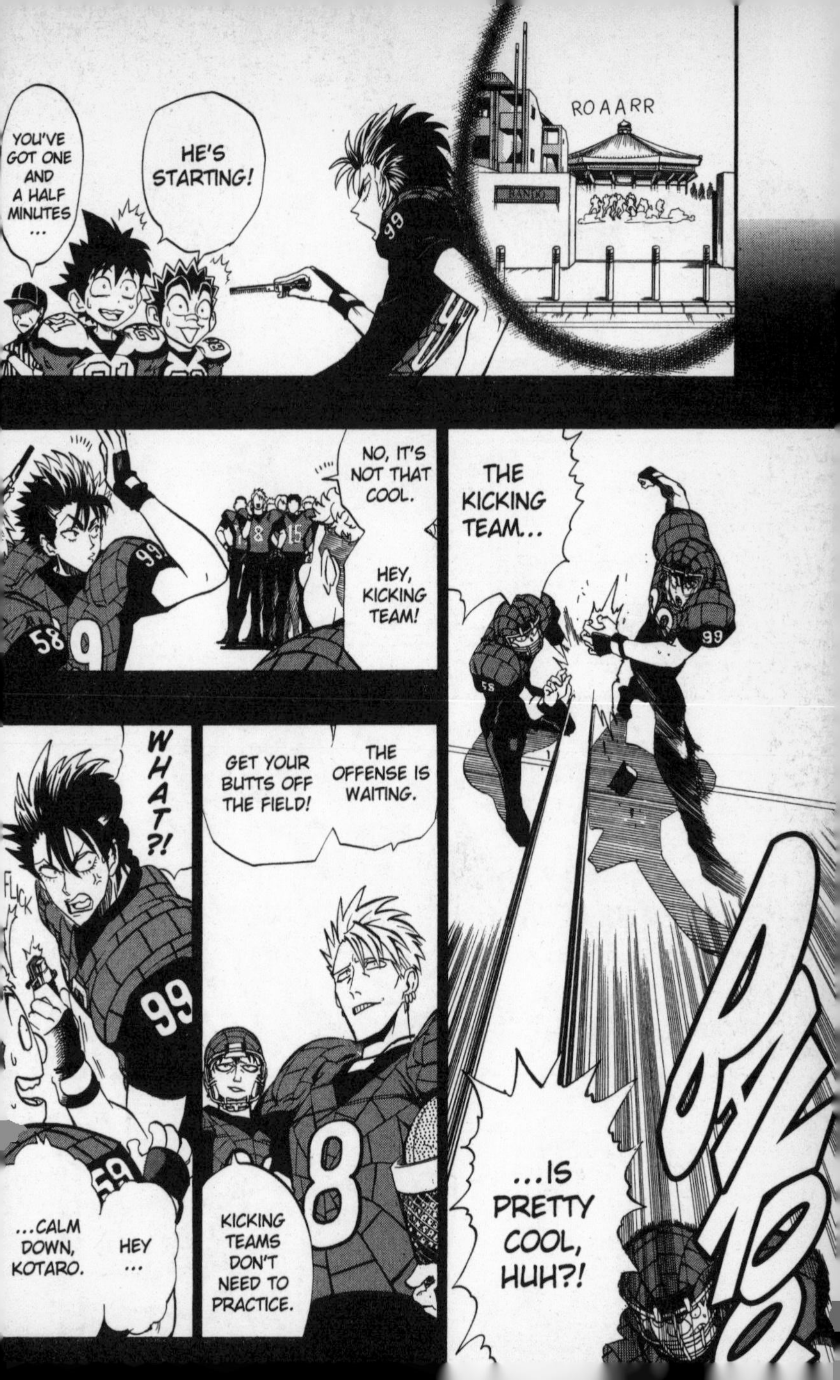
ROAARR
HE'S STARTING!
YOU'VE GOT ONE AND A HALF MINUTES...
THE KICKING TEAM...
...IS PRETTY COOL, HUH?!
NO, IT'S NOT THAT COOL.
HEY, KICKING TEAM!
THE OFFENSE IS WAITING.
GET YOUR BUTTS OFF THE FIELD!
KICKING TEAMS DON'T NEED TO PRACTICE.
WHAT?!
FLICK
HEY...
...CALM DOWN, KOTARO.

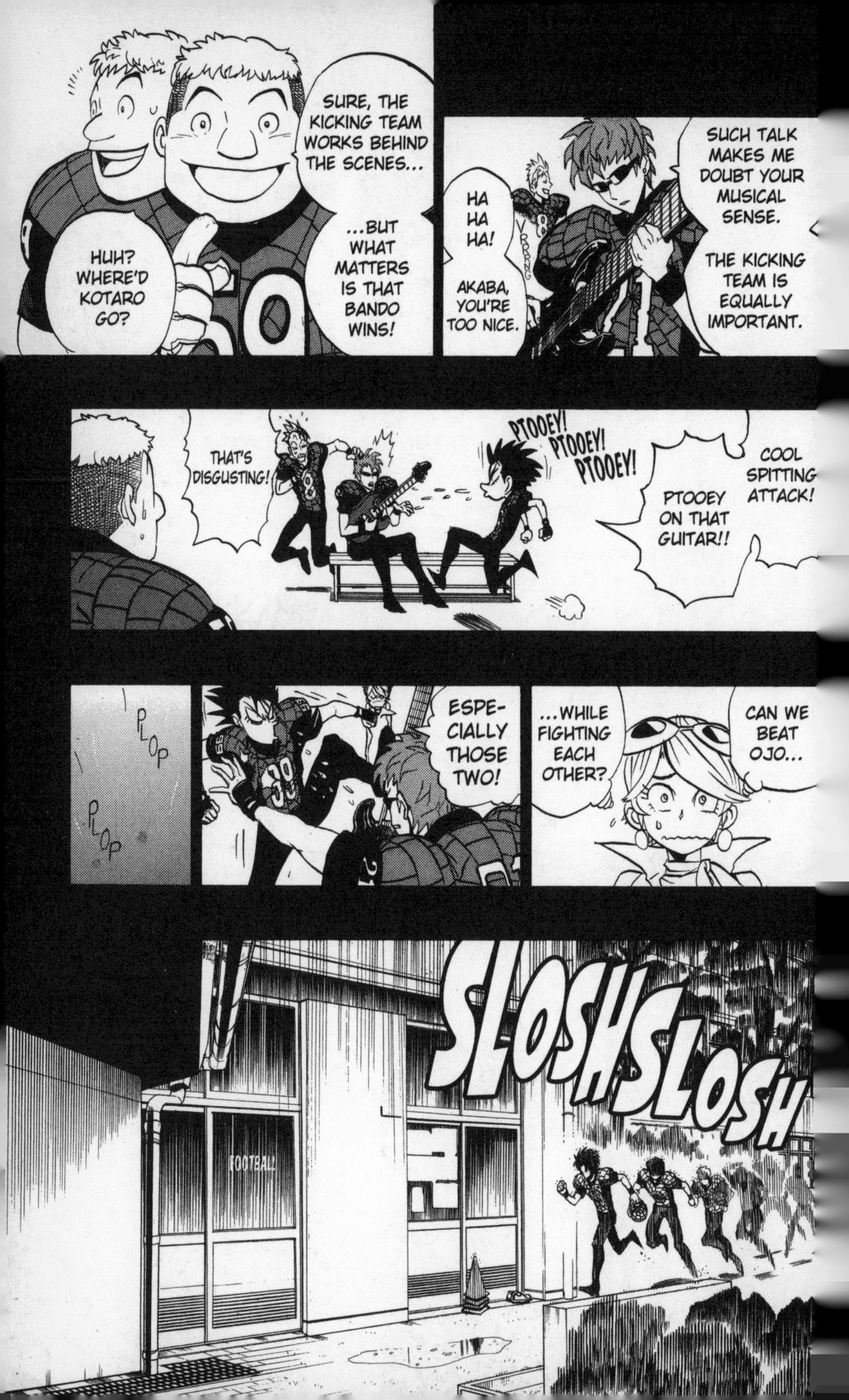
SUCH TALK MAKES ME DOUBT YOUR MUSICAL SENSE.
THE KICKING TEAM IS EQUALLY IMPORTANT.
VRRRNG
HA HA HA!
AKABA, YOU'RE TOO NICE.
SURE, THE KICKING TEAM WORKS BEHIND THE SCENES...
...BUT WHAT MATTERS IS THAT BANDO WINS!
HUH? WHERE'D KOTARO GO?
COOL SPITTING ATTACK!
PTOOEY ON THAT GUITAR!!
PTOOEY! PTOOEY! PTOOEY!
THAT'S DISGUSTING!
CAN WE BEAT OJO...
...WHILE FIGHTING EACH OTHER?
ESPE-CIALLY THOSE TWO!
PLOP
PLOP
SLOSH SLOSH
FOOTBALL

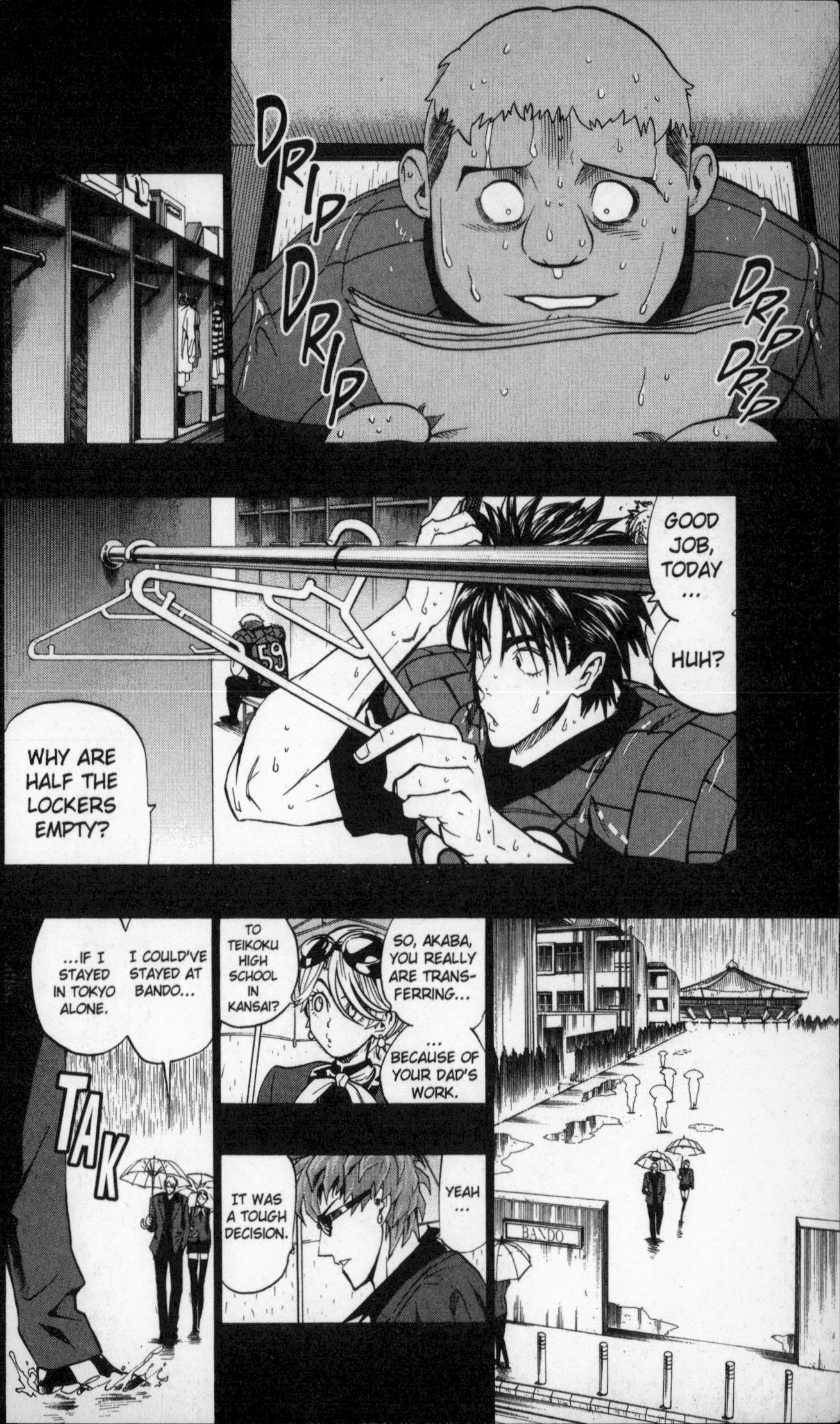
DRIP DRIP DRIP DRIP
DRIP DRIP DRIP DRIP
GOOD JOB, TODAY ...
HUH?
WHY ARE HALF THE LOCKERS EMPTY?
BANDO
SO, AKABA, YOU REALLY ARE TRANSFERRING...
TO TEIKOKU HIGH SCHOOL IN KANSAI?
... BECAUSE OF YOUR DAD'S WORK.
YEAH ...
IT WAS A TOUGH DECISION.
I COULD'VE STAYED AT BANDO...
...IF I STAYED IN TOKYO ALONE.
TAK

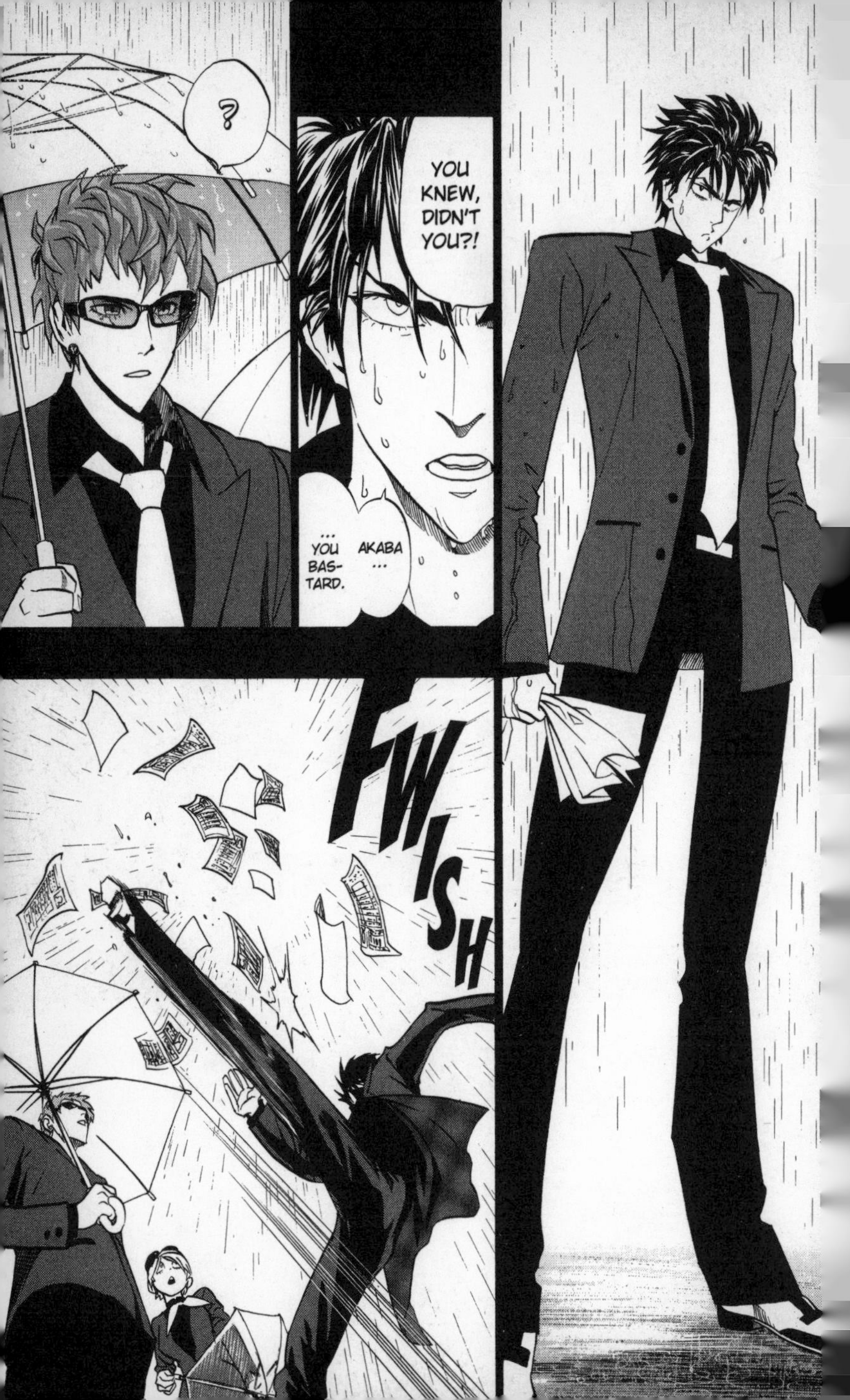
YOU KNEW, DIDN'T YOU?!
AKABA ... ... YOU BAS-TARD.
?
FWISH

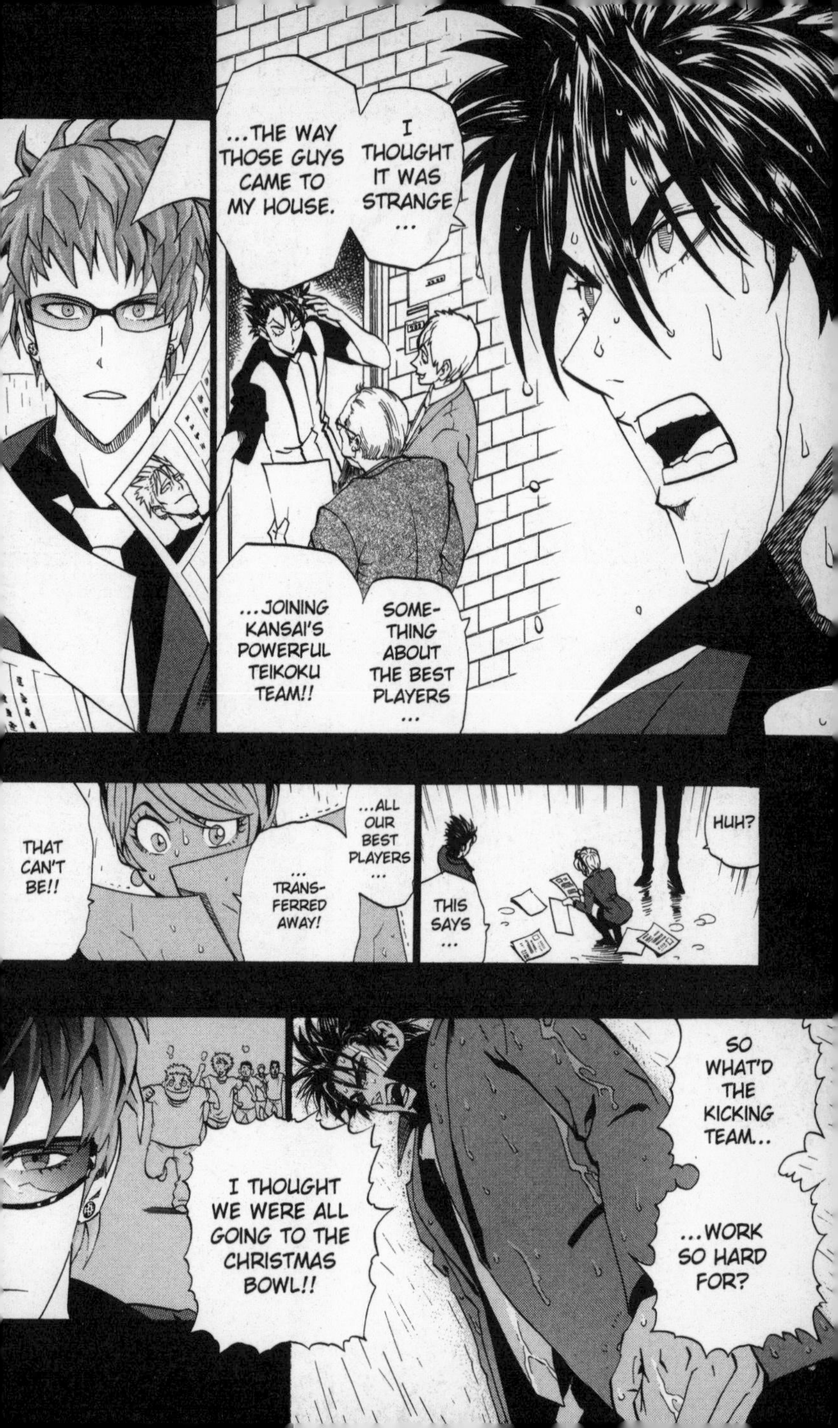
I THOUGHT IT WAS STRANGE...
...THE WAY THOSE GUYS CAME TO MY HOUSE.
SOME-THING ABOUT THE BEST PLAYERS...
...JOINING KANSAI'S POWERFUL TEIKOKU TEAM!!
HUH?
THIS SAYS...
...ALL OUR BEST PLAYERS...
...TRANS-FERRED AWAY!
THAT CAN'T BE!!
SO WHAT'D THE KICKING TEAM...
...WORK SO HARD FOR?
I THOUGHT WE WERE ALL GOING TO THE CHRISTMAS BOWL!!

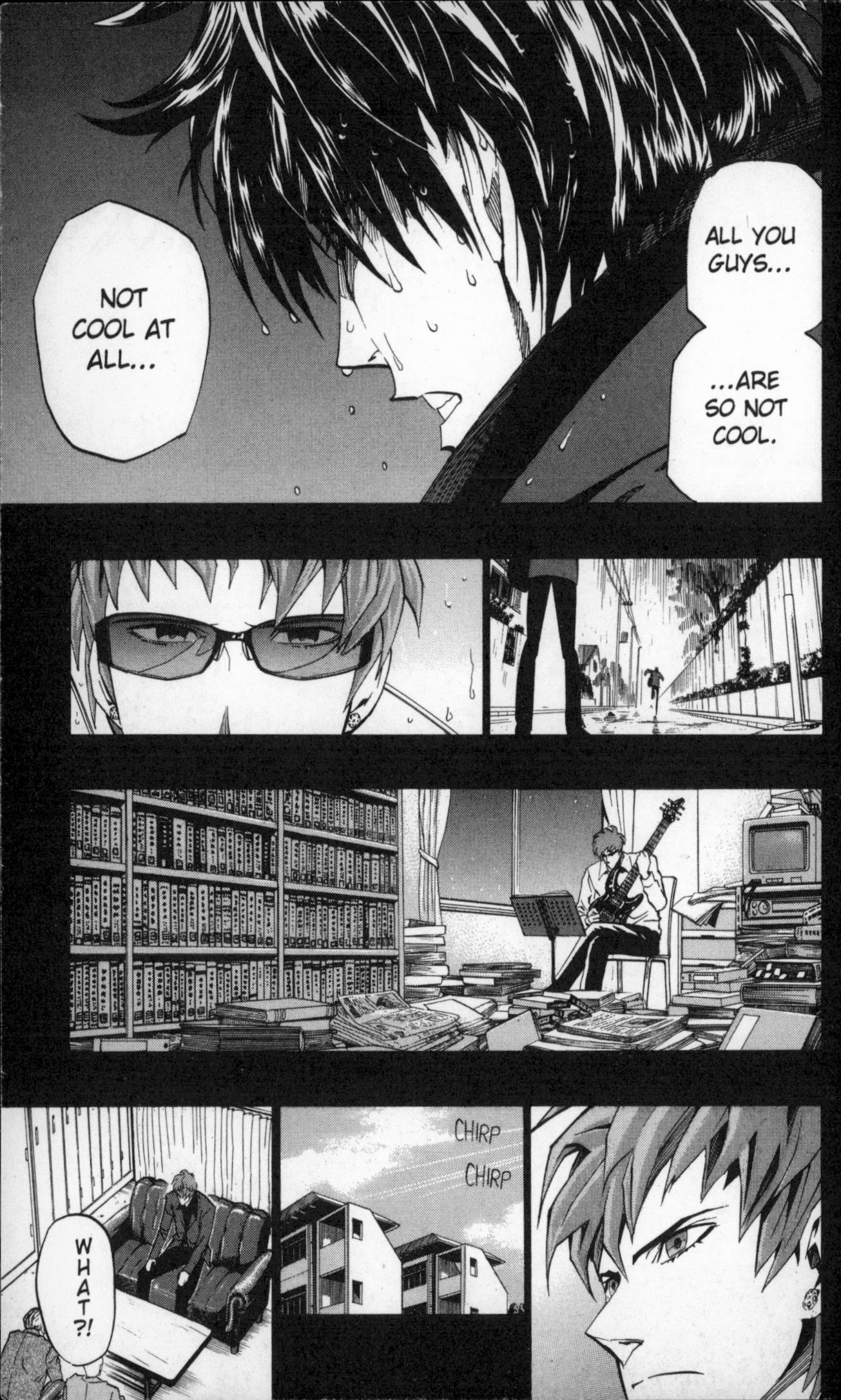
ALL YOU GUYS...
...ARE SO NOT COOL.
NOT COOL AT ALL...
CHIRP
CHIRP
WHAT?!

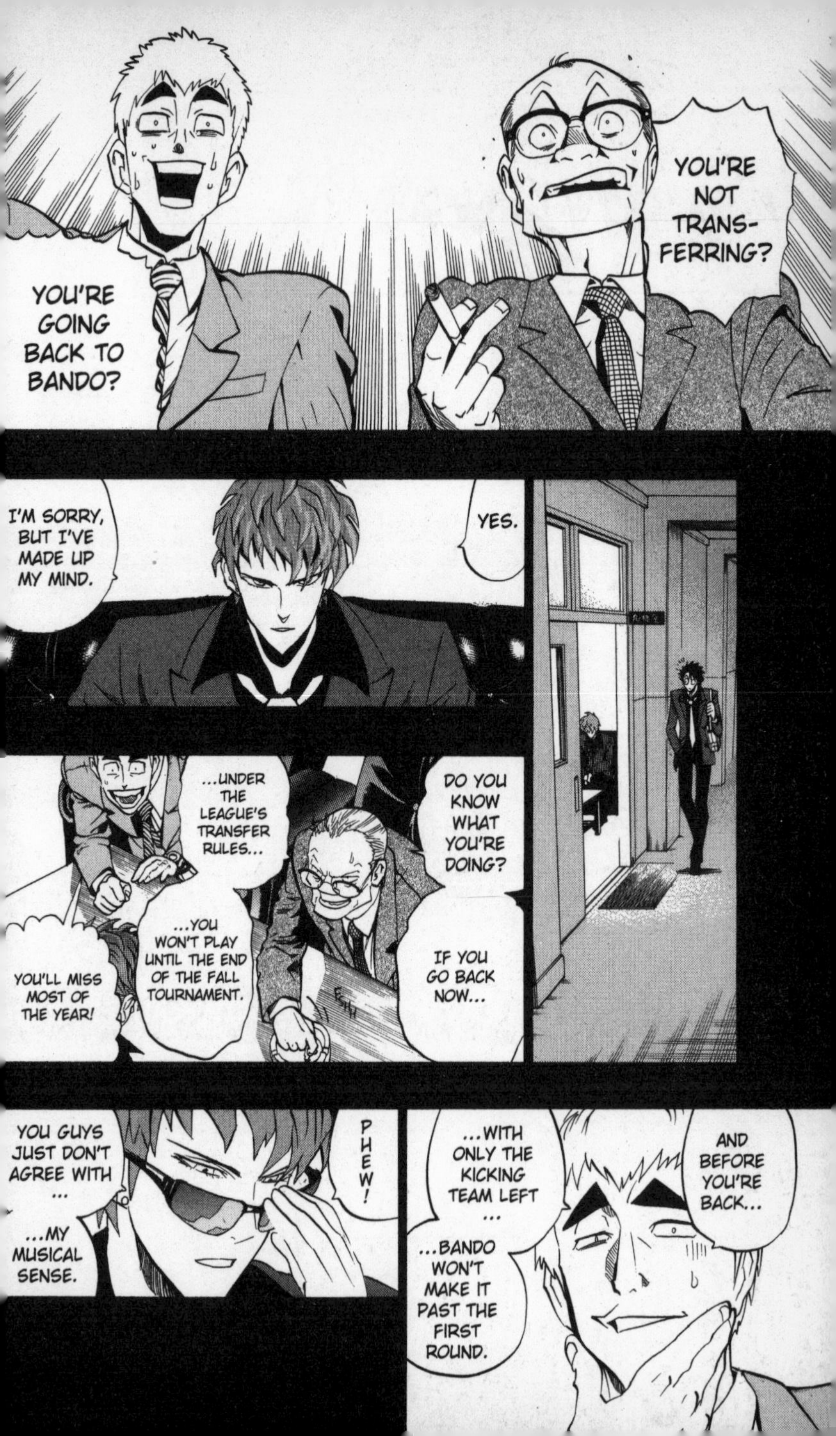
YOU'RE NOT TRANS-FERRING?
YOU'RE GOING BACK TO BANDO?
YES.
I'M SORRY, BUT I'VE MADE UP MY MIND.
DO YOU KNOW WHAT YOU'RE DOING?
...UNDER THE LEAGUE'S TRANSFER RULES...
IF YOU GO BACK NOW...
...YOU WON'T PLAY UNTIL THE END OF THE FALL TOURNAMENT.
YOU'LL MISS MOST OF THE YEAR!
AND BEFORE YOU'RE BACK...
...WITH ONLY THE KICKING TEAM LEFT...
...BANDO WON'T MAKE IT PAST THE FIRST ROUND.
PHEW!
YOU GUYS JUST DON'T AGREE WITH...
...MY MUSICAL SENSE.

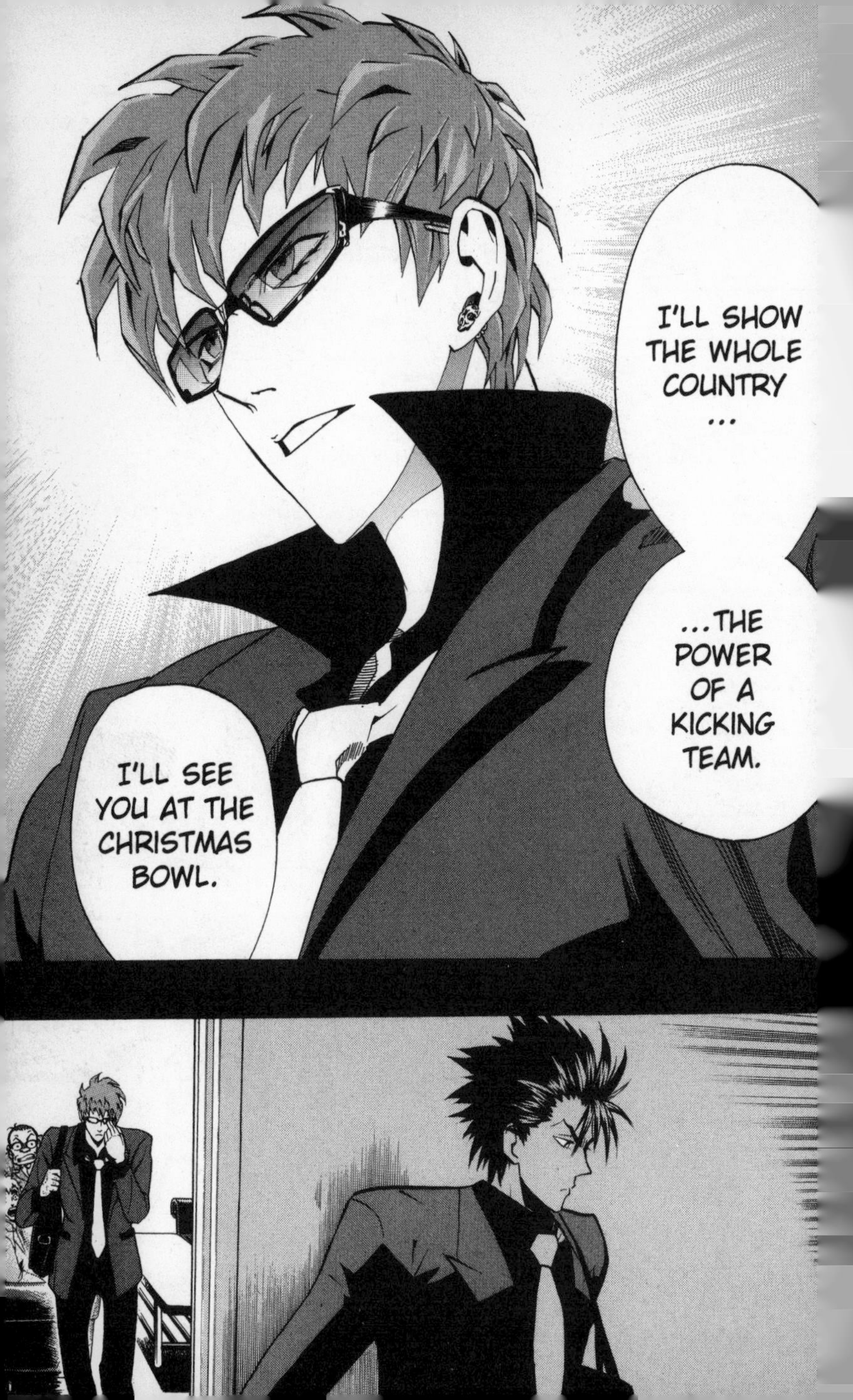
I'LL SHOW THE WHOLE COUNTRY ...
...THE POWER OF A KICKING TEAM.
I'LL SEE YOU AT THE CHRISTMAS BOWL.

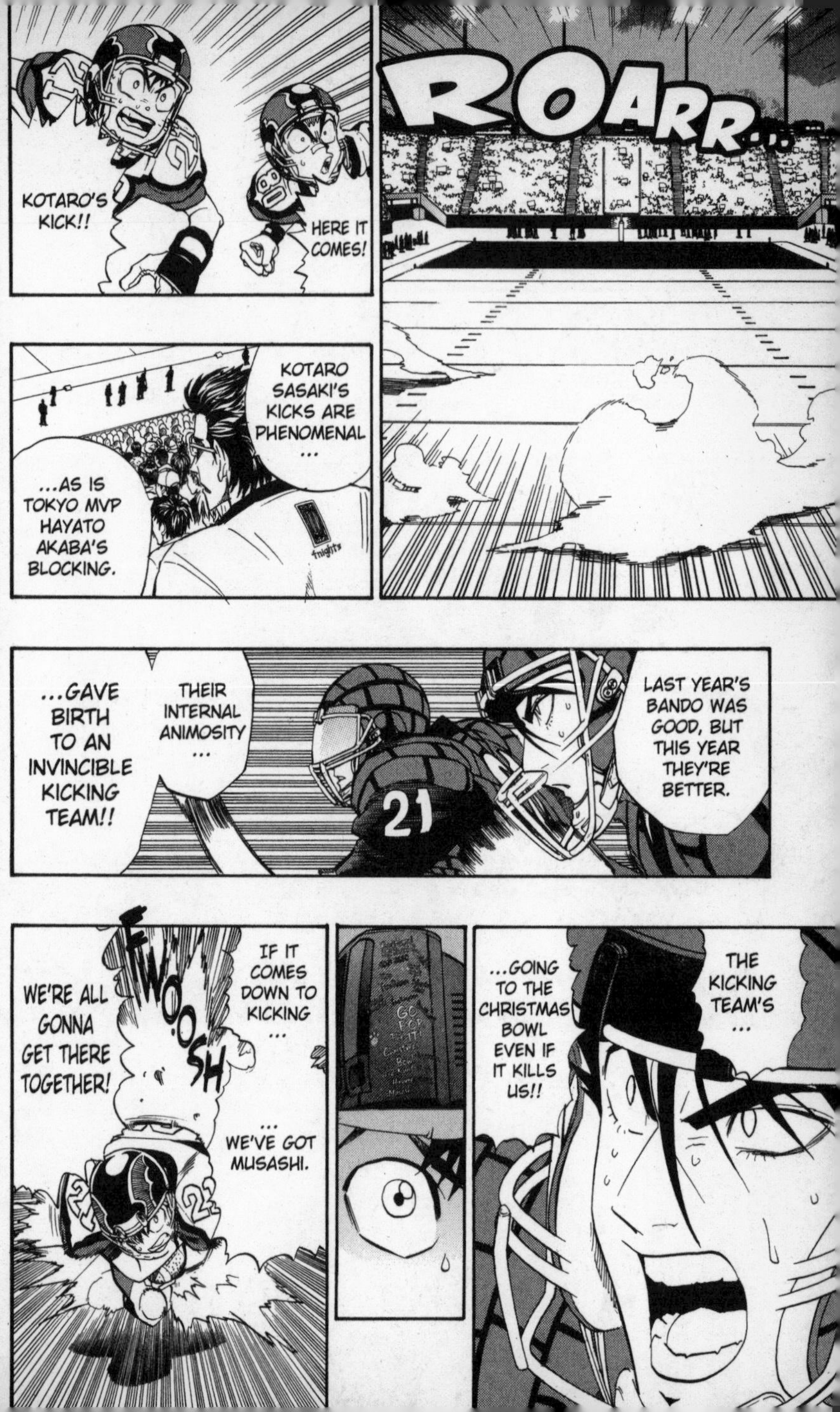
ROARR...
HERE IT COMES!
KOTARO'S KICK!!
KOTARO SASAKI'S KICKS ARE PHENOMENAL ...
...AS IS TOKYO MVP HAYATO AKABA'S BLOCKING.
LAST YEAR'S BANDO WAS GOOD, BUT THIS YEAR THEY'RE BETTER.
THEIR INTERNAL ANIMOSITY ...
...GAVE BIRTH TO AN INVINCIBLE KICKING TEAM!!
THE KICKING TEAM'S ...
...GOING TO THE CHRISTMAS BOWL EVEN IF IT KILLS US!!
IF IT COMES DOWN TO KICKING ...
... WE'VE GOT MUSASHI.
FWOOSH
WE'RE ALL GONNA GET THERE TOGETHER!

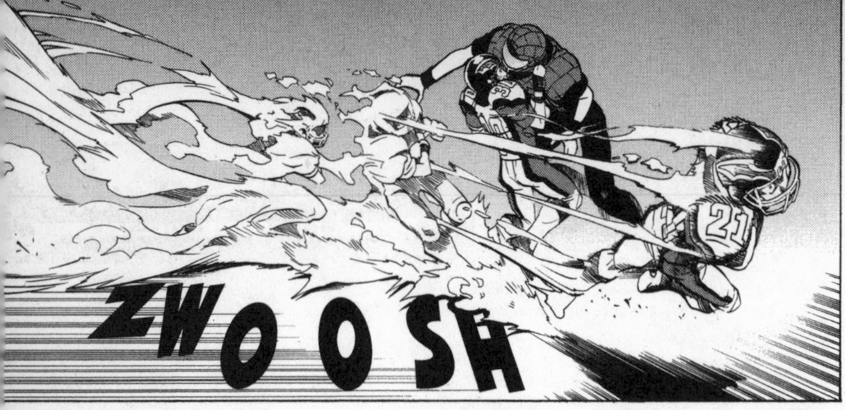
ZWOOSH
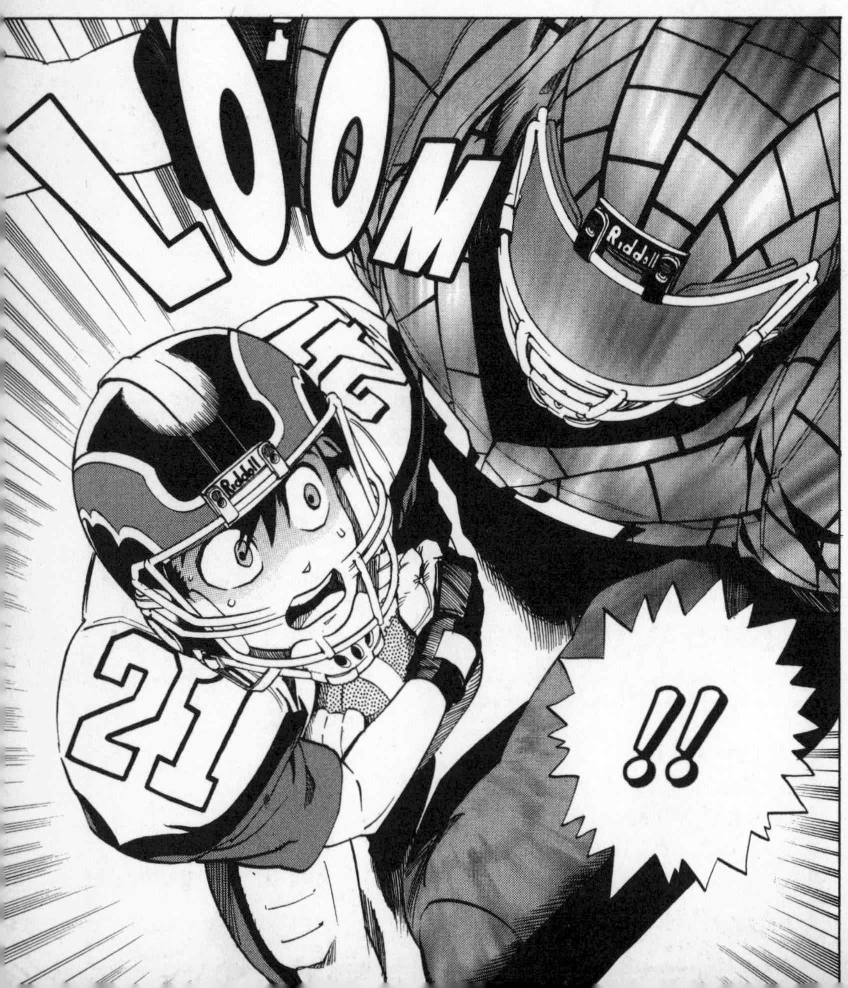
LOOM
!!

Eyeshield 21 Survey Corner

Devil Bat 021

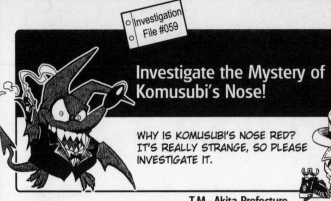

Investigation File #059

Investigate the Mystery of Komusubi's Nose!

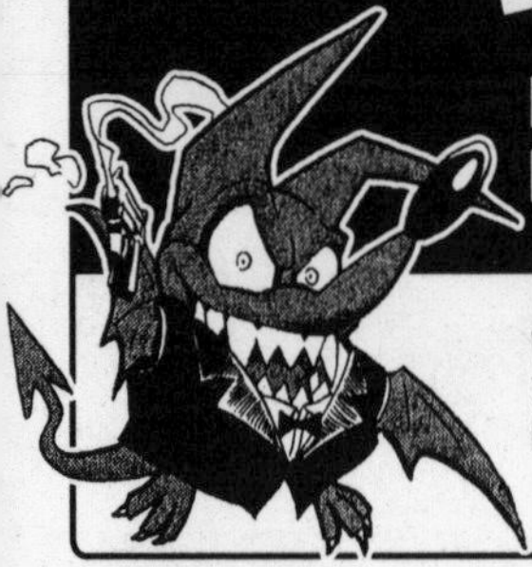

WHY IS KOMUSUBI'S NOSE RED? IT'S REALLY STRANGE, SO PLEASE INVESTIGATE IT.

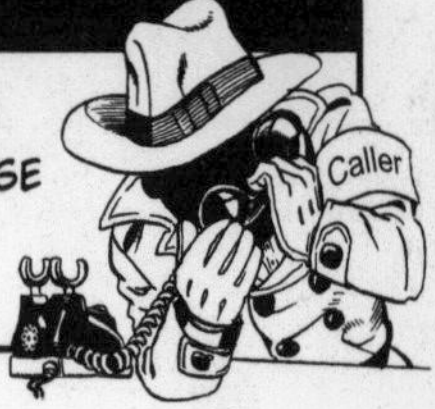
Caller

T.M., Akita Prefecture

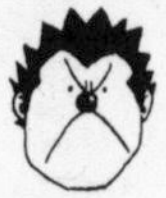

UMPH.

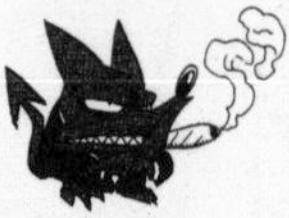

UM...YOUR TURN, KURITA. TRANSLATE THAT FOR US.

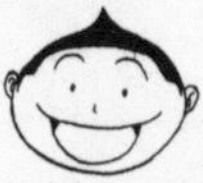

HE SAID, "BECAUSE I'M ALWAYS PUSHING MYSELF AS HARD AS I CAN."

Send your queries for Devil Bat 021 here!!

Devil Bat 021
Shonen Jump Advanced/Eyeshield 21
c/o VIZ Media, LLC
P.O. Box 77010
San Francisco, CA 94107

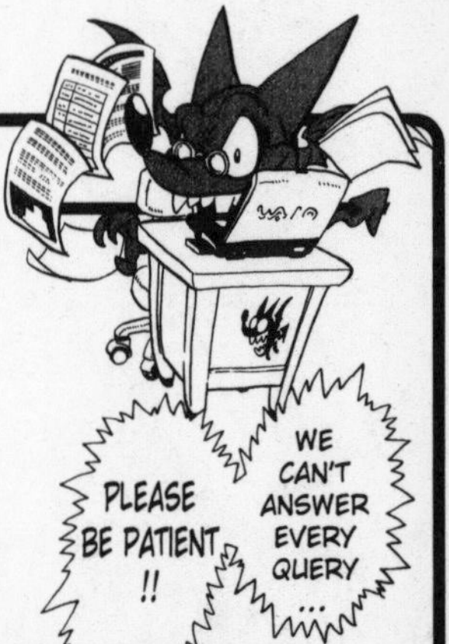
PLEASE BE PATIENT!!
WE CAN'T ANSWER EVERY QUERY...

THE FINAL TO SEE WHO ADVANCES AND WHO GOES HOME!

THE GAME'S ALREADY IN FULL SWING!

YEAH!

Chapter 160 A Challenge to the Real Thing

...THE REAL...

...EYESHIELD 21?

IS TOKYO'S MVP...

...HAYATO AKABA...

IT THOUGHT IT WAS AT FOUR THIS *MORNING!*

HOW COULD YOU THINK *THAT*?!

SORRY ...

...I GOT THE KICKOFF TIME WRONG.

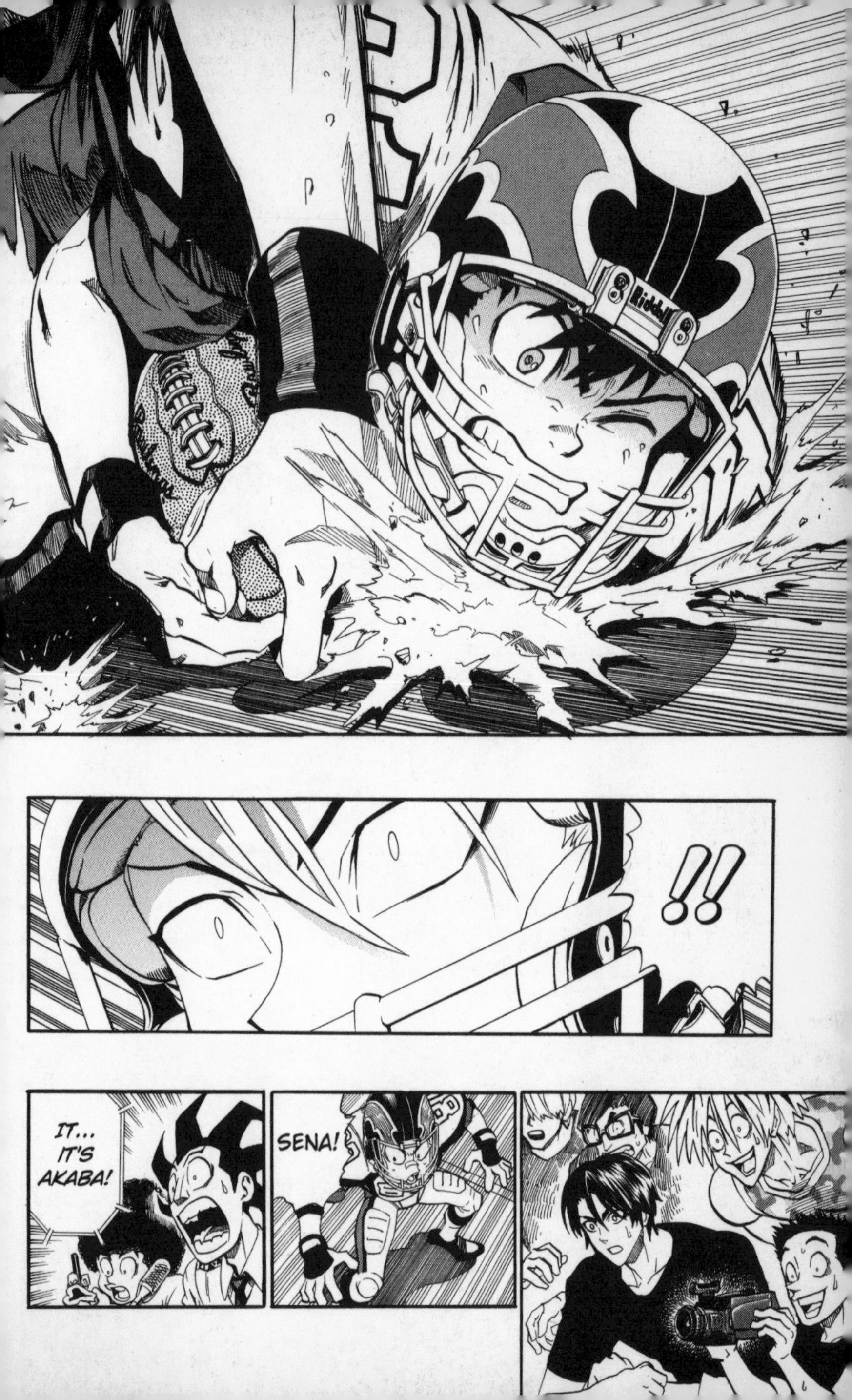
!!
SENA!
IT... IT'S AKABA!

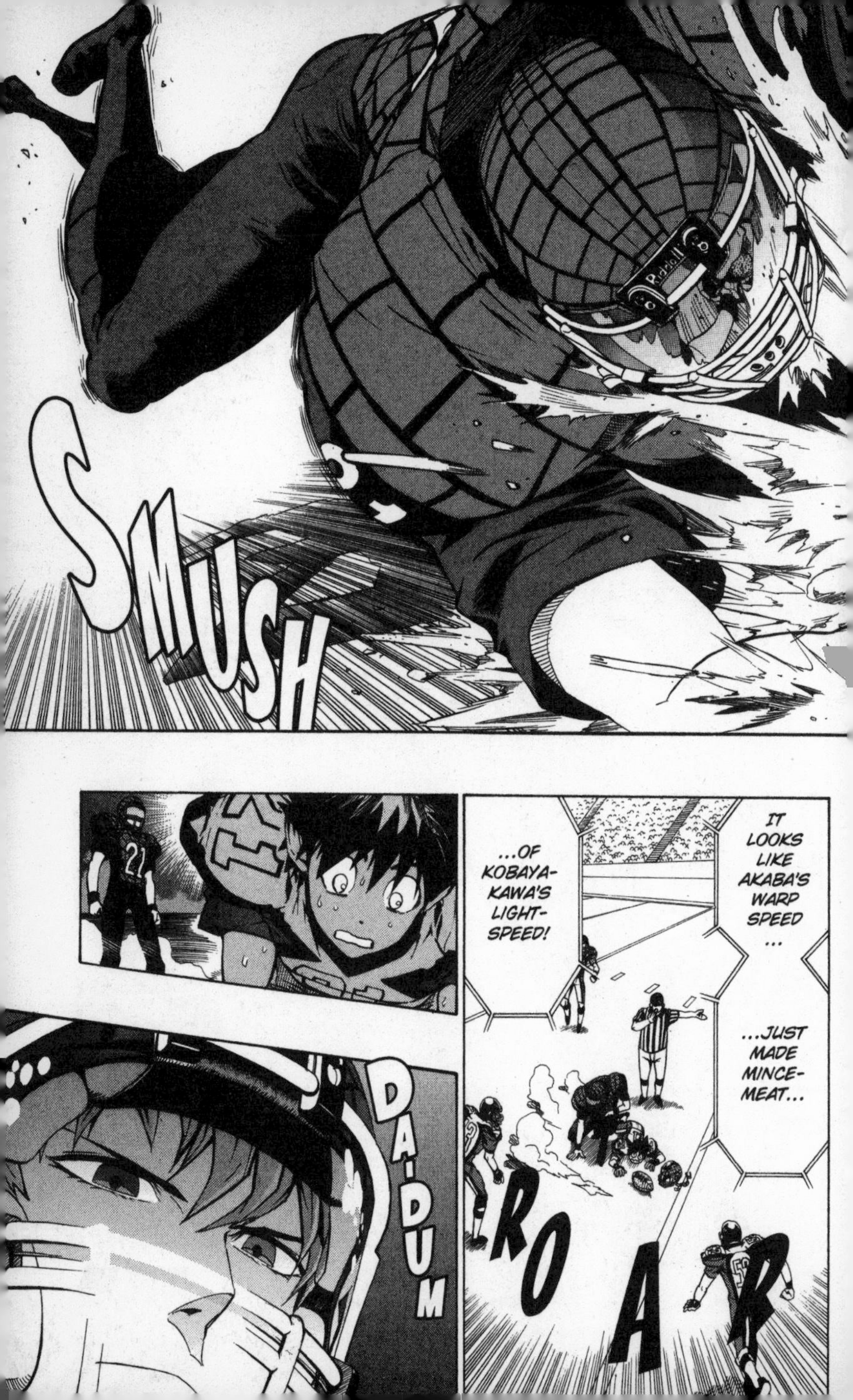
SMUSH
IT LOOKS LIKE AKABA'S WARP SPEED ...
...JUST MADE MINCE-MEAT...
...OF KOBAYA-KAWA'S LIGHT-SPEED!
ROAR
DA-DUM

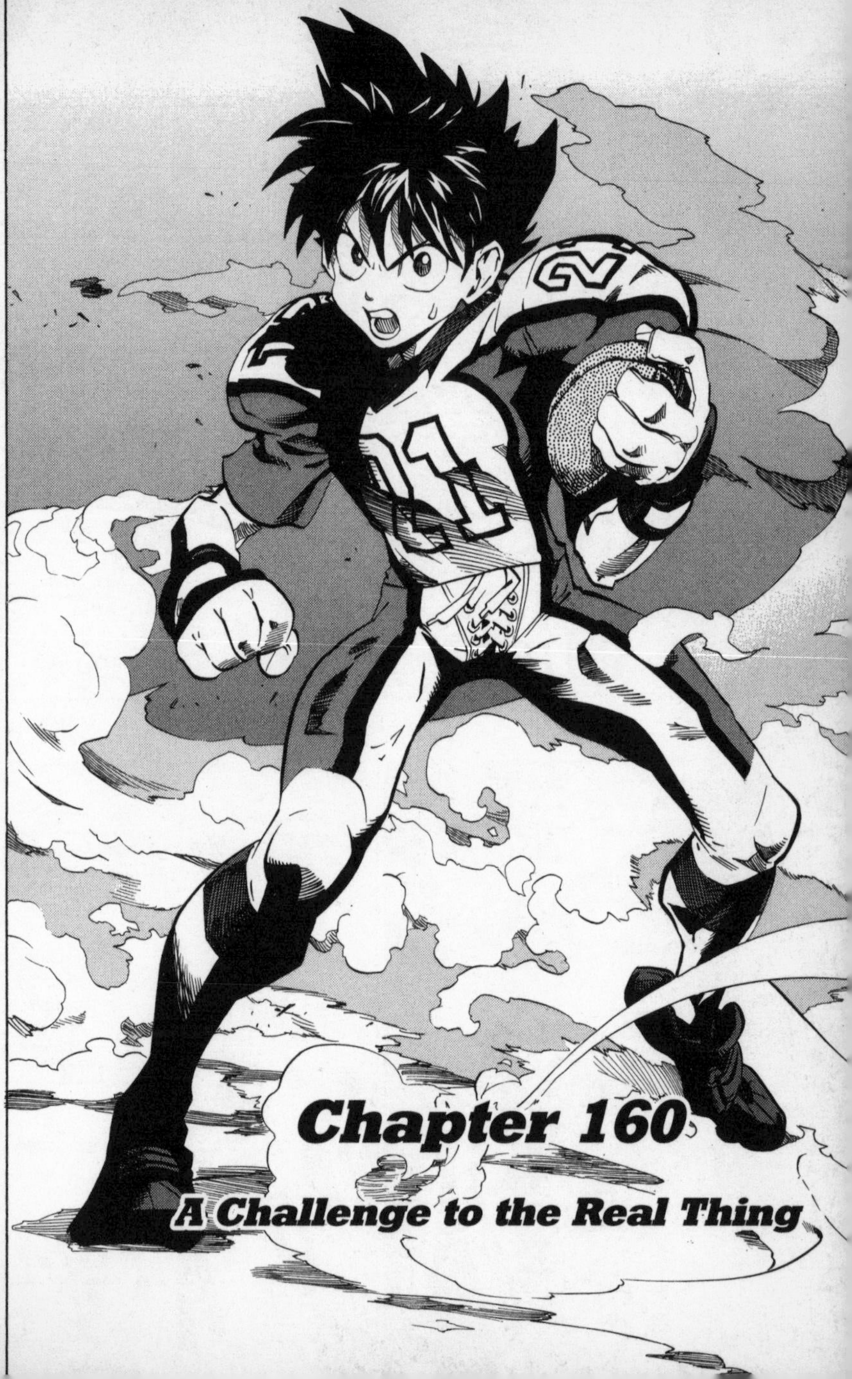

21
Chapter 160
A Challenge to the Real Thing

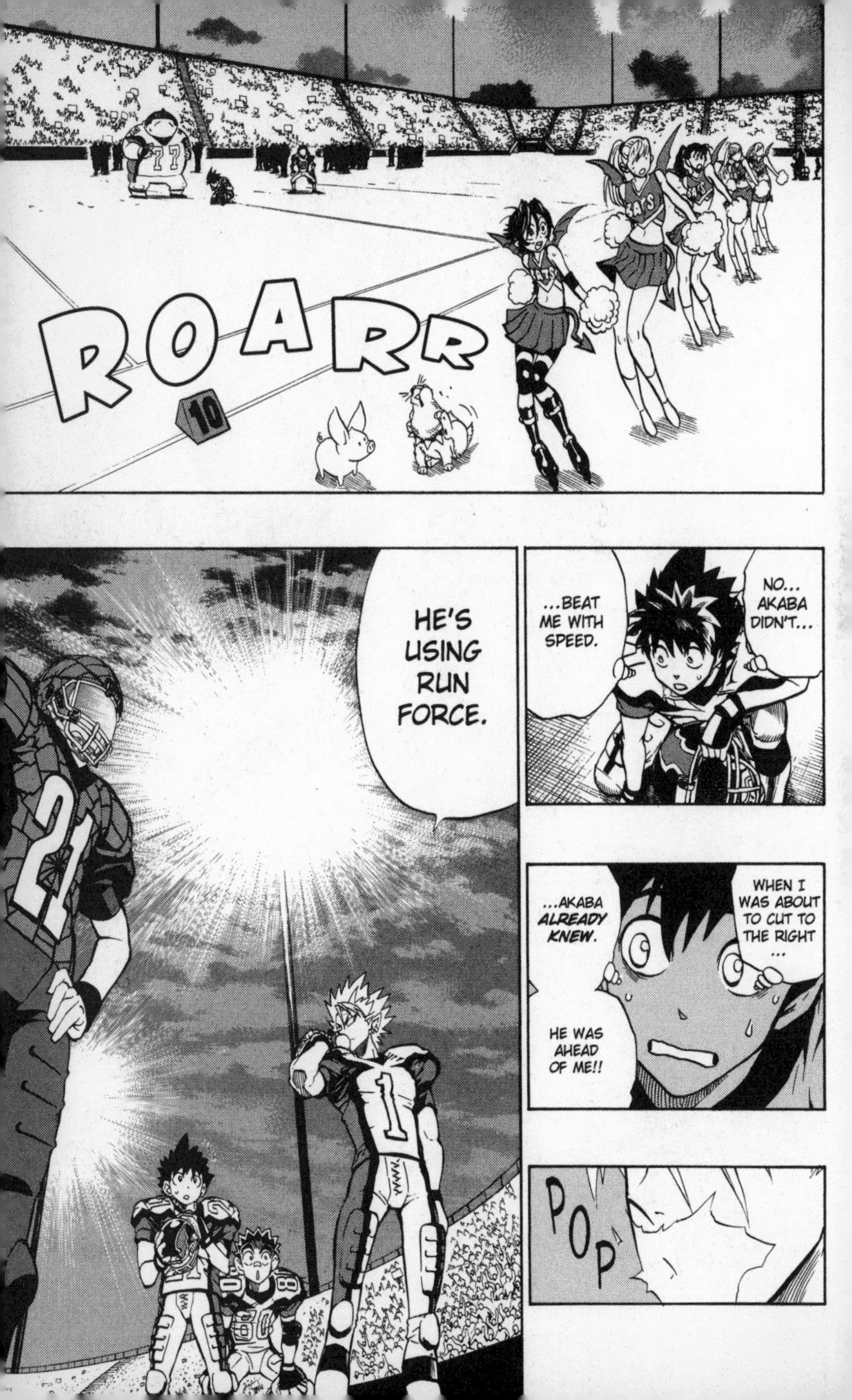
ROARR
10
NO... AKABA DIDN'T...
...BEAT ME WITH SPEED.
WHEN I WAS ABOUT TO CUT TO THE RIGHT...
...AKABA *ALREADY KNEW*.
HE WAS AHEAD OF ME!!
POP
HE'S USING RUN FORCE.

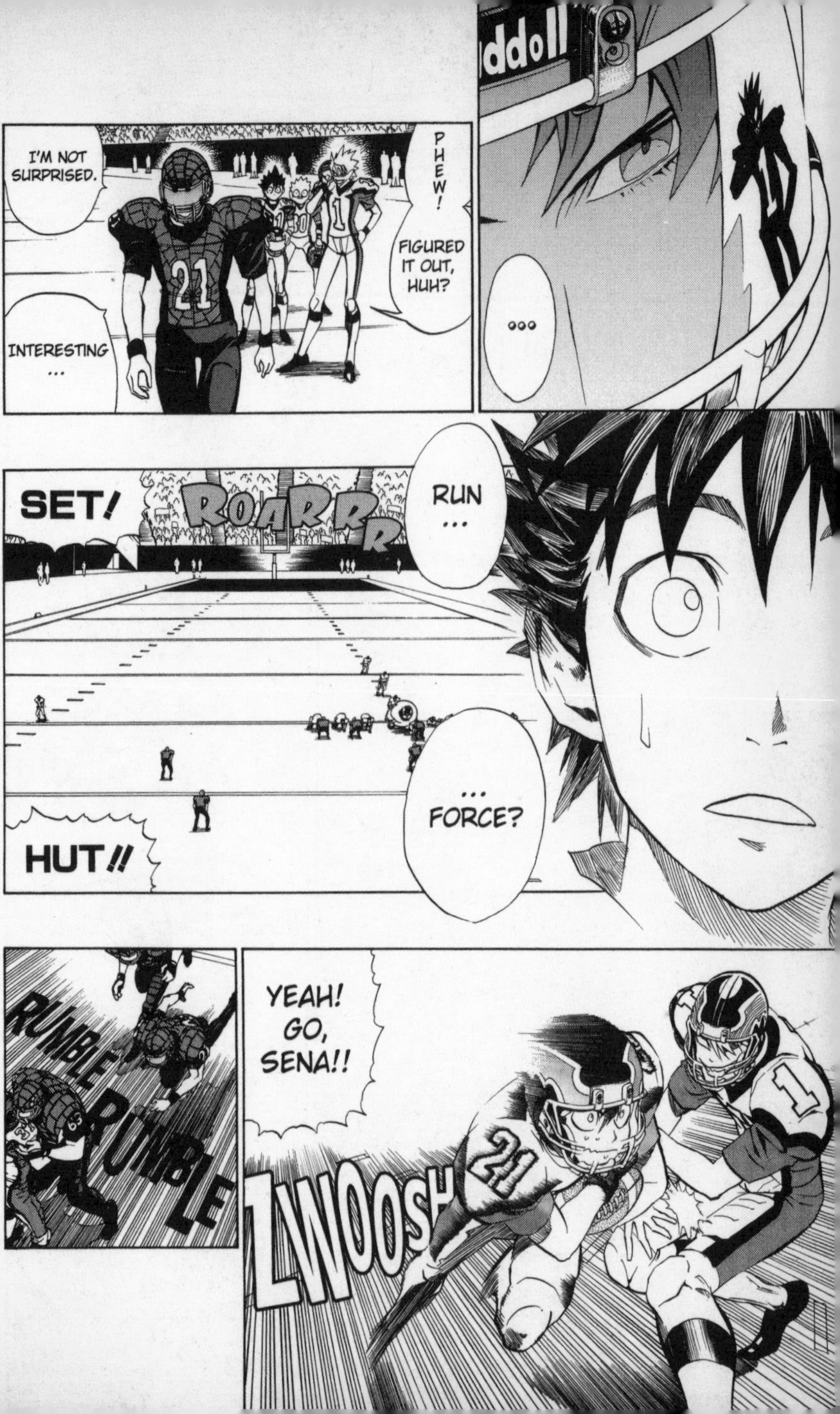
...
PHEW!
FIGURED IT OUT, HUH?
I'M NOT SURPRISED.
INTERESTING...
RUN...
...FORCE?
SET!
ROARRR
HUT!!
YEAH! GO, SENA!!
ZWOOSH
RUMBLE
RUMBLE

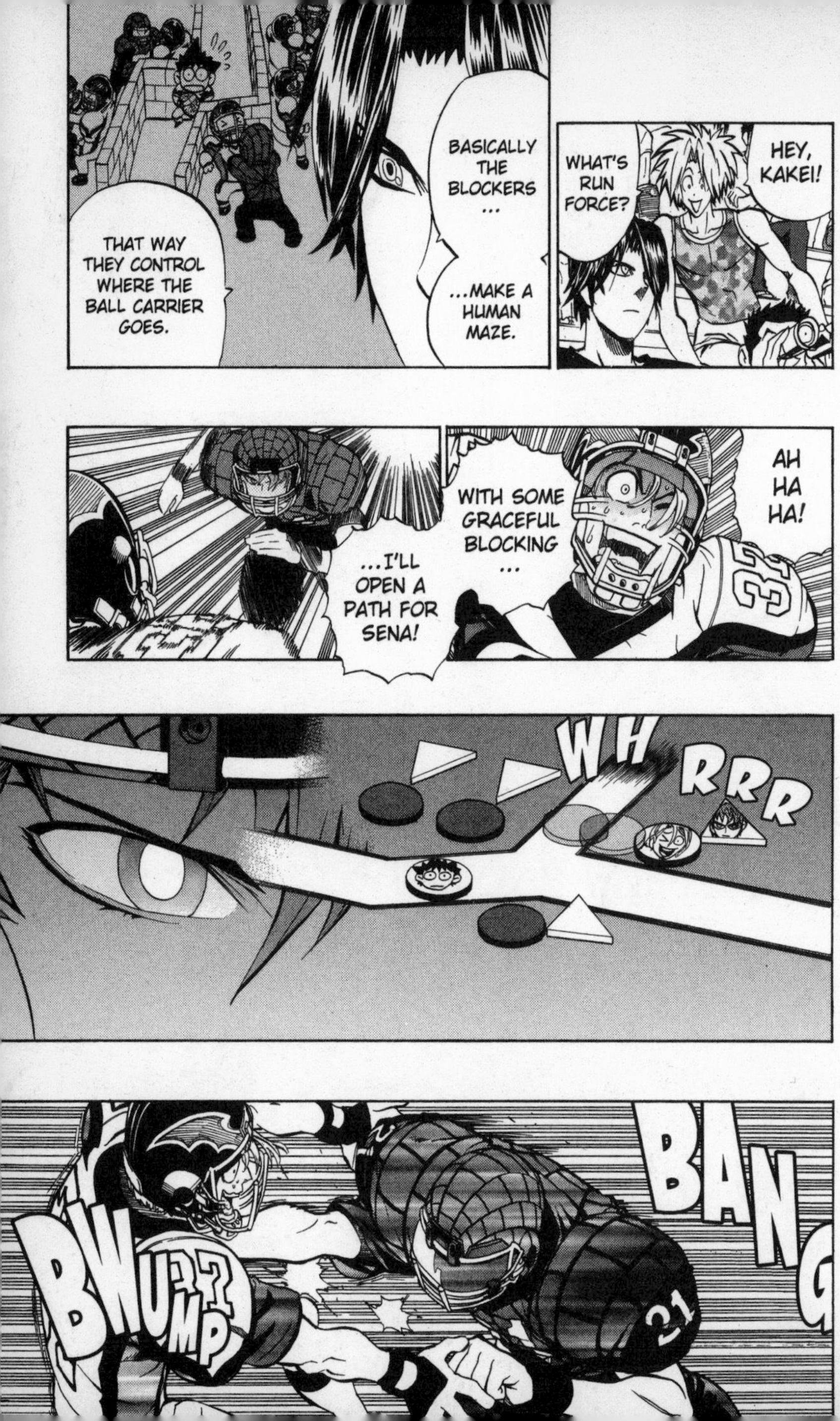
HEY, KAKEI!
WHAT'S RUN FORCE?
BASICALLY THE BLOCKERS...
...MAKE A HUMAN MAZE.
THAT WAY THEY CONTROL WHERE THE BALL CARRIER GOES.
AH HA HA!
WITH SOME GRACEFUL BLOCKING...
...I'LL OPEN A PATH FOR SENA!
WHRRR
BANG
BWUMP

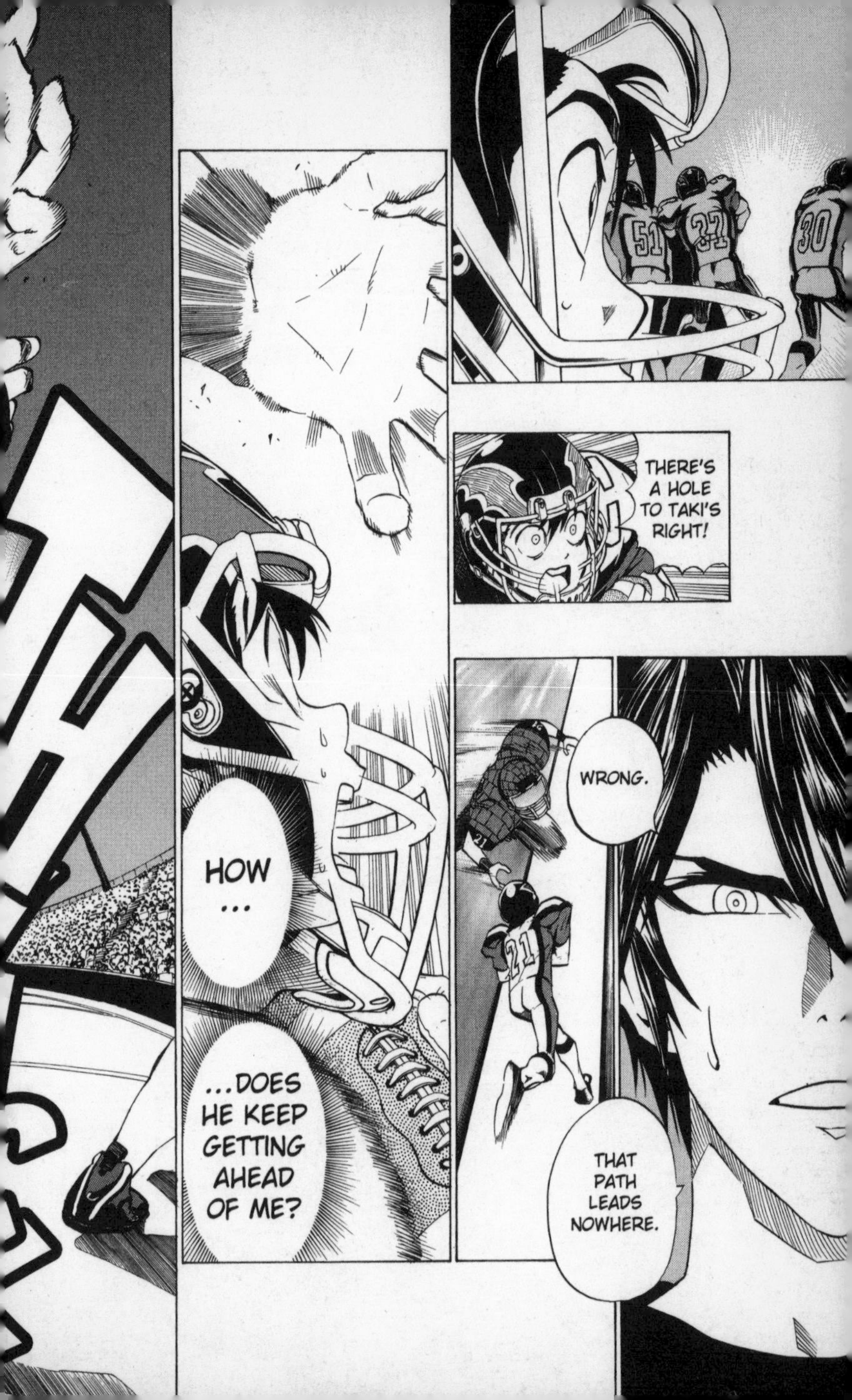
THERE'S A HOLE TO TAKI'S RIGHT!
WRONG.
THAT PATH LEADS NOWHERE.
HOW ...
...DOES HE KEEP GETTING AHEAD OF ME?

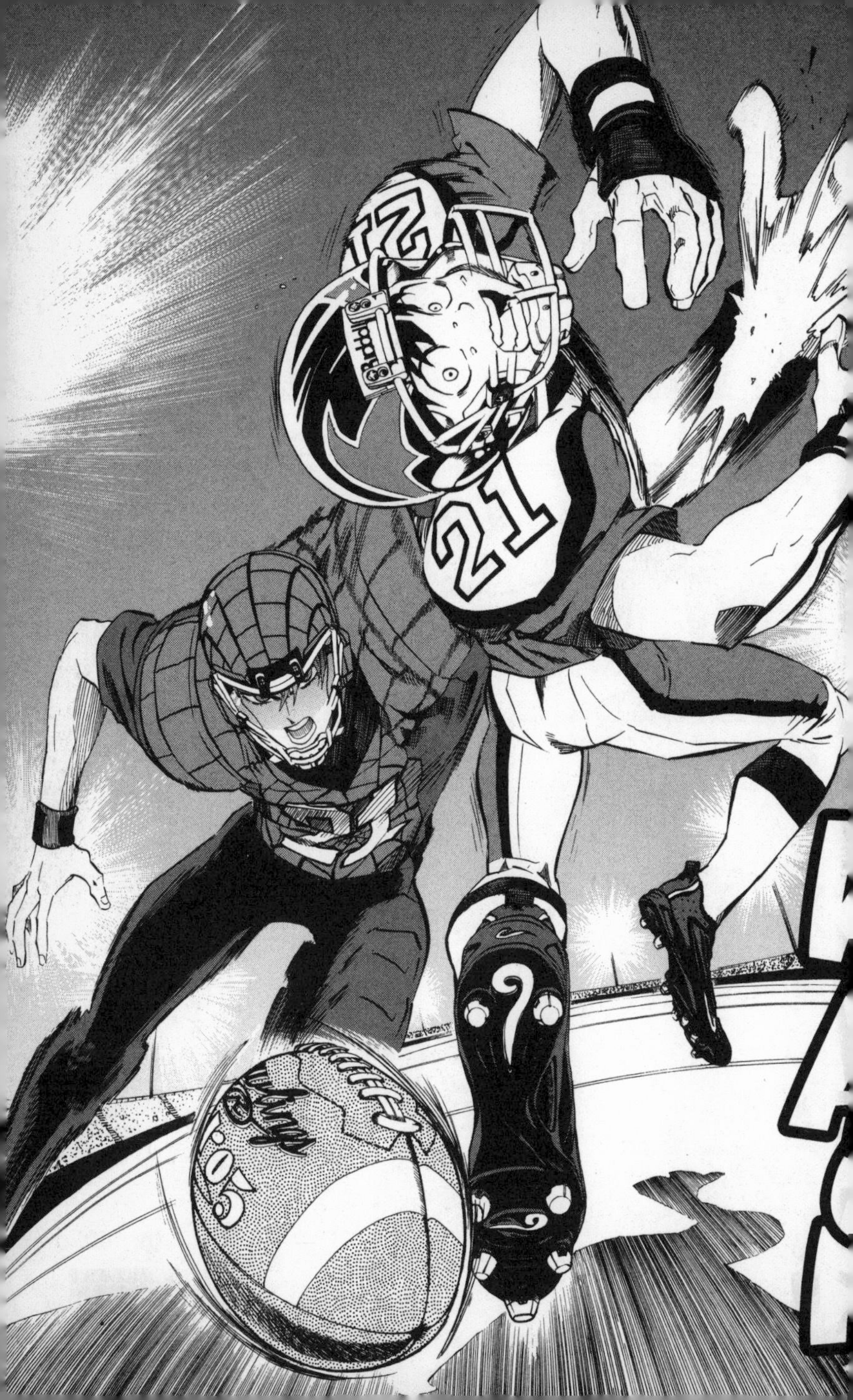

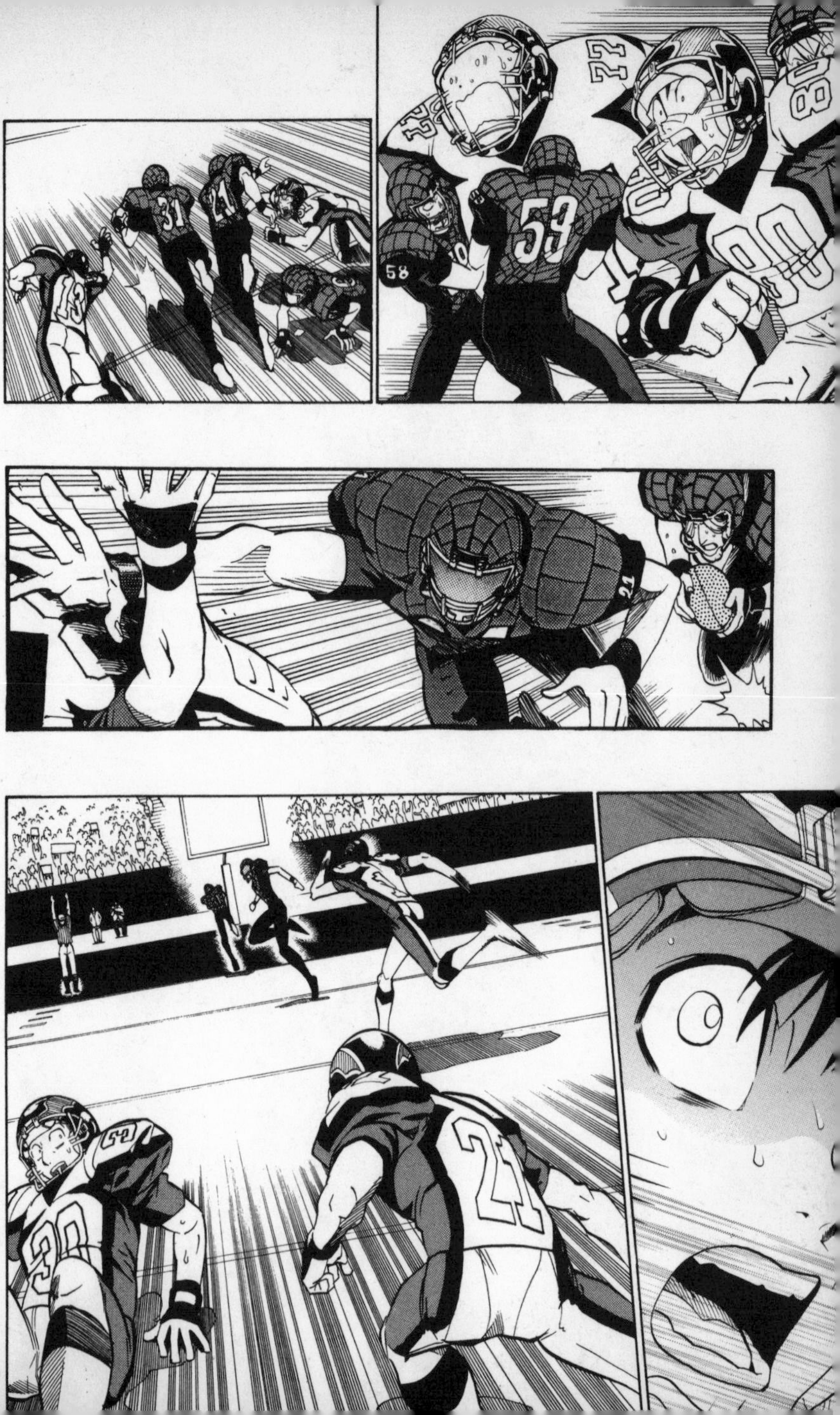

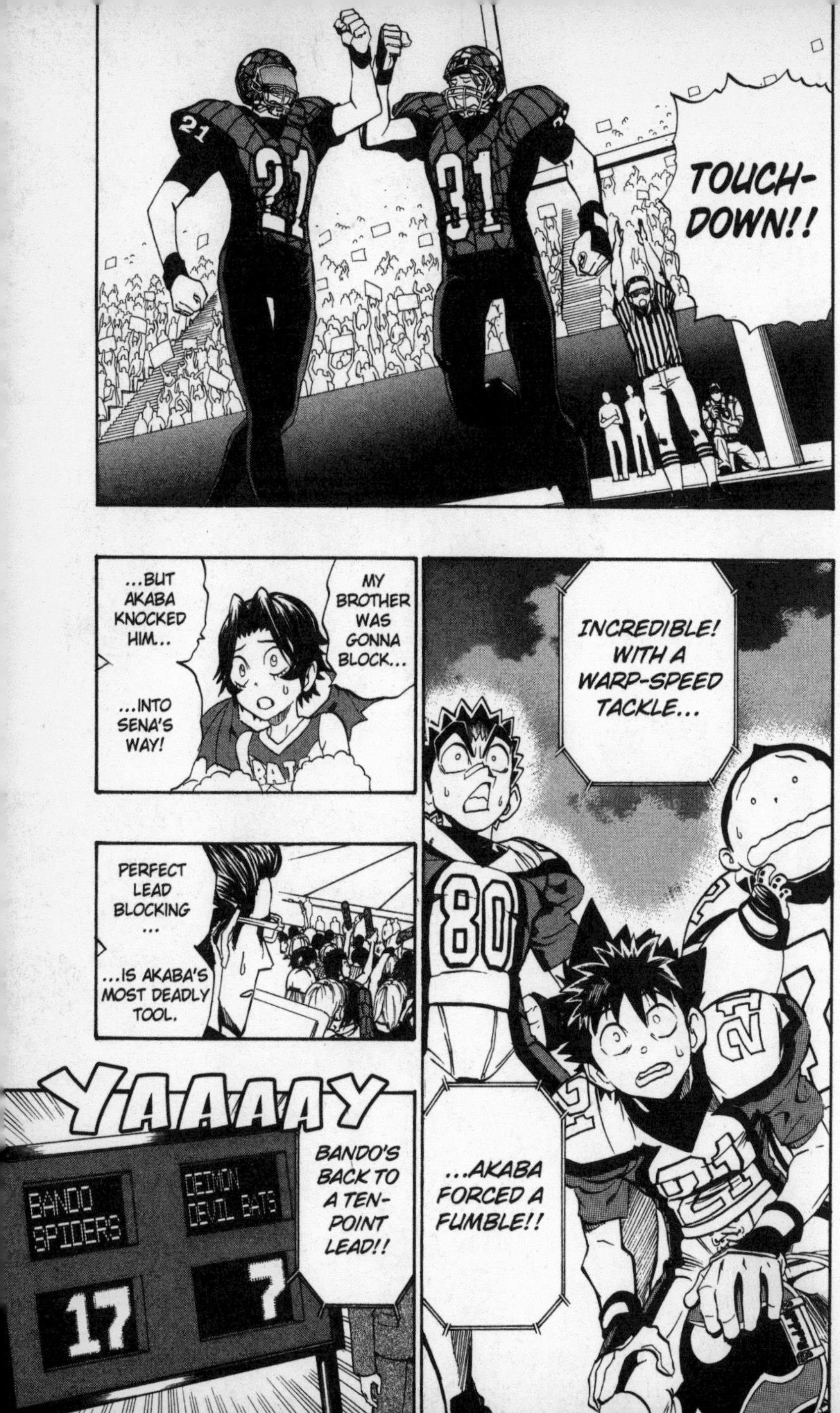
TOUCH-DOWN!!
INCREDIBLE! WITH A WARP-SPEED TACKLE...
...AKABA FORCED A FUMBLE!!
MY BROTHER WAS GONNA BLOCK...
...BUT AKABA KNOCKED HIM...
...INTO SENA'S WAY!
PERFECT LEAD BLOCKING...
...IS AKABA'S MOST DEADLY TOOL.
YAAAAY
BANDO'S BACK TO A TEN-POINT LEAD!!
DEIMON DEVIL BATS
BANDO SPIDERS
7
17

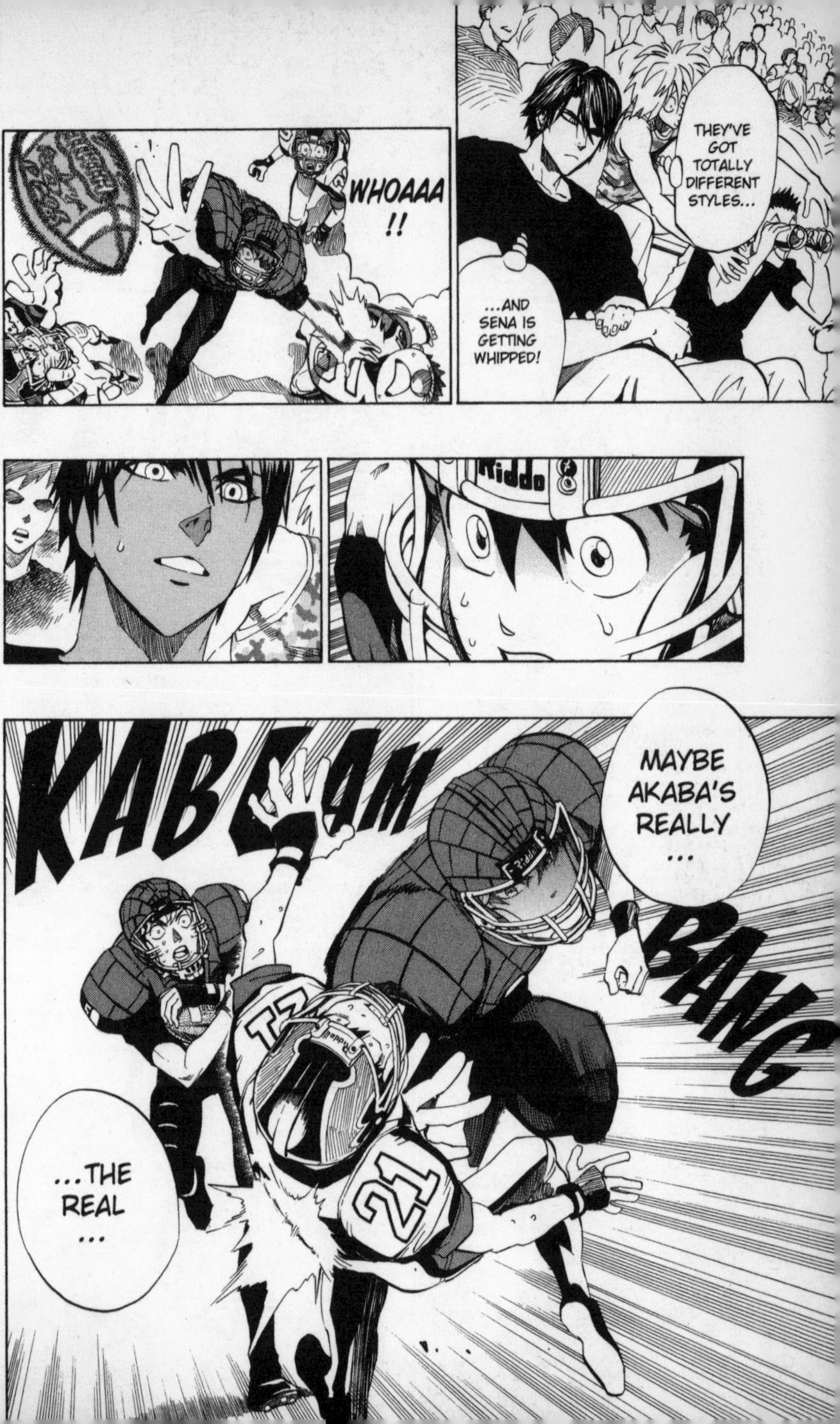
THEY'VE GOT TOTALLY DIFFERENT STYLES...
...AND SENA IS GETTING WHIPPED!
WHOAAA!!
MAYBE AKABA'S REALLY...
BANG
...THE REAL...

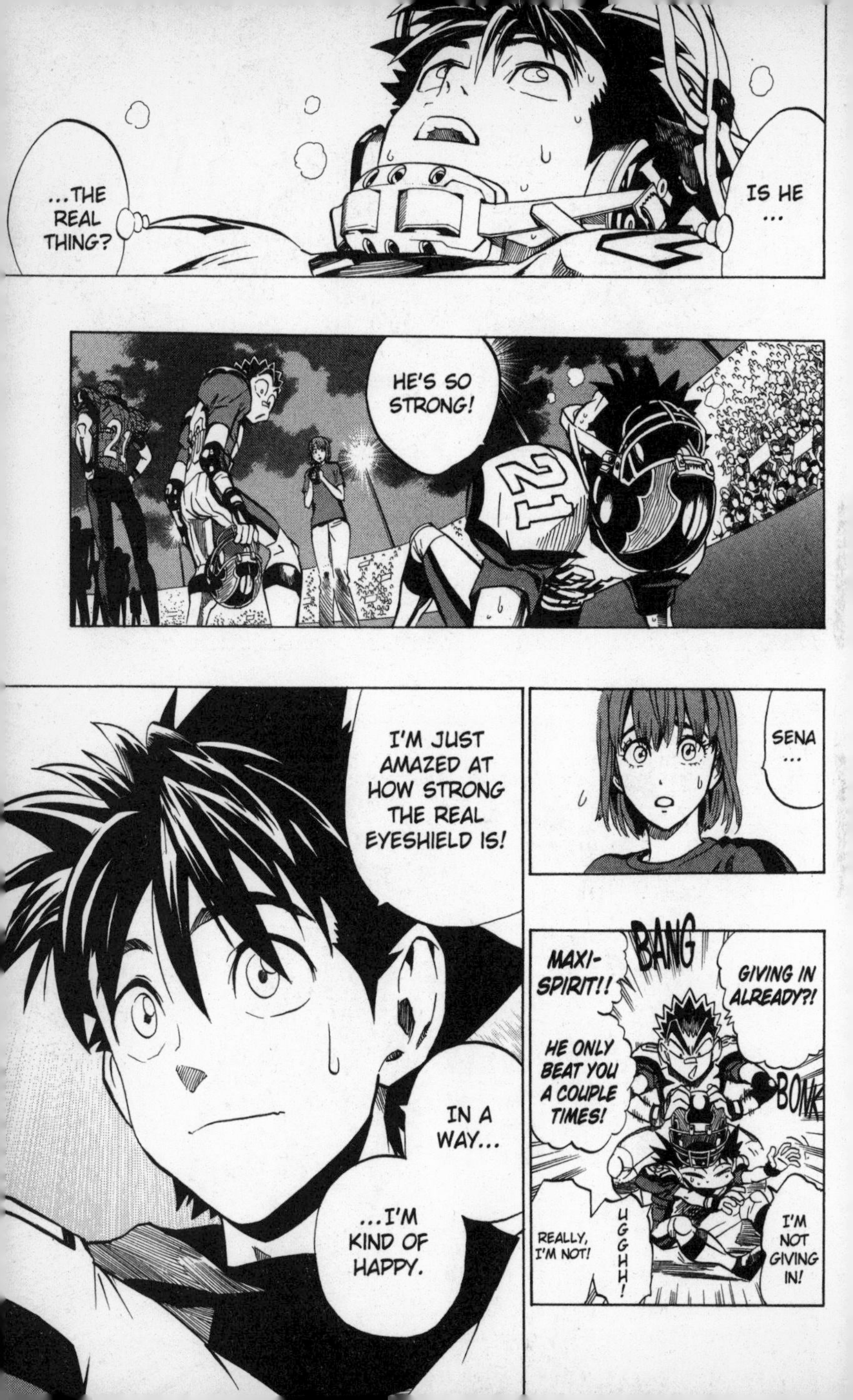
IS HE ...
...THE REAL THING?
HE'S SO STRONG!
SENA ...
GIVING IN ALREADY?!
BANG
MAXI-SPIRIT!!
BONK
HE ONLY BEAT YOU A COUPLE TIMES!
I'M NOT GIVING IN!
UGGHH!
REALLY, I'M NOT!
I'M JUST AMAZED AT HOW STRONG THE REAL EYESHIELD IS!
IN A WAY...
...I'M KIND OF HAPPY.

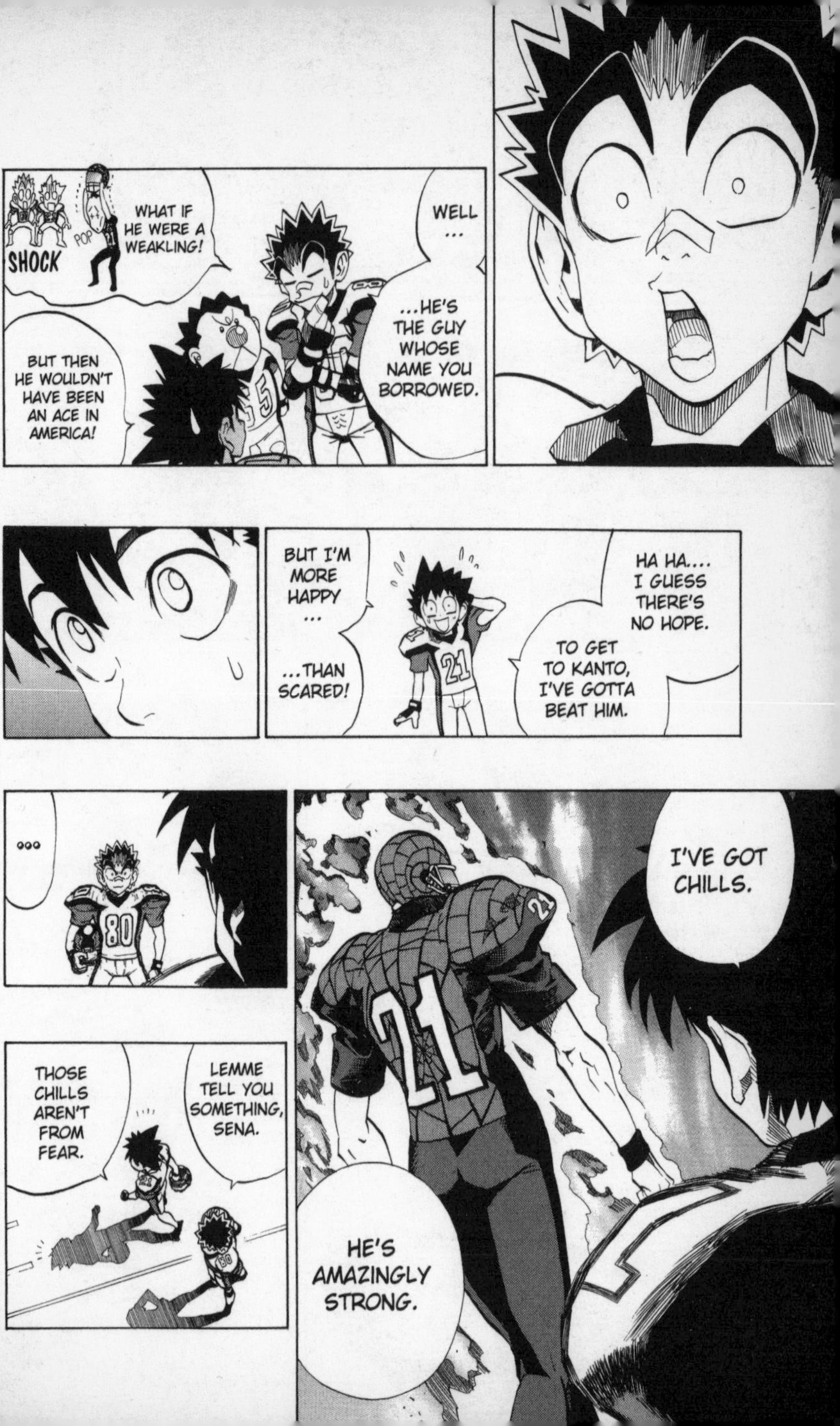
WELL ...
...HE'S THE GUY WHOSE NAME YOU BORROWED.
WHAT IF HE WERE A WEAKLING!
POP
SHOCK
BUT THEN HE WOULDN'T HAVE BEEN AN ACE IN AMERICA!
HA HA.... I GUESS THERE'S NO HOPE.
TO GET TO KANTO, I'VE GOTTA BEAT HIM.
BUT I'M MORE HAPPY ...
...THAN SCARED!
I'VE GOT CHILLS.
HE'S AMAZINGLY STRONG.
...
LEMME TELL YOU SOMETHING, SENA.
THOSE CHILLS AREN'T FROM FEAR.

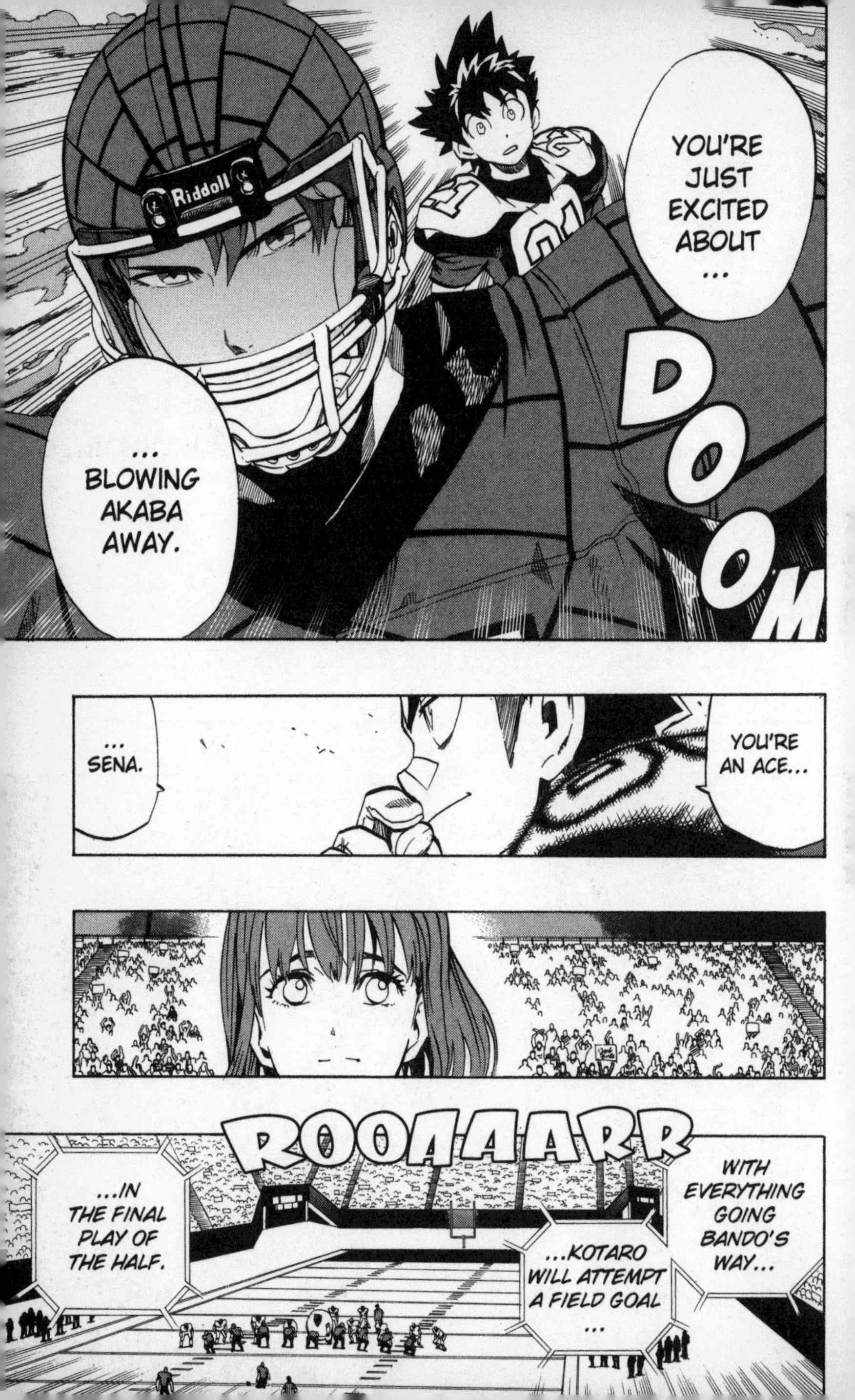
YOU'RE JUST EXCITED ABOUT ...
DOOM
... BLOWING AKABA AWAY.
YOU'RE AN ACE...
... SENA.
ROOAAARR
WITH EVERYTHING GOING BANDO'S WAY...
...KOTARO WILL ATTEMPT A FIELD GOAL ...
...IN THE FINAL PLAY OF THE HALF.

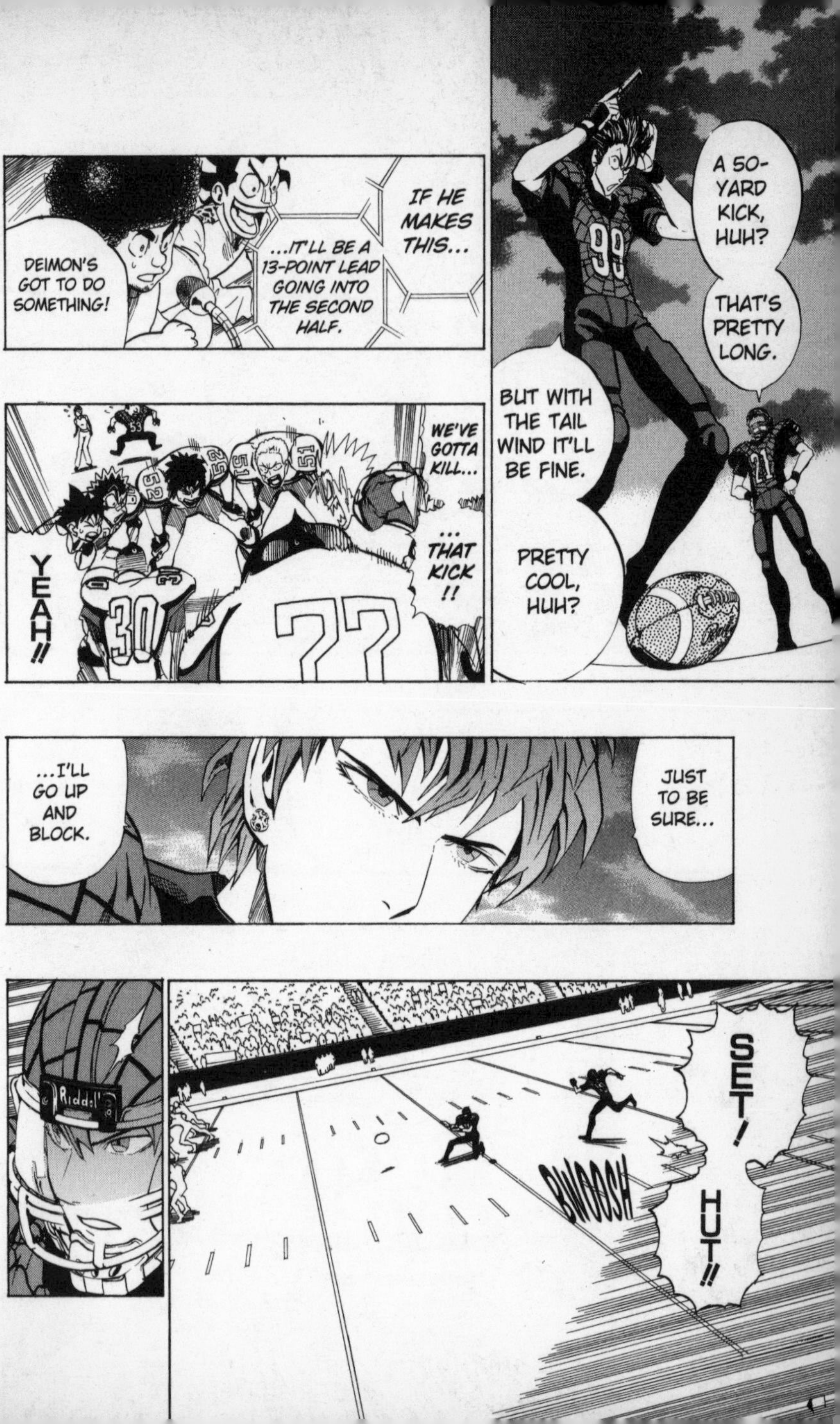
A 50-YARD KICK, HUH?
THAT'S PRETTY LONG.
BUT WITH THE TAIL WIND IT'LL BE FINE.
PRETTY COOL, HUH?
IF HE MAKES THIS...
...IT'LL BE A 13-POINT LEAD GOING INTO THE SECOND HALF.
DEIMON'S GOT TO DO SOMETHING!
WE'VE GOTTA KILL...
...THAT KICK!!
YEAH!!
JUST TO BE SURE...
...I'LL GO UP AND BLOCK.
SET!
HUT!!
BWOOSH

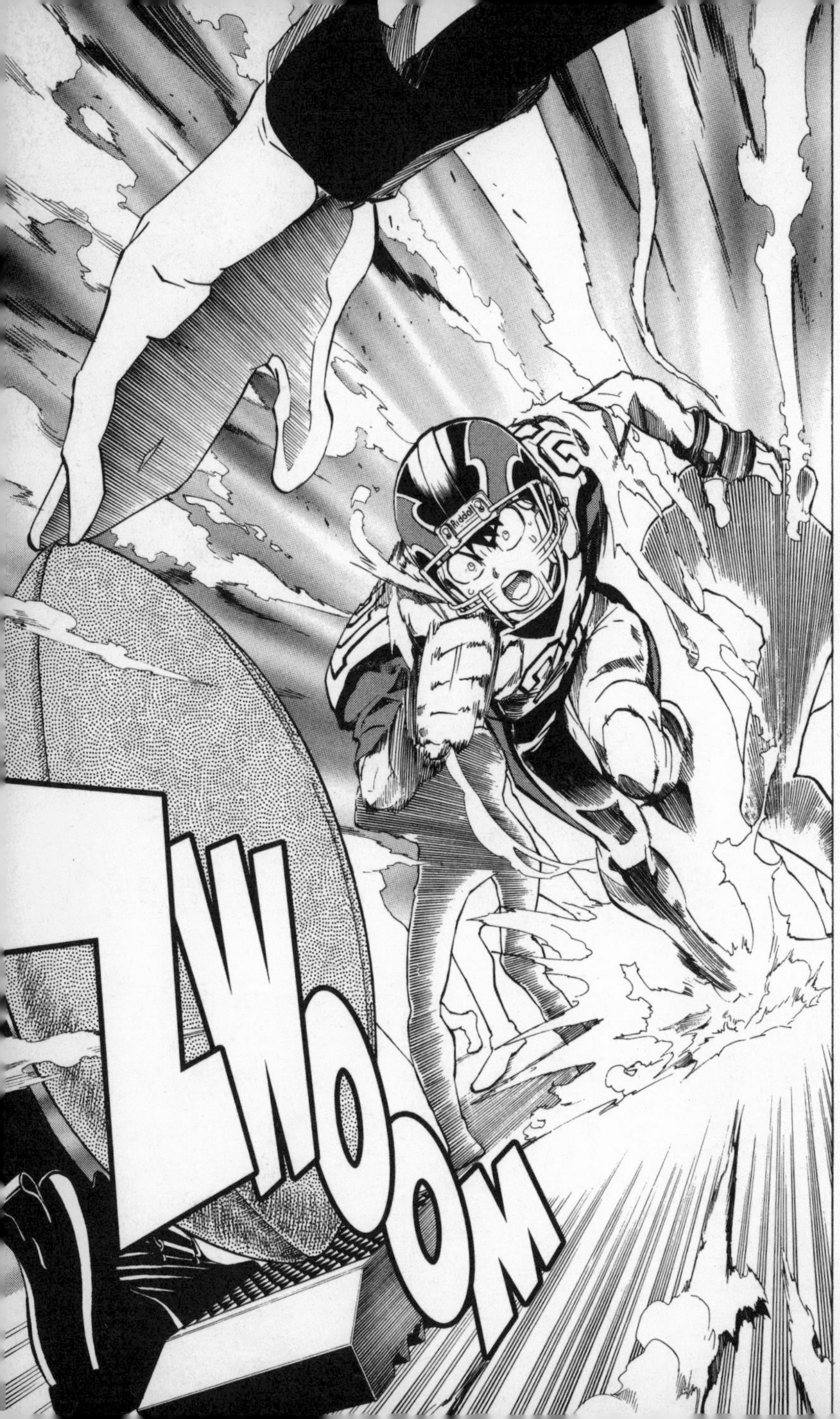
ZWOOM

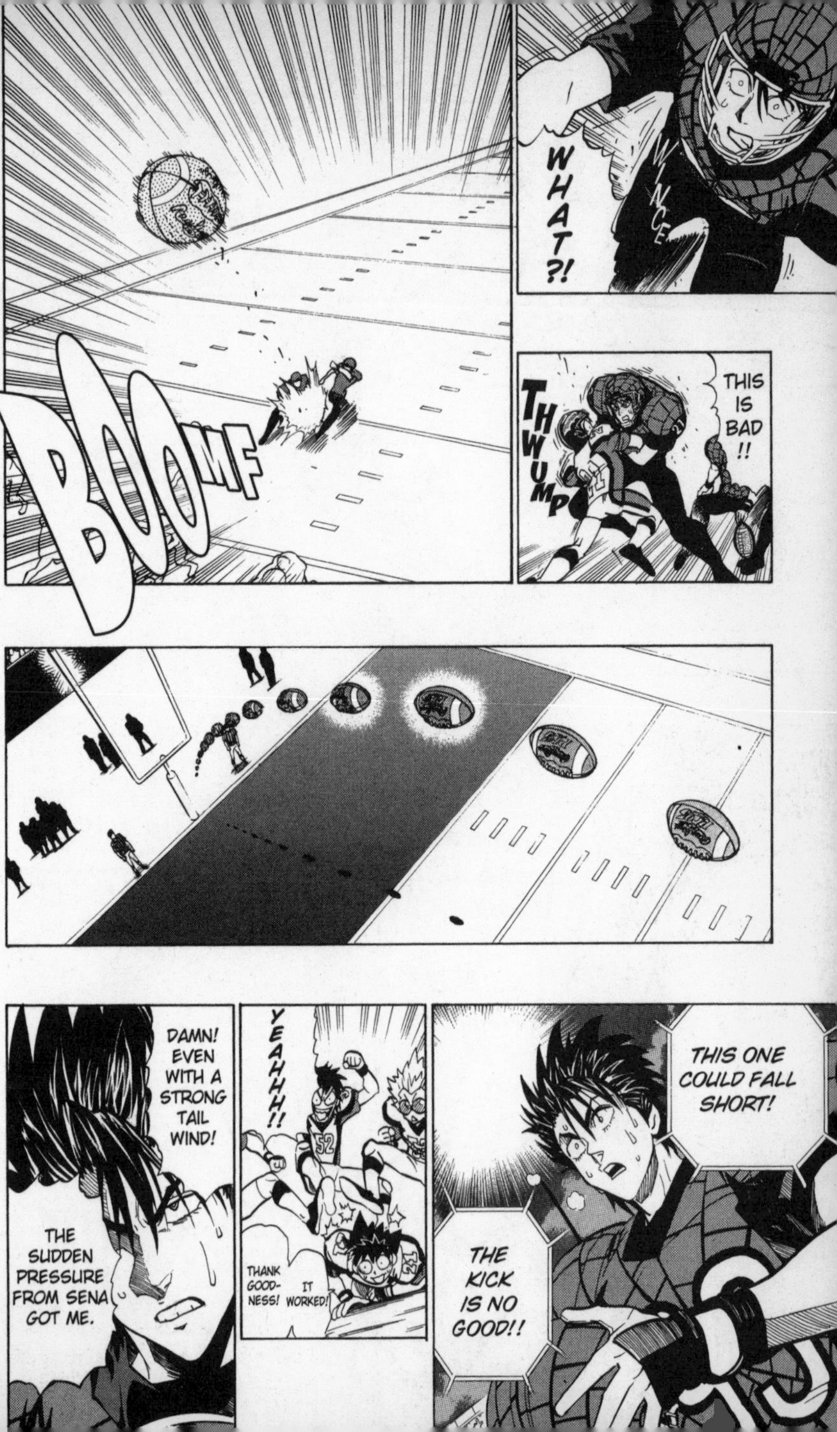
WHAT?!
WINCE
THIS IS BAD!!
THWUMP
BOOMF
THIS ONE COULD FALL SHORT!
THE KICK IS NO GOOD!!
YEAHHH!!
THANK GOOD-NESS!
IT WORKED!
DAMN! EVEN WITH A STRONG TAIL WIND!
THE SUDDEN PRESSURE FROM SENA GOT ME.

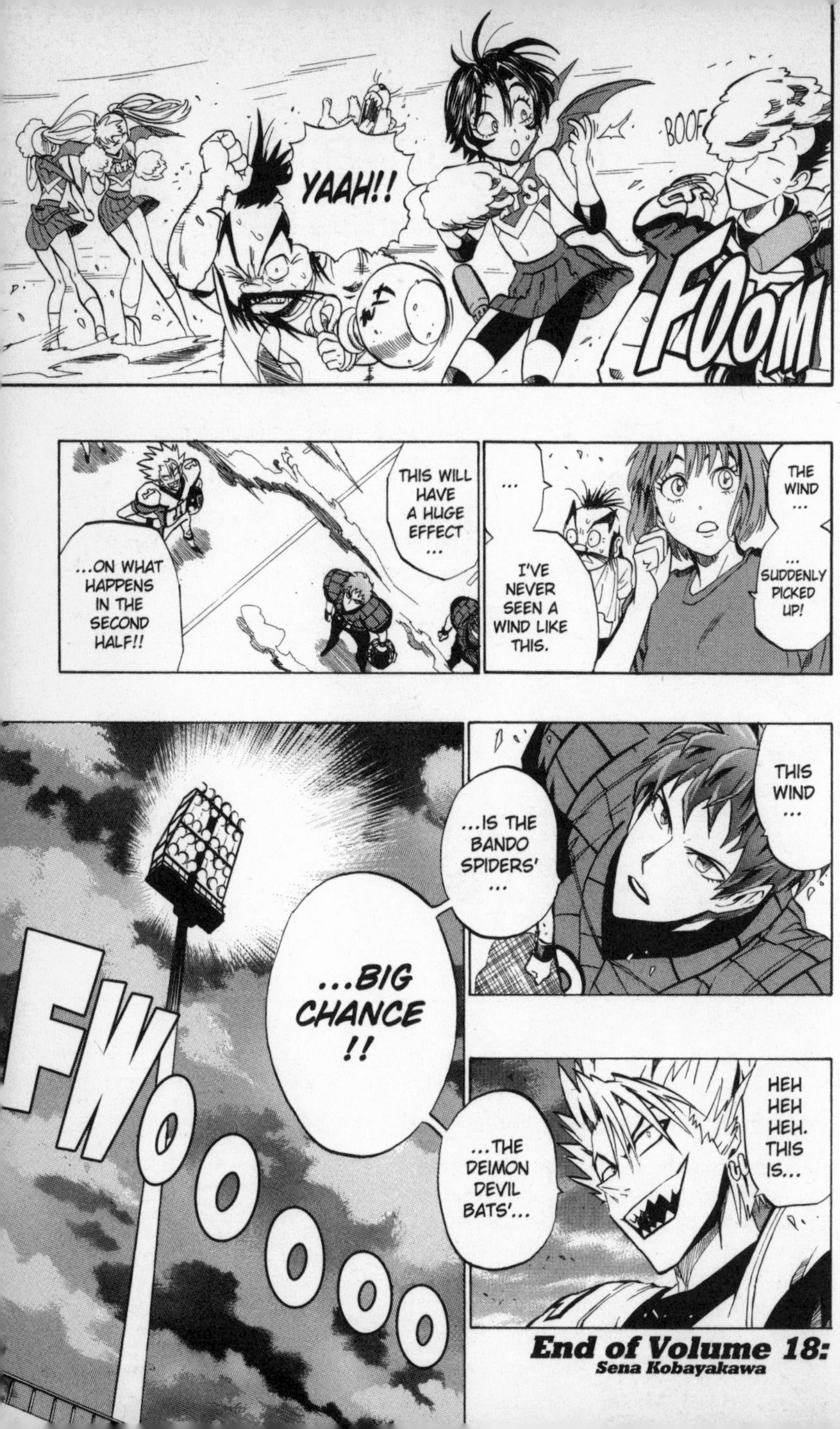
BOOF
FOOM
YAAH!!
THE WIND ...
... SUDDENLY PICKED UP!
...
I'VE NEVER SEEN A WIND LIKE THIS.
THIS WILL HAVE A HUGE EFFECT ...
...ON WHAT HAPPENS IN THE SECOND HALF!!
THIS WIND ...
...IS THE BANDO SPIDERS' ...
HEH HEH HEH. THIS IS...
...THE DEIMON DEVIL BATS'...
...BIG CHANCE !!
FWOOOOOO

End of Volume 18:
Sena Kobayakawa

Deluxe Biographies of the Supporting Cast

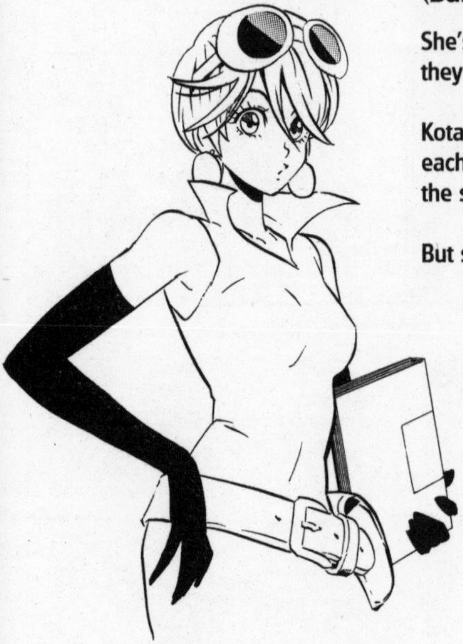

Juri Sawai (Bando Spiders Manager)

She's been friends with Kotaro ever since they were kids.

Kotaro has asked her out ***three times***, and each time, she's sighed and said, "You say the silliest things!"

But she's never actually turned him down.

Captain of the Genshijin Fighters

Besides football, he's really good at ***throwing the javelin***. He also takes pride in being able to ***start a fire by rubbing sticks together***.

If you really think about it, neither of those things is that strange, but people think of him as a kind of ***caveman*** anyway.

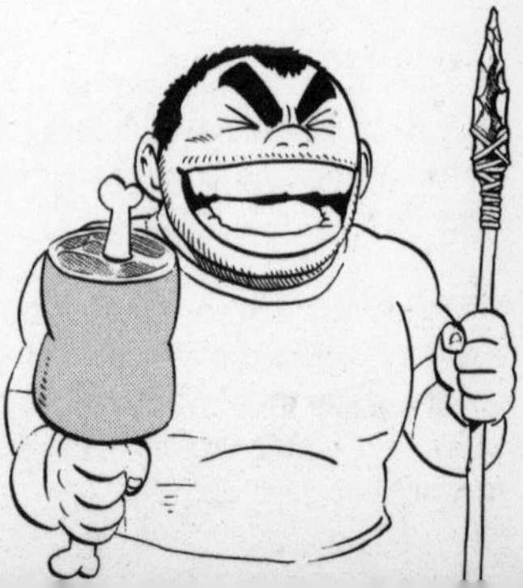

Healthy Bath Center

This is the bath that the sports teams from Kyoshin High School use. Its unique health effects are listed below.

1. Recovery from fatigue.
2. Cleansing of one's body.

It's easy to miss, but number two isn't really a unique effect.

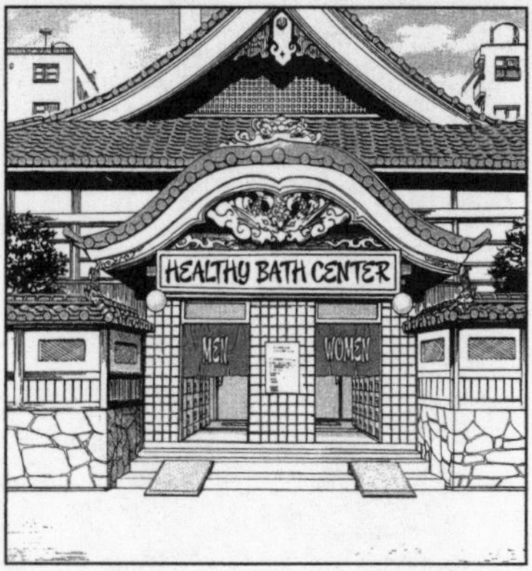
HEALTHY BATH CENTER
MEN
WOMEN

Captain of Bando's Kicking Team

He has been a constant supporter of the ***plain and sober*** kicking team, believing that it works behind the scenes.

For some reason, he's really noticed Ishimaru. ***He feels a strange affinity to him.***

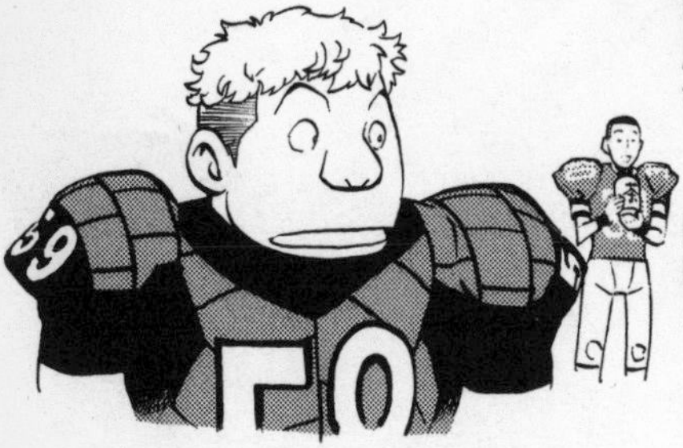

The Scouts

They work for Teikoku High School by hunting down athletes and luring them away from other teams.

When they tried to convince Akaba to join them, they were coolly told an allegory about a guitar that had its strings cut. When they ***didn't understand what Akaba meant,*** they gave up.

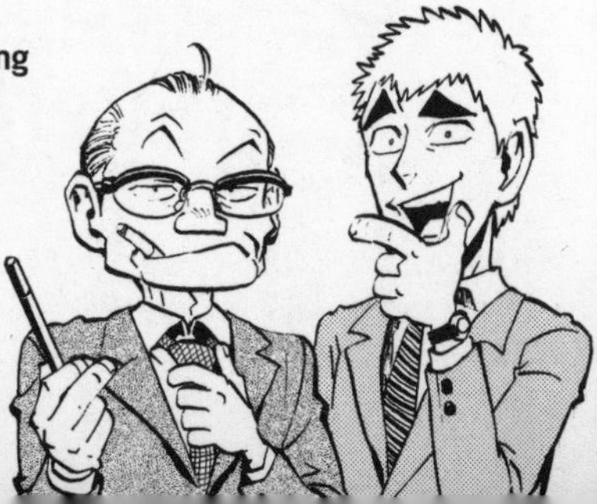

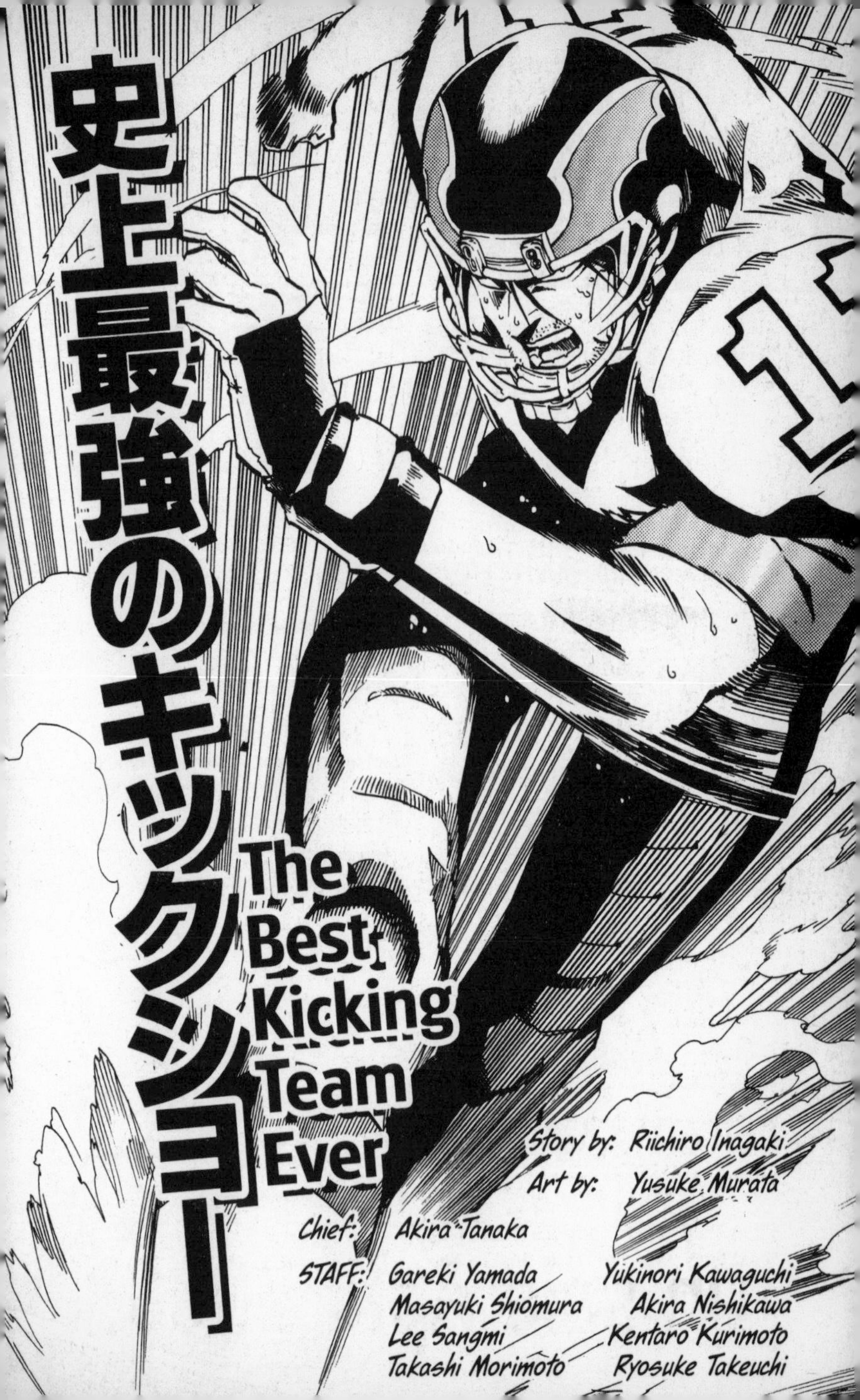
史上最強のキックショー
The Best Kicking Team Ever
Story by: Riichiro Inagaki
Art by: Yusuke Murata
Chief: Akira Tanaka
STAFF: Gareki Yamada
Yukinori Kawaguchi
Masayuki Shiomura
Akira Nishikawa
Lee Sangmi
Kentaro Kurimoto
Takashi Morimoto
Ryosuke Takeuchi

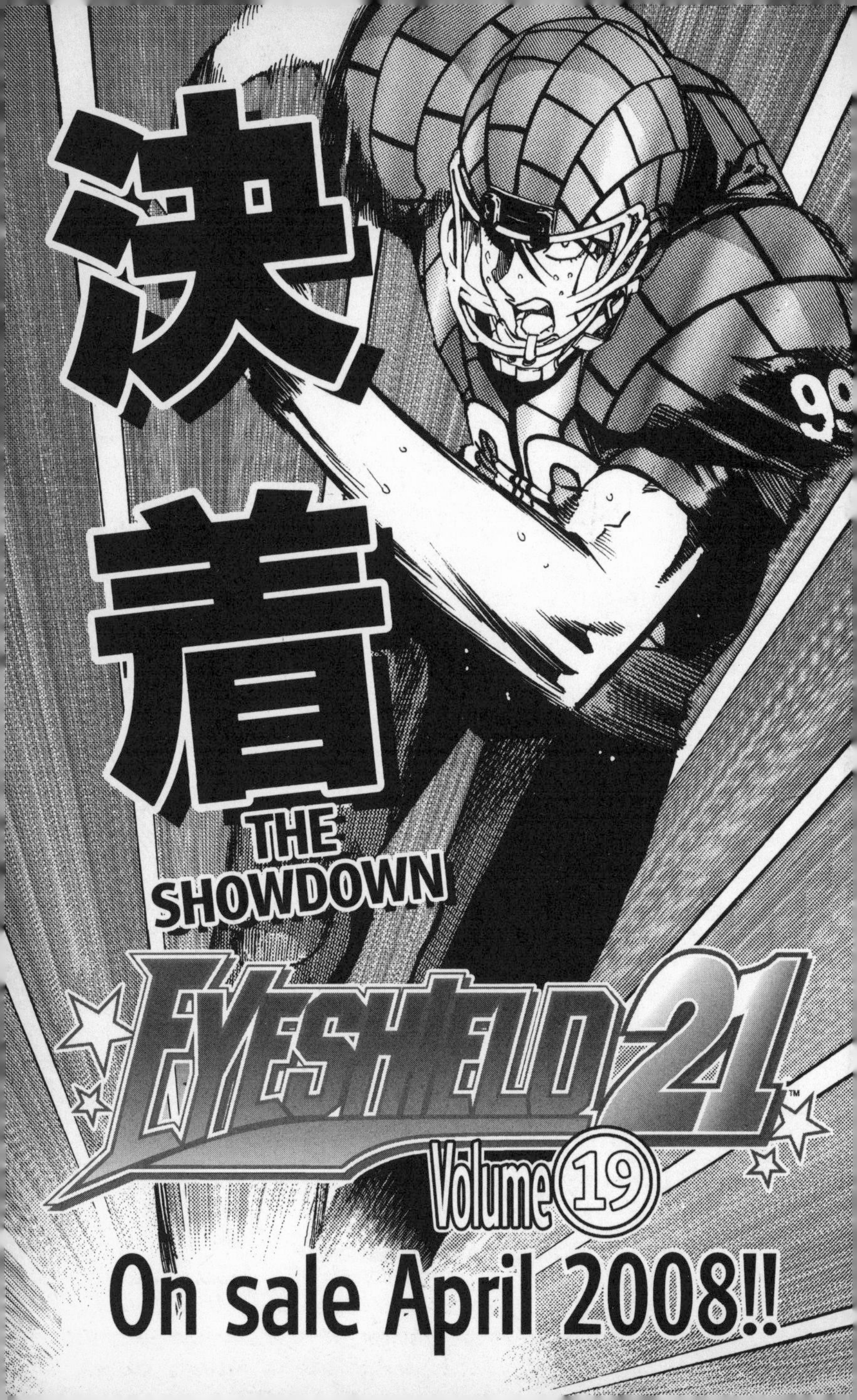
決着
THE SHOWDOWN
EYESHIELD 21™
Volume 19
On sale April 2008!!

EYESHIELD 21
Vol. 18: Sena Kobayakawa
The SHONEN JUMP ADVANCED Manga Edition

STORY BY RIICHIRO INAGAKI
ART BY YUSUKE MURATA

English Adaptation & Translation/Craig & Hime Kingsley, HC Language Solutions, Inc.
Touch-up Art & Lettering/James Gaubatz
Cover & Graphic Design/Sean Lee
Editor/Urian Brown

Editor in Chief, Books/Alvin Lu
Editor in Chief, Magazines/Marc Weidenbaum
VP of Publishing Licensing/Rika Inouye
VP of Sales/Gonzalo Ferreyra
Sr. VP of Marketing/Liza Coppola
Publisher/Hyoe Narita

Printed in the U.S.A.

Published by VIZ Media, LLC
P.O. Box 77010
San Francisco, CA 94107

SHONEN JUMP ADVANCED Manga Edition
10 9 8 7 6 5 4 3 2 1
First printing, February 2008

THE WORLD'S MOST
CUTTING-EDGE MANGA
SHONEN
JUMP
ADVANCED
www.shonenjump.com

VIZ
media
www.viz.com

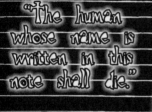

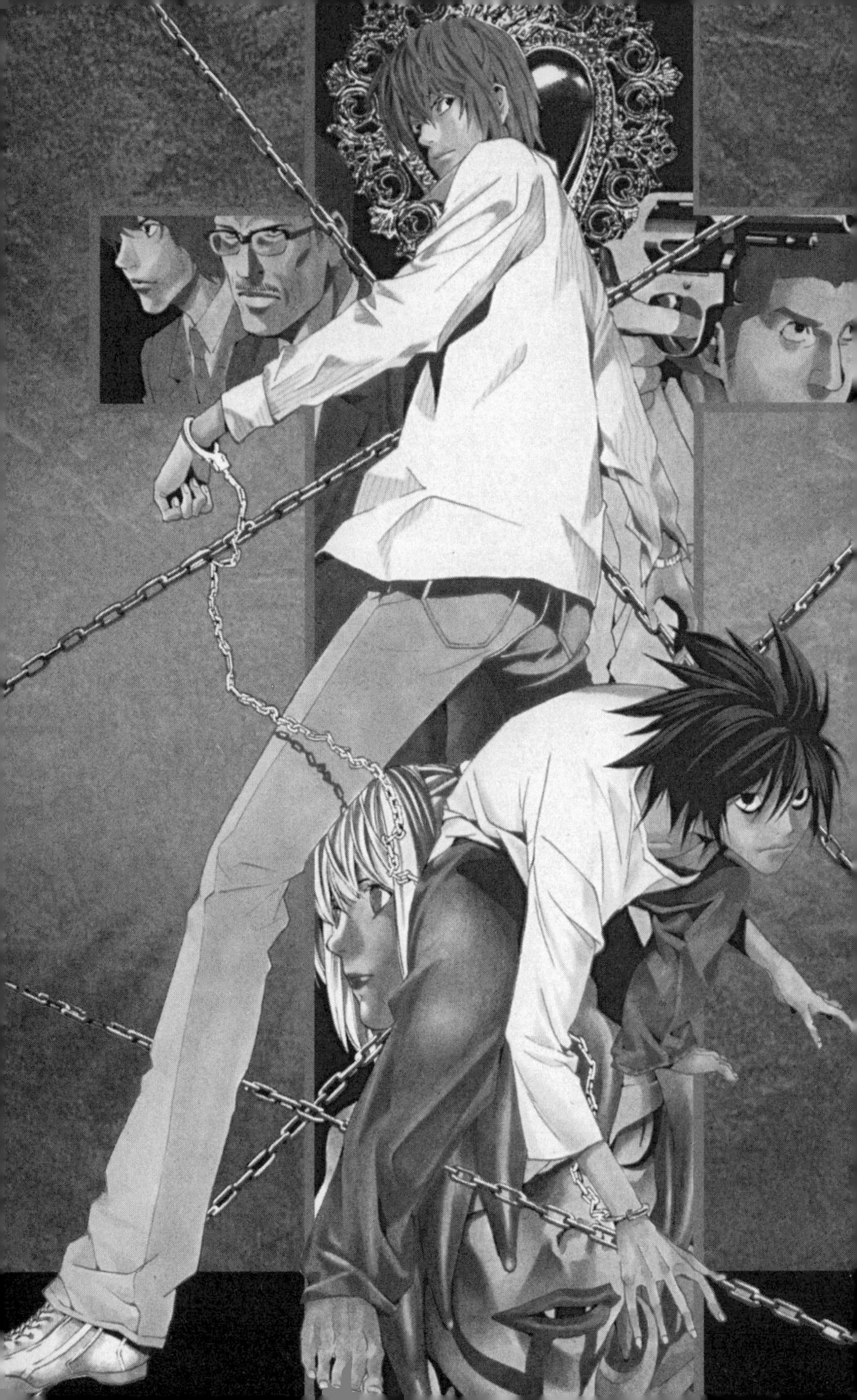

Tell us what you SHONEN JUMP manga!

Our survey is now available online.
Go to: *www.SHONENJUMP.com/mangasurvey*

Help us make our product offering better!

THE REAL ACTION
STARTS IN...

SHONEN JUMP

THE WORLD'S MOST POPULAR MANGA
www.shonenjump.com